T0298949

Trade Unions in Asia

Asia has undergone a rapid transformation over the past decade as many countries have embraced globalization, promoting a substantial improvement in living standards for the majority of workers. Nevertheless, the 1997–1998 Asian Financial Crisis and the resulting surge in unemployment has demonstrated the inherent weaknesses of the global economic system and the negative impacts of a development approach based solely on economic growth. Asian workers often lack adequate legislative protection and institutional support, meaning that trade unions represent one of the few institutions capable of promoting some measure of equity and social justice. This book examines the role played by trade unions in Asia, with particular focus on how they have organized to represent workers and the strategies they have adopted. Economies considered include Japan, South Korea, Taiwan, Hong Kong, Singapore, China, India, Vietnam, Thailand and Indonesia. It is argued that in the developed economies sectoral shifts away from manufacturing toward services and knowledge-based work is putting pressure on unions to develop new strategies to represent workers, whilst in the developing economies the vulnerability of workers in a globalized world is constraining the growth of unionism. Overall, this book provides a comprehensive account of the role of trade unions in Asia today.

John Benson is Professor and Head of the School of Management at the University of South Australia. He is the author/editor of nine books and over eighty journal articles and book chapters. He has had extensive consultancy experience with unions, business enterprises and government departments. His major research interests include Japanese management and unions, the restructuring of Chinese industry, outsourcing, and knowledge workers.

Ying Zhu is the Director of the Master of HRM Programme and an Associate Professor in the Department of Management and Marketing, the University of Melbourne, Australia. He has published a number of books, chapters and journal articles covering industrial relations, human resource management, cross-cultural management, business and economic development in East Asia and Australia. His recent publications include *Unemployment in Asia* (co-edited with John Benson, Routledge, 2005) and *Management in Transitional Economies: from the Berlin wall to the Great Wall of China* (co-authored with Malcolm Warner, Vincent Edwards, Gennadij Polonsky and Danijel Pucko, Routledge, 2005).

Routledge Studies in the Growth Economies of Asia

Trade Unions in Asia

An economic and sociological analysis

Edited by
John Benson and Ying Zhu

LONDON AND NEW YORK

First published 2008
by Routledge
2 Park Square, Milton Park, Abingdon, Oxon OX14 4RN

Simultaneously published in the USA and Canada
by Routledge
711 Third Avenue, New York, NY 10017, USA

*Routledge is an imprint of the Taylor & Francis Group,
an informa business*

Typeset in Times New Roman by
HWA Text and Data Management, Tunbridge Wells

British Library Cataloguing in Publication Data
A catalogue record for this book is available from the British Library

Library of Congress Cataloging-in-Publication Data
Trade unions in Asia / edited by John Benson and Ying Zhu.
      p. cm. – (Routledge studies in the growth economies of Asia series)
   Studies from a workshop held at the University of Melbourne in March
   2006.
   Includes bibliographical references and index.
   1. Labor unions – Asia – Congresses. 2. Industrial relations – Asia –
   Congresses. 3. Globalization – Economic aspects – Asia – Congresses.
   I. Benson, John, 1948- II. Zhu, Ying, Ph. D.
HD6796.T73 2008
331.88095-dc22   2007048598

ISBN10: 0–415–41007–X (hbk)
ISBN10: 0–203–92649–8 (ebk)

ISBN13: 978–0–415–41007–6 (hbk)
ISBN13: 978–0-203–92649–9 (ebk)

Contents

Illustrations

Figures

Tables

Contributors

John Benson is Professor and Head of the School of Management at the University of South Australia. Prior to taking up his present appointment, John was Chair of the MBA Programme in International Business at the University of Tsukuba, Japan, after having spent many years as a Reader in the Department of Management, University of Melbourne, Australia. His major research interests are Japanese management and unions, the restructuring of Chinese and Vietnamese industry, outsourcing and knowledge work. John has published numerous papers and monographs and his most recent edited monographs are *Unemployment in Asia* (Routledge, 2005) with Ying Zhu and *Women in Asian Management* (Routledge, 2006) with Vimolwan Yukongdi.

Janaka Biyanwila is a lecturer in Industrial Relations at the University of Western Australia.

Andy W. Chan is an Associate Professor of Department of Management and Marketing at The Hong Kong Polytechnic University. His research areas are HRM and industrial relations in Hong Kong and China. His publications appear in *British Journal of Industrial Relations*, *Economic & Industrial Democracy*, *Human Relations*, *Industrial Relations*, *International Journal of HRM*, *International Journal of Management Reviews*, and *Journal of Vocational Behavior*. He has also published books on HRM and labour management and is also a frequent contributor to local mass media including television and newspapers on employment matters.

Vincent Edwards is visiting professor at the Faculty of Economics, University of Ljubljana and was until recently Professor of International Management at Buckinghamshire Chilterns University College. His research has focused on management and corporate change in transforming economies. He has published a number of co-authored books as well as articles in *Asia Pacific Business Review*, *International Journal of Human Resource Management*, *The Leadership & Organization Development Journal*, *Journal of Euromarketing*, and *International Journal of Entrepreneurial Behaviour & Research*. He is on the editorial board of the *Journal for East European Management Studies* and *Economic and Business Review for Central and Eastern Europe*.

Howard Gospel is Professor of Management at King's College, University of London; a Research Associate at the Centre for Economic Performance, London School of Economics; and a Fellow of the Said Business School, University of Oxford. His research interests include the development of employer labour policy, corporate governance and human resource management, forms of employee representation, and training and development. He has published on these topics in historical and contemporary contexts and with an international and comparative perspective.

Samanthi Gunawardana is completing her PhD on the employment systems of Sri Lanka's Export Processing Zones, at the University of Melbourne. She is an Assistant Professor in International and Comparative Employment Relations in the Department of Labor Studies and Employment Relations at Pennsylvania State University. Her research interests include gender and the political economy of development in South Asia, and comparative employment.

Joe Isaac is a Professorial Fellow in the Department of Management and Marketing at the University of Melbourne. Formerly Professor of Economics at the University of Melbourne and later at Monash University where he was Deputy Chancellor. Joe was a Deputy President of the Australian Conciliation and Arbitration Commission from 1974 to 1987 and more recently has worked as a consultant to ILO Jakarta on wage issues.

Chris Leggett is Professor of Management in the School of Management at the University of South Australia. He has researched and taught in many countries and specializes in the industrial relations of East and Southeast Asian countries.

Anh Phan has been working since 2004 at Buckinghamshire Chilterns University College, UK on his doctoral research into business training in small Vietnamese firms. A Vietnamese from Hanoi, he earned his master's degree from the Asian Institute of Technology, Thailand. He possesses working experience in the local private business sector as well as in several international organizations. His current interests include the influence of business training on firm performance, traditional cultural values in management and the integration of information technology in business.

Nagiah Ramasamy is currently a doctoral candidate in the area of industrial relations, at the Universiti Putra Malaysia. He has taught in the areas of human resource management, industrial relations and business management at both undergraduate and postgraduate levels, at local and overseas institutions of higher education, over the last 16 years. His early work experiences were in accounting, followed by a career change to personnel management, in the manufacturing and services sectors. His research interests include Malaysian industrial relations and exploring the role of trade unions in corporate governance. Nagiah has presented a number of papers on Malaysian trade unions at local forums.

Chris Rowley is the inaugural Professor of Human Resource Management at the Cass Business School, City University. He is the founding Director of the new, multi-disciplinary and internationally networked *Centre for Research on Asian Management*, the Editor of the leading journal *Asia Pacific Business Review* and the founding book Series Editor of 'Studies in Asia Pacific Business' and 'Asian Studies: Contemporary Issues and Trends'. Professor Rowley researches in a range of areas, including international and comparative human resource management and Asia-Pacific management and business. He has an extensive list of publications including over 20 edited and sole-authored books.

K. R. Shyam Sundar is a Reader in the Department of Economics, Guru Nanak College of Arts, Science and Commerce affiliated to Mumbai University, Mumbai. He has done research work on various themes in industrial relations and labour economics such as industrial conflict, trade unions, labour flexibility, labour laws, labour reforms, collective bargaining, labour statistics. He has published research articles and book reviews in well-known journals in India such as *Indian Journal of Labour Economics* and *Indian Journal of Industrial Relations, Economic and Political Weekly*. He has been a Visiting Scholar at the International Institute of Labour Studies, ILO, Geneva. He recently completed two major research reports on the labour flexibility debate in Europe and labour regulation in Maharashtra.

Sari Sitalaksmi is a staff member at the Faculty of Economics, Gadjah Mada University, Indonesia. She is currently undertaking a PhD programme in the Department of Management and Marketing, University of Melbourne, Australia. The topic of her dissertation is 'Managing transformation at state-owned enterprises and their employment relations: The case of Indonesia'. Her particular research interests are industrial relations, human resource management, and management of state-owned enterprises (SOEs).

Malcolm Warner is Professor and Fellow Emeritus at Wolfson College and Judge Business School, University of Cambridge. He has published extensively on management, industrial relations and HRM in Asia. He has been, in the last few years, the Editor-in-Chief of the *International Encyclopedia of Management*, 8 vols (Thomson Learning, 2002). His most recently edited books are *Human Resources Management in China Revisited* (Routledge, 2005) and (with Grace O. M. Lee) *Unemployment in China* (Routledge, 2006). A new monograph, written together with Grace O. M. Lee, *The Political Economy of the SARS Epidemic: The Impact on Human Resources, Labour Markets and Unemployment in East Asia* was published by Routledge in 2007. He is currently Co-editor of the *Asia Pacific Business Review.*

Kil-Sang Yoo is a Professor at the Korea University of Technology and Education and President the Korea International Migration Association. He received his PhD in Economics from the University of Hawaii in 1988. He has served as a Vice President of the Korea Labor Institute, President the Korean Social Security Association, Vice President of the Korean Labor Economics Association, and an Assistant Director of the Economic Planning Board of Korean government. He has played an important role in developing labor policies as a researcher and as policy advisors to the President of Korea and Minister of Labor in Korea. Kil-Sang played a key role in designing the Korean employment insurance system.

Vimolwan Yukongdi is a senior lecturer in human resource management in the School of Management and Information Systems at Central Queensland University. Vimolwan holds a PhD degree from the University of Melbourne, a Master of Business Administration from the University of Pittsburgh, and a Bachelor of Business Administration (Magna Cum Laude) from Assumption University. Vimolwan has worked in the consulting and oil industries. She has taught at universities in Australia, New Zealand, and Thailand. She has held academic appointments at the University of Melbourne, University of Newcastle, Massey University, Assumption University, and Bangkok University. She recently co-edited with John Benson a monograph entitled *Women in Asian Management* which was published by Routledge in 2006.

Ying Zhu is Associate Professor and the Director of the Master of Human Resource Management in the Department of Management and Marketing, the University of Melbourne. He was educated at Peking University where he took his International Economics bachelor degree in 1984, then held the post of Economist and Research Fellow in the Research Office of Shenzhen Special Economic Zone Development Company. He completed a PhD at the University of Melbourne in 1992. His teaching and research interests include international human resource management, international business, economic development in East Asia, and the political economy of globalization. He has published extensively on the topics of international human resource management, employment relations in Asia, labour law and regulations in Asia, and economic development in Asia.

Preface

Trade unions in Asia have often been depicted as controlled by less than democratic regimes or individual employers and where some semblance of independence existed they were seen as nascent or transitional. Yet, such a depiction does little to provide the reader with an understanding of the roots of trade unionism in various Asian economies, the struggles they have endured and the benefits they have brought to workers. Moreover, such a depiction may now be out of date as many Asian economies have embraced the processes of globalization and have witnessed a rapid transformation of their societies. The ensuing economic growth has led to a substantial improvement in living standards for many workers.

The aim of this book is to fill this knowledge gap and provide the reader with a clearer understanding of the background, structure, operations and outcomes of trade unionism in Asia. We have chosen twelve economies that range from the highly developed through to those that have more recently commenced this process. Within these broad parameters some of these economies are undergoing political and institutional transformation while others have long-standing political traditions with well-established institutions. Indeed the choice of the term economy to represent the various case studies illustrates the present day political realities in Asia. The twelve economies chosen to be included in this volume was based on providing a variety of contexts which would represent the issues referred to above. The developed economies included are Japan, South Korea, Taiwan, Hong Kong, Singapore and Malaysia while the others are China, India, Sri Lanka, Vietnam, Thailand and Indonesia.

In the developed economies sectoral shifts towards services and knowledge work has meant that manufacturing, the traditional organizing base for trade unions, is in decline and this coupled with attitudes of young workers places pressure on trade unions to develop new strategies and avenues for the representation of their members. In all these economies institutions and regulations have been developed to guide employment and regulate labour markets, and a degree of protection and support for workers exists. In contrast, in the developing economies the shift from agricultural pursuits to manufacturing and the vulnerability of workers in the globalized world means that the growth of trade unions has been constrained and that traditional forms of unionism may be less relevant. In these economies labour market institutions and regulations are generally poorly developed and little support is provided to unemployed workers.

Yet to study these economies in isolation from much of the literature and our understanding of trade unions in more advanced Western economies will limit the value of this comparative analysis. We therefore start this volume with a chapter that explores the theories, research and paradigms that have emanated from trade union research in these advanced Western economies. This provides both a backdrop and a tool of analysis for our discussion on trade unions in Asia. This has meant that a common frame of reference or structure has been adopted for each chapter. This has allowed each chapter to have a common set of tables, to canvass a common set of issues, and to consider a variety of explanations for the structure and trajectory of trade unions in this region.

The contributing authors in this volume are all specialist in the economies they examine. They have access to both the English and domestic literature, statistics and government reports. We would like to thank them for their dedication and their contributions to this book and to the workshop that was held at the University of Melbourne in March 2006. This workshop and the overall project were funded by the Centre for Human Resource Management at the University of Melbourne for which we are extremely grateful. We would also like to thank Saadia Carapiet for her editorial input and liaison with the individual chapter contributors and Barbara Brougham for her editing of the final draft of the volume. Their efforts have improved the content, consistency and presentation of the chapters considerably. Finally, we are grateful for the support we have received from Routledge and their willingness to publish on this important issue. We hope that this volume will create further interest in trade unions in Asia and will lay the groundwork for a more comprehensive understanding of trade unions more generally.

John Benson and Ying Zhu
October 2007

1   Trade unions in Asia

Organization, strategy and issues

John Benson and Ying Zhu

Introduction and key questions

Asia has undergone a rapid transformation over the past two decades as many Asian economies[1] have embraced the processes of globalization. Over this period the inflow of foreign capital into the region, the level of internal trade amongst these economies, and trade with other parts of the world have increased substantially. The ensuing economic growth has led to an improvement in living standards for many workers. This economic growth has attracted considerable attention and has resulted in a significant volume of research being undertaken that seeks to explain the rapid growth and also to assess the impact of this growth on society (see for example: World Bank 1993; Leipziger 1997; Mugtada and Basu 1997).

Economic development in these economies has, however, been uneven and many workers have been excluded from the gains that have flowed from globalization. For these workers their lack of relevant skills and the intense competition for jobs has meant that low paid work or unemployment have become their only alternatives. Moreover, in many cases the impact of globalization has been beyond the control of workers and national economies. This was well illustrated by the events surrounding the 1997–8 Asian financial crisis (Asian Crisis) which highlighted the vulnerability of national systems that have fully embraced globalization (see McLeod and Garnaut 1998). The resultant unemployment and the social consequences of this unemployment in the Asian economies (see Benson and Zhu 2005) demonstrated the inherent weaknesses of the global economic system and the negative impacts of a development approach based solely on economic growth.

For Asian workers these negative impacts of globalization have been exacerbated by the lack of adequate legislative protection and institutional support systems (Rowley and Benson 2000). This has meant that trade unions represent one of the few institutions capable of achieving some measure of equity and social justice for workers. Trade unions can do this through workplace representation and bargaining and also through their capacity to play a wider role in influencing economic, legislative and social reforms. Yet, such a role is problematic as in many Asian economies trade union activities have been severely constrained. This raises the question of whether globalization has improved the potential of Asian trade unions to independently represent workers and whether their prospects are likely to improve in the future.

Whilst a considerable volume of research has been undertaken on trade unions and industrial relations in Asian economies, much of this research has focused on single economies and researchers have not sought to locate their findings within the context of trade union developments in the wider Asian region. This is understandable given the obstacles facing trade union researchers in many Asian economies. While some of these studies make reference to the earlier literature on trade union development in advanced industrial economies, this has not been the norm. As a consequence, the contribution of these studies to trade union theory has been limited, although again this is understandable given the criticisms of those who use Western theories as explanations for Asian phenomena. While much of this earlier research is rich in detail the rapid economic development in these economies has meant that much of what we know about trade unions may now be out of date. It is for these reasons that we sought to undertake the task of mapping out the development, organization and strategies of Asian trade unions.

The attempt to add an Asian perspective to trade union theory, as well as provide a wider comparative analysis of trade unions in Asia, was the starting point for this book. Clearly such a task would be beyond the expertise of any one researcher, so we brought together leading researchers on trade unions in various Asian economies to write the individual case studies. Yet we realized that this would do little more than update the current literature while remaining silent on the issues raised above. To address this problem a workshop was held at the University of Melbourne in March 2006 where experts on Asian trade unions discussed these issues and debated what would constitute the most appropriate research framework.

The outcome of these discussions led to four key questions being adopted to guide the case studies of the various economies. First, how have Asian trade unions organized to represent workers? Second, what do Asian trade unions do? Third, what impacts have Asian trade unions had on workers and businesses? Fourth, how can the trajectory of trade unions in individual Asian economies be explained? By adopting a uniform approach, a comparative analysis can be undertaken both between the individual case study economies, as well as extending the analysis to accommodate a discussion that has the potential to contribute to the wider trade union literature.

Structure and framework

Twelve economies in Asia were chosen to investigate the questions underpinning this book. As trade unions are a product of industrialization, any analysis of trade unions in Asia must accommodate the various stages of economic development that exist in this region. One proxy for the level of development is the distribution of employment between the agricultural, industrial and service sectors. Where employment in the agricultural sector is low it can be reasonably assumed that the level of industrialization and economic development is higher. The economies chosen and the employment figures in each sector are presented in Table 1.1.

Table 1.1 Breakdown of employment in case study economies 2005

Employment (%)			
Economy	*Agriculture*	*Industry*	*Services*
Japan[a]	4.6	27.8	67.7
South Korea*	6.4	26.4	67.2
Taiwan*	6.0	35.8	58.2
Hong Kong*	–	10.4	89.4
Singapore[b]	–	24.0	76.0
Malaysia[d]*	14.5	36.0	49.5
China[b]*	49.0	22.0	29.0
India[b]*	60.0	17.0	23.0
Sri Lanka[c]*	38.0	17.0	45.0
Vietnam	56.8	37.0	6.2
Thailand	49.0	14.0	37.0
Indonesia[e]*	46.5	11.8	41.7

Source: globalEDGE, Michigan State University. Online. Available at HTTP <http://globaledge.msu.edu/ibrd/CountryStats.asp> (accessed 26 May 2007).

Notes
* estimate; a – 2004, b – 2003, c – 1998, d – 2000, e – 1999

On the basis of sectoral employment, the developed economies are Japan, South Korea, Taiwan, Hong Kong and Singapore and Malaysia[2] while the developing economies are China, India, Sri Lanka, Vietnam, Thailand and Indonesia. In most of the developed economies the sectoral shifts towards services and knowledge work means that manufacturing, the traditional organizing base for trade unions, is in decline and this, coupled with attitudes of young workers, places pressure on trade unions to develop new strategies and avenues for the representation of their members. In all these economies, institutions and regulations have been developed to guide employment and regulate labour markets, and a degree of protection and support for workers exists. In contrast, in developing economies the shift from agricultural pursuits to manufacturing has been accompanied by governments placing severe restrictions on the formation and activities of trade unions in an attempt to be more competitive in a globalized world. This may mean that traditional forms of unionism may be less relevant. In these economies labour market institutions and regulations are poorly developed and little support is provided to unemployed workers. Within this group a further distinction can be made as China and Vietnam are socialist states that are in the process of transition towards market-based economies.

This breakdown by employment of the 12 economies is important if the strategies adopted by trade unions in the various economies are to be explained. The economic health of the 12 case study economies over the past decade varies significantly and cuts across the developed/developing divide. The three fastest growing economies over the period 1996 to 2005 – China, Vietnam and India (see Table 1.2) – are developing economies, whilst the next group of growth economies were mature economies at the start of this period (Singapore, Malaysia, South Korea and Taiwan). Moreover, although Thailand had only experienced modest growth over the past decade, its unemployment rate was low compared with those economies with higher economic growth. This case illustrates that the relationship between growth and unemployment is moderated by the sectoral shifts taking place in employment as economies move from an agricultural base to a more industrial and service structure.

It is important to recognize, however, that these broad economic parameters only tell part of the story. Trade unions in Asia have faced many challenges. Governments of all persuasions have sought to constrain their development and activities out of a fear that such an institution represents a serious political, economic and social threat. This has, in some cases, led to institutionalized violence against trade unions and their members. It may also mean that less efficient labour legislation may result (World Bank 1995: 86). It is for this reason that we asked all contributors to this book to commence their study with a section on context and history, where many of these issues relating to the concept of trade unionism can be outlined and discussed.

The economies represented in this volume are typical of those that have undertaken or are going through significant economic restructuring and transition. Many of these economies have had periods of foreign occupation and some have maintained the institutions that were established during these times. Indeed, with

Table 1.2 Real GDP growth and unemployment in case study economies, 1996–2005

Economy	Real GDP growth	Unemployment
Japan	1.3	4.5
South Korea	4.5	4.2
Taiwan	4.5	3.7
Hong Kong	3.9	5.4
Singapore	5.5	2.7
Malaysia	4.7	3.2
China	8.6	4.6
India	5.6[a]	6.0[b]
Sri Lanka	4.2	9.0
Vietnam	6.3	6.2[c]
Thailand	3.4	1.8
Indonesia	2.9	7.1

Source: Case study, Chapters 3 to 14

Notes
a – 1991–2004; b – 1980–2004; c – 1996–2004

the exception of China and Vietnam most 'East Asian states have adopted, in broad outline at least, systems of labour law that reflect the form and content of the systems of Western countries' (Cooney *et al.* 2002: 3). On the other hand, all the economies considered in this volume have a set of unique conditions that underpin their political, social and economic systems, and which have led to a variety of approaches to trade unions.

The structure adopted for each case study consists of six sections. Each chapter commences with a brief introduction and relevant background information for the particular economy. This is followed by an overview of the economic and social context of each case study state, a historical outline of the development of trade unions and an overview of trade union membership. A third section explores union types and structure, which allows for a general description of the predominant union form to be presented, an assessment to be made of the degree of independence and some discussion on how workers are organized. This is then followed by a section that explores what the unions do, focusing both on processes, such as collective bargaining, and economic and non-economic outcomes. The fifth section of each chapter then attempts to explain the development, structure and strategies of trade unions within their national context. The final section of each chapter considers the future of trade unions and the challenges they face. This standardized format also extends to the information provided in each chapter, with a detailed table being included for each of the four substantial sections of the chapter. It should be noted, however, that we did not want to be overly prescriptive and so each chapter will have some variations around these themes.

Given the objectives of the book to contribute more widely to the trade union literature and to provide a comparative analytical framework, it was necessary to begin with a more conceptual chapter that would introduce the key issues. Chapter 2 therefore provides the justification for the chapter framework outlined above as well as providing the comparative analysis to link this text to the wider trade union literature. Chapter 2 begins with an overview of classical and contemporary trade union theories that have grown out of the study of trade unions in advanced industrialized economies. As pointed out by Gospel (Chapter 2), the 'intention is not to impute Western notions to these countries, but rather to suggest a basis of ideas and comparison'.

This is followed by a section that challenges the traditional craft/occupational, industrial, general and enterprise categories and introduces other ways to view union structure and government. A third section then considers what trade unions do and how they do it; and a fourth section suggests a number of possible explanations for the development of trade unions in advanced industrial economies. Chapter 2 finishes by suggesting three tentative conclusions that may provide some 'context for and stimulate questions about Asian countries' and their trade unions.

The case study economies

The economic histories of the case study economies all followed similar trajectories, although variations occurred across time. When broken down by the developed/developing classification some clear similarities emerge. The developed economies all industrialized rapidly from the 1960s, although Japan was a little earlier and Malaysia somewhat later. High levels of GDP growth were achieved in this time and unemployment tended to be low. Much of this growth was driven by the manufacturing sector and only in the 1990s did this growth falter due to the Asian Crisis, as in the case of Korea, or the rationalization of production to offshore sites in the case of Taiwan. Japan's fall was more complex and continued through much of the 1990s and the early part of the twenty-first century.

In contrast, the six developing economies have all experienced rapid growth for much of the past two decades. China and Vietnam undertook major restructuring of state-owned enterprises and moved to more market-based economies. The Asian Crisis had little long-term impact on these economies. In a similar fashion, Indonesia and Thailand instituted a series of economic reforms, deregulated their economies and promoted foreign direct investment (FDI) during this period. These economies suffered badly with the onset of the Asian Crisis, although it was only Indonesia that took some time to recover. Steady, although generally lower, economic growth is now occurring in these economies. The social, political and institutional contexts of these 12 economies did, however, differ and it is these aspects that will now be briefly considered.

Japan represents the most developed and economically successful of the case study economies, experiencing four decades of significant economic growth from the early 1950s. In the 1990s this pattern came to an end following the collapse of the 'bubble economy' in the late 1980s, the emergence of a number of Asian manufacturing competitors and the 'hollowing out' of Japanese domestic manufacturing. During this period unemployment more than doubled and was particularly high amongst the young and older workers. The ageing population has highlighted the plight of older unemployed workers who often do not have adequate pension cover and so rely on paid employment. As pointed out by Benson in Chapter 3 much of the decline in manufacturing has been taken up with employment in the services sector, although these jobs have often been temporary and part-time and so have presented a major challenge to trade unions.

South Korea represents a similar trajectory to the early post-war development of Japan. South Korea's early success commenced with the manufacturing sector and the economy increasingly became integrated into world markets. This global integration was to take its toll with the onset of the Asian Crisis. The government was forced to turn to the International Monetary Fund for emergency credit which, in turn, imposed significant structural reforms on the financial, corporate and labour sectors. Unlike Japan, however, South Korea recovered quickly and unemployment has fallen significantly, although not quite to pre-Crisis levels. Nevertheless as Rowley and Yoo point out in Chapter 4, masking this rapid economic development has been a history of trade union repression.

Taiwan, in a similar fashion to South Korea, commenced its industrial develop-ment in the 1960s and enjoyed two decades of high economic growth accompanied by low levels of unemployment. By the late 1980s the growth rate of industrial production had commenced to fall, although much of the excess labour generated was absorbed by the growth in the service sector. Nevertheless, from the mid-1990s unemployment has steadily risen as Taiwanese companies rationalized their domestic production and relocated offshore, particularly to mainland China. Zhu, in Chapter 5, points out that this economic uncertainty coupled with the political instability in the relationship between Taiwan and mainland China has created an unstable operating environment for trade unions.

Hong Kong represents one of the leading *laissez faire* economies in the world. While officially re-integrated into China as a Special Administrative Zone in 1997, Hong Kong remains outside many of the controls of China. During the past two decades Hong Kong has de-industrialized and re-commercialized leaving many unskilled workers out of mainstream employment. This, according to Chan in Chapter 6, has placed pressure on trade unions to find ways to protect these workers and develop more job opportunities.

Singapore has been a high growth economy since the 1960s, although this growth had been more modest over the past decade. As Leggett points out in Chapter 7, with few natural resources the government has placed a strong emphasis on human resources, high levels of labour market participation and productivity. Singapore is essentially an 'administrative state' and this has proved a major challenge to the development of trade unions. Industrial relations was constrained and in the latter part of the twentieth century the emphasis was placed on human resource planning in an endeavour to improve Singapore's competitive position within an increasingly globalized world.

Malaysia, like many of the developing economies represented in this volume, achieved substantial growth over the past two decades with a rapid shift away from agriculture. In this respect it is more like the developed economies, where growth over the last decade has been more modest. This growth was uneven across the economy and in certain sectors the import of foreign labour was necessary to meet the increased demand. The Asian Crisis dampened demand and led to a three-fold increase in retrenchments from the previous year. Yet, many of these retrenched workers were employed in the informal sector or were foreign workers who returned home after losing their jobs and as such had only a minor effect on the official unemployment figures. Despite economic growth, the nature of industrial relations in Malaysia, according to Ramasamy and Rowley in Chapter 8, has remained firmly within the control of the government and the major employers in an attempt to maintain the attractiveness of Malaysia as a destination for foreign investment.

The first of the developing economies to be considered in this volume is China. China represents an economy in transition as it continues to experience high levels of economic growth, industrial production and substantial foreign investment. This success has seen the official unemployment figures remain remarkably low, although it is suspected that the real figure would be considerably higher. One of the most serious problems facing China is the large number of unskilled workers unemployed. This is further compounded by the limited training opportunities available and the under-developed nature of the external labour market. This has meant that retrenched workers are likely to experience long periods of unemployment on minimum income support. While these conditions would normally constitute fertile grounds for trade unions, the Chinese unions, according to Warner in Chapter 9, appear to have had difficulty adjusting to the new realities.

India like China has experienced considerable, although somewhat lower, economic growth over the past two decades. Foreign direct investment and, consequently, industrial production have risen and this has led to the development of a class of well-paid workers. Nevertheless, India remains a relatively poor country. One legacy of the 200 years of British rule has been the adoption of a federal-democratic-pluralist political model that has led to constitutional rights for workers such as the freedom of association. As pointed out by Shyam Sundar in Chapter 10 there has, however, been little political support for trade unions in recent times and the market power of employers has given them the dominant edge.

Sri Lanka has experienced modest economic growth over the past two decades. This growth, however, has co-existed with high levels of unemployment, particularly among women and young people. Like India, Sri Lanka was under British control for 150 years, during which time British-styled institutions and laws were introduced. A major difference is that Sri Lanka has been involved in an ongoing conflict with the Tamils over their demand for a separate state. This has proved difficult for trade unions as some unions maintain a close connection with the Tamils, which makes a united union approach difficult. According to Gunawardana and Biyanwila in Chapter 11, the state's capacity has been restrained by the ethnic war and this has led to a serious external constraint on trade union activity.

In Vietnam the reform agenda, known as *Doi moi,* commenced in the mid-1980s and has transformed the economy into a socialist market state in a similar fashion to that of China. Economic growth over the past two decades has been substantial, although lower than that achieved by China. As pointed out by Edwards and Phan in Chapter 12, this has led Vietnam to become a more open society with greater employment and business opportunities. Nevertheless, trade unions have had difficulty in adapting to this transformation as they attempt to represent their members' interests whilst maintaining support for the ruling party. This has been made difficult as political reform has lagged well behind market reform.

The high level of economic growth over the past two decades has transformed Thailand from an agrarian economy into an export-oriented developing nation. This growth was most pronounced in the late 1980s and early 1990s where growth averaged 9 per cent per annum. The economy was badly affected by the Asian Crisis which saw growth halved for the next decade, although unemployment remained remarkably low. Like many of the developing economies represented in this volume, a sizeable proportion of the Thai labour force are employed on a part-time or self-employed basis. This has been exacerbated, according to Yukongdi in Chapter 13, by the influx of migrant workers from neighbouring countries which has led to a variety of peripheral forms of employment, such as subcontracting and part-time employment, being used to replace permanent employment which in turn represents a major challenge for trade unions.

As with the other developing economies, Indonesia experienced rapid economic growth in the late 1980s and early 1990s; although most of this growth ceased after the onset of the Asian Crisis in the late 1990s. Unlike most of the other developing economies affected by the Crisis, Indonesia was slow to recover and has not regained the momentum of the 1990s. Unemployment has continued to rise and is now over three times that of the period 1986 to 1995. The increase in unemployment is a result of the political and social instability that followed the Crisis as Indonesia sought to democratize and increase regional autonomy. As Isaac and Sitalaksmi point out in Chapter 14, this context, coupled with repressive legislation makes it difficult to predict the outcomes for trade union activity.

Conclusion

The economies represented in this volume have all experienced rapid economic growth at some stage of their development. The developed economies have, in general, more mature institutions, more modest economic growth, and more stable industrial relations. In contrast, the developing economies have undergone rapid economic growth for much of the past two decades, and have been restructuring their economies, which has led to a marked decline in the agricultural labour force, and a subsequent increase in urbanization. In these economies there remains, or has developed, a significant informal work sector which has absorbed many of those displaced through the restructuring process. The institutionalization of employment and social security through legislative and other means remains underdeveloped in many of the these economies.

While the divide between the developed and the developing economies can be blurred, as in the case of Malaysia, it is an important distinction as it allows us to make some assessment of the key factors that influence trade union development and activity. Nevertheless, all the economies have a range of unique factors which have guided their economic and social development, including their industrializing strategies, their promotion of various human resource policies, their unique history and context, as well as their prevailing political ideologies and structures. In choosing these economies we were aware of the need to provide some representation based on these factors. It is within these broad social, economic and political contexts that the analysis of trade unions in these economies is undertaken.

Notes

1 The term economy is used as some of these economies are economic regions and not sovereign countries.
2 We have classified Malaysia as a developed economy. It is clearly different to the other developing economies, but lags a little behind the other developed economies on the basis of its sectoral composition.

References

Benson, J. and Zhu, Y. (eds) (2005) *Unemployment in Asia*, London: Routledge.

Cooney, S., Lindsey, T., Mitchell, R. and Zhu, Y. (2002) *Law and Labour Market Regulation in East Asia*, London: Routledge.

Leipziger, D. (ed.) (1997) *Lessons from East Asia*, Ann Arbor, MI: University of Michigan Press.

McLeod, R. and Garnaut, R. (eds) (1998) *East Asia Crisis: From Being a Miracle to Needing One?* London: Routledge.

Mugtada, M. and Basu, P. (1997) 'Macroeconomic policies, growth and employment expansion: the experience of South Asia', in A. Kahn and M. Mugtada (eds) *Employment Expansion and Macroeconomic Stability Under Increasing Globalization*, Basingtoke: Macmillan Press.

Rowley, C. and Benson, J. (eds) (2000) *Globalization and Labour in the Asia Pacific,* London: Frank Cass.

World Bank (1993) *The East Asian Miracle: Economic Growth and Public Policy*, New York: Oxford University Press.

World Bank (1995) *Workers in an Integrating World*, New York: Oxford University Press.

2 Trade unions in theory and practice

Perspectives from advanced industrial countries

Howard Gospel

Introduction

This chapter is in two parts. The first part considers a number of classic and contemporary theories of trade unions and their behaviour. This draws mainly on theories and insights which have been derived from the long history of unions in advanced industrial countries. The second part sets these theories and insights against the historical and contemporary situation in such countries, drawing on readily available data. The intention is to provide background for the other chapters in this volume which consider unions in Asian countries. From the outset, however, it should be stated that the intention is not to impute Western notions to these countries, but rather to suggest a basis of ideas and comparisons.

There are a number of potential positive results of such an enterprise. Comparisons can help us not only understand foreign systems, but also better understand our own system. They can make us aware about the relativity and the diversity of institutions across countries. On the basis of this, one can consider possibilities for transference (borrowing from other countries) and convergence (moving in the same direction as other countries or, by contrast, in different directions). There are also pitfalls from such an enterprise. We must be wary of the nominalist fallacy; in other words thinking that because something has the same name in one country it is the same kind of institution and performs the same function in another country. Equally one must be aware of the homogeneity fallacy; in other words we must be careful not to do injustice to the complexity and diversity within different countries. Above all perhaps, we should beware of the nationalist fallacy, namely a tendency to think we are better than other countries or, indeed, sometimes that we are worse. This does not mean there are no universals and judgements cannot be made, for example about the desirability of the right to organize in a trade union, but we should be cautious of many such judgements. In this respect, also, comparative study increasingly makes us think about complementarities; in other words, how institutions in a country may fit together and produce outcomes which are optimal for that country.

Union types

Over the years there have been many theories, inductive and deductive, about trade unions, their nature and basic purpose. We review these classical and contemporary theories to provide possible insights and contexts for the later chapters on Asian countries.

The Webbs (1894) classically defined a trade union as 'a continuous association of wage earners for the purpose of maintaining or improving the conditions of their employment' (the Webbs 1894: 1). To be a union, therefore, there has to be continuity over time and involvement in regulating conditions of employment. This is still a useful starting point for defining a trade union. However, it prompts one immediate question, namely union independence from the employer or the state. This is often a difficult line to discern, but here we see independence from the employer or the state as a crucial defining aspect of trade unions. We are not therefore concerned with employer-controlled 'company unions', but we do include enterprise-based unions and also so-called staff associations which meet other aspect of the Webbs' (1894) criteria. Unions have varying degrees of dependence on the state or they may develop from state-dependent to more independent organizations. Some examples of these differing stages of independence are considered in this volume.

Another early and classic statement of trade unions and one which is still pertinent today is to be found in the writings of Perlman (1928) in the US. Perlman is concerned to stress the role of unions in terms of job control. Writing in the context of the US experience, he argues that most employees are predominantly aware of the scarcity of jobs and limited opportunities for ordinary people. Given this, unions are interested in trying to control jobs and secure them for their members at a particular reserve price. Thus, they seek to establish 'property rights' in jobs and to impose a set of common rules around them. According to Perlman (1928) and those who have followed his analysis, unions and their members are much less interested in the control of industry or political action *per se*. This notion of the central purpose and nature of unions fits very much with the US context, and with the notion of 'pure and simple' or 'bread and butter' or 'business' unionism, where the essential nature of unions is seen as attempting to maintain and improve the conditions and working lives of members. However, it is difficult or even impossible for unions to be entirely job orientated and to be entirely divorced from the political context within which they operate.

Other classical theorists take a more moral view of unions. Veblen (1904) and Tannenbaum (1951), drawing on ideas from the sociologist Durkheim (1893), see in trade unions a reaction to industrialization and urbanization. Unions, they argue, came into existence to counter the dislocation and alienation caused by such processes. In this view, the essential role of unions was to produce a sense of belonging and solidarity among workers and to promote these relations as an end in themselves. Though not intended by these theorists, somewhat similar notions of unions as an integrating force were also advanced by statist and fascist type regimes in the early part of the twentieth century in countries such as Italy,

Germany, and Spain. This prompts questions as to whether such ideas, stressing the moral and integrative nature of unions, have any applicability to any of the Asian countries considered in the following chapters.

This sort of moral notion of unions overlaps with variants of confessional unionism. In other words, religions have been interested in defining and promoting certain types of employee collective representation. For example, the Catholic Church has seen trade unionism as a moral force giving workers a voice and introducing justice into the workplace (Pope Leo XIII *Rerum Novarum* 1891 and John Paul II *Laborem Exercens* 1981). According to this doctrine, workers have a right to join and participate in unions and unions can contribute to justice in the workplace and in the wider society. But, equally, unions and their members have responsibilities towards employers and towards society to work fairly and cooperatively. Again, this prompts questions in Asian countries of how Buddhist, Confucian, Islamic, and other religions have viewed unions and their central purpose and how in turn this has affected union philosophy and behaviour.

Reverting to notions of unions as essentially economic organizations, a strong statement of the ultimately economic purpose of trade unions is to be found in the writings of Dunlop (1944). Starting from a neoclassical economic framework, this theorist sees unions as essentially about optimizing a combination of wages and employment. In other words, what unions are basically about is obtaining the highest possible wage, subject to the constraint of not putting too many members out of work. In a classic debate, Ross (1948) contests this and suggests that unions, their leaders and members, cannot and do not make these calculations. Unions are best seen as organizations made up of leaders and members. Leaders are concerned above all with the survival of the union and with the survival of themselves as leaders. Members are concerned with comparisons with other workers and with ideas of relative fairness. Basically, in terms of what union leaders do, they seek to deliver benefits of a kind which compare favourably with those obtained by similar workers. This suggests that unions are not maximizers or optimizers in some economic way, but they are satisficers in a more political sense in that they seek to satisfy their members and deliver fair and comparable terms and conditions.

Somewhat similar themes have been developed by other theorists. Hence, Michels (1911) promoted the idea that within voluntary organizations, such as unions, there is an inevitable tendency towards oligarchy as leaders come to entrench their positions and subvert any original more radical purpose of unions. Later Lester (1958), observing US unions in the early post-Second World War decades, expressed this slightly differently and with more approval. He argued that, in their early stages, union leaders and members may have radical ideas about asserting control of production and transforming society; but, as they mature, they come to stress recognition by employers and other significant groups and consequently stability, respectability, and partnership. Herein lies a stage theory of unions which prompts the question as to whether such stages are being or are likely to be passed through by unions in Asian countries as union systems evolve.

Of course, from the nineteenth century onwards, there were those on the left who saw unions through the prism of class relations, revolutionary politics, and the wider transformation of society. Marx (1867) and Marx and Engels (1848) saw unions as arising out of the separation of the means of production and the development of labour as a commodity. Employers bought labour power in the market, but always had a problem of extracting actual labour or effort from the labour they had purchased. Given the commoditization of labour and the extraction of value, contradiction and conflict was inevitable. However, for Marx and many of his followers, though trade unions might in some circumstances help further revolutionary change, in practice they embodied a limited union consciousness rather than a class consciousness and they tended towards accommodation with capitalist society.

The Leninist (Lenin 1902) notion of unions, long dominant in Communist countries, accepted that unions could play a role in bringing about transformation, but once Communism was established, their role was to promote workers' interests subject to party control and to act as a transmission mechanism between the party and the workers. These views of unions contrast strongly with other left-wing notions of unions such as those espoused by syndicalist type theorists who believed that what unions should be about was direct action, from the bottom up, which would encroach on management control and establish workers' control (Sorel 1908; Gramsci 1921–6).

From this left-wing, especially Marxist–Leninist, perspective, two questions are pertinent for this volume: (1) do these political type notions help us understand unions in Asian countries? (2) where such ideas were once predominant, in countries such as China and Vietnam, how powerful have they been in shaping present-day realities?

By contrast to these revolutionary type notions of unions, and reverting back to a broad typification of most of the other theories referred to above, a dominant perspective on unions in the West has been of a liberal-pluralist kind. According to this view, democratically-based unions are a fundamental feature of industrial societies of a liberal, pluralist, and democratic kind. Their essential role, be it economic or social or moral, is to provide checks and balances at work. Indeed, in the broader political economy, unions reflect the existence of such liberal notions and also more widely provide important national checks and balances which are fundamental to liberal societies. Kerr and his colleagues (1960) predicted that over time there would be a convergence on this model. The question then becomes: are unions in Asia and other parts of the world converging on some sort of liberal-pluralist model or is this a strictly Western notion based on Western philosophy and experience?

Up to now we have outlined a diverse set of perspectives on unions. A recent overview of unions in Europe provides a useful way of integrating some of these earlier classical theories in a limited number of major types. Drawing on Hyman (2001), one may identify three ideal types or models of unions. First, there are *market*-orientated unions where unions are essentially economic actors pursuing economic goals. Under this model, unions seek to improve the welfare of members, especially through collective bargaining within the labour market. According to this model, unions essentially tend towards a sort of business union model. Second, there are *class*-orientated unions. Such unions are deemed to be vehicles of class struggle and their role is to promote working class interests and the transformation of society in a revolutionary direction. Third, there are *society*-orientated unions. Here unions may be seen essentially as social actors or social partners, engaged in a social dialogue and operating in a social democratic context. Their role is to strengthen the voice of workers in the broader society and act as a force for social, moral, and political integration.

Of course, in practice, unions may face in a number of directions and there can be mixtures of different types of unions within a country. Hence, unions may focus on the market, but may also wish to play a broader role in society. Market unions cannot ignore the political context. Equally, class-orientated unions must deliver economic benefits to members if they are to attract and keep large numbers of ordinary workers in membership. An important caveat here is that, though some of these types can be combined within the one union, combining all three different types is well-nigh impossible within any one organization. However, all three different types may co-exist (albeit uneasily) within one country.

Hyman's (2001) trilogy of market, class, and social unionism can be used to map the trajectory of unions over time. Hence, unions in countries such as the UK, the US, and Australia, started out with a strong market orientation; through the early twentieth century onwards they moved in a more class direction; more recently, over the last quarter-century, some have moved in a more social partnership direction or back towards more market goals. By contrast, France had an early tradition of class-based unionism and still today provides an interesting example of many different types of unions (market, social democratic, and class) which co-exist side by side. In Germany, after the Second World War, unions moved quickly from a class to a more market and social direction. This typology offers some potentially useful pointers for how we view unions in Asian countries and how in practice they are developing.

Union structure and government

The traditional view of union structure is to see unions as craft/occupational, industrial, general, and enterprise. Craft unions organize workers with a set of usually closely related skills and try to do so throughout the industries where such workers may be employed. An example of this might be electricians/electrical workers. Occupational unions are somewhat similar and organize throughout an occupation. The term occupational tends to be used more of white collar or professional workers, such as teachers or nurses. Industrial unions organize throughout an industry and seek to organize all the workers, vertically up and down, in that industry, regardless of their skill or occupation. An example here might be railway or steel or mine workers. By contrast, general unions seek to organize wherever they can and cover a wide range of crafts, occupations, and industries. Enterprise unions organize within the confines of one organization, be it a private company or a public organization and seek to organize all classes of employees within the boundary of the enterprise.

A further way to see structure is in terms of whether unions are closed or open (the Webbs 1897: 88; Commons 1909; Ulman 1955; Turner 1962). Closed unions restrict membership to one class of workers and do not seek to organize broader groups. They usually represent a well-defined category of workers and are focused on protecting the position and benefits of such workers, especially relative to other workers. Examples might be occupations such as airline pilots or doctors and other examples might be enterprise unions which organize exclusively within the boundaries of one firm. By contrast, open unions take a wider view of their area of recruitment and seek to organize and represent broader groups of workers, both horizontally across occupations and industries and vertically up and down hierarchies. Such unions take a more general and less relative view of the terms and conditions of their members. Historically, closed unions have often tended to open up and come to recruit similar workers who have skills which might complement or substitute for those of existing members. After having done this, they might then close down again and not go so far as to become completely open and general unions (Turner 1962; Sako 2006).

Increasingly, in the context of declining membership, many unions in Western countries have become open and general. This has, for example, happened in the US and Germany where unions had traditionally often been confined to one occupation or industry. Having opened up in this way, these unions have then been organized into sub-groups or divisions within a bigger union. This opening up has some advantages, especially where traditional industries and areas of membership are contracting and/or blurring, and it also gives unions greater political clout. However, it may also have disadvantages in that unions become very unwieldy, it becomes difficult to service members, and internal conflict within the union may ensue.

In most countries there also exist peak organizations which are confederations or umbrella bodies which have many independent unions in membership and which seek to represent their interests, in particular in the political sphere. In some countries, these are 'encompassive' to use Visser's (1990) term and there is only one confederation. In other countries, they are less comprehensive and there may be several confederations to which different unions affiliate. Such divisions have existed on various lines: for example, divisions by occupations with different confederations for blue and white collar workers; splits on political lines with confederations of unions from across the political spectrum; and schisms on confessional lines with different confederations for unions from different religions. We will see considerable difference across Asian countries in this respect, but it should be borne in mind that Visser (1990) suggests that more encompassive union movements tend to have greater strength and higher membership.

We have already briefly touched on union government when we referred to possible tendencies towards oligarchical control by union leadership. In practice, the governance and degree of democracy in a union depends on a whole series of factors, such as size, checks and balances in union constitutions, membership type and participation, membership identification, and where and how key decisions are made. In practice, in most unions there is constant tension between administrative rationality and democratic or representational rationality. Much of the literature would suggest that, though there may be costs to democracy, more democratic unions are desirable in themselves and are also more likely to better represent members economically and politically (Lipset *et al.* 1956; Child *et al.* 1973; Edelstein and Warner 1979).

Another dimension of unions is their relations with the state. The involvement of the state has varied significantly between countries and over time in all countries, not least in Asia (Frenkel 1993). As already stated, in Western market economies unions have tended to be largely autonomous of the state, though legally dependent on it for certain rights and protections. Of course, at points in time, as in fascist Germany and Italy in the interwar years, independent unions were abolished and replacement organizations created under state control. Also, as stated, this was the role of unions in Communist countries, under Marxist-Leninist notions of trade unions. Increasingly in many Western countries, the state has come to take less interest and to show something like indifference to unions, at least in the private sector in countries such as the US, the UK, and France. In Asia, as we will see from the following chapters, there is a considerable spread, from state-repressive, to state-incorporationist, to state-autonomous and sometimes even state-indifference.

What do unions do and how do they do it?

This section focuses on concepts and trends in two areas. First, it deals with the methods used by unions. Second, it considers the outcomes and effects of union actions.

Reverting to the classic works of the Webbs (1894, 1897), they point to various means whereby unions seek to maintain and improve terms and conditions of employment. First, they identify 'mutual insurance', that is, the provision by unions of various kinds of benefits such as provision for unemployment, sickness, and pensions. Unions still sometimes provide such benefits, though not on a significant scale in most Western countries. However, in the Scandinavian countries, engagement in national welfare states provides an important base and support for unions. In other countries, unions provide some newer benefits, such as insurance for union members and credit card facilities.

Second, the Webbs (1894, 1897) talk about 'unilateral regulation', that is, workers acting collectively, autonomously, and informally to control aspects of their working lives. This used to be very common, especially in the case of craft and occupational union members who established so-called 'restrictive practices' at work. However, over many years, employers have refused to tolerate this sort of union action. It now exists in a fairly robust form only among certain professionals such as doctors and university academics, who still often have considerable autonomy in their jobs, especially in the public sector.

Third, the Webbs (1894, 1897) focus on 'collective bargaining', which we might define as bilateral action with an employer to establish and administer a set of common rules for a group of workers and which regulate work and employment. Through the post-Second World War period, this particular method came to be the dominant mechanism for negotiating with employers in most countries. Increasingly, though, as union power has waned in many countries, collective bargaining has begun to blur with joint consultation. Unions are consulted, as much or more than they are bargained with. As a result of this, we also include here joint consultative type bodies.

The dividing line between collective bargaining and joint consultation is a difficult one to draw. Also, it will depend on the context as to whether unions bargain or consult on certain issues. Here we include in our consideration of trade unions those organizations which otherwise meet the criteria of being a union, but which have a significant joint consultation element in their activity. This means that we consider joint consultation committees, such as works councils, where these meet other desired definitional requirements.

Fourth, in their classic typology, the Webbs (1894, 1897) refer to political lobbying or what they call 'legal enactment'. In other words, unions look to and lobby the state to provide benefits for workers of various kinds. These may cover basic laws which allow unions to operate and also benefit both on-the-job (health and safety) and off-the-job (unemployment benefits, pensions) conditions. Ultimately, the Webbs (1894, 1897) believed that legal enactment offers many advantages in terms of its relative permanency and comprehensiveness. In practice, we have indeed seen legal protections and arrangements tend to grow over time, often as the other mechanisms have declined (Simitis 1987; Supiot 2001; Piore 2002).

As to what unions actually do and what impact they achieve, there is a broad and detailed literature on the effects of unions in OECD countries which is too extensive to review here. However, a few general points may be made which will enable us to put Asian developments into some context.

Unions can have a broad set of effects. Some of these are clearly substantive, related to economic effects on wages, productivity, profitability, and prices. Some effects are more concerned with procedural outcomes and primarily concern questions of voice and justice. Other effects are political at both the micro and macro levels. (See Metcalf 2003, for a useful international overview.)

In terms of economic effects, research has shown that when unions organize a particular firm, industry, or occupation, they usually have a positive effect on wages. Of course, in turn this can affect prices, and union activity did so significantly at some points in time in OECD countries, especially in the 1970s. Unionism can also affect jobs, since employers may well lower employment levels as wages rise or shift jobs away from unionized employment. More recently, the positive effect of unions on wages has been reduced, in large part reflecting the greater openness of national economies to international trade and the difficulty of passing wage increases on in prices (Gospel 2005; Brown 2006). However, vigorous union activity is still an issue, especially in the public sector in many countries.

Historically, when unions have been strong, they have also had a potentially negative effect on profitability, demanding that economic rents be shared more equally with union members. In recent years, in OECD countries, the effect of unions on profitability has also been weakened, however, again reflecting the greater openness of economies to international competition and the reduced scope for union rent seeking. The effect which unions have on productivity has been much debated, especially since the classic US study in the 1980s by Freeman and Medoff (1984). On the one hand, unions can have a negative effect by introducing various kinds of restrictive practices and discouraging employer innovation. On the other hand, they can have a positive effect, by reducing labour turnover, inducing investment in skills, providing a shock and check on employers, and inducing the latter to substitute capital for labour. Research in different countries produces different results: in the US, unions might have had a small positive effect; in the UK, historically, they probably had a small negative effect. For reasons already given, however, unionism in both these countries has now been reduced to a zero effect. Unions and works councils in Germany seem to have a small positive effect (Metcalf 2003).

There is less literature on other effects of unions. In terms of justice, they seem to have an effect on narrowing income differentials, at least between union members, though there is always the possibility that they will increase differentials of union members over non-members. They can have a positive effect on training, again though this may be for union members at the expense of non-members. Above all, they can have a positive effect on representation at work by giving members a voice and helping them in grievances and disputes with employers. This may not mean that union members finish up happier, however, since expectations may rise and they may become more demanding (Metcalf 2003; Guest and Conway 2004).

Finally, we revert to the political effect of unions and the debates outlined above. At various times, unions have had a destabilizing political effect. This was particularly the case in the West after the First World War and to a lesser extent after the Second World War. Unions also had a destabilizing effect in countries such as France, the UK, and Italy during the 1960s and 1970s period of high inflation. However, though, unions have been able to bring down governments, they have rarely played a major part in transforming whole political systems. Against this must be set the fact that unions can also have a stabilizing political effect. Here we refer once again to the Kerr *et al.* (1960) thesis: unions give voice; in turn this legitimizes political processes, and adds to stability.

Explanations of broad trends in advanced industrial countries

We have already touched on some broad trends in the discussion above. Here we explore these further so as to provide some broad comparative contexts for the following chapters on unions in Asian countries.

In terms of union membership, there have been considerable differences in levels and trends across countries over time. Generalizing, however, we can attempt some broad conclusions. Before the First World War, union membership was low in most countries and was confined to a few craft and industrial unions.

Membership grew significantly over the First World War period, reflecting full employment, rising prices, and government and employer reliance on unions in exceptional circumstances. Levels of membership reached around a quarter to a third of workers in countries such as the UK, France, Germany, and the US. Thereafter, in the depression of the interwar years, union membership fell significantly, and did not start to pick up again until the mid-1930s. However, in countries such as Germany and Italy, state-dominated unionism replaced true unions. After the Second World War, there was an explosion of trade unionism in most major industrial societies, reflecting new freedoms and postwar economic expansion. Union membership rose to higher levels than ever in the past, rising beyond a third of the labour force in many countries.

From this point onwards, a split occurred. Union membership in the US started to decline from the early 1960s onwards. By contrast, in the 1960s and 1970s, it rose in much of Europe, largely reflecting price inflation and the spread of union membership to new sectors, such as public sector and white collar workers. Membership reached around half the working population in the UK and Australia, and much higher levels in the Scandinavian countries. However, soon after, it began to fall in France. Thereafter, membership fell in most countries, from the late 1970s/early 1980s onwards, as price inflation fell, unemployment rose (at least temporarily), the composition of industry changed, and countries become more open to foreign competition. The fall in membership was not uniform, however, and in some countries, such as those of Scandinavia, membership was maintained and in some cases even rose.

One consequence of the loss of membership, as we have already seen, is that union structure began to change and there has been an increase in the opening up of unions, union mergers, and the growth of conglomerate unions. There has also been a debate as to the ways forward for unions. Some argue that unions should concentrate on expanding their market share in sectors where they are still strong and seek to better service existing members and 'infill' any gaps in membership. Others argue that they should seek to move into new sectors, such as private sector services, if they are to have a future. Some argue that the way forward for unions is to stress more radical agendas, emphasizing the organization and building of alliances with community groups, representing women, minorities, and students. Others, including many union leaders, believe that in a changed economic climate unions should look towards social partnership with employers and the state as a way of gaining recognition and producing positive benefits for all parties. Still others have argued that there is an increasing trend towards a kind of new enterprise unionism, based as much on joint consultation as on collective bargaining, and that trade unions need to recognize and build on this. (See Turner 1991, Frege and Kelly 2004, Benson and Gospel 2006 for summaries of these trends and debates.) As we will see, these analyses have resonances in, and implications for, unions in Asian countries.

In terms of union methods, little survives in the modern world of unilateral regulation. Employers are not prepared to allow union members to have much untrammelled say in regulating terms and conditions. It might be argued that little now survives of mutual insurance. It is true that some union benefits still exist and unions have tried to devise new ones, such as banking and insurance facilities. It is also true that in some countries unions play an important part in administering state insurance systems. For example, this in part explains the high levels of union membership in some Scandinavian countries and provides an essential underpinning for weak union membership in France. Hence, union methods now come down largely to collective bargaining and political lobbying.

In terms of collective bargaining, there have been a number of broad trends in OECD countries. First, with only a few exceptions, there has been a tendency towards more decentralized collective bargaining. In the private sector, company or workplace bargaining has long been predominant in the US. The UK also moved early in this direction. Other countries, such as France and Italy, have also moved towards greater decentralization. Even in Germany, where various kinds of coordinated bargaining have traditionally been very strong, the tendency is to do more at local level. Even in the public sector, in some countries, there is a trend towards more decentralization.

Second, there has a been a shrinking of the issues which are subject to collective bargaining and in some countries an increase in joint consultation, especially where enterprise committees and works councils exist. Third, in terms of the use of the strike in collective bargaining, this has seen a long-term downward trend in most countries in the private sector. However, the public sector in countries such as France, the UK, and Germany can still see significant strike action.

In terms of political action, it is more difficult to discuss broad trends. Unions continue to lobby and agitate for the supports offered by a welfare state legally and socially. In many countries, they also have links with political parties of the Left. However, lobbying and agitation is probably increasingly a phenomenon of public sector unions. Links with political parties remain significant, but some loosening of such links is discernible in countries such as the UK, France, and Italy.

Conclusions

Three tentative conclusions can be drawn which provide some context for and stimulate questions about unionism in Asian countries. These also prompt certain caveats about comparisons.

First, many different types of unions in terms of ideology, structure, and governance have existed over time. Some insights may be drawn from Western countries where unions developed early, but these should not be taken as inevitable trajectories or models necessarily to be emulated or followed. Also, as we will see in subsequent chapters, there are in Asia alternative types of unions which workers, employers, and governments may take as models. However, it should be noted that transferring models from one country to another is not usually possible and, if attempted, usually results in significant modification of the original.

Second, union membership and power have ebbed and flowed, but for the most part in the advanced industrial countries it has recently undergone a long-term secular decline. The extent of this has led some commentators to believe that a definitive turning point has been reached in which union membership and power are very unlikely ever to re-emerge (Fernie and Metcalf 2005). This prompts interesting questions about the Asian countries surveyed in this volume: are they likely to see a rise of union membership and power or are they likely to see a foreshortened version of the Western story; or will the trajectory of development be completely different?

Third, it is not possible to talk about convergence and divergence of national systems, especially not over such broad areas as comparing North American, European, and Asian systems. There may be elements of convergence, but equally there are considerable diversity and divergence, to the extent that some scholars have talked about a convergence on greater diversity within countries and between systems (Katz and Darbishire 2000).

References

Benson, J. and Gospel, H. (2006) 'The emergent enterprise union? A conceptual and comparative analysis', mimeo, Australia: University of Melbourne and London: King's College.

Brown, W. (2006) 'The influence of product markets on industrial relations', working paper, Cambridge: Department of Economics, Cambridge University.

Child, J., Loveridge, R. and Warner, M. (1973) 'Towards an organizational study of trade unions', *Sociology*, 7(1): 71–91.

Commons, J. (1909) 'American shoemakers 1648–1895: a sketch of industrial evolution', *Quarterly Journal of Economics*, 24: 39–84.

Dunlop, J. (1944) *Wage Determination Under Collective Bargaining*, New York: Macmillan.

Durkheim, E. (1893) *The Division of Labour*, New York: Free Press.

Edelstein, J. D. and Warner, M. (1979) *Comparative Union Democracy*, New Brunswick, NJ: Transaction Books.

Fernie, S. and Metcalf, D. (2005) *Trade Unions: Resurgence or Demise?* London: Routledge.

Freeman, R. and Medoff, J. (1984) *What Do Unions Do?* New York: Basic Books.

Frege, C. and Kelly, J. (2004) *Varieties of Unionism: Strategies for Union Revitalization in a Globalizing Economy*, Oxford: Oxford University Press.

Frenkel, S. (ed.) (1993) *Organized Labor in the Asia-Pacific Region*, Ithaca, NY: Cornell University Press.

Gospel, H. (2005) 'Markets, firms, and unions: a historical-institutionalist perspective on trade unions', in S. Fernie and D. Metcalf (eds) *The Future of Trade Unions*, London: Routledge.

Gramsci, A. (1921–6; compiled 1978) *Selection from His Political Writings*, London: Lawrence & Wishart.

Guest, D. and Conway, N. (2004) 'Exploring the paradox of unionised worker dissatisfaction', *Industrial Relations Journal*, 35(2): 102–21.

Hyman, R. (2001) *Understanding European Trade Unionism: Between Market, Class, and Society*, London: Sage.

Katz, H. and Darbishire, O. (2000) *Converging Divergencies: Worldwide Changes in Employment Systems*, Ithaca, NY: Cornell University Press.

Kerr, C., Dunlop, J., Harbison, F., and Myers, C. A. (1960; 1973 edn) *Industrialism and Industrial Man*, London: Penguin.

Lenin, V. I. (1902) 'What is to be done?', in V. I. Lenin, *Collected Works*, compiled 1961, Moscow: Foreign Language Publishing Press.

Lester, R. A. (1958) *As Unions Mature*, Princeton, NJ: Princeton University Press.

Lipset, S. M., Trow, M. and Coleman, S. J. (1956) *Union Democracy*, New York: Free Press.

Marx, K. (1867) *Das Kapital*, vol. 1, Hamburg: Otto Meissner.

Marx, K. and Engels, F. (1848; 1961 edn) 'The Communist manifesto', in *Collected Works*, Moscow: Foreign Language Publishing Press.

Metcalf, D. (2003) 'Unions and productivity, financial performance, and investment: international evidence', in J. Addison and K. Schnabel (eds) *International Handbook of Trade Unions*, London: Edward Elgar.

Michels, R. (1911; 1955 edn) *The Iron Law of Oligarchy*, New York: Dover.

Perlman, S. (1928) *A Theory of the Labour Movement*, New York: August M. Kelly.

Piore, M. (2002) 'The reconfiguration of work and employment relations in the United States at the turn of the century', paper prepared for International Labour Organisation Symposium, Lyon, 2002.

Ross, A. (1948) *Trade Union Wage Policy*, Berkeley, CA: University of California Press.

Sako, M. (2006) *Shifting Boundaries of the Firm: Japanese Company – Japanese Labour*, Oxford: Oxford University Press.

Simitis, S. (1987). 'Juridification of labor relations', in G. Teubner (ed.) *Juridification of Social Spheres,* Berlin and New York: De Gruyter.

Sorel, G. (1908; 2004 edn) *Reflections on Violence*, New York: Dover Books.

Supiot, A. (2001) *Beyond Employment*, Oxford: Oxford University Press.

Tannenbaum, F. (1951) *A Philosophy of Labor*, New York: Knopft.

Turner, H. A. (1962) *Trade Union Growth, Structure, and Policy*, London: Allen & Unwin.

Turner, L. (1991) *Democracy at Work: Changing World Market and the Future of Unions,* Ithaca, NY: Cornell University Press.

Ulman, L. (1955) *The Rise of the National Trade Union*, Cambridge, MA: Harvard University Press.

Veblen, T. (1904; 1994 edn) *The Theory of the Business Enterprise*, New York: Dover Publications.

Visser, J. (1990) *In Search of Inclusive Unionism*, Deventer: Kluwer.

Webb, S. and Webb, B. (1894) *History of Trade Unionism*, London: Longman.

Webb, S. and Webb, B. (1897) *Industrial Democracy*, London: Longman.

3 Trade unions in Japan

Collective justice or managerial compliance

John Benson

Introduction

Since the 1950s Japanese trade unions have been predominantly enterprise based with union federations uniting workers at the industry and national levels. This enterprise focus has led to claims that Japanese trade unions are little more than company unionism or a third arm of management (Cole 1971; Galenson and Odaka 1976; Tokunaga 1983; Kawanishi 1992; Matsuzaki 1992). For these critics enterprise unions lack the independence from management and the industrial power necessary to represent workers adequately and to achieve the gains made by occupational and industrial unions.

Others, however, have argued that the criticism of this form of unionism overlooks the gains made by Japanese unions in the bargaining process (Shirai and Shimada 1978) and that Japanese unions operate within a skilled internal labour market (Koike 1988). Galenson and Odaka (1976: 637) concede that the strength of enterprise unions are their closeness to their constituency and it is this context that led Taira (1977: 101–2) to argue that unions organized along enterprise lines exhibit the most appropriate form to enhance workers' interests. As Shirai and Shimada (1978: 253) contend, it is not easy to justify the poor evaluation of Japanese unions given their significant achievements.

The debates of these writers, however, took place within an expanding Japanese economy when unemployment was low and a shortage of skilled labour existed. In the past 15 years a different economic context has arisen where wage gains have been considerably harder for unions to achieve, where unemployment has increased substantially and where globalization has made the market for Japanese goods highly competitive. It is thus time to revisit what we know about the Japanese enterprise union and to provide a more contemporary assessment of this form of union organization. In doing so this chapter will explore how this form of organization developed, the types of activities Japanese enterprise unions engage in and their impact, and how the present state of Japanese unions can be explained. The following section will set the scene for this analysis by providing the context and history of Japanese enterprise unionism.

Context and history

Economic and social context

Japan is an archipelago stretching some 3,000 kilometres and covering an area of 378,000 square kilometres. Japan's population in 2005 was a little over 127 million people, the majority of whom reside in urban areas along the coast. Japan is a stable, liberal/pluralistic society which operates under a complex set of cultural and legislative rules. Product market regulations, as with many other regulations, are generally moderate, although they serve to protect the interests of Japanese domestic companies. Agriculture has rapidly declined in its share of employment and now most workers are employed in the services sector. GDP per capita is high at over US$35,000 in 2004 which places Japan among the wealthiest nations in the world. Income distribution has been quite even when compared with most industrialized nations, although the past 15 years have seen an increase in income inequality with now approximately 25 per cent of households earning nearly 75 per cent of total income.

Real GDP growth has slowed considerably over the past 10 years and has averaged a little over 1 per cent per year. This is in stark contrast to the 10 per cent per annum average growth rates of the 1950s and 1960s and the 5 per cent average growth rates of the 1970s and 1980s. Much of this decline in economic activity was caused by poor consumer demand and the rising competitiveness of other countries. This led many Japanese manufacturers to relocate parts of their operations overseas, particularly to other Asian countries. This 'hollowing out' of manufacturing saw employment in this sector fall from 15.5 million in 1991 to 12.2 million in 2002. This represented a fall in employment of 3.3 million employees, or 21.3 per cent of the manufacturing workforce (Benson 2005: 40).

While the loss of jobs was compensated by an increase in service sector employment of 3.58 million employees (24.8 per cent) many of these jobs were temporary or of a part-time nature. This shift partly accounts for the rapid increase in non-regular employment in Japan; and the lower wages paid to these workers have raised concerns about 'whether such employment can support career development and family aspirations' (Whittaker 2004: 30). These events led to a doubling of the unemployment rate compared with the previous 10 years and, in 2005, unemployment stood at 4.5 per cent of the labour force. Summary details are presented in Table 3.1.

Accompanying these economic changes have been a number of important social changes that have impacted on trade unions in a variety of ways. More women are now in the workforce, for example, and this has resulted in a significant rise in double-income households. Nevertheless, the ageing of the population and the decline in the birth rate[1] have meant that the working age population has declined in recent years. This has been exacerbated by the rise in the number of young people not making an immediate transition from school to full-time employment, a number which stood at about 4.2 million young people in 2002. Of this group

Table 3.1 Contextual factors – Japan

General statistics	
Population1 (2005)	127.4 million
Area (square kilometres)[1]	377.9 thousand
Employment by sector (%)[1] (2002) Agriculture Industry Services	5.0 25.0 70.0
Urban population (% of total population)[2]	66.0
GDP per capita[3] (2004)	US$35,882
Income inequality (high, medium or low) Gini coefficient[4] (2002)	Medium 0.4983
Real GDP growth (%)[5] 1986–1995 1995–2005	3.2 1.3
Unemployment (%)[5] 1986–1995 1996–2005	2.5 4.5

Summary description	
Product market regulation[6] (1998)	Medium
Political context (Liberal/pluralistic, state unitarist [Communist, non-Communist])	Liberal/pluralistic
Political stability (high, medium or low)	High

Sources
1 GlobalEDGE, Michigan State University (http://globaledge.msu.edu/ibrd/ CountryStats.asp), accessed 21 April 2006.
2 World Bank, 'Japan at a Glance' (http://web.worldbank.org), accessed 21 April 2006).
3 'Recent Trends and Prospects for Major Asian Economies', *East Asian Economic Perspectives*, Special Issue, 17(1), Table 2.1.
4 Ministry of Health, Labour and Welfare survey in 2002. See Shigeaki, S. (2006) 'The Income Gap and Social Stratification in Japan', *Japan Spotlight*, March/ April: 12–15.
5 OECD (2006) 'Economic, Environmental and Social Statistics', *Factbook 2006*, Paris: Organisation for Economic Cooperation and Development; OECD (2005) *Economic Outlook*, No. 78, 19 December, Paris: Organisation for Economic Cooperation and Development.
6 Nicletti, G., Scarpetta, S. and Boyaud, S. (2000) 'Summary Indicators of Product Market Regulation with an Extension to Employment Protection Legislation', OECD Economic Department Working Papers, No. 226, Paris, Organisation for Economic Cooperation and Development, Table A3.6: 79. In this report Japan = 1.5 compared with the USA = 1.0 and Italy = 2.3.

1.9 million have been labelled as 'freeters' (young people working in temporary jobs), 1.7 million as young people without work, and 0.6 million young people not in work. Several surveys have also suggested that young people have less enthusiasm for work and are more willing to switch jobs (JILPT 2006a).

Trade union history and development

The rapid industrialization and economic growth that occurred after the Meiji Restoration in 1868 transformed many feudal workers to wage labour and led to a severe shortage of skilled workers. These conditions created the prospects for the emergence of trade unions, although the reservoir of cheap agricultural labour coupled with *samurai* acting as subservient 'model labourers' (Hirschmeier and Yui 1975: 310) meant that it would be some years before a viable union movement would emerge. In these early years attempts by some workers to win improvements in wages and working conditions by engaging in strike action were met with strong opposition and managerial appeals to workers' loyalty and sense of family (Hirschmeier and Yui 1975: 311). Where these appeals failed, the state violently suppressed any sign of worker dissent, as was illustrated in the attempted organization of a union by the Tokyo *ricksha* men in 1883 (Lockwood 1968: 557).

In the late 1880s trade unions among printers, iron-workers and other craft workers were formed, although most were short lived (Kuwahara 1993: 241). In part this was due to opposition from employers and the government and, in part, due to 'fluctuating membership' and a lack of funds (Garon 1987: 18). For the state this opposition was seen as necessary so as to prevent the rise of socialism. While numerous other attempts to form unions occurred in the 1890s (Marsland 1989: 29–45), labour would remain largely unorganized until the end of World War I. During the intervening years numerous strikes took place and, in most cases, were met with heavy-handed action from the government and the military. By the end of the Tokyo streetcar strike in 1912 little was left of the fledgling union and socialist movement (Garon 1987: 31).

After the end of World War I the trade union movement began to develop (Nakamura 1993: 5), although union membership advanced slowly (Lockwood 1968: 558). In 1919 Japan signed the Treaty of Versailles which guaranteed the right of workers to organize. Later in that year Japan became a foundation member of the International Labour Organization (Garon 1987: 43; Harari 1973: 10). Notwithstanding these international developments, a number of large-scale strikes occurred in the 1920s and in 1931 the highest number of strikes was recorded to date (Kuwahara 1993; 242; Nakamura 1994: 7).

At this time there were 818 unions representing 7.9 per cent of the workforce (Hazama 1997: 49). The majority of these unions were organized along industrial or craft lines, although about one-third of all unions were organized on an enterprise basis (Sakurabayashi 1985: 72–3; Weinstein 1994: 55). The highest union membership achieved in this period was in 1936 when 420,000 employees were members of unions (Shinoda 1997: 191). At this time, in an attempt to contain strike activity and the growing union movement, the government, as part of their mobilization policy, dissolved all trade unions and absorbed them into the Industrial Association for Serving the Nation. The aim of this organization was to control the radical elements in the workforce and at the enterprise level acted as a defacto local bargaining mechanism and an employee welfare system

(Hart and Kawasaki 1999: 37). Overall, during the 1930s the development of unions was handicapped by political events, particularly legislation which limited their activities and their legal status (Lockwood 1968: 559).

Following World War II, trade union membership grew rapidly and major industrial action, led by industrial unions, commenced almost immediately (Farley 1950: 82–167). While strikes in the early post-war years were often short and peacefully settled, over time strikes were increasingly met with stronger resistance from employers. Militant industrial union activists were dismissed and employers supported a more cooperative, enterprise-based union structure. While such unions had existed earlier[2] (Marsland 1989: 151–5; Kawanishi 1992: 30; Weinstein 1994: 55), they were now strongly supported by management in terms of recognition and provision of facilities (Tokunaga 1983; Gordon 1985; Matsuzaki 1992). This move away from a class orientation and towards more of a market position, as pointed out by Gospel in Chapter 2, also occurred in Germany at the same time. In the case of Japan the focus had to be at the enterprise level as, for the most part, unions were not included in the developing broader social partnership arrangements.

Japanese trade union density reached a peak of 55.8 per cent (6,655,000 members) in 1949 due, in large part, to the support of the Allied Command (Fujimura 1997: 299). This support, coupled with the strong economic growth over the next four decades would lead to a growth in the numbers of enterprise unions and workers joining unions. The number of unions reached a high of 74,579 in 1984 (Kuwahara 1993: 224) while the number of union members was highest in 1994 with some 12,699,000 workers belonging to trade unions, although by this time the union density rate had fallen to 24.1 per cent (Fujimura 1997: 299).

Union types and structure

Since the 1950s, over 80 per cent of union members have been part of an enterprise union which has exclusive representation within the company, although in some companies a weaker, second enterprise union or industrial-type union also exists (Kawanishi 1992; JIL 2000: 90). Nevertheless, most unionized enterprises have only one union representing employees (Inagami 1988) and this type of union accounts for over 95 per cent of all unions (Taishiro 2000: 23). Local unions may be formed within the individual plants of the enterprise, although they are directly linked to the enterprise union. Enterprise unions dominate companies with more than 1,000 employees and the unionization rate was 47.7 per cent in these companies in 2005. In contrast, only 1.2 per cent of companies that employ less than 100 workers were unionized in 2005. In both cases the rate had fallen from 61.0 per cent and 2.0 per cent respectively since 1990 (JILPT 2007: 71). The unionization rate also varied significantly by industry. Industries where the unionization rate was 50 per cent or more in 2004 included electricity, gas and water, government, and financing and insurance while real estate, agriculture and the service sector had rates of unionization below 10 per cent (MPMHAPT 2004).

The enterprise structure of Japanese unionism means that the major objectives of these unions have been the pursuit of economic goals such as job security, increased wages and improved working conditions, goals which have traditionally been pursued through collective bargaining. These goals and the enterprise structure of unions is the 'form of unionism most consistent with the activities of individual firms' (Matsuzaki 1992: 50). For this reason, the unions can be broadly classified as business or market-based organizations (Perlman 1928). This form of unionism can be contrasted to social-democratic and revolutionary types of unions where unions seek a wider role in society or provide opposition to class interests (Hyman 2001).

Nevertheless, as Hyman (2001) points out, all unions are influenced by a range of factors related to markets, society and class and, as a consequence, union strategy will vary over time. By organizing at the enterprise level, Japanese unions have been able to maintain a high degree of independence from the state and have not sought corporatist type arrangements from any of the major political parties. They have, however, sought and encouraged cooperative arrangements with employers as part of their broader market-based strategies. In these endeavours, according to Cole (1971: 228) 'it becomes difficult for the union to represent effectively the interest of its members, as distinct from the interests of the company'. As Mouer (1989: 120) asserts, Japanese 'unions have shifted their attention from the distributive or egalitarian interests of individual workers to administering personnel policies on behalf of management in the name of higher incomes and a larger pie for all workers'. Some unions have, however, elected to present some semblance of managerial challenge and maintain a degree of independence from management, although these have been in the minority (Benson 1995, 1996).

Most full-time, regular workers in a company are eligible to join the union and this includes front-line supervisors and managers up to the level of subsection head (Koike 1988: 251). Until recently, union membership did not normally extend to part-time employees, many of whom are women. Thus the typical union member in Japanese enterprise unions is a full-time male employee and the organizing policies of enterprise unions have served to protect this core group of male workers. Union officials are drawn almost exclusively from the membership, with some of the more senior officials on leave from the company and working full-time for the union (Shirai 1983: 119). In these cases the approval of the company is normally required (Inagami 1988), and it is not uncommon for these officials to be drawn from 'low ranking supervisors' (Tokunaga 1983: 321).

Many enterprise union leaders have gone on to more senior positions with the company. This latter point is illustrated by the results of a survey conducted by the Japan Federation of Employers' Association which found that over 15 per cent of directors of large enterprises were former union officials (Ballon 1992: 42). The closed shop is prevalent in union workplaces and union dues are often deducted from employee wages. The major share of these dues is retained by the enterprise union and is spent on the employment of officials and various union campaigns and activities. Companies also provide the union with a range of facilities, often at little or no cost (Inagami 1988). In this context the unions' '...continued existence and development are tied to the prosperity of the enterprises' (Hanami 1981: 94).

Enterprise unions normally belong to an industrial federation which, in turn, will be affiliated to a more general peak union organization (Matsuda 1993: 193–4). The major national peak union federation is the Japanese Trade Union Confederation (Rengo), which is made up of 54 industrial union federations (Rengo 2006). The present day Rengo was formed from an amalgamation in 1989 of the private sector Rengo and unions belonging to three public sector peak union bodies. Rengo itself was the product of a merger in 1987 of unions belonging to five private sector peak union bodies (Shinoda 1997: 196–7). The amalgamations have taken place as part of an effort to unite the union movement, provide a single union voice, and increase trade union membership. Total unity has not been achieved, however, and two other major peak union bodies have emerged – the National Confederation of Trade Unions (Zenroren), a more militant and political body, and the National Trade Union Council (Zenrokyo). Together these three peak bodies accounted for 75.6 per cent of total union membership in 2003, with Rengo accounting for 85.5 per cent of the union membership affiliated to these associations.

In 2005 the number of unions in Japan stood at 61,178, a decline of 15.3 per cent from 1990 and 18.0 per cent from the record number of 74,579 unions that existed in 1984 (JILPT 2007: 70). A similar decline occurred with the number of union members. In 2005 the total number of union members was 10,014,000 which represented a decline in membership of 17.3 per cent from 1990 and 20.2 per cent from the record membership of 12,699,000 in 1994 (JILPT 2007: 70). Union density in 2005 stood at 18.7 per cent, down significantly from the 25.2 per cent of workers who were members in 1990 (as at June 30; JILPT 2007: 70). Summary statistics are presented in Table 3.2. This rate varied substantially depending on company size; companies employing 1,000 or more employees had an average union density of 47.7 per cent compared with only 1.2 per cent for companies with less than 1,000 employees (JILPT 2007: 71). All three peak bodies have lost members in recent years; between 2000 and 2003 membership fell by 6.9 per cent, 4.2 per cent and 36.4 per cent for Rengo, Zenroren and Zenrokyo respectively (EIRO 2001, 2005). This loss of membership and the corresponding loss of funds have circumscribed and reduced the effectiveness of these bodies.

The loss of members has sparked a number of activities at all levels of Japanese unions. At the enterprise level, some unions have sought to expand their membership base by attempting to recruit more women, part-time workers and managers, as well as workers in subsidiary and subcontracting companies. This trend had commenced in the 1990s and, according to Inagami (1995), 10.6 per cent of unions were attempting to organize part-time workers and 12.1 per cent of unions had started to organize managers. This strategy was seen as essential if unions were to maintain membership in the wake of an increasing percentage of workers employed on a part-time or temporary basis; from 18.8 per cent in 1990 to 29.1 per cent in 2004 (MHLW 2005). In a small number of cases enterprise unions have also extended their coverage to take in workers from other related

Table 3.2 Japanese trade unions

General statistics	
Number of unions[1]	
1990	72,202
2004	61,178
Number of union members[1,2]	
1990	12,265,000
2005	10,138,000
Union density (%)[1,2]	
1990	25.2
2005	18.7

Summary description	
Union type	
Main	Economic/market
Secondary	Political
(Economic/market, political, other)	
Union structure	
Main	Enterprise
Secondary	Industrial
(Occupational, industrial, general, enterprise)	
Unity of peak organization (high, medium or low)	Medium
State control of unions (high, medium or low)	Low
Involvement in collective bargaining (high, medium or low)	Medium–low

Sources
1 JILPT (2006) *Japanese Working Life Profile 2006/2007*, Tokyo: Japan Institute for Labour Policy and Training.
2 Ministry of Health, Labour and Welfare, *Basic Survey on Labour Unions*, in JILPT (2006) 'International Comparison of Labour Statistics', Tokyo: Japan Institute for Labour Policy and Training.

firms within the corporate group (*Keiretsu*) (Sako and Sato 2000; Sako 2006) while others have allowed members transferred to subsidiaries to maintain their union membership and about a third of all unions have allowed temporary employees to join (JIL 2002: 14). Industrial union federations have also sought to halt the declining membership by merging with other industrial unions and by setting up occupational type trade unions, unions for agency workers and more general community type unions (EFILWC 2005: 18). At the level of the peak federations, Rengo has established 'regional unions' where part-time workers can join as individual members (JILPT 2005: 21).

What do unions do?

In seeking their essentially economic objectives Japanese enterprise unions have traditionally placed strong reliance on collective bargaining at both the company and industry levels. Collective bargaining is an appropriate mechanism for this form of unionism as the key objectives of economic rewards and welfare benefits can be achieved by trading off aspects of work such as job control, increased work flexibility and the introduction of new work forms and technology. Underpinning this bargaining has always been a tacit understanding that employment security was guaranteed (Benson and Debroux 2000).

Collective bargaining in Japan over wages and other monetary conditions developed a unique form in the 1950s. Groups of unions would lodge their wage demands and if these were not met would simultaneously stage repeated, short industrial action. This system became known as the spring wage offensive or *shunto* and led to a system of industry and national level coordination of enterprise wages (Sako 1997; Suzuki 1997: 78). Such a coordinated system was important as enterprises where strike action was taking place would not lose market share to their competitors and, as the industrial action was short, it would not threaten the viability of the company (Nimura 1994: 81). Claims were thus formulated at the industry and national level, with collective bargaining taking place at the industry and/or enterprise level around March each year. Notwithstanding the brief bargaining period, particular unions would lead the bargaining and set standards that weaker unions could adopt. The similarity of wage settlements across enterprises and industries demonstrated the influence of union federations and the wage settlements were based on macro-economic conditions as much as enterprise considerations (Nikkeren 1999; Tachibanaki and Noda 2000: 99).

Although at times there was some disquiet with this system, particularly with the way wage increases were calculated (Nimura 1994: 82), it remained intact for the next four decades and was able to deliver real wage increases for most union members, as well as the working population in general. During the 1990s, with the economy experiencing very low growth rates and increasing global competition, wage settlements became more dispersed and local enterprise considerations more important. In 1999 *shunto* failed to deliver a real wage increase (Weathers 2003: 127) and in 2000 nominal wages remained static.

By the late-1990s the prolonged period of economic downturn led many employers and some unions to question the relevance of this multi-employer approach (Suzuki 1997: 79; Kawamoto 2000: 18). In 2002 the end of *shunto* as a major uniform wage fixing mechanism was accepted by Japanese unions (Rengo 2002). The collapse of *shunto* as a unified system meant that the notion of socially accepted wage standards had essentially disappeared from the Japanese system of wage determination (Nakamura 2007).

The demise of *shunto* meant that the collective determination of wages and working conditions moved to a more enterprise-based system (Weathers 2003: 128). A more enterprise-focused system had, however, been developing from the early 1990s and paralleled the decline in union membership and the economic downturn. Companies had been expanding their joint consultative arrangements such that by 1997 four out of five unionized enterprises (78.1 per cent) had such mechanisms in place compared with 73.5 per cent of unionized enterprises in 1992 (JIL 2000: 94).

At this time (1997) larger companies were found to be more likely to have such mechanisms in place: 92.8 per cent of those companies that employed between 1,000 and 4,999 workers and 100.0 per cent of those companies that employed 5,000 or more workers (JIL 2000: 94). In the same year, with the exception of wages, issues were more likely to be discussed through some form of joint consultation (JIL 2000: 95). Even in the case of wages only 58.9 per cent of unionized companies undertook collective bargaining compared with 52.0 per cent of unionized companies discussing this matter through some joint consultation process.

By 2002, 80.6 per cent of unionized enterprises had joint consultative arrangements in place (JILPT 2006c: 74). As in earlier years these activities were concentrated in large enterprises (98.3 per cent and 97.4 per cent respectively) and again, with the exception of wages (58.1 per cent and 40.3 per cent respectively) were the main mechanism in the settlement of working conditions (JILPT 2006c: 74–5). Although the line between collective bargaining and joint consultation is somewhat artificial, these findings do illustrate the decentralization of Japanese industrial relations in recent years.[3]

Joint consultation was strengthened by the revised Labour Standards Law (1998) which introduced statutory management–worker committees for the revision of working hours (Yamakawa 1998). These joint consultation arrangements occurred at the same time Japanese companies were looking to develop a more individualistic approach to enterprise HRM policies. Notwithstanding the impact of the sustained economic downturn, it is the case that the move from collective bargaining to joint consultation has occurred simultaneously with hours of work, including the level of unpaid overtime, increasing after falling for much of the past 10 years. There has also occurred in recent years an increase in short-term employment with lower hours and less ancillary benefits. Many of these short-term employees are now recruited through employment agencies, and companies are making more use of the dual system for training which includes on-the-job training and training at occupational colleges.

The present system of wage determination remains firmly tied to collective bargaining in unionized companies. With the demise of *shunto* as a unified 'national' system, collective bargaining now predominantly takes place at the enterprise level. Moreover, as many companies have experienced financial difficulties over the past decade, unions have been forced to trade off wage increases for some guarantees concerning employment levels. Employers have, since about 1999, also sought to align wage increases with business performance (EFILWC 2005: 6–7). This has been particularly the case with the lump-sum bonuses awarded twice a year. While some employers have also attempted to extend performance criteria to monthly basic wages, it remains the case that this wage component remains strongly linked to age, length of service and ability.

Scheduled hours of work are also primarily determined by collective bargaining, again now at the company level. Despite the hours of work falling in some industries, in general, unions have not made any major gains in this area in recent years. Nevertheless, there does appear to be some increase in the diversity of working hours among Japanese companies. This may be partly a result of some local bargaining that has occurred with the demise of *shunto* as a national system, but is also due to the 2001 *Social Agreement on Employment* between Rengo and Nikkerein, the then peak employer body. The *Social Agreement* commits the parties to making 'comprehensive efforts to maintain employment', on the one hand, while 'workers would accept shorter working hours and lower wages' on the other (EFILWC 2005: 9). Such an agreement was, at least in part, a response to the growing unemployment at the time and the union movement's key objective of maintaining employment levels.

The resultant industrial action that flows from collective bargaining is low in Japan by international standards. Working days lost in the period 1998 to 2002 averaged one day per thousand workers, compared to an average of two working days lost for the period 1993 to 1997 (EFILWC 2005: 22). The number of disputes has fallen from 2,071 in 1990 to 737 in 2004 (JILPT 2006c: 75). The reason for disputes has also changed. In 1990, 46.2 per cent of all disputes involved wage increases; by 2004 this percentage had fallen to 19.3 per cent of all disputes. In contrast, disputes involved discharge and re-instatement rose from 1.9 per cent in 1990 to 20.9 per cent of all disputes in 2006 (JILPT 2007: 75). Paralleling this decline has been a sharp rise in the number of individual disputes that require formal counselling and settlement. In 2005, some 176,429 individual civil applications were lodged with the appropriate agencies compared with 41,284 applications in 2001. This represents an increase of 327.4 per cent over five years (JILPT 2006c: 74). Over one quarter of these disputes (26.1 per cent) involved termination of employment, with another 14.0 per cent relating to a deterioration of employment and working conditions (JILPT 2006c: 74).

In short, Japanese unions have moved from a unified collective bargaining system to one more focused at the enterprise and where joint consultation is now the preferred form of resolving most issues. This is illustrated in Table 3.3 which provides a summary of the present situation in Japan. With the decline in the number of unions and the fall in union density, the extent of collective bargaining can be classified as moderate and is limited, in general, to the larger companies. Industrial disputes are low, both by international and Japanese standards. While the degree of state intervention in employment protection can only be classified as medium, a trend to more individual dispute resolution, using civil law, has began to replace some of the traditional protection provided by unions.

For most of the last five decades real wages have increased, although as pointed out by Hart and Kawasaki (1999: 44), real wage increases have been well below productivity increases. In the two periods where negative productivity growth occurred (1975 and 1992) wages continued to grow, although subsequently there was a fall for a short period in real wages. What has been the effect of union activity on the growth of wages? Tachibanaki and Noda (2000) found that wages did not significantly differ between union members and other workers, although they did find unions were associated with marginally higher wages for female workers. Hart and Kawasaki (1999: 42) have cited studies which show the major

Table 3.3 What do Japanese unions do?

Activities	
Extent of collective bargaining[1,2] (high, medium or low)	Medium
Level of collective bargaining[1,2] (high, medium or low)	
National	Low
Industry	Low–medium
Enterprise	High
Extent of joint consultation[1,2] (high, medium or low)	High
Industrial disputes[1,2,3]	
Working days lost per 1,000 employees (2003)	<1
Relative assessment (high, medium or low)	Low
Degree of state intervention in employment protection (high, medium or low)	Medium

Sources
1 JILPT (2006) *Japanese Working Life Profile 2006/2007*, Tokyo: Japan Institute for Labour Policy and Training.
2 JILPT (2005) *Labour Situation in Japan and Analysis: Detailed Exposition 2005/2006*, Tokyo: Japan Institute for Labour Policy and Training.
3 MHLW (2003) *Survey on Labour Disputes*, Tokyo: Ministry of Health, Labour and Welfare.

factors in determining the size of wage increases are the demand and supply for labour, consumer prices and general business conditions.

On the other hand, several studies have found that union firms tend to be significantly less profitable than their non-union counterparts (Benson 1994; Brunello 1992). While this could be explained by union firms being less productive, research evidence to support this theory has been mixed (Muramatsu 1984; Brunello 1992; Benson 1994). An alternative explanation is that unions may well force employers to pay higher wages; and more recent studies have shown that unions are associated with significantly higher wages for male employees (Hara 2003; Noda 2007). Indeed, Noda (2007: 26) has pointed out that the average male wage was 11 to 20 per cent higher in unionized companies.

Union members may receive a range of non-monetary benefits from union membership. Japanese unions have since the 1950s been willing to moderate wage demands to ensure job security for their members. Tachibanaki and Noda (2000: 100–1) point to findings that unions have a significant effect on working hours and severance payments. Results from their study indicate that unions in some instances have reduced working hours by 5.3 per cent and increased severance payments by 28 per cent. In addition, they note that workers in unionized firms perceive that they have a stronger voice, although this does not appear to lead to higher job satisfaction or a lower propensity to leave. A recent study by Noda (2007) has also observed that unions resist the lowering of working conditions and are slower at making employment adjustments than non-unionized counterparts during periods of economic decline.

A problem with the above findings is that unionized firms have been simply defined as those with a union presence. In some cases, however, Japanese enterprise unions appear to be actually an extension of management (Cole 1971; Galenson and Odaka 1976; Kawanishi 1992; Matsuzaki 1992; Tokunaga 1983) rather than independent organizations representing workers. To overcome this problem Benson (1996) has classified unions according to their structural and functional independence. This results in unions being classified into four types: company, enterprise, oligarchic and independent. The findings seem quite clear: more independent unions are more likely to bargain over management practices, work less hours and receive higher overtime payments, and are more likely to have participation arrangements such as suggestion schemes. Workers in these unions did, however, take more industrial action and have higher levels of absenteeism.

Explaining the development, structure and strategies of trade unions

Japanese enterprise unions are organized on an enterprise basis, engage in many of the key activities at this level and form the basic unit within a federation structured trade union movement. In many ways this sets them apart from trade unions in most industrialized economies, although in some of these economies enterprise unionism to varying degrees also exists. This section will consider why Japanese unions are structured in this way using the four explanations that were outlined in Chapter 2. A summary of these explanations is presented in Table 3.4.

Historical traditions

The first explanation pertaining to the structure of Japanese trade unions is that the structure represents certain historical traditions. Such an explanation would receive support from Whitley (1992) who argues that the structure of the modern Japanese company is a product of pre-industrial history and the industrialization process. This can be seen in the high levels of trust and collective identities that exist in the modern Japanese company which Whitley (1992: 182) traces back to the Tokugawa period. Given the general hostility towards industrial unionism, enterprise structures may well have been the only form acceptable to employers. However, given the fact that only a third of all unions were organized along enterprise lines in the 1930s and that the dominance of this structural form has only been the case since the 1950s it is likely that other factors are more important.

Political context

The second explanation for the union structure is the political context and the degree of liberalization and autonomy granted to worker organizations. The industrial unions that developed during the US occupation had increasingly engaged in industrial action that was, as discussed earlier in this chapter, strongly resisted by employers and the state. This occurred at a critical juncture of economic and political events which encouraged the state, the US occupation authorities and employers to restructure unions along enterprise lines (Whitley 1992: 37). At the

Table 3.4 Explaining Japanese trade union development, structure and strategy

Political context	
Degrees of liberalization and autonomy (repression, tolerance, support, indifference)	Indifference
Relations with the state (dependent, independent)	Independent
Markets	
Openness (imports + exports as % of GDP)[1]	25.1 (Low)
Degree of competition (high, medium or low)	High
Financial markets	
Openness to market financing	Medium
Ownership[2] (group, institutional, foreign, dispersed)	Dispersed
Labour markets	
Demand elasticity (relates to ability of employers to pass on wage increases in prices – high, medium or low)	Low–Medium
Employers	
Concentration (top 100 companies as a percentage value of total)	Medium
Employer organization membership (high, medium or low)	High
Multinational (high, medium or low)	Low
Unitarist or pluralist perspective	Pluralist

Sources

1 GlobalEDGE, Michigan State University. Online. Available HTTP: <(http://globaledge.msu.edu/ibrd/CountryStats.asp> (accessed 20 April 2006).

2 'Welcome M&As in Japan', *Japan Spotlight*, January/February, 2006: 6–25.

same time, the productivity movement was being established in Japan with its underlying principle of sharing enterprise gains between employers, workers and consumers. This was accepted by workers as a means of ensuring job security, and served to reinforce an enterprise union structure as it was at the enterprise level that productivity programmes would be developed.

The role of the employer

This observation leads to a consideration of the role of employers in shaping union structure. It can be argued that an enterprise union focus was promoted by Japanese employers as this was seen to be an important way of overcoming the 'excesses' of industrial and ideologically based unionism that were seen as responsible for the wave of strike action in the late 1940s and early 1950s. As highlighted by Dore (1990: 328), as industrial unions became more militant, 'second' unions were covertly supported by employers who were willing to recognize their legitimacy.

Moreover, this was consistent with the principles underpinning the emerging productivity movement and was seen as a way of more closely aligning the interests of workers with those of the company. This led to employers providing resources for the enterprise unions, and these unions, with some guarantees of job security, were prepared to work with management to ensure the success of the company. Thus, while external influences were important, it was the employers' strong support for this type of unionism which proved to be a decisive factor in ensuring the unions continuation and growth.

Competition and globalization

Employers' strategies cannot, however, be divorced from the environment in which they operate. This leads to a fourth explanation of Japanese union structure: the economic contexts of competition and more lately globalization. Japanese firms operate in, and have done so for many years, a highly competitive domestic market. Through the *Keiretsu/s* Japanese companies have a high degree of vertical integration and are usually focused on a particular industry. This industrial structure has resulted in intense competition between firms. In turn this competition has led to an emphasis on market share, which can be achieved by a unique product, a focus on quality (and to a lesser extent price), and improvements in productivity. All of these are company-based objectives that are assisted by a union structure in which collective bargaining frameworks are enterprise based. Wider union concerns have been regarded as less important and achievable by union federations at the industry or ideological levels.

More recently, although not an explanation of union structure *per se*, globalization has reinforced enterprise union structures both within Japan and in offshore operations.

Conclusions

This chapter has examined Japanese unions and their key activities. A particular focus of this chapter has been on how the dominant form of unionism developed in Japan. Japanese unions are structured on an enterprise basis and although many belong to an industrial federation, and in turn a peak union body, there is no sense of a common ideology or solidarity between unions. Unions in Japan engage in collective bargaining and face many of the challenges that unions in other industrialized countries face. These challenges include decreasing union membership, declining relevance to younger workers, a fall in the significance of collective bargaining, and an increasing number of employers embracing a globalized market perspective.

What then is the future of Japanese enterprise unions? The present climate provides a clear indication of the weakness of the enterprise union model. Nevertheless, it is unlikely that this model will change in the near future as can be seen by the unwillingness of unions to attempt to provide a more inclusive union structure by recruiting more part-time and women workers. While there are some possibilities for change, as shown by the emergence of several general or industry type unions, and unions that go beyond the one company to service workers in associated companies and networks, the evidence to date indicates that these initiatives are the exception and are unlikely to be part of a general trend. Of course large companies will continue to be highly unionized but with the demographic changes taking place in Japan, coupled with cutbacks in pensions, it is likely that an increasing number of workers will fall outside unions and the protection and benefits they can provide.

Notes

1 The fertility rate in Japan in 2005 stood at 1.25. See JILPT (2006b: 4).
2 Sakurabayashi (1985: 72–3) claimed that in the period 1926 to 1930 enterprise unions represented 38 per cent of total membership. Similarly, Weinstein (1994) estimated that in 1930 when total union membership was 354,312 some 127,463 workers or 36 per cent of union members belonged to an enterprise union. At this time industrial unions were the major union form covering 46 per cent of union members with craft unions covering an estimated 7 per cent. See Table 1.1.
3 In 2004 the number of unionized enterprises that had joint consultative arrangements in place was reported as 37.3 per cent (JILPT 2007: 72). It is difficult to understand why such a significant drop took place from 2002 and suggests some problem with the sampling and/or the response rate. Given this uncertainty I have reported only the 2002 figures in the main text.

References

Ballon, R. (1992) *Foreign Competition in Japan: Human Resource Strategies*, London: Routledge.

Benson, J. (1994) 'The economic effect of unionism on Japanese manufacturing enterprises', *British Journal of Industrial Relations*, 32(1): 1–21.

Benson, J. (1995) 'Japanese unions: managerial partner or worker challenge? *Labour and Industry*, 6(2): 87–102.

Benson, J. (1996) 'A typology of Japanese enterprise unions', *British Journal of Industrial Relations*, 34(3): 371–86.

Benson, J. (2005) 'Unemployment in Japan: globalisation, restructuring and social change', in J. Benson and Y. Zhu (eds) *Unemployment in Asia*, London: Routledge.

Benson, J. and Debroux, P. (2000) 'Japanese trade unions at the crossroads: dilemmas and opportunities created by globalization', *Asia Pacific Business Review*, 6(3/4): 114–32.

Brunello, G. (1992) 'The effect of unions on firm performance in Japanese manufacturing', *Industrial and Labour Relations Review*, 45(3): 471–87.

Cole, R. (1971) *Japanese Blue Collar: The Changing Tradition*, Berkeley, CA: University of California Press.

Dore, R. (1990) *British Factory – Japanese Factory*, Berkeley, CA: University of California Press.

EFILWC (2005) *Industrial Relations in the EU, Japan and the USA, 2003–2004*, Dublin: European Foundation for the Improvement of Living and Working Conditions.

EIRO (European Industrial Relations Observatory) (2001) *2001 Annual Review for Japan*, Online. Available HTTP: <http://www.eiro.eurofounf.eu.int> (accessed 24 May 2006).

EIRO (European Industrial Relations Observatory) (2005) *Industrial Relations in Japan 2003–2004*, Online. Available HTTP: <http://www.eiro.eurofounf.eu.int> (accessed 24 May 2006).

Farley, M. (1950) *Aspects of Japan's Labor Problems*, New York: John Day Company.

Fujimura, H. (1997) 'New unionism: beyond enterprise unionism?', in M. Sato and H. Sato (eds) *Japanese Labour and Management in Transition*, London: Routledge.

Galenson, W. and Odaka, K. (1976) 'The Japanese labour market', in H. Patrick and H. Rosovsky (eds) *Asia's New Giant: How the Japanese Economy Works*, Washington: Brookings Institution.

Garon, S. (1987) *The State and Labor in Modern Japan*, Berkeley, CA: University of California Press.

Gordon, A. (1985) *The Evolution of Labour Relations in Japan*, Cambridge, MA: Harvard University Press.

Hanami, T. (1981) *Labour Relations in Japan Today*, Tokyo: Kodansha.

Hara, H. (2003) 'Kumiai ha nanno tameni?: fukyo taisaku to chingin wo megutte [What is a labour union for?: anti-recession measures and wages], in *Rengo Rodo Kumiai Nikansuru Isiki Chosa Hokokusho [Survey Report on Awareness of Labour Unions]*, Tokyo: Japanese Trade Union Confederation, Research Institute for Advancement of Living Standards.

Harari, E. (1973) *The Politics of Labour Legislation in Japan*, Berkeley, CA: University of California Press.

Hart, R. and Kawasaki, S. (1999) *Work and Pay in Japan*, Cambridge: Cambridge University Press.

Hazama, H. (1997) *The History of Labour Management in Japan*, Basingstoke: Macmillan.

Hirschmeier, J. and Yui, T. (1975) *The Development of Japanese Business: 1600–1973*, London: George, Allen and Unwin.

Hyman, R. (2001) *Understanding European Trade Unionism: Between Market, Class and Society*, London: Sage.

Inagami, T. (1988) *Japanese Workplace Industrial Relations*, Tokyo: Japan Institute of Labour.

Inagami, T. (1995) *Seijuku Shakai no Nakano Kigyobetsu Kumiai [Enterprise Unions in a Mature Society]*, Tokyo: Japan Institute of Labour.

JIL (2000) *Japanese Working Life Profile 2000: Labour Statistics*, Tokyo: Japan Institute of Labour.

JIL (2002) *Formation of Labor Unions and Responses to Management Crises – Industrial Relations in the Late 1990s (Summary)*, Tokyo: Japan Institute of Labour.

JILPT (2005) *Labor Situation in Japan and Analysis: Detailed Exposition 2005/2006: Labour Statistics*, Tokyo: Japan Institute for Labour Policy and Training.

JILPT (2006a, 16 January) Japan Labor Flash No. 53, Online. Available HTTP: < http://www.jil.go.jp/emm/whatjlf.htm>.

JILPT (2006b, 15 June) Japan Labor Flash No. 63, Online. Available HTTP: < http://www.jil.go.jp/emm/whatjlf.htm>.

JILPT (2006c) *Japanese Working Life Profile 2005/2006: Labour Statistics*, Tokyo: Japan Institute for Labour Policy and Training.

JILPT (2007) *Japanese Working Life Profile 2006/2007: Labour Statistics*, Tokyo: Japan Institute for Labour Policy and Training.

Kawamoto, H. (2000) 'The 2000 spring labour-management wage negotiations', *Japan Labor Bulletin*, 39(9): 18.

Kawanishi, H. (1992) *Enterprise Unionism in Japan*, London: Kegan Paul International.

Koike, K. (1988) *Understanding Industrial Relations in Modern Japan*, London: MacMillan.

Kuwahara, Y. (1993) 'Industrial relations in Japan', in G. Bamber and R. Lansbury (eds) *International and Comparative Industrial Relations*, Sydney: Allen and Unwin.

Lockwood, W. (1968) *The Economic Development of Japan*, Princeton, NJ: Princeton University Press.

Marsland, S. (1989) *The Birth of the Japanese Labor Movement*, Honolulu, HI: University of Hawaii Press.

Matsuda, Y. (1993) 'Japan', in S. Deery and R. Mitchell (eds) *Labour Law and Industrial Relations in Asia*, Melbourne: Longman Cheshire.

Matsuzaki, H. (1992) 'Japanese business unionism: the historical development of a unique labour movement', *Studies in Human Resource Management and Industrial Relations in Asia, No. 1*, Sydney: University of New South Wales.

MHLW (2005) *Monthly Labour Survey*, Tokyo: Ministry of Health, Labour and Welfare.

MPMHAPT (2004) *Labour Force Survey*, Tokyo: Ministry of Public Management, Home Affairs, Posts and Telecommunications.

Mouer, R. (1989) 'Japanese model of industrial relations: warnings or opportunities?', *Hitotsubashi Journal of Social Studies*, 21: 105–24.

Muramatsu, K. (1984) 'The effect of trade unions on productivity in Japanese manufacturing industries', in M. Aoki (ed.) *The Economic Analysis of the Japanese Firm*, Amsterdam: Elsevier Science Publishers.

Nakamura, K. (2007) 'Decline or revival?: Japanese labor unions', *Japan Labor Review*, 4(1): 7–22.

Nakamura, T. (1993) *A History of Showa Japan: 1926–1989*, Tokyo: University of Tokyo Press.

Nakamura, T. (1994) *Lectures on Modern Japanese Economic History: 1926–1994*, Tokyo: LTCP International Library Foundation.

Nikkeren (1999) *The Current Labour Economy in Japan*, Tokyo: Japan Federation of Employer Associations.

Nimura, K. (1994) 'Post-second world war labour relations in Japan', in J. Hagan and A. Wells (eds) *Industrial Relations in Australia and Japan*, St Leonards, NSW: Allen and Unwin.

Noda, T. (2007) 'Effects of enterprise labour unions: reviewing the effects on wages and employment adjustment', *Japan Labor Review*, 4(1): 23–40.

Perlman, S. (1928) *A Theory of the Labor Movement*, New York: August M. Kelly.

Rengo (2002) *Rengo Hakusho [Rengo White Book]*, Tokyo: Japanese Trade Union Confederation.

Rengo (2006) Japanese Trade Union Confederation. <http://www.jtuc-rengo.org> (accessed 6 May 2006).

Sako, M. (1997) 'Shunto: the role of employer and union coordination at the industry and inter-sectoral levels', in M. Sako and H. Sato (eds) *Japanese Labour and Management in Transition: Diversity, Flexibility and Participation*, London: Routledge.

Sako, M. (2006) *Shifting Boundaries of the Firm: Japanese Company – Japanese Labour*, Oxford: Oxford University Press.

Sako, M. and Sato, H. (2000) 'Union networks in the extended enterprise in Japan: evidence from the automobile and electrical machinery industries', paper presented at the International Industrial Relations Association Congress, Tokyo, May–June.

Sakurabayashi, M. (1985) *The Organization and Functions of the Industrial Association for Serving the Nation*, Tokyo: Ocha-no-mizu-shobo.

Shinoda, T. (1997) 'Rengo and policy participation: Japanese-style neo-corporatism', in M. Sako and H. Sato (eds) *Japanese Labour and Management in Transition*, London: Routledge, 187–214.

Shirai, T. (1983) 'A theory of enterprise unionism', in T. Shirai (ed.) *Contemporary Industrial Relations in Japan*, Madison, WI: University of Wisconsin Press.

Shirai, T. and Shimada, H. (1978) 'Japan', in J. Dunlop and W. Galenson (eds) *Labour in the Twentieth Century*, New York: Academic Press.

Suzuki, F. (1997) 'Labour relations, trade union organizations, collective bargaining, and labour management consultation', in Deutscher Gewerkschaftsbund (DGB) and Japanese Trade Union Confederation (JTUC) (eds) *Future of Work, Future of Social Welfare State, Future of Trade Unions*, Tokyo: Rengo.

Tachibanaki, T. and Noda, T. (2000) *The Economic Effects of Trade Unions in Japan*, London: Macmillan.

Taira, K. (1977) 'In defence of Japanese enterprise unions', *Japan Echo*, 4(2): 95–109.

Taishiro, T. (2000) *Japanese Industrial Relations*, Tokyo: Japan Institute of Labour.

Tokunaga, S. (1983) 'A Marxist interpretation of Japanese industrial relations, with special reference to large private enterprises', in T. Shirai (ed.) *Contemporary Industrial Relations in Japan*, Madison, WI: University of Wisconsin Press.

Weathers, C. (2003) 'The decentralization of Japan's wage setting system in comparative perspective', *Industrial Relations Journal*, 34(2): 119–34.

Weinstein, D. (1994) 'United we stand: firms and enterprise unions in Japan', *Journal of the Japanese and International Economies*, 8: 53–71.

Whitley, R. (1992) *Business Systems in East Asia: Firms, Markets and Societies*, London: Sage.

Whittaker, D. (2004) 'Unemployment, underemployment and overemployment: re-establishing social sustainability', *Japan Labor Review*, 1(1): 29–38.

Yamakawa, R. (1998) 'Overhaul after 50 years: the amendment of the labour standards law', *Japan Labour Bulletin*, 37(11): 5–12.

4 Trade unions in South Korea

Transition towards neocorporatism?

Chris Rowley and Kil-Sang Yoo

Introduction

Trade unions, industrial relations and economic development have been closely related in South Korea (Korea). During the development era from the early 1960s to the mid-1980s Korea successfully transformed from one of the poorest nations in the aftermath of World War II and the Korean War to a booming economy and modern nation-state. Its 'economic miracle' generated overall real annual gross domestic product (GDP) growth rates of more than 8 per cent on average per annum and export growth rates of a phenomenal 30 per cent (Rowley *et al.* 2002) and expanded employment (Rowley *et al.* 2005).

The Korean model of economic development had some distinct characteristics (Rowley and Bae 1998). Aspects related to trade unions included military governments that encouraged change and growth through a series of five-year economic and social development plans. Authoritarianism dominated the operation of the economy and business, and supported a strategy of export-led industrialization that used the abundant and cheap labour. To enhance competitiveness by maintaining lower wage costs and longer working hours, the government adopted a 'labour exclusive' policy whereby labour was not considered an important factor in policy. The labour movement was under the control of the government, with wages and working hours determined by employers. This is one reason why the employer favoured authoritarian industrial relations: although lacking fairness, it did not cause serious overt industrial relations conflict until the 1980s.

However, economic and social development changed the sense of values and attitudes of younger generations. These grew up in much better circumstances than their parents, were highly educated and resisted the prevailing ethos. Conflicts with the old industrial relations system began to erupt in the 1980s. The Declaration of Democratisation in 1987 suddenly removed a protective shield from the authoritarian industrial relations and touched off massive disputes and labour movement growth. Also, there was organizational change, shifting from a state-sponsored single union federation at the national level and enterprise unions, to twin federations and also industry and occupational unions.

This situation has been portrayed as 'an unsteady mix of pluralism, corporatism and clientelistic paternalism in South Korean industrial relations' (McNamara 2002: 154). Kim and Bae's (2004) three-stage categorization of the industrial relations system echoes McNamara: pre-1987 state corporatism; 1987–91 exploratory pluralism; post-1997 experiment with social corporatism. Trade unions have experienced many ups and downs since, especially during the 1997 Asian Financial Crisis, and are still searching for a new paradigm of more constructive industrial relations.

In this chapter we explore various facets of Korean trade unions. The relevant context and history are outlined, followed by union types and structure, what unions do and their impact.

Context and history

During the Japanese colonial period (1910–45) employers exploited and discriminated against Korean workers. Therefore, the labour movement was anti-foreign capital and defiant toward employers and government and was connected with the independence movement. The Korean War (1950–3) and the division of the Korean peninsula were crucial factors contributing to the evolution of an authoritarian industrial relations environment.

After the Korean War, concern with communism grew in South Korea. As many trade union leaders had connections with the communists, the labour movement was treated as possibly serving the interests of North Korea. Consequently, only the anti-communist labour movement was granted legal approval. Therefore, so-called 'yellow' unions (with leaders controlled by management and the authorities) developed. Collective bargaining and union actions were strictly restricted. Even research and teaching on labour issues at colleges and universities were monitored and actually prohibited.

South Korea had few natural resources, and thus adopted an export-led industrialization strategy from the 1960s. Economic growth was the top priority under the slogan of 'growth first, distribution later', and a series of military authoritarian governments from 1961 oversaw the emergence of a form of capitalism based on a particular variety of large-scale diversified business conglomerates (the *chaebol*) and close inter-linkages with government (Rowley and Bae 1998; Rowley *et al.* 2002). The labour movement and basic labour rights were restricted for this export-led economic development strategy and competitiveness via low wages and tight control. Therefore, unions were too weak to voice the discontent of members and represent their demands. In sum, unions were harshly suppressed by a containment policy which considered the labour movement harmful to economic success.

However, with economic development and improvements in living standards, opposition developed, especially from the late 1970s. Even though formal union activities were strictly checked, a strong labour movement emerged, as seen in outbreaks of 'wildcat' strikes. These were often met with the clubs of the *kusadae*, mobs hired by companies (Lee 1993). Furthermore, from the mid-1980s, politicians, students, scholars and unionists all demanded political democratization and guarantees of labour rights.

With the 1987 regime change to democracy, restrictions on the labour movement slackened and latent anger and frustration emerged in the form of defiant unions and the organizing of strikes. A major reason for this was that the fruits of the economic miracle had not been distributed fairly and workers now demanded wage rises to compensate. However, the 1997 Asian Financial Crisis hit Korea hard, and the country faced national insolvency and turned to the International Monetary Fund (IMF) for assistance. The IMF required a fundamental restructuring of the economy and labour market in return.

When the Crisis hit, President-elect Kim Dae-Jung established the Korean Tripartite Commission in January 1998 to boost cooperation among the representatives of labour, management, political parties and government. In 1998 the Commission agreed on the *Social Agreement for Overcoming the Economic Crisis* covering 90 items. The key contents included the immediate enactment of dismissals for managerial reasons and a worker dispatch scheme for increasing labour market numerical flexibility, legalization of teachers' unions, workplace councils for public servants, extension of the employment insurance system and union rights to engage in political activities for the enhancement of basic labour rights, strengthening employment stabilization and unemployment policies, and the promotion of management transparency and corporate restructuring.

Immediately after signing this social pact, the Korean Confederation of Trade Unions (KCTU) leadership faced criticisms from members. This resulted in the resignation of the chairperson and other leaders, and the KCTU withdrew from the Commission. The KCTU left and rejoined the Commission several times, although it stopped participating in 1999, and instead demanded direct labour-government negotiations. The Federation of Korean Trade Unions (FKTU) has participated in the Commission, even though it withdrew for a period in 2005 and 2006.

From June 1998 public interest groups were added as Commission members and gained a firm legal status through enactment of the *Tripartite Commission Act* in 1999, excluding political parties from membership. The Commission has dealt with issues concerning working hours, irregular workers, job creation, labour-related laws and IR. Even though the Commission produced the *Social Agreement on Job Creation* in 2004, all the social partners have not implemented the agreements because each partner had no real intention to fulfil its role in creating jobs, but asked other partners to do something. This showed that mutual trust and concession of each social partner is more important the Social Agreement itself.

Even though the social pact helped economic recovery, there has been a criticism of the need for the Commission as there have been only a few productive outputs since its inception. Korea has no political and cultural background for developing social dialogue among its social partners, however, and the Commission provides a main social dialogue body in Korea. Many economic and social issues, such as reforming IR, labour market systems and social insurance, economic systems and developing policy measures for lifelong learning, creating more and better jobs, and 'flexicurity' (flexibility and security) of the labour market and many labour-related laws have been and are being dealt with at special sessions of the Commission.

Thus, the political and economic context of trade unionism went from authoritarian governments to democracy and economic 'miracle' to seeming 'mirage' with the 1997 Crisis, although the economy quickly bounced back. The environment surrounding the labour market rapidly changed (Rowley *et al.* 2005). Employment patterns diversified. After the Crisis, temporary and part-time workers rapidly increased, while regular workers decreased, which had an impact on unions. An outline of contextual factors, including demographic, employment and economic, is presented in Table 4.1.

Brief history of trade unions

In the nineteenth century wage earners began to appear in Korea and the early labour movement was led mainly by miners and dockers, with the Sungjin Dock

Table 4.1 Contextual factors – Korea

General statistics	
Population[1] (2005)	48.3 million
Area (square kilometres)[1]	99.5 thousand
Employment by sector (%)[1] (2005)	
Agriculture	7.9
Industry	18.6
Services	73.5
Urban population (% of total population)[2]	80.8%
GDP per capita[2] (2004)	$14,162 (US)
Income inequality (high, medium or low)	Low
Gini coefficient[2] (2004)	0.310
Real GDP growth (%)[1]	
1986–1995	8.7
1996–2005	4.5
Unemployment (%)[1]	
1986–1995	2.7
1996–2005	4.2
Summary description	
Product market regulation (1998)	Medium
Political context (liberal/pluralistic, state unitarist [Communist, non-Communist])	Liberal/pluralistic
Political stability (high, medium or low)	High

Sources
1 Korea Labor Institute, *2005 KLI Labor Statistics, 2005* and *Monthly Labor Review*, No. 16 (April 2006), 2006.
2 Korea National Statistical Office, http://www.nso.go.kr.

Workers Union in 1898 the first union (Lee 1993). During the early nintheenth century the factory system started and Japanese colonization propelled production systems and an increase in factory workers and labour organizations (Lee 1993; Kwon and O'Donnell 2001; Kim and Bae 2004). Union activities were related to the independence movement against Japan, and so union leaders and activities were severely oppressed. Thus, it was natural that unions undertook underground activities and some cooperated with the communists. Following independence in 1945, the unions were divided by ideology into two national union centres: the rightist Korea Federation of Trade Unions (KFTU) and the leftist National Congress of Korea Trade Unions.

Immediately after the Korean War the government enacted the *Trade Union Act* (TUA) of 1953. While this became the legal basis of activities, unions were not able to escape from political restrictions. Policy related to unions was designed to ensure industrial peace and minimize their influence. One of the measures was to have unions affiliate with an industrial federation under a single, government-sponsored, national centre. Thus, the KFTU was reorganized as the FKTU. The FKTU played the role of a junior partner of the state and management until 1987 under the 'growth first, distribution later' and anti-communism stance, and showed tendencies to be supportive of government and management. A succession of legal revisions followed, mainly to weaken union activities by tight control based on hierarchical labour–management relationships at the enterprise level (Kim 1997).

It was the political transition to democracy in 1987 that marked a turning point for unions. Increased union organization and wage increases gave rise to a boom in unionization and strikes. Such a growth of union organization meant the employer-dominated industrial relations could not be sustained and unions became a major player in national politics and the economy (Lee 1998).

Overview of trade union membership

As Korea industrialized, union numbers and membership grew. The number of unions increased from 2,634 in 1965 to 4,091 in 1975 and membership from 301,000 to 750,000, while unionization density rates increased from 11.6 per cent to 15.8 per cent. However, when the government took a harder stance on union activities, numbers and density dropped. Union numbers fell to 2,635 in 1980 and 2,551 in 1985, slightly increasing to 2,742 by June 1987, while density decreased to 14.7 per cent, 12.4 per cent and 11.7 per cent over those time periods. Only membership increased, going from 948,000 to 1,004,000 and to 1,050,000 in those years due to an increase in the labour force.

Post-1987, unions grew rapidly in number, membership and density rates (see Table 4.2). For example, union numbers increased in just six months from 2,742 to 4,103 between June and December 1987, almost doubling to 7,883 by December 1989. However, union numbers, membership and density began to decline again after 1989. Membership fell steadily for several reasons. First, large company membership, where it was relatively easy to organize workers, had reached high

Table 4.2 Korean trade unions

General statistics	
Number of unions[1]	
1986	2,675
1987	4,103
1990	7,698
2004	6,107
Number of union members[1]	
1986	1,035,890
1987	1,267,457
1990	1,886,884
2004	1,536,843
Union density (%)[1]	
1986	16.8
1987	18.5
1990	18.4
2004	10.6

Summary description	
Union type	
Main	Economic/market
Secondary	Political
(Economic/market, political, other)	
Union structure	
Main	Enterprise
Secondary	Industrial, occupational
(Occupational, industrial, general, enterprise)	
Unity of peak organization (high, medium or low)	Medium
State control of unions (high, medium or low)	Low
Involvement in collective bargaining (high, medium or low)	Medium–low

Source: 1 Korea Labor Institute (2005), *2005 KLI Labor Statistics*, Seoul.

levels while small and medium enterprises (SMEs) were slow to organize. For example, in 1989 density rates were 85 per cent in firms with 500 employees or more and 77.8 per cent in firms with 300–499 employees, falling to 77.1 per cent and 71 per cent respectively in 1997. Unionization rates in SMEs were lower and did not increase (except for very small firms), e.g. 57.7 per cent and 55 per cent for firms with 100–299 employees, 23.8 per cent and 20.7 per cent for firms with 30–99 employees, and 9.9 per cent and 11.4 per cent for firms with 10–29 employees in the same two periods. This illustrates the difficulties in organizing workers in SMEs under an enterprise union system. The major interest of workers in SMEs was to maintain employment, not to organize unions. Second, as the communist regimes in Eastern Europe collapsed, so from the late 1980s the ideological foundation for activists who had led union organization was eroded. Third, double-digit wage growth post-1987 prompted concern about possible economic problems and stricter control of militant unions.

Unionization started to increase again after the Asian Crisis hit. Against the wave of dismissals and restructuring of the economy and employment, unions tried to organize workers. Legalization of teaching staff unions was another source of membership growth. The Korean Teachers and Educational Workers Union (*chunkyojo*) existed before legal approval, with the teachers' right to organize recognized in 1998 and coming into force in 2000.

As the labour market stabilized from 2001, union membership began to fall once more from 2002. As shown in Table 4.2, the number of trade unions, memberships and the unionization rate declined to 6,107; 1,537,000 and 10.6 per cent respectively by 2004. The major reason for the drop in unionization was the dismantling of the employment of regular workers as many employers tended short-sightedly to reduce labour costs by downsizing regular employment and outsourcing work (Yoo 2006). For example, from 2001 to 2005 regular employees decreased by 419,000 while non-regular employees increased by 1,848,000.

Union types and structure

The single union national centre of the FKTU was challenged after 1987. Enterprise unions in industrial complexes started providing physical and financial support to one another to mutually increase their bargaining power, giving rise to collective labour associations that encompassed an entire region. Such regional trade union associations, or Councils, started out in Seoul and gradually spread to other major industrial complexes in the region. The new unions launched ten regional and seven occupational trade union councils in 1988 for worker solidarity, transcending the borders of enterprise unions. Councils focused on information exchange and mutual support among enterprise unions in a region or sector and were organized one after another. The Councils launched the Korea Trade Union Congress (KTUC, *chunnohyup*). The KTUC was suppressed by the government and its leaders were arrested as multiple unions were still illegal.

The FKTU's cooperative attitude toward government and management resulted in a significant number of unions breaking away and joining the Korean Council of Trade Union Representatives (KCTUR, *chonnodae*) in protest. The KCTUR was an emerging nucleus of the labour movement, while the KTUC was weakening under government suppression. The KCTUR comprised numerous occupational trade union councils and large-scale enterprise unions, becoming the foundation for the KCTU, with 862 unions and 420,000 members (26 per cent of total union membership). The combined councils founded a national centre step by step: the Korean Council of National Trade Unions in 1989, the Korean Council of Trade Union Representatives in 1993 and the KCTU in 1995.

As multiple unions, even at the national level, were still illegal, the government tried to prevent this new national centre forming. The KCTU was not registered as an authorized union; but, while the KCTU was not *de jure* legally authorized, it was *de facto* recognized, as demonstrated by the fact that its leaders took part in the Presidential Commission on industrial relations reform in 1996 and in the

Tripartite Commission in 1998. With the labour law revisions in 1998 authorizing multiple unions at the national (or industrial) level, the KCTU gained legal authorization from 2000. The KTUC remained highly critical of the cooperative and non-democratic style of the FKTU and advocated a hard-line stance and democratic operation totally independent from management. The confrontational stance of the KCTU made it attractive to workers and it expanded. In 2004, out of 1,537,000 total union members, the FKTU had 780,000 (56.5 per cent) and the KCTU 668,000 (43.5 per cent).

The TUA (1953) did not regulate the structure of unions. However, between 1964 and 1987 the structure was affected by the government in a succession of legal revisions. The TUA revised in 1963 intended to create an industrial union system, seeing it as easier to control, and so restricted enterprise unions. However, policy changed and a revised TUA in 1973 deleted the clauses supporting industrial unions. The TUA revised in 1980 enforced enterprise unions more expressly as these alone were permitted, and industry-based unions were prohibited. The major reason for this was to weaken union power. Enterprise unions could affiliate with an industrial federation, but it was not an industry-based union movement. The TUA was revised again in 1987, deleting provisions permitting the establishment of unions only at the enterprise level, and allowing industry-based unions in order to guarantee workers rights of association and collective bargaining. Nevertheless, an enterprise union system prevailed until recently.

The establishment of industry-based, or at least occupational, unions had been an objective of the labour movement, not least as enterprise unions were limited in organizational power and economy of scale in operations and budgets, with weak financial standing inadequate to support activities. By 1996, however, only four trade unions were industry-based at the national level, with just 91,000 members (5.7 per cent of total union membership). The conversion of enterprise to industry unions was initiated by the KCTU and started with the Korean Federation of Hospital Unions becoming the Korean Health and Medical Union in February 1998. Prior to this the Korean Teachers and Educational Workers Union was launched in 1989 as a single-industry union, but was not legal until 2000. The National Medical Insurance Union (currently the Korea Social Insurance Union), the Journalists' Union, the Banking and Financial Union, and the Railroad Workers Union, followed in transition to industry unions.

In terms of occupational unions, in 1994 the National Science and Technology Union and the Regional Health Insurance Union were the first, followed by the Mutual Credit Fund Union in 1996 and the National Universities Employees' Union, the Democratic Union for Bus Services, and the Research and Professional Union in 1997.

With the Asian Crisis and consequent layoffs and unemployment, both union centres strengthened efforts to build an industrial or occupational union system. Hundreds of enterprise-level metal workers unions joined in the Korea Metal Workers' Federation of the KCTU, forming a metal workers' industrial union in 2000. However, transformation to industrial or occupational unions faces opposition. For example, leaders of the powerful enterprise unions with large memberships in the manufacturing sector have been reluctant to concede their strong power and bargaining rights, while management are also opposed.

The strategy of the KCTU is to convert enterprise unions to industrial unions as soon as possible, however. In December 2005 industrial unionists accounted for about 30 per cent of total union membership, rising by May 2006 to 54.2 per cent, a majority for the first time. In June 2006 three powerful automobile enterprise unions (Hyundai, Kia and GM-Daewoo), which had been strongly opposed, declared they would transform themselves into a metal industry union in 2006.

This organizational transition has been one of the strategies adopted by unions to achieve economies of scale through mergers and consolidation to keep pace with the changing external environment. Globalization, rapid technological development and enhanced labour market flexibility are driving the evolution of the labour movement. This organizational conversion is also a shift from the existing decentralized collective bargaining structure toward a more centralized one. The effect of such change on the internal politics of unions, management and industrial relations remains to be seen.

The Korean government retained the long tradition of single unionism by prescribing only a single union at all (national, industrial, occupational, enterprise) levels. The main rationale was that multiple unions would compete and fight for the initiative of the labour movement and that resultant splits and conflicts would cause confusion and disorder in industrial relations.

However, many union leaders have strongly supported multiple unions. To reinforce the autonomy and accountability of labour and management and to achieve more democratic industrial relations, labour-related law revisions in 1996 permitted multiple unions for higher (national, industrial, occupational) level organizations in 2000 and unit business establishment level in 2002. The methods and procedures for collective bargaining, such as unifying the bargaining channel between labour and management, were to be developed. Thus, a multiple union system at enterprise level was postponed by five years in 2001 and by a further three years in 2006.

What do unions do?

The Korean constitution and labour laws guaranteed the right to collective bargaining for employees, although this was restricted and wages and working conditions were usually determined by employers before 1987. Post-1987, labour–management bargaining developed. Unions placed a strong emphasis on collective bargaining. Yet, because employers and unions had no experience of collective bargaining, it was usually accompanied by labour disputes. Employers and unions played 'zero-sum' games while engaged in bargaining, and distrust was worsened through collective bargaining. The basic strategy of unions was to 'strike first, bargain later'. Between 1987 and 1989, an overwhelming proportion of labour disputes involved illegal union activities, which declined from the early 1990s with collective bargaining becoming the central mechanism for deciding wages and working conditions. After the 1997 Crisis raised unemployment rates and threatened job security, employment-related issues became the focus of collective bargaining.

The characteristics of collective bargaining in South Korea

Collective bargaining has the following characteristics in South Korea. First, the national level organizations of employees and employers (the Korea Employers Federation, KEF) set their desirable pay increase rate and its rationale annually which serves as an important reference figure for bargaining. The unions tend to suggest figures based on the average increase in the rate of living costs in urban areas, while the employers suggest figures using national productivity per employee rates. The data used to calculate both rates are not fully reliable and there is often a wide gap between suggestions. For example, in 1990 the KCTU and the FKTU demanded 23.3 per cent and 17.3 per cent respectively while the KEF suggested 7 per cent, with a final average negotiated increase of 9 per cent.

Second, the bargaining and negotiated rate are influenced significantly in other firms by the leading large companies (as pattern setters). Unions tend to be very concerned with the bargaining results of companies in the same industry. Thus, national level trade unions usually support, and sometimes illegally intervene in, collective bargaining in such leading companies to gain higher wage increases: one reason why such firms frequently experience severe labour disputes.

Third, collective bargaining is basically carried out at the enterprise level as a result of enterprise unionism. In 2003 enterprise-level bargaining accounted for 78.1 per cent, and occupational and industry-level bargaining for 16.1 per cent, of collective bargaining (Korea Labor Institute 2005). One of problems with enterprise-level bargaining is a wider wage gap between firms: large firms can afford to accept relatively high increases while SMEs cannot. Thus, large firms with strong unions tend to have higher wage rises, while SMEs without unions tend to have lower wage increases. For instance, the average wage level at firms with less than 50 employees was 90 per cent of that of firms with 500 employees or more until 1986, collapsing to about 60 per cent in 2006.

Fourth, collective bargaining practice is not well established. Unions often demand high wage increases, payment for strikers and full-time officials, participation in company decisions and guarantees for activities during working time. Sometimes they also make political and social demands, such as the release of arrested unionists and revisions of labour laws, enterprise governance, taxes, health insurance, national pensions and education. In reality, these demands cannot be negotiated at the bargaining table.

On the other hand, employers tend to disclose incorrect business performance, thus reducing trust in management. Unions, in most cases, insist on all demands being met and threaten strikes that are illegal as agreements should be ratified through a membership vote. For instance, in 2005 only 50.9 per cent of unions voted on collective bargaining agreements (Kim 2006). In cases where the collective bargaining agreement is rejected by members it leads to employer distrust of union representatives and conflicts between union leaders and members, which may result in unstable union leaderships and IR.

Fifth, collective bargaining issues have changed with economic and labour market circumstances. Until 1997 the major issues were wage rates, payments during strikes and for full-time officials, participation in personnel and disciplinary decision committees, guarantees of activities during working time and the closed shop. After the Crisis issues turned to employment security. This is indicated by the fact that the proportion of labour disputes due to disagreements on wages was around 50 per cent until 1997, more than halving to 21.7 per cent in 1998, falling again to 18.8 per cent in 2000 and just 12.1 per cent in 2004. On the other hand, disputes due to disagreements on employment security increased to 65.4 per cent, 66.8 per cent and 83.5 per cent over the same period (Korea Labor Institute 2005).

Prior to democratization in 1987 labour policy was subordinate to economic development and disputes were dealt with not as labour issues, but as national security issues. Thus, labour laws were characterized by restriction and suppression. Post-1987, however, many union claims have been enacted in various legal revisions to protect labour rights and improve the quality of working life.

The TUA was revised in 1987 to maintain and improve working conditions as well as the economic and social status of workers by securing rights of association, collective bargaining and collective action, and to contribute to the maintenance of industrial peace and economic development by preventing and resolving disputes through the fair adjustment of IR. This revision included the following:

- The provision that there be unions only at the enterprise level was deleted so as to guarantee rights of association, collective bargaining and collective action.
- To promote collective bargaining the regulations on the delegation of authority to conduct bargaining or to conclude a collective agreement were relaxed, and the 'registration' required for the delegation was changed to 'notification'.
- By revision of the *Labor Dispute Adjustment Act*, the scope of prohibited public services and defence corporations was narrowed to encourage autonomous and voluntary resolution of issues, and provisions on voluntary adjustments were introduced to encourage autonomous and voluntary adjustment of disputes.
- The revision of the *Labor Standards Act* in 1989 expanded its scope of application to all businesses or workplaces with five or more employees and weekly working hours were reduced from 48 to 44.
- In 1993 the *Employment Insurance Act* was enacted to implement the employment insurance system in 1995.

Both employers and unions recognized that revisions of labour-related laws were needed to meet international standards: employers wanted labour flexibility while trade unions wanted improved labour rights. Confronted with these two opposite voices on revisions the government tried to build a social consensus.

The Labor Law Research Committee, launched in 1992 as an advisory body to the Minister of Labor and the Presidential Commission on industrial relations reform, launched in 1996 as an advisory body to the President, were attempts to discuss labour issues and gain social consensus on revising laws. These attempts were intended to emphasize both the autonomy and accountability of labour and management to achieve democratic industrial relations, and to match global standards.

In order to achieve these goals, the following was set as the direction to be taken in legal revisions:

- deregulating the labour market and higher flexibility
- laying the foundation of autonomous bargaining between labour and management
- rationalizing disputes and mediation processes
- reforming unreasonable institutions and practices
- rationalizing labour administration
- creating the foundation for sound industrial relations based on participation and cooperation (Ministry of Labor 1997).

Although there was failure to reach agreement on the revisions, the experiences and know-how accumulated did serve as an important basis for legal changes afterwards and the later Tripartite Accord in 1998.

The revision of labour-related laws in 1996 integrated the TUA and the *Labor Dispute Adjustment Act* in the *Trade Union and Labor Relations Adjustment Act*. The details are as follows. First, the provision prohibiting union political activities was deleted, with unions regulated by law just like any other social organization. Second, multiple unions were permitted for higher level organizations in 2000 and enterprise level in 2002 (postponed by the 2001 revision, and thus multiple unions were permitted from 2007). Third, employers were prohibited from remunerating full-time union officials, a punishable 'unfair labour practice'. Fourthly, the prohibition on third-party intervention was lifted and the persons or organizations from which unions or employers could seek support were specified and others were prohibited from intervening in, manipulating or instigating collective bargaining or industrial action. Fifthly, employers had no obligation to pay workers participating in industrial action and unions were prohibited from taking industrial action to demand wage payments during industrial action. An overview of what Korean unions do can be seen in Table 4.3.

Wage increases

Economic outcomes include wage increases. Korean wage levels were stable until 1987, when they rose rapidly. The average monthly wage of 351,000 won in 1986 increased by 676 per cent to 2,373,000 won by 2004, while manufacturing industry rates increased by 776 per cent from 294,000 to 2,280,000 won. Between

Table 4.3 What do Korean trade unions do?

Activities	
Extent of collective bargaining (high, medium or low)	Low
Level of collective bargaining (high, medium or low)	
National	Low
Industry	Low
Enterprise	High
Industrial disputes[1]	
Working days lost per 1,000 employees (2003)	90.2
Relative assessment (high, medium or low)	High
Degree of state intervention in employment protection (high, medium or low)	Medium

Source: 1 Korea Labor Institute (2005), *2005 KLI Labor Statistics*, Seoul.

1987 and 2004 the average nominal wage increase rate was 11.3 per cent (reaching 14.6 per cent between 1987 and 1996) and the average real wage increase rate was 6.1 per cent between 1987 and 2004 (reaching 8.1 per cent between 1987 and 1996). Wages grew rapidly by 17.7 per cent during 1987–92, then slowed somewhat, but remained at double-digit rates until turning negative in 1998 due to the Crisis. The economic recovery from 1999 brought back double-digit wage growth, with levels becoming stable since 2000.

These wage increases were due to the influence of a strong and defiant labour movement using collective bargaining and strikes. Wage increases had been the dominating issue in most negotiations from 1987 to the mid-1990s. The tide of wage strikes was an expression of frustration and anger that workers had been kept on low wages until then. These wage increases somewhat satisfied this and workers started to reduce their claims.

As unions influenced wages, impacts on gender (Rowley and Kang 2005) and firm size emerged. For example, the ratio of the average wage of female to male workers improved from 48.9 per cent in 1986 to 62.1 per cent in 1997, but stagnated at 62.3 per cent by 2004. Wage differential by firm size widened. In 1986 the average wage in firms with 10–29 employees was 90 per cent of that in firms with 500 employees or more, declining to 72.6 per cent in 1992, 72.3 per cent in 1997 and 60.3 per cent by 2004. This is because the majority of unions are enterprise-based and represent regular employees in large enterprises.

Large vs small, temporary vs full time

Unions are basically regular employee and large firm oriented. Thus, the outcomes of collective bargaining do not tend to go to vulnerable workers who are not organized in unions. A criticism is that unions take care of only high-paying regular workers in large companies at the sacrifice of low-paid workers in SMEs. This is indicated in the widening wage gap between firm sizes post-1987. For instance, the average wage level of firms with 10–29 employees compared with that of firms with 500 employees or more fell from 90 per cent in 1986 to 60.3 per cent in 2004.

Also, unions in large monopolistic companies have strengthened the employment stabilization of their members and resisted employment restructuring plans. Employers have responded by reducing regular employment and utilizing contract-based temporary workers. This has resulted in decreases in regular employment and sharp increases in irregular employment. During 2001–05 the number of regular employees decreased by 419,000 while irregular employment soared by 1,848,000. At the same time the distribution of earnings, measured by the Gini coefficient, improved from 0.335 in 1986 to 0.277 in 1997, but deteriorated post-Crisis to 0.311 in 2003 (Korea Labor Institute 2005).

Hours of work

Another important outcome was working hour reductions. Following union demands the *Labor Standards Act* was revised in 1989 and 2004 to gradually reduce legal weekly working hours. These began to decline from 48 to 44 by 1990 to 40 by 2005. However, actual working hours are the longest among OECD member countries, although decreasing gradually since 1987, from 52.5 in 1986, falling most rapidly to 48.2 by 1990. The Crisis stimulated further reductions, from 47.3 in 1996 to 45.9 in 1998, although economic recovery in 1999 led to increases, to 47.9 in 1999, albeit with decreases since 2000 to 45.7 by 2004. However, levels remain notoriously high. For example, a study of the world's 71 largest cities found Seoul's employees worked the most hours (2,300, some 50 per cent more than in Paris) per year (Briscoe 2006).

Labour disputes

Non-economic outcomes of the unions include labour disputes. The number of labour disputes was low, fewer than 100 per year during the 1960s and 1970s, slowly rising to about 200 a year up to 1987. Then the number rose very sharply, from 276 in 1986 to 3,479 in 1987. Even though disputes decreased to 1,873 in 1988 and 1,616 by 1999, they became longer and larger in scale. Thus, the number of lost workdays increased very substantially from 72,000 in 1986 to 6,947,000 in 1987, remaining high at 5,401,000 in 1988 and 6,351,000 in 1989. The amount of production lost by labour disputes increased from 54 billion won in 1987 to 73 billion won in 1988 and hit a peak of 136 billion won in 1989. Of course, these sorts of 'costs' figures are biased in that they do not include the 'savings' of not running businesses and the fact that production may be made up quickly afterwards.

The number of labour disputes sharply decreased to 322 in 1990 and to just 78 by 1997, while the number of lost workdays due to disputes also decreased to 4,487,000 and to just 445,000 in 1997 and the number of lost workdays per 1,000 employees due to labour disputes fell from 410 to just 33. The amount of production lost due to labour disputes decreased from 31 billion won in 1990 to 16 billion won in 1997.

The fallout from the Asian Crisis led to union resistance and increased labour disputes to 129 in 1998 and 250 in 2000, rising further to 462 in 2004 before declining to 289 in 2005. The number of lost workdays due to labour disputes increased to 1,452,000 in 1998 and 1,894,000 in 2000, and then began to decrease. The number of lost workdays per 1,000 employees due to labour disputes increased to 118 in 1998 and fell to 90 by 2003 (Korea Labor Institute 2005).

During 1987–89 most labour disputes involved illegal activities. The proportion of legal disputes was just about one-fifth, 20.4 per cent in 1988, rising to just less than one-third, 31.5 per cent in 1989. The major reason was that union leaders did not accept existing laws. For instance, the most common reason for classification as an illegal strike was the lack of legitimacy in purpose (with strikes commonly staged for political reasons or demands beyond management control, such as revisions of laws and social reforms) or procedure (most commonly for breaching mediation preceding industrial relations arbitration processes prior to strikes). Illegal disputes resulted in the arrest of large numbers of union leaders and members, and this became another reason for illegal disputes – demanding the release of arrested colleagues. However, with increasing illegal disputes being seen as threatening competitiveness, from about 1990 unions sought to work more cooperatively with the management. In spite of this, the proportion of legitimate labour disputes remained at around 60 per cent until 1994 and then increased to about 80 per cent from 1995.

According to the Ministry of Industry and Resources, the average annual production loss due to labour disputes since 1990 is 1,817 billion won and the average export loss due to labour disputes is US\$ 569 million (Korea Labor Institute 2005). Another outcome of the increasingly active labour movement is that unions have significantly contributed to the development of national political democracy and corporate transparency. Unions have participated in the decision-making processes within companies and have also raised their voices on political and social issues. These union activities helped transform business management from authoritarian and opaque cultures to more democratic and transparent ones, and have thereby contributed to some democratization of industry. Linked to these activities is greater industrial participation and involvement of workers at the enterprise level.

The Labour-Management Council system

The Labour-Management Council (LMC) system is one institutionalized channel available to promote communication and cooperation between employees and management, facilitate participation in business administration and improve labour rights and the status of employees. This system was introduced by the *Labour-Management Council Act* (1980). The act was replaced by the *Act on Promotion of Worker Participation and Cooperation* (1997). LMCs at workplaces or businesses employing 30 persons or more hold regular (on a quarterly basis) meetings composed of equal numbers (usually three to ten) of representatives from labour and management. When unions represent the majority of employees, union leaders become employee representatives.

Three types of matters are dealt with in LMCs: consultation, resolution and reporting. Employers consult on improvements in productivity, employee welfare and working conditions. Employers and employees together develop the basic plan for training and skills development, establishment and management of welfare facilities and company welfare funds for employees. Employers report on personnel policy and business plans, performance and prospects. However, the LMC system and collective bargaining have different goals in that the former is aimed at pursuing the common benefit of the employer and employee, whereas the latter is fundamentally based on the contradictory positions of the employer and employee.

Development, structure and strategies of trade unions

Prior to 1987 the FKTU and its member unions were tightly repressed by the government. Policies and activities were generally subordinate to government, from which the FKTU received financial support. Thus, unions had little autonomy and were criticized for being 'yellow' unions. However, from the late 1970s a stronger, independent labour movement began to emerge. This movement resulted in wildcat strikes and the connection with the political democratization movement. Democracy provided opportunities for forming new unions and resulted in the KCTU.

Unions have acquired a full degree of liberalization and autonomy since 1987, with independence from government and management. The FKTU particularly has tried to reform itself to compete with the KCTU. Even though the FKTU is more cooperative than the KCTU with government and management, it still enjoys full autonomy. An overview of Korean trade union development can be seen in Table 4.4.

There are three trends in the activities and strategies of Korean unions. First, union leaders have begun to realize that in order to survive in the competitive international market the antagonistic relationship between the labour and management should be converted to a more collaborative one. Confrontation and distrust between the two parties can help discourage business investment and destroy jobs. In 2006 the FKTU President joined the Minister of Industry and Resources and many business people in 'road shows' trying to attract foreign investment into Korea. It was the first time union leaders had tried to attract foreign investment with government and business leaders.

Second, there are some trends of convergence in the activities and strategies of unions. The two national level unions are trying to promote industrial unionism to improve the organizational power of the labour movement. Thus, long-rooted enterprise unionism is being gradually transformed. Uncoordinated decentralization based on enterprise unionism is being changed towards more centralized industrial unionism. However, because of the long tradition of enterprise unionism, it may be a difficult, slow change. The trend toward industrial unionism is an attempt to harmonize the decentralization and centralization of union organization. Also, behind the scenes there has been dialogue between the two national level unions

Table 4.4 Explaining Korean trade union development, structure and strategy

Political context	
Degrees of liberalization and autonomy (repression, tolerance, support, indifference)	Indifference
Relations with the State (dependent, independent)	Independent
Markets	
Openness (imports + exports as % of GDP)	70.3
Degree of competition (High, Medium or Low)	High
Financial markets	
Openness to market financing	High
Ownership (group, institutional, foreign, dispersed)	Dispersed
Labour markets	
Demand elasticity (relates to ability of employers to pass on wage increases in prices – high, medium or low)	Low
Employers	
Concentration (top 100 companies as a percentage value of total)	High
Employer organization membership (high, medium or low)	High
Multinational (high, medium or low)	Medium
Unitarist or pluralist perspective	Pluralist

Source: Korea Labor Institute (2005), *2005 KLI Labor Statistics*, Seoul.

to unify them, but it will take a long time for a unified national union to result because each national centre wants to subsume the other.

Third, Korea has tried to encourage social dialogue among labour, management and government since 1998 with the conviction that a consensus-building mechanism is necessary to create 'win–win' IR. After the social pact in 1998 the Korea Tripartite Commission failed to meet the expectations of labour, management and government. Nevertheless, each party is trying to develop social partnerships in various ways.

Until the 1970s Korea had adopted the strategy of protecting infant industries. As such industries began to gain international competitiveness, Korea opened its markets to the world. Especially from the 1980s, such an open-door policy was a key policy direction. In the process of joining the OECD and restructuring the economy after the Crisis, the speed of openness accelerated. Korea opened its financial markets and now several financial institutions are owned by foreign investors. The share of exports and imports as a part of GDP – 70.3 per cent in 2004 – indicates a high degree of openness in the Korean economy, implying substantial levels of competition in global markets.

Since the Korean market is exposed to a high degree of competition, it is not easy for employers to pass on wage increases in prices. This is a commonly made and historical argument. Instead, employers in large companies tend to pass on rises to subcontractors, which reduces the contractors', often SMEs, profits and wages. This is one of the reasons for the wide wage gap between large firms and the SMEs.

It has often been argued that Korean economic development was underpinned by a Confucian work ethic and its values, which produced characteristics such as emphasis on education, leadership in government and consensus formation, which later mixed with Western Christian ethics to produce '… an amalgam of family or collective-orientated values of the East and the pragmatic, economic-goal orientated values of the West' (Lee 1993: 246). Additionally, there was the '… close, sometimes collusive ties between government and private capital …' (McNamara 2002: 2).

Until the early 1990s most Korean employers who were the first generation of company founders were authoritative and labour exclusive, preferring top-down decision-making processes. These attitudes resulted in massive labour disputes and confrontations with angry and defiant unions post-1987. Employers were not accustomed to having dialogue and negotiations with unions. They were antagonistic to unions and felt their control threatened by calls for participation in business management, wage increases and payments during disputes.

Confronted with union collective activities, employers recognized that they had to jointly respond and formed the Korean Association of Industrial Organisations in 1989, representing employers in responding to unions. It failed in responding successfully and ceased its activities in 1992, and the Korea Employers Federation (KEF) became the counterpart to the unions at the national level. For example, annually the KEF suggests for employers basic guidelines and strategies for collective bargaining and positions on enactment and revision of labour-related laws, tries to persuade the government, politicians and the public and negotiates with unions.

In response to wage increases and strong unions, most employers followed labour market numerical flexibility strategies. They adopted labour-cost saving approaches, such as speeding up automation, improving wage flexibility by introducing performance-based pay systems instead of seniority-based systems, global outsourcing, downsizing by layoffs, freezing new regular employment and using temporary employment, outsourcing non-core jobs by establishing small independent companies within firms, moving-out production to low-wage countries, and reducing domestic investment and increasing foreign investment. The results are a decrease in stable jobs and an increase in unstable employment, early retirement, high (especially youth) unemployment and a deterioration of earnings distribution. On the other hand, some employers have adopted a labour-management partnership strategy by sharing information and engaging in dialogue with employees. In these companies some trade unions had 'no labour disputes' declarations and even accepted wage setting without collective bargaining.

Conclusions

Since 1987 unions in Korea have gone through numerous changes in legal status, organization, structure, position and acceptance. Nowadays unions have a role as important social partners. However, the rampant distrust between labour and management, as well as the repetitive use of illegal force in collective bargaining and forceful intervention in disputes, indicate that the institutionalization of industrial relations is yet to be completed. The confrontational industrial relations of the late 1980s has continued. There remain high levels of strikes and loss of working days, production (US$2 billion annually) and exports (US$1 billion annually). Moreover, approximately 20 per cent of union strikes are illegal.

In sum, the relevance, position and role of unions in Korea has evolved along an uneven path. They have moved from anti-colonial groups via opposing military government and pro-democracy bodies to the organizations that they are today. Korean unions retain their high profile in the media and amongst policy makers and politicians due to their strike actions and demands and apparent impacts on business, especially overseas investors.

Bibliography

Briscoe, S. (2006) 'Taxis, restaurants and rent make London most expensive place to live', *Financial Times*, 10 August, p. 3.

Kim, D. (2006) 'The analysis on the wage negotiation in 2005', *Monthly Labor Review* (in Korean), 16: 3–14.

Kim, D. and Bae, J. (2004) *Employment Relations and HRM in South Korea*, London: Ashgate.

Kim, H. (1997) *Korean Labor Laws* (in Korean), Seoul: Pakyoungsa.

Korea Labor Institute (2005) *2005 KLI Labor Statistics*, Seoul: Korea Labor Institute.

Kwon, S. and O'Donnell, M. (2001) *The Chaebol and Labour in Korea: The Development of Management Strategy at Hyundai*, London: Routledge.

Lee, M. B. (1993) 'Korea', in M. Rothman, D. Briscoe and R. Nacamulli (eds) *Industrial Relations Around the World*, Berlin: de Gruyter, pp. 245–69.

Lee, W. (1998) 'Industrial relations: retrospect on the past decade and policy directions for the 21st century', in Lee Won-duck and Kang-shik Choi (eds) *Labor Market and Industrial Relations in Korea*, Soeul: Korea Labor Institute, pp. 51–118.

McNamara, D. (2002) *Market and Society in Korea: Interest, Institution and the Textile Industry*, London: Routledge.

Ministry of Labour (1997) *White Paper of Labor 1996*, Seoul: Ministry of Labour.

Park, Y. and Leggett, C. (2004) 'Employment relations in the Republic of Korea', in G. Bamber, R. Lansbury and N. Wailes (eds) *International and Comparative Employment Relations*, London: Sage, pp. 306–28.

Rowley, C. (2002) 'South Korean management in transition', in M. Warner and P. Joynt (eds) *Managing Across Cultures: Issues and Perspectives*, London: Thomson Learning, pp. 178–92.

Rowley, C. (2005) 'Context, development and interactions in the HRM system in South Korea', *Journal of Comparative Asian Development*, 4(1): 105–33.

Rowley, C. and Bae, J. (1998) (eds) *Korea Businesses: Internal and External Industrialisation*, London: Frank Cass.

Rowley, C. and Bae, J. (2001) 'The impact of globalisation on HRM: the case of South Korea', *Journal of World Business*, 36(4): 402–28.

Rowley, C. and Bae, J. (2002) 'Globalisation and transformation of HRM: the case of South Korea', *International Journal of Human Resource Management*, 13(1): 522–49.

Rowley, C. and Bae, J. (2003) 'Culture and management in South Korea', in M. Warner (ed) *Culture and Management in Asia*, London: Routledge, pp. 187–209.

Rowley, C. and Bae, J. (2004a) 'Macro and micro approaches to HR development: context and content in South Korea', *Journal of World Business*, 39(4): 349–61.

Rowley, C. and Bae, J. (2004b) 'HRM in South Korea' in P. Budhwar (ed.) *Managing Human Resources in Asia-Pacific*, London: Routledge, pp. 35–60.

Rowley, C. and Bae, J. (2004c) 'HRM in South Korea after the Asian Crisis: emerging patterns from the labyrinth', *International Studies of Management and Organization*, 31(1): 52–82.

Rowley, C. and Kang, H. R. (2005) 'Women in management in Korea: advancement or retrenchment', *Asia Pacific Business Review*, 11(1): 100–19.

Rowley, C. and Kim, J. (2001) 'Managerial problems in Korea: evidence from the nationalised industries', *International Journal of Public Sector Management*, 14(2): 129–48.

Rowley, C. and Kim, J. (2005) 'Dual commitment: determinants and theoretical perspectives', *Asia Pacific Business Review*, 11(2): 203–21.

Rowley, C. and Kim, J. (2006) 'Commitment to company and labour union: empirical evidence from South Korea', *International Journal of Human Resource Management*, 17(4): 673–92.

Rowley, C., Sohn, T. W. and Bae, J. (2002) (eds) *Managing Korean Business: Organization, Culture, Human Resources and Change*, London: Routledge.

Rowley, C., Yoo, K.S and Kim, D. H. (2005) 'Unemployment and labour markets in South Korea: globalisation, social impacts and policy responses', in J. Benson and Y. Zhu (eds) *Unemployment in Asia*, London: Routledge, pp. 58–78.

Yoo, K. (2005) *Industrial Relations and Human Resource Development* (in Korean), Seoul: Korea Labor Institute.

Yoo, K. (2006) *Reality and Policy Options for Irregular Employment* (in Korean), The Presidential Committee on Job Strategy. Seoul: Korea Labor Institute.

5 Trade unions in Taiwan

Confronting the challenge of globalization and economic restructuring

Ying Zhu

Introduction

The trade union movement in Taiwan has experienced three stages of transformation in the past five decades. A period of repression under the Nationalist Party's (Kuomintang, KMT) authoritarian rule between the late 1940s and 1980s, then a period of active growth as part of the process of democratization in the late 1980s and early 1990s, and the current stagnation period influenced by economic restructuring and globalization.

The issue of trade unions has been very political in Taiwan, whether as a tool for the ruling KMT government during the martial law period in the past, or as a vehicle for promoting democracy in the society, as well as in the workplace in more recent years. Political parties, including the former ruling party of KMT, now as the major opposition party, as well as the former opposition party, the Democratic Progressive Party (DPP), now the ruling party in the government, have long tried and continue to try to influence union organizations for political reasons.

The changing political landscape has exerted a profound impact on the union movement, given the shift of political power and economic resources from one party to another, each of which tends to favour different union organizations. Political confrontation between different unions has been the inevitable result of party politics.

Economically, the process of globalization and the restructuring of the Taiwanese economy has forced the trade unions to cope with new challenges, such as the increasing number of companies moving to Mainland China and other economies in East and South-east Asia, which has prompted the downsizing and retrenchment of Taiwanese workers, the introduction of new technologies and the need for upgrading the skills of the Taiwanese labour force, and an emerging services sector with relatively few and dispatched employees. Uncertainty and change in both the political and economic environment have, in fact, divided the trade unions and weakened their power for influencing policy at the national level and bargaining at industry and firm levels.

In his research on understanding European trade unionism, Hyman (2001) identifies three types of trade unions: (1) trade unions as labour market actors labelled as business unionism focusing on the market; (2) trade unions as vehicles of anti-capitalist mobilization fighting in a class struggle; (3) trade unions as agents of social integration labelled as integrative unions emphasizing 'social partnership'. However, in reality, all trade unions face in three directions (Hyman 2001: 3). Unions cannot ignore market forces and they have a central concern to regulate the wage–labour relationship. Meanwhile, they have to organize workers fighting for collective interests and establishing a collective identity that divides workers from employers.

In addition, unions also exist and function within a social framework that they may aspire to change but that constrains their current choices (Hyman 2001: 4). In other words, unions are part of society. Hyman (2001: 4) claims that all three models typically have some purchase; but in most cases, actually existing unions have tended to incline towards an often contradictory admixture of two of the three ideal types. The question is, then, how do Taiwanese trade unions fit into the observed models?

It is important to illustrate the historical evolution of the trade union movement in Taiwan and identify the dilemma trade unions are confronting now. This chapter tackles the key questions raised in Chapter 2 of this book. In order to adequately address these issues, the chapter is comprised of the following sections: the next section covers contextual and historical issues, including the evolution of the trade union in Taiwan under different political and economic environments, and an overview of union membership. Following this is a section that identifies union types and structure, their external relationship with the state, business/market and society as a whole and the inter- and intra-union relationships. The fourth section highlights the major activities of trade unions, such as their involvement in collective bargaining, legal enactment, social benefit and employee protection. A fifth section explains the development, structure and strategies of trade unions currently in terms of confronting the pressure from political changes, economic uncertainties and competition. Finally, the chapter concludes by illustrating the possible future of the union movement in Taiwan and some general implications for underpinning theory, as well as policy considerations.

Context and history

Before getting into the details of the history of the trade union movement in Taiwan, Table 5.1 presents an overview of contextual factors in Taiwan. Under the economic restructuring, the tertiary sector makes up more than 58 per cent of the total workforce, while the secondary sector makes up 36 per cent and the primary sector makes up 5.5 per cent. By the end of 2005, the total GDP reached US$346 billion and GDP per capita was US$15,676, making Taiwan one of the leading economies in East Asia. Taiwan has experienced a long period of positive economic growth, even during the Asian Crisis when other East Asian economies suffered. On the other hand, the unemployment rate remained relatively low compared with other developed economies (see Zhu 2005: 81).

Taiwan has a relatively open economy compared with other East Asian economies. In particular, since the World Trade Organization accession in

Table 5.1 Contextual factors – Taiwan

General statistics	
Population (million, 2005)	22.7
Size of the territory	340,000 square km

Proportion (labour force) in:
  Primary
  Secondary
  Tertiary
	
	5.49%
	36.02%
	58.49%

GDP per capita (2005)	US$15,676
Total GDP (2005)	US$346.4 billion

Growth rates:
  Average for 1985–95
  Average for 1995–2005
	
	7.3%
	4.5%

Unemployment:
  Average for 1985–95
  Average for 1995–2005
	
	1.6%
	3.7%

Summary description	
Openness and degree of competition: International trade (import + export)	H I: US$381,051 million + E: US$355,843 million
World Bank regulation index	No. 47 rank

Political context:
  System of regime
 	
  Political stability
	
	Transformed from authoritarian to
	democracy
	M: early stage of democracy and possible
	confrontation with Mainland China

Source: Monthly Bulletin of Labor Statistics, January 2007, Taipei: Council of Labor Affairs, Executive Yuan, Republic of China.

Note
H – high, M – medium, L – low.

December 2001, Taiwan has enjoyed a continuing growth of international trade and is ranked as the sixteenth largest trading nation in the world (*Taiwan Yearbook 2006*). In addition, the World Bank regulation index ranks Taiwan forty-seventh in the world as being open and easy for business activities (World Bank 2007).

The trade union movement in Taiwan

The trade union movement in Taiwan has experienced three stages of transformation: an early period of repression (1940–80), a period of active growth (late 1980s to early 1990s), and the current stagnation. Each of these stages is discussed next.

The trade union movement during the period between the late 1940s and early 1980s was basically under the control of the KMT through local government, legislation and the nomination and election of union officials. The formulation of labour laws also effectively outlawed strikes. All the union branches were under the 'supervision' of the Chinese Federation of Labor (CFL). However, the CFL did not conduct a single election for its congress or its executive officers between 1950 and 1975. The reason was given that the CFL was a national organization and because Mainland China was occupied by the Communists, a national congress could not be held (Frenkel *et al.* 1993). Therefore, officials of the CFL 'supervised' union affairs, persuading union representatives and other union functionaries to act in line with KMT policy (Minns and Tierney 2005).

By 1950, there were 175 union branches representing 7.9 per cent of non-agricultural employees (Lee 1988: 186). Union growth was relatively slow until 1975, however, when the *Trade Union Law* was amended (Lee 1988: 186). The old *Trade Union Law* (1929) required that unions be established in workplaces in most sectors when there more than 50 employees. This threshold was reduced to 30 employees in 1975.

In addition, new legislation, namely the *Labour Standards Law* of 1984, gave workers the opportunity to join an occupational union as a means of contributing to, and receiving, various social insurance benefits. Hence, increasing numbers of those who were self-employed or who worked for small and medium enterprises (SMEs) joined the occupation- based unions.[1]

Furthermore, the expansion of the secondary industry from 28 per cent of employees in 1970 to 42.3 per cent in 1984 made unionization more likely (Lee 1988). By 1984, the number of unions had reached 1,924 and they represented 22.8 per cent of the non-agricultural workforce (Lee 1988). As Lee (1988) claims, the CFL also helped the government to build external relationships with other international union organizations when Taiwan was forced to relinquish its seat in the United Nations in 1971 and was isolated internationally.

In fact, major changes of both economic and political environments in general, and the trade union movement in particular occurred in the 1980s (Bello and Rosenfeld 1996). After over three decades of rapid industrial expansion, the supply of land and labour became limited, causing a rapid increase in labour costs and land prices in Taiwan (Zhu *et al.* 2000). As a consequence, many labour-intensive industries relocated from Taiwan to low-cost countries, especially in South-east Asia and Mainland China. Government policy also encouraged the development of technology-intensive and service-oriented industries in order to maintain economic development momentum (Zhu *et al.* 2000).

As Lee (1995: 101) claims, during the period of economic restructuring in the 1980s and early 1990s, not only did the structure of the economy change quickly, so also did industrial relations, human resource management practices, and government labour policies (see Ng and Warner 1998: 152). The system became more complex and formal, and the government policy shifted toward a more pro-labour orientation. The outcome was that the government amended several labour laws in the 1980s, including the *Collective Agreement Law* in 1982, the *Labour Disputes Law* and the *Labour Insurance Act* in 1988, and the *Vocational Training Act* in 1983 (Lee 1995: 101; Chen 1998: 155–6). It also enacted new laws such as the *Labour Standards Law* in 1984 (last amended in 1996), the *Employment*

Service Act in 1992, and the *Equal Rights in the Workplace Act* in 1993 (Lee 1995: 101; Chen 1998: 155–6).

The government expanded the range of worker benefits through the creation of a social welfare system. For instance, the *National Health Insurance Law* of 1994, the *Law for the Protection of People with Mental and Physical Disabilities* of 1997, and the *Rules for the Implementation of the Payment of Unemployment Insurance Benefits* of 1998 were implemented in the 1990s (Wang and Cooney 2002; Zhu 2005). Some of the rules relating to unemployment benefits were a response towards the influence of the Asian financial crisis in 1997/98 (see Zhu and Warner 2001).

On the political front, pressure for democratization had become overwhelming and the lift of martial law in 1987 marked the beginning of the end of the old political system. Before lifting martial law, there was increasing pressure on the KMT to liberalize the political environment.

Starting around 1984, the trade union movement became more active as part of a social movement against pollution and nuclear power and in favour of consumer protection (Ying 1990). As part of this social movement, workers sought improved working conditions and the right to form new unions (Ying 1990).

The only open opposition party, the DPP, was established in September 1986. Though it was illegal, the party was allowed to survive. The following month, marital law was lifted, an event accompanied by a lifting of the ban on strikes and the reduction of restrictions on travel to Mainland China. These events, together with the emergence of a free press and competition between political parties, demonstrated by the establishment of the Labor Party in 1987, indicated that Taiwan was changing rapidly and moving to a more open and democratic political position. In late 1986, the opposition parties won two of the five seats reserved for union representatives in the legislative branch of the government (Cheng 2003). These changes pushed the government to adopt a more pro-labour policy and new legislation was introduced, as mentioned previously.

In this changing political landscape, the union movement played a significant role. While the KMT initially retained control of most government institutions, it continued to lose electoral support, culminating in its defeat to the DPP in the 2000 presidential elections (Wang and Cooney 2002) when many newly established independent unions supported the formation of a new government.

In Taiwan, unions are distinguished between industrial and occupational unions. The *Trade Union Law* requires that there be only one union per workplace and employees of different manufacturing occupations belong to the same union. Employees in smaller establishments have tended to join occupational unions based outside the workplace, which is location-based, same-occupation unionism (Frenkel *et al.* 1993: 170).

Union membership increased sharply by 58.1 per cent between the end of 1986 and the end of 1989, compared with an increase of 33.8 per cent in the seven-year period ending in 1986 (Frenkel *et al.* 1993). In particular, the increase among occupational unions was more than doubled between the end of 1986 and the end of 1989. Meanwhile, the union density increased from 20.4 per cent in 1979 to 32.6 per cent in 1989 and the number of national federations increased to five (Frenkel *et al.* 1993).

Frenkel *et al.* (1993) point out several reasons for this increased activity: First, the lifting of martial law in 1987 acted as a catalyst for many people to participate in public affairs. Thus, many employees joined occupational unions because their workplaces lacked statutory support or because their employers opposed unions despite the law. Second, the opportunity to contribute to and obtain from various social insurance benefits as union members, as stipulated by the *Labour Standards Law* of 1984, proved very attractive. Third, the official definition of occupation became narrower in 1984 following the enactment of the *Labour Standards Law*, and consequently new unions had to register to cover the new occupational groups (Cooney 1996).

The union movement in Taiwan has stagnated in recent years. There has been a limited increase in unions and union density remained at 36.9 per cent in 2005 (see Table 5.2). Many reasons led to these outcomes and the following sections illustrate these trends through further examination of union types and structure, their routine activities and their developmental strategies.

Union types and structure

As indicated at the beginning of the chapter, a changing political landscape, such as the democratic movement in the late 1980s and 1990s, and the changing of the government from the old ruling party of KMT to the new ruling party of DPP in 2000, has had a profound impact on the union movement because the shift of political power and economic resources from one party to the other favoured some union organizations but not others. Political confrontation between different union organizations became inevitable due to the influence of party politics.

The relationship between trade unions and the state was very close in one form or another in the period both before and after regime change. Under KMT rule, the official trade union, the CFL, controlled virtually all registered labour unions and all unionized workers in Taiwan (Minns and Tierney 2005). The KMT financially supported the CFL at the county, provincial and national levels and paid the rent on all of the Federation's offices (Ho 1990). The KMT also had the power to dissolve unions within the CFL if there was an indication of subversive behaviour. Most union leaders were KMT members and they were elected or appointed with KMT support. From time to time, those union branches were used as a KMT political base to support KMT candidates in local elections. Therefore, the CFL was an instrument of KMT party policy (Minns and Tierney 2005).

Given such strong support by the state, the CFL enjoyed a great number of union members. In terms of union density, Taiwan has been higher than other Asian neighbours, for instance, much higher than that of South Korea, which is one of the most advanced economies with an influential union movement in East Asia. However, the high union density in Taiwan does not reflect the true identity of trade unions as the representative of working men and women. Compared with South Korea, which has been regarded as a symbol of an advanced economy with

Table 5.2 Taiwanese trade unions

General statistics	
Number of unions (end of 2005)	4,310
Number of union members (end of 2005)	2,986,804
Union density (end of 2005)	36.95%
Level of collective bargaining	L
Summary description	
Main union type	Transformed from more political-oriented to less political and more economic/market-oriented
Main union structure	General Federations of Unions (national) Federation of Unions (city and county) Industrial Unions Occupational (craft, location-based) Unions Enterprise Unions (since 1997) Combination Unions (since 1997)
Extent of unity of peak organization	L
State control of unions	Changed from H to M
Involvement in collective bargaining	L

Note
H – high, M – medium, L – low.

strong union influence in East Asia, Taiwan has a low level of worker militancy and experienced few strikes during the post-World War II period due to multiple factors. As mentioned earlier, martial law and state control were in part responsible for this. In addition, other factors, such as an emerging middle class, mass labour intensive production carried out by small and medium family businesses with less union influence, and state-owned enterprises (SOEs) with subordinated unions might also be contributing factors.

The most significant example of the union movement was the establishment of the so-called independent union organization – the Taiwan Labour Front. It was born in 1984 to provide free legal consultations with unionists. The Taiwan Labour Front started campaigns in 1992 to enhance the autonomy of unions, to extend the *Labour Standards Law* to service sector employees and to minimize the offshore relocation of Taiwan's manufacturing capital (Minns and Tierney 2005). Since the 1990s, it has been affiliated with key representatives of 11 large and potentially powerful union organizations and finally formed another counter-KMT-supported Federation – the Taiwan Confederation of Trade Unions (TCTU) in 1998. However, this so-called independent union was affiliated with the DPP's anti-KMT movement in the past and it has been recognized by the new DPP government as a legitimate union organization since 2000. This new national Federation includes 18 industrial unions with more than 280,000 members (Cheng 2003).

The changes occurred not only among the anti-KMT camps, but also within the KMT-controlled CFL. In 2000, the outcome of the CFL leadership election was success, not on the part of candidates nominated by the KMT, but for long-term militant unionists involved in the democratic movement, such as Lin Huei-kwung, the leader of the 1988 railway workers' struggles. Lin was elected as President, and Wang Juan-ping, a long-term Labour Party and Labour Rights Association member, was elected as Assistant General Secretary (Minns and Tierney 2005).

Under their leadership, the CFL emphasized its new direction and stressed the need to maintain distance from party politics and truly represent and protect its members' interests and needs. However, due to its historical ties with the KMT, in particular at the enterprise branch level, it was hard for the CFL to be fully independent. In fact, after the election of the new leadership of the CFL, two groups moved away from the CFL to form separate organizations under the leadership of KMT members who were also member of the national legislature (Xu 2000).

Therefore, it is hard to assert that the trade union movement in Taiwan is independent from the intervention or influence of political parties or vice versa. Some relatively independent union organizations in Taiwan are rather small in size and extremely limited in influence (Minns and Tierney 2005). However, there has been increasing awareness that trade unions should truly represent and protect members' interests and need to keep their distance from party politics (Xu 2000; Pan 2004). In fact, most trade union strategies and policies currently are related to those concerns and more detailed analysis will be provided in the later sections.

Table 5.2 demonstrates the current structure and membership of trade unions in Taiwan. According to Taiwan's *Monthly Bulletin of Labour Statistics, March 2006* (Council of Labour Affairs 2006), the total number of unions was 4,308 by the end of 2005. The total number of union members was 2,986,804. Union density was 36.95 per cent. As mentioned earlier, the *Labour Union Law* stipulates the union structure in Taiwan. Although the law has been amended four times since 1929, the fundamental principles remain intact. According to the law, the trade unions' structure is comprised top-down vertically from General Federations of Unions at national level, to Federations of Unions at city and county level, then to industrial unions and occupational unions at the grassroots level.

A 1997 amendment to the *Labour Union Law* added two new types of unions: enterprise unions and combination unions. Enterprise unions and industrial unions are different by official definition, though confusion has been generated from time to time. Industrial unions are established within one industry sector, but branches are established in each workplace with more than 30 employees. Even within one company, they cannot form one branch across different workplaces. The KMT government used this legislation to reduce the power of unions by enforcing circumstances providing less strength and unity. The 1997 amendment allowed more 'independent' unions to be formed at enterprise level. They are not branches or part of existing industrial unions, but independent unions established within one enterprise. In addition, the so-called combination unions are another type of new formation of union organization created through the association of employees in related industry sectors or skills. They are also not part of traditional systems of industrial unions and occupational unions.

Generally speaking, by allowing more separate union organizations to be formed at the grassroots level, the government created competition among different types of union organizations, which led to less united union power. However, the willingness to allow different types of unions does show that the government encourages freedom of association and political openness, according to Mr Liu, President of Taipei Federation of CFL (Wu 2000).[2]

Nevertheless, in recent years, competition and hostility have emerged among different union organizations, divided by different ideologies, associating with different political parties, espousing separate political and economic goals, and forming different union structures. For instance, the number of General Federations of Unions increased from 25 in 2000 to 58 in 2005. Meanwhile, the number of Federation of Unions at city and county level also increased from 20 to 25. However, the total number of union members did not change very much, increasing from 2,868,330 in 2000 to 2,986,804 in 2005, indicating a fracturing of the membership (Council of Labour Affairs 2006).

There are increasing power struggles among peak union organizations and there is no one voice representing the interests of working men and women in Taiwan. Consequently, an increasing sense of uncertainty and frustration has appeared among trade union leaders as well as ordinary members regarding the general direction and well-being of the trade union movement in Taiwan.[2]

The matter of state control of union movement has changed gradually, in particular after the change of regime in 2000. The new DPP government adopted rather indirect measures to influence their favoured union organizations, but were not very friendly towards union organizations associated with the KMT. Preferences for one union over another influenced funding and the selection of union leaders to join the advisory committees at the Council of Labour Affairs and other government agencies. As mentioned earlier, the increasing awareness of trade union leaders about the need to be independent from the interference of the party politics has encouraged all unions to distance themselves from either the ruling or the opposition party. Therefore, there is a trend for state control of the union movement in Taiwan to move from very high and direct to relatively medium and indirect.

In terms of the issue of collective bargaining, it has been always very weak in Taiwan (see Table 5.3). There are historical reasons for this, such as the control of the KMT regime in the past, as well as structural reasons, such as union fragmentation and lack of unity among peak union organizations. For many years, both the old KMT government and the new DPP government believed that the detailed issues of industrial relations, such as wages, working conditions, insurance and so on should be regulated through the intervention of government, but not direct negotiation between unions and employers. Only in this way could economic development on the one hand and social stability on the other be maintained in a balanced way. Therefore, the institutional environment did not encourage collective bargaining (Pan 2004).

Table 5.3 What do Taiwanese trade unions do?

Activities of Taiwanese trade unions	
Extent of collective bargaining	L
Level of collective bargaining	Industry and enterprise levels
Extent of joint consultation	L
Strikes, working days lost per 1,000 employed	L
Degree of state intervention in employment protection	H

Note
H – high, M – medium, L – low.

According to Taiwan's *Monthly Bulletin of Labour Statistics, March 2006*, the total number of collective agreements in Taiwan fluctuated from 289 in 1990 to 301 in 2000, then to 255 in 2005. Among the total number of collective agreements, 32 per cent (82 agreements) belonged to the public sector and 68 per cent (173 agreements) belonged to the private sector in 2005. Given there were more than 4,000 union organizations in Taiwan in 2005, the number of total collective agreements only covered 6 per cent of total union organizations. Therefore, it is obvious that the unions' involvement in collective bargaining in Taiwan is very low.

What do unions do?

Union activity in Taiwan has to be differentiated according to the influence of the political system, the ownership and size of the business, and labour market changes. For example, there is a history of separate union activity between unions within the state institutional system and unions outside the system (that is, the so-called illegal unions).

In addition, a large number of union branches were established among SOEs with relatively higher union membership compared with a smaller number of union branches and membership among SMEs and foreign-invested enterprises (FIEs) (Pan 2004).

Furthermore, following economic development and later restructuring, the labour market also changed from time to time. The fragmentation of the labour force, for instance, the differences between skills as well as occupations and between local workers and foreign workers, led to different types of union actions with similar or different purposes.

As we reviewed in the earlier section on historical background, the intervention of the state in the industrial relations system provides some basic protection measurements for individual workers through legislation on the one hand, but may repress any attempt for collective action through unions on the other (see Table 5.4). Individual workers might feel protected by the government and eschew anti-government organizations, such as supporting the communists and their activities, while the power of the trade unions and their unity and collective action could be controlled and limited by the government.

Therefore, unions as part of the state-led industrial relations system had a limited power to organize collective action in the workplace. The role of unions within such a system has been labelled as welfare unionism because social functions, vocational training and other welfare activity such as insurance schemes is provided by the government, a phenomenon identical to the trade unions' role in Mainland China (Pan 2004).

In Taiwan, similar to the situation in Mainland China, a large number of union branches were established among SOEs that were invested and controlled by the state directly. A small proportion of unions among SMEs and FIEs were mainly small in size and less influential, with a limited function of providing welfare, such as labour health and unemployment insurance, and different pension schemes (Pan 2004). In addition, family-owned businesses adopted paternalist management systems by emphasizing mutual commitment and loyalty in order to eliminate a confrontational style of union–management relations.

Table 5.4 Explaining Taiwanese trade union development, structure and strategy

Contexts of the Taiwanese trade union	
Political context:	
Degrees of liberalization and autonomy	The society has transformed from authoritarian to democratic.
	The attitude towards union movement has changed from repression to tolerance and a certain degree of support.
	Party politics influence union movement substantially.
Economic context:	
Product markets	H trade as % of GDP H degree of competition
Financial markets	H level of openness to market financing H level of state ownership M level of family ownership M level of foreign ownership M level of institutional ownership
Labour markets	
Demand elasticity (relates to ability of employers to pass on wage increases in prices – high, medium or low)	M
Employer organization membership	M
Multinational	M
Unitarist vs. pluralist	Unitarist (majority)

Note
H – high, M – medium, L – low.

In fact, many of those union members within family-owned SMEs, as well as to a certain degree FIEs, joined the occupational unions for the purpose of being covered by social insurance schemes, but not for other union activities as illustrated in the earlier section.

As for the even smaller proportion of 'illegal unions', they have emerged outside the state-controlled industrial relations system as an 'independent union movement' in their own terms but illegal by government definition since the 1980s (Cheng 2003).

As presented in the earlier part of this chapter, the so-called independent union organization, the Taiwan Labour Front was born in 1984 to provide free legal consultations with unionists. The Taiwan Labour Front has been involved in many activities since its establishment, such as providing legal aid to workers and unions involved in legal disputes, publishing a monthly bulletin, the *Labourer*, to criticize injustice in the workplace and in society, uniting other unions to carry out strikes and public demonstrations targeting either individual companies or government regulations, campaigning for amending the *Labour Standards Law* and the *Labour Union Law* by providing their own draft to the legislature, and finally formed their own anti-KMT Union Federation – the Taiwan Confederation of Trade Unions (TCTU) in 1998. Most 'illegal unions' became legal union organizations after the regime change in 2000 (Cheng 2003).

Nowadays, there is increasing competition among different union organizations, namely the traditional unions used to following the former regime of the KMT, relatively recent union establishments mainly associated with the new ruling party of the DPP, and some other small-sized 'independent unions'. The complexity of union organizations generates multiple voices with similar, as well as different purposes.

For example, the agenda of the formerly powerful CFL includes the following: firstly, to eliminate the influence of the KMT as the historical source of party politics and to establish free and independent elections of leadership at different levels within a CFL system; secondly, to monitor DPP government policy carefully and to lobby the legislature to amend the laws in order to encourage the expansion of union independence, abolishing the limitation on unions being restricted to one within a single workplace and allowing union branches to be formed across workplaces and locations; thirdly, to fully develop and engage collective bargaining at both industry and enterprise levels by empowering union branches through allowing greater autonomy; fourthly, to reduce hours of work from 48 per week to 44 (compared with other OECD economies and neighbouring countries, the working-hour in Taiwan is still very high, second to South Korea in the East Asian region), reduce the number of foreign workers entering Taiwan in order to increase employment opportunity for local workers, and promote comprehensive social insurance and pension schemes in order to cope with the increasing pressure of unemployment due to industrial restructuring and relocation as well as an ageing population; fifthly, to promote the new draft of the *Law of Equal Right at Workplace* and to push the government and the legislature to establish this law as early as possible in order to protect workforce diversity in the workplace, in particular, the interests of women and other disadvantaged groups (Yang 2000).[2]

Other activities with broader social and economic implications are also part of the union's agenda, such as improving health and safety standards, considering the relationship between the environment and the well-being of workers, and upgrading workers' skills by lobbying the government for more investment in vocational training, as well as helping to realize the goal of human resource development through the unions' own vocational training centres (Yang 2000).[2]

Foreign workers and unions' responses

The employment of foreign workers in Taiwan has been an issue since the late 1980s when labour-intensive industries faced serious economic difficulties due to an appreciating currency, increasing levels of wages and a shortage of labour (Minns and Tierney 2005). As a consequence, in 1989, the government permitted major construction projects to engage foreign workers. The number of foreign workers reached a peak in Taiwan in 2002 with more than 300,000 foreigners employed in the economy, coming mainly from Southeast Asian countries such as the Philippines, Indonesia, Thailand and Vietnam (Minns and Tierney 2005).

These foreign workers work in semi-skilled and unskilled jobs in factories and on construction sites, and as domestic servants. They are paid the minimum monthly wage and generally exploited by labour hire brokers who charge significant placement fees (Tierney 2002). According to labour union law, foreign workers are eligible to join Taiwan's labour unions, but are neither allowed to form their own unions nor seek office within unions (Minns and Tierney 2005). As a result, there is little or no involvement of foreign workers in Taiwan's unions.

However, foreign workers have organized industrial action against discrimination and exploitation from time to time with the support of several organizations friendly to organized labour. They have occasionally demanded the strengthening of legal sanctions against racial discrimination and the revision of labour union laws to allow foreign workers to establish independent unions. They are very vulnerable employees, however, and industrial action is difficult. Strike action and complaints can be punished by a loss of contract and deportation. In addition, since their tenure in the country is limited by legislation to two years, with an option for a third, industrial action is fraught with the danger that permission to stay in Taiwan might be revoked or not extended (Minns and Tierney 2005).

The responses of the mainstream Taiwanese union movement towards the foreign workers' struggle have been rather negative and unhelpful. Generally speaking, as Minns and Tierney (2005) note, neither the union leaders nor the Taiwanese rank and file have been interested in solidarity with the struggle of the foreign workers. Tierney (2002) points out that this has been a consequence of the structural weakness of the union movement as a whole and of the robust xenophobic ideology that consistently blames foreign workers for Taiwan's growing unemployment problems (also see Zhu 2005). In addition, this has been a consequence of the willingness of the State to perpetuate immense political divisions within the working class (Minns and Tierney 2005).

Outcomes of union efforts

The outcomes of union activities can be divided into economic and non-economic categories. As for the economic outcomes, the overwhelming phenomenon has been the increase in wage rate, in terms of both the minimum wage rate, as well as the nominal wage rate. Non-economic outcomes include the amendment of industrial relations legislation, such as a reduction of working hours from 48 to 42 per week in recent years (Pan 2004), more freedom and diversity of union establishments, new programmes on job creation, and training with increasing funding. There have been increased opportunities for unions to be involved in the process of democratization and decision-making, such as more union leadership being involved in the government advisory committees, and participating in the legislature through direct involvement as elected members or indirect influence by means of public hearings and lobbying activities.

Explaining the development, structure and strategies of trade unions

The challenges facing the union movement are both external and internal. In terms of external challenges, the process of globalization and competition from other economies, in particular in the East Asian region, has led to painful industrial restructuring with many casualties.

The union movement is confronting these challenges in a variety of ways, including new strategies in three major areas, according to the Taiwanese union movement, which is now under new leadership (Pan 2004).

Union operational procedure

There is a need to develop effective union operational processes, in particular to encourage new members from areas outside the traditional industrial sectors. The new leadership of Taiwanese trade unions has emphasized the importance of being independent and truly representing workers' interests, thus eschewing close association with political parties and government. In terms of providing benefits to union members, trade unions have looked to a more flexible welfare policy in order to cope with the current workforce with its diverse terms of employment and working patterns (Pan 2004).

In addition, the new union operational process is focused on developing a new pattern based on the philosophy of 'social partnership'. A sense of duality – that unions could be good partners of business at the same time as they serve the interests of their members – should be an acceptable union response to confront the challenges of globalization and industrial restructuring (Wu 2000).

Collective bargaining

A related task is to fully develop and engage in collective bargaining, which has been marginalized and neglected due to lack of government policy, as well as a paucity of union initiatives (Pan 2004). Following the move away from a strong central government, including political and economic intervention in the operation of trade unions, to market competition and less state involvement in the operation of business and unions, trade unions must to learn how to protect union members' interests effectively and independently. Collective bargaining is one of the most important ways in which workers can protect their interests by negotiating economic benefits and other conditions, but it is at an infant stage in Taiwan (Pan 2004). Both the skills and strategies of negotiation, as well as knowledge of the economic environment and the way of obtaining information about the economic situation of companies need to be improved.

Union structure

Improvement of union structure, adequate financial arrangements, including reforming membership fees (the current level of 1 per cent of wage rate is too low and not sufficient to cover unions' activities), as well as members' education and internal democracy within union organizations are all required. A trend towards grassroot orientation with increasing focus on developing community-based unions would lead to a more democratic and flat union structure.

Political participation

One way to address issues in terms of the unions' relationships with the government is to encourage union members to engage in independent political participation and actively engage in the processes of formulating new policy and legislation (Pan 2004). The political participation of union leaders is not an individual political gain for those leaders, but an entire plan as part of union engagement strategies. Due to rapid changes of political and economic environments in Taiwan and the world, different interest groups are keen to be involved in the process of decision making at different levels of society. Trade unions must engage in this process actively in order to make sure that the majority of working men and women in society are protected and their voices are heard (Pan 2004).

Conclusion

The future of the trade union movement in Taiwan is rather blurred and uncertain. On the one hand, the union movement is currently experiencing substantial political freedom and autonomy, for the first time in Taiwanese history. On the other hand, the processes of globalization, economic restructuring and industrial relocation are making capital more mobile and market forces more powerful, with a concomitant increase in union movement vulnerability.

To answer the general question raised in the Chapter 2, we can see change for Taiwan with some characteristics distinguishing Taiwan's union movement from the models presented by Hyman (2001) as well as Gospel (2005). For instance, a union movement with a strong political orientation toward class struggle has not evolved. Taiwanese unions' political orientation has, instead, been used by the regime and party politics and the unions do not pursue outcomes related to cherished ideologies. Instead they are using the union organization for political and economic gain to benefit their own group, not as a vehicle to mobilize members to participate in a class struggle. The unions' agenda is inward looking and inherently selfish as is evidenced by their attitude towards foreign workers and the internal power struggles among different peak union bodies and their leadership.

Mainstream unions in Taiwan, as most unions in other countries, have adopted more economically-oriented strategies and behaviours, with the emphasis on the 'social partnership' and 'dual responsibility' of the workers and the employers. But the model in Taiwan is very different from the union movement in either Europe (trade unions as agents of social integration labelled as integrative unions emphasizing 'social partnership') or the United States (trade unions as labour market actors labelled as business unionism focusing on the market) (see Hyman 2001: 3). Taiwanese unions look more like a combination of both, a response to the fact that the Taiwanese workplace is managed in a very unitary style and unions are afraid of companies closing down their business operations in Taiwan. They tend, therefore, to be more cooperative with management in order to avoid the consequences of not cooperating.

The movement of business infrastructure to more favourable locations is a challenge of globalization and confronts not only the union movement and its activities in Taiwan and other countries, but also academic researchers in the industrial relations field, forcing them to rethink future development and patterns of union movement in different parts of the world.

Notes

1 Author's interview with Ms Huang, General Secretary of Taipei Hotel Occupational Union, 16 May 2006.
2 Author's interview with Mr Liu, President of Taipei Federation of CFL, 18 May 2006.

References

Bello, W. and Rosenfeld, S. (1996) *Dragons in Distress: Asia's Miracle Economies in Crisis*, San Francisco, CA: Institute for Food and Development Policy.

Chen, S. J. (1998) 'The development of HRM practices in Taiwan', in C. Rowley (ed.) *Human Resource Management in the Asia Pacific Region: Convergence Questioned*, London: Frank Cass.

Cheng, T. S. (2003) *Trade Unions' Research: The Examples of the United States, Japan and Taiwan*, Kaoshiung: Liwen Publishing House.

Cooney, S. (1996) 'The new Taiwan and the old labour law: authoritarian legislation in a democratised society', *Comparative Labour Law Journal*, 18: 1–61.

Council of Labor Affairs (2006) *Monthly Bulletin of Labor Statistics, Taiwan Area*, March, Taipei: Council of Labor Affairs, Executive Yuan.

Frenkel, S, Hong, J. C. and Lee, B. L. (1993) 'The resurgence and fragility of trade unions in Taiwan', in S. Frenkel (ed.) *Organized Labor in the Asia-Pacific Region: A Comparative Study of Trade Unionism in Nine Countries*, Ithaca, NY: ILR Press.

Gospel, H. (2005) 'Markets, firms, and unions: a historical-institutionalist perspective on trade unions', in S. Fernie and D. Metcalf (eds) *The Future of Trade Unions*, London: Routledge.

Ho, S. Y. (1990) *Taiwan – After a Long Silence: The Emerging New Unions of Taiwan*, Hong Kong: Asia Monitor Research Centre.

Hyman, R. (2001) *Understanding European Trade Unionism: Between Market, Class, and Society*, London: Sage.

Lee, J. S. (1988) 'Labor relations and the stages of economic development: the case of the Republic of China', in Institution for Economic Research (1988), *Proceedings of the Conference on Labor and Economic Development*, Taipei: Institution for Economic Research, China Productivity Center.

Lee, J. S. (1995) 'Economic development and the evolution of industrial relations in Taiwan, 1950–1993', in A. Verma, T. A. Kochan and R. D. Lansbury (eds) *Employment Relations in the Growing Asian Economies*, London: Routledge.

Minns, J. and Tierney, R. (2005) 'Class and class struggle in Taiwan', *Chengda Laodong Xuibao*, 18: 79–117.

Ng, S. H. and Warner, M. (1998) *China's Trade Unions and Management*, London: Macmillan and New York: St Martins Press.

Pan, S. W. (2004) 'The influence of economic globalization on Taiwan's trade union movement', *Furen Xuizhi*, 38: 111–30.

Taiwan Yearbook (2006) *Taiwan Yearbook 2006*, Taipei: Government Information Office.

Tierney, R. (2002) 'Foreign workers and capitalist class relations in Taiwan: a study of economic exploitation and political isolation', *Bulletin of Labour Research*, 12: 125–65.

Wang, H. L. and Cooney, S. (2002) 'Taiwan's labour law: the end of state corporatism?' in S. Cooney, T. Lindsey, R. Mitchell and Y. Zhu (eds) *Law and Labour Market Regulation in East Asia*, London and New York: Routledge.

World Bank, (2007) *Doing Business in Taiwan, China*, The World Bank Group: www.doingbusiness.org/ExploreEconomies.

Wu, S. L. (2000) 'Re-thinking Taiwan's trade unions in the 21st century', *The Chinese Federation of Labour News*, 5: 11–19.

Xu, G. X. (2000) 'The development of national federation of trade unions: diversity and independence?' *The Chinese Federation of Labour News*, 7: 1–2.

Yang, R. C. (2000) 'The independent way of the Chinese Federation of Labour', *The Chinese Federation of Labour News*, 5: 1–5.

Ying, H. S. (1990) *Taiwan – After the Long Silence: The Emerging New Unions of Taiwan*, Hong Kong: Asia Monitor Research Centre.

Zhu, Y. (2005) 'Unemployment in Taiwan: globalization, regional integration and social changes', in J. Benson and Y. Zhu (eds) *Unemployment in Asia*, London and New York: RoutledgeCurzon.

Zhu, Y. and Warner, M. (2001) 'Taiwan business strategies *vis-à-vis* the Asian Financial crisis', *Asia Pacific Business Review*, 7(3): 139–56.

Zhu, Y., Chen, I. and Warner, M. (2000) 'HRM in Taiwan: an empirical case study', *Human Resource Management Journal*, 10(4): 32–44.

6 Trade unions in Hong Kong

Worker representation or political agent?

Andy W. Chan

Introduction

Hong Kong is a cosmopolitan and highly urbanized society. It is widely recognized as one of the world's leading exponents of a *laissez faire* economy. The roles of trade unions in Hong Kong are similar to that of developed economies in many aspects, including bargaining for labour interest *vis-à-vis* employers, assisting workers in labour disputes, providing services to members, and participating in wider social issues. One unique characteristic of Hong Kong's union movement is its close relationship with the political struggle in China for several decades. Though union density is not very low in Hong Kong, unions are traditionally deemed weak and feeble in terms of their influence in the workplace (England 1989; Turner *et al*. 1991; Levin and Chiu 1993; Chan and Snape 2000).

This chapter looks at the recent development and changing posture of trade unions in Hong Kong which has undergone rapid changes economically and politically during the last two decades. The first section briefly examines the political and economic contexts in which unions operate, including the new political system established following Britain's return of Hong Kong's sovereignty to China in 1997, and the changing economic structures. The second section offers a brief history of union development and membership and then analyses types of unions, union centres, and unionization across economic sectors. Then what Hong Kong unions do and have done, especially in the past few decades, is examined. Next is an analysis of recent developments and strategies of unions in relation to the characteristics of Hong Kong's employers and employment practices. The conclusion discusses how Hong Kong's unions are likely to further develop and reposition themselves in response to the dilemma of representing labour in terms of employment regulation and conditions as opposed to acting for political interests.

Context and history

After 155 years of British rule (1842–1997), Hong Kong was returned to China as a Special Administrative Region (SAR) on 1 July 1997 with guarantees that the 'previous capitalist system and way of life shall remain unchanged for

50 years'.[1] This implies that the existing economic, legal and social systems will be maintained; and Hong Kong enjoys a high degree of autonomy except in defence and foreign affairs.

Hong Kong is headed by the Chief Executive. Accordingly to the *Basic Law*, the Chief Executive is elected by a broadly representative Election Committee composed of 800 Hong Kong residents and appointed by the Chinese Central Government. The Chief Executive leads the SAR and decides on government policies and issues executive orders. He also signs bills passed by the Legislative Council to promulgate laws. He is advised on major policy decisions by the Executive Council whose members are appointed by the Chief Executive from the principal officials, Legislative Council members, and other public figures. At present, there are 15 non-official members.[2]

Mr Tung Chee-hwa was elected the first Chief Executive and served from 1997 to 2002. After being elected for a second term, he resigned in 2005 and Mr Tsang Yam-kuen became the SAR's second Chief Executive. Overall the political principle of 'one country, two systems' has worked quite well since 1997 as the Chinese government has tried not to intervene in Hong Kong's internal affairs; with the exception of influencing aspects of the political system, especially the methods of electing the Chief Executive and the Legislative Council.

In Hong Kong, three major political powers dominate the Legislative Council: the pro-Beijing DAB (the Democratic Alliance for the Betterment of Hong Kong); the pro-democracy DP (Hong Kong Democratic Party); and the pro-business LP (Liberal Party). The DAB has on many occasions allied with the LP to support the sitting government and thus their leaders have frequently been chosen as Executive Council members. The DP and other pro-democracy parties, on the other hand, have tended to oppose the SAR government on many public policies and none of their leaders have been appointed to seats in the Executive Council. In general, the pro-government groups prefer gradual change in the political system while the pro-democracy groups strive for quick reform and direct elections rather than the system of appointees put in place by China.

Thus, Hong Kong is a liberal, pluralistic and stable society. Governance is not truly democratic; but since it came under the control of China in 1997, Hong Kong has become a unique capitalistic city within the communist country (see Table 6.1).

By 2005, there were a total of 6.97 million people residing in a compact city with an area of 1,100 square kilometres. Despite limited natural resources and its small physical size, Hong Kong's economy has had an excellent record for the past 40 years. Its gross domestic product (GDP) grew at an average rate of 3.9 per cent in real terms per annum during the past decade. Per capita GDP reached US$25,600 (Table 6.1), second only to that of Japan in Asia and higher than that of many Western countries. Hong Kong is ranked eleventh in the world's most competitive environments.[3]

Hong Kong experienced hyper-growth from the 1960s to the mid-1980s with an influx of capital and overseas buyers. It rapidly developed export-led industrialization, mainly in manufacturing garments and later in light industrial

Table 6.1 Contextual factors – Hong Kong

General statistics	
Population[1] (2005)	6.97 million
Area (square kilometres)[2]	1.10 thousand
Employment by sector (%)[2] (2005)	
Agriculture	0.3
Industry	5.2
Construction	8.0
Services	86.5
Urban population (% of total population)	almost 100.0
GDP per capita[3] (2005)	US$25,600
Income inequality	Medium–high
Gini coefficient[4]	0.453 (1986)
	0.518 (1996)
	0.533 (2006)
Real GDP growth (%)[3, 5]	
1986–1995	6.4
1995–2005	3.9
Unemployment (%)[3, 5]	
1986–1995	1.9
1996–2005	5.4

Summary description	
Product market regulation	
Political context	Liberal/pluralistic; a capitalist city within a communist country
Political stability	High

Sources
1 Census and Statistics Department, Hong Kong 'Hong Kong Statistics'. Online. Available HTTP http://www.censtatd.gov.hk/hong_kong_statistics/statistics_by_subject/index.jsp (accessed on 17 August 2006).
2 Census and Statistics Department, Hong Kong (2006) *Hong Kong in Figures 2006 Edition*, February.
3 Census and Statistics Department's *Hong Kong Annual Digest of Statistics (1996 to 2005 editions)*. Tables on gross domestic product (GDP) and tables on unemployment rates are used, respectively, to compute the figures of GDP growth and unemployment rates.
4 Census and Statistics Department (1992) *1991 Population Census Main Report; and Census and Statistics Department (2007) Population Census 2006 Main Report – Volume I*, Hong Kong: Census and Statistics Department.
5 Census and Statistics Department, Hong Kong 'Hong Kong Statistics'. Online. Available HTTP <http://www.censtatd.gov.hk/hong_kong_statistics/statistical_tables/index.jsp?charsetID=1&subject ID=2&tableID=006> (accessed on 17 August 2006).

products. Its GDP grew in real terms about 10 per cent per annum in the period 1961–84. The number of workers being employed in manufacturing establishments increased from 230,000 in 1961 to 593,000 in 1971, and then to 904,000 in 1981.[4] At the end of the 1970s, China adopted an open-door policy and Hong Kong became more prosperous with rapid growth in service industries including import/ export, retail and eating establishments.

In the 1980s, Hong Kong experienced a decline in the manufacturing sector after three decades of rapid growth. Retail, trading and financial services competed for workers with the manufacturing sector. People started to change from blue-collar to service sector employment because of the higher wages, greater status and promotion prospects. Many industrialists started to move their factories to the Guangdong Province of China for lower labour and operations costs. Since then, Hong Kong is no longer an export-oriented, low-wage manufacturing economy, and the largest employers in the private sector are retail, restaurants, trading and financial services (Wong 1994).

In the past two decades, Hong Kong has further developed as a tourist and financial centre. Simultaneously, the manufacturing industry has been experiencing further contraction due to increased relocation of production plants into various cities of the Chinese mainland. Changes in the relative share of the GDP and employment between the manufacturing and service sectors reflect this economic shift. The contribution of the 'industry' sector (including manufacturing, mining, and construction industries) to Hong Kong's whole GDP fell from 31 per cent in 1970 to 17 per cent in 1990, and then to only 13 per cent in 2000. Also, the manufacturing sector's percentage share of employed workers decreased from 47 per cent in 1971 to 36 per cent in 1990, and to 14 per cent in 2005.[5]

In contrast, the service sector (including retail, trading, hotels, transport, business, community and personal services) has prospered, with its relative contribution to Hong Kong's GDP rising from 60 per cent in 1970 to 76 per cent in 1991 and then to 87 per cent in 2000. Total employed persons in the service sector increased gradually, with 1.37 million in 1985 to 2.1 million 1995 and 3.4 million in 2005. The sector's share in the total workforce advanced from 54 per cent in 1985 to 72 per cent in 1995 and 86 per cent in 2005.

Such a restructuring of the economy led to a changed pattern of inter-sectoral distribution of the workforce and occupational structures. Employment has shifted towards white-collar occupations such as clerical and professional work. Specifically, the relative share of production workers in the employed workforce fell from 43 per cent in 1987 to 35 per cent in 1991 and 17 per cent in 2001. By contrast, the percentage of professionals and managers in the workforce rose from 12 per cent in 1987 to 28 per cent in 1991 and 32 per cent in 2001.[6]

Immediately after the establishment of the SAR, Hong Kong experienced a series of crises causing economic recession. In late 1997, the Asian Financial Crisis caused all sectors to suffer, including the prosperous property sector. Waves of redundancies occurred and many people lost jobs, including frontline workers and middle managers in various trades. Another major crisis was the outbreak of severe acute respiratory syndrome (SARS) in early 2003. The disease was a serious blow to all service industries in that period. In fact, the unemployment rate reached 8.6 per cent in the second quarter of 2003, a historical high in Hong Kong.

To resolve these crises, the government became more proactive in its policies to fit the changing economic structures. It introduced new policies to attract investors, both from overseas and from mainland China. For instance, it cooperated with business groups to develop the Digital Harbour; it successfully persuaded the Walt Disney Company to build a theme park to boost tourism. The Chinese government supported Hong Kong and signed the Mainland and Hong Kong Closer Economic Partnership Arrangement (CEPA) so that selected Hong Kong manufacturers could export their products to the Mainland with zero tariff and professionals, including accountants and lawyers, could practise in China. About 29,000 new jobs were created within the first two years of CEPA.[7] Hong Kong's economy gradually recovered, with annual unemployment rates dropping from the peak 7.9 per cent in 2003 to 6.8 per cent in 2004, and to 5.6 per cent in 2005.[8]

For the past two decades, the Hong Kong economy has experienced a process of de-industrialization and re-commercialization (Chan *et al.* 2000). The grassroots workforce has suffered most. Many unskilled workers and middle-aged labourers, without training or experience in the service sector, could not easily find jobs. Their family incomes were severely reduced. The distribution of wealth in the territory has become increasingly uneven with the Gini coefficient rising from 0.453 in 1986 to 0.518 in 1996, and to 0.533 in 2006 (see Table 6.1). This disparity in wealth contributed to dissatisfaction among working people. Social organizations and labour unions repeatedly took militant action to demand more job opportunities.

Brief history of trade unions

Being a city in southern China, Hong Kong cannot avoid being subject to China's political influence, so the early development of Hong Kong unions was really an extension of the wider political–labour movement inside China (England and Rear 1981). The power struggle between the two rival union centres, the pro-Communist Hong Kong Federation of Trade Unions (FTU) and the pro-Nationalist Hong Kong and Kowloon Trade Unions Council (TUC) began in the 1950s. The two union camps continue to compete with one another to recruit members and have extended the politics from the Mainland to Hong Kong. This is one reason why workplace representation has not been pursued with great vigour in Hong Kong (England and Rear 1981), as the two union centres seldom worked together to pursue labour rights. The result was a long period of industrial peace from the 1950s to the 1980s, with no large-scale strikes except for a series of incidents in May 1967 when labour disputes in two factories led to widespread action. Leaders of the FTU actively participated in this confrontation. Work stoppages, street-rioting and even bombs appeared. Over fifty people died in the confrontation which lasted for a few months (England and Rear 1981). Immediately after this incident, the government started to uphold its role as 'protector of labour' by actively promulgating labour legislation concerning working hours, child labour and work safety. It also improved policies on social welfare, medical care and education. England (1989) thus concluded that the 1967 industrial action marked a major watershed in the development of industrial relations and social policies in Hong Kong.

Union membership grew steadily in the 1970s and reached a peak in 1977, with 404,000 registered members. One important factor contributing to the growth was the Chinese government's open-door policy towards Western businesses. Many workers joined FTU affiliates as a patriotic gesture of identification with their mother country. Another reason was the growth of white-collar unions in the service sector, such as those formed by teachers, social workers, civil servants and the staffs of public utilities (Levin and Jao 1988).

Before the 1980s, the FTU and TUC shared union power in Hong Kong. After the signing of Sino-British Declaration in the mid-1980s, the TUC lost many members because of the union's pro-Taiwan stance. The FTU became the largest union with steady growth in membership. The establishment of a pro-democracy union centre, the Hong Kong Confederation of Trade Unions (CTU), in 1990 marked a new era in union development in Hong Kong. The CTU adopted proactive and radical strategies in representing workers' rights against employers in labour disputes. Its affiliated unions and membership size both increased steadily. It has become the FTU's major competitor in recruitment and leadership in the 'union industry'.

The influence of union centres and their leaders on social and political issues has increased significantly over the past two decades. Since the 1980s, along with other unions, the FTU has been active with the pro-Beijing lobby, including the DAB. The CTU on the other hand maintains close ties to the pro-democracy forces including the DP. In past two decades, the DAB and the DP were direct competitors in the political arena and elections. Unions also participated in electoral politics and some active labour advocates were elected as Legislative Council members (Chiu and Levin 2000). They could then exert significant influence on the government's decisions on labour policy. However, given the polarization of political parties and union affiliation to adversarial camps, unions have unavoidably become politically and organizationally divided.

Hong Kong has experienced slow union membership growth over the past two decades (refer to Table 6.2). Union membership increased faster in the period 1985–1995 than in 1995–2005; there was an increase of about 61 per cent between 1985 and 1995, and only about 11 per cent between 1995 and 2005.

Union types and structure

Registered unions in Hong Kong are predominately industrial and occupational unions. Industrial unions can be found in the major economic sectors including manufacturing (garments, plastics, and electronics) and non-manufacturing industries (construction, retail, restaurants, and banking). As many factories were relocated to the Mainland, the total number of workers in manufacturing decreased, along with union membership. Occupational unions are concentrated in the community and business services, as they are mainly civil servants or professional employees who organize unions to safeguard their sectoral interests. The largest unions represent teachers, nurses, and civil servants. Occupational unions in the business sector are formed by tourist guides, real estate agents and

Table 6.2 Trade unions in Hong Kong

General statistics	
Number of unions[1,2]	
1990	452
2005	686
Number of union members[1,2]	
1990	468,746
2005	655,159
Union density (%)[2,3]	
1990	18.8
2005	20.6
Summary description	
Union type	
Main	Economic/market
Secondary	Political
(Economic/market, political, other)	
Union structure	
Main	Industrial
Secondary	Occupational
(Occupational, industrial, general, enterprise)	
Unity of peak organization (high, medium or low)	Medium
State control of unions	Low
Involvement in collective bargaining	Low

Sources:

1 Registrar of Trade Unions, *Hong Kong, Annual Departmental Report (1990 to1994)*, Hong Kong: Government Printer.

2 Registry of Trade Unions, Labour Department, *Annual Statistical Report (1995 to 2005)*, Hong Kong: Labour Department.

3 Commissioner for Labour, *Annual Departmental Report (1990 to 2002)*, Hong Kong: Government Printer.

financial planners but they are quite inactive in the union movement. There still exist a few craft unions for older, traditional skilled workers such as woodwork carvers, rattan workers and tailors. Many craft unions were founded half a century ago and only a few remain.

By 2005, there were about 50 enterprise unions established by employees in large public utilities such as transport, gas, electricity, telecommunications, and in large retail chains (Registry of Trade Unions 2005). Many of them were active in representing employees at the workplace level and in organizing industrial actions. For instance, large-scale strikes have been organized by pilots and flight attendants of the Cathay Pacific Airline, staff of the Hong Kong Telecommunications, and drivers of bus companies in the past two decades.

There are also general unions which, due to historical development, recruit across industrial and occupational boundaries. They are mainly found in the manufacturing, trading and transport sectors. The Hong Kong Union for Chinese Workers in Western Style Employment, with 24,000 members, is the largest general union. It was founded in 1949 and successfully recruited various categories of office workers when Hong Kong shifted to a service economy.

Unions in Hong Kong have been typically small because of the political division, employer sponsorship of company unions and the ease of registration of small unions (England 1989: 128–30; Chan and Snape 1996). Average union membership was only 955 in 2005. Over the past two decades, registered unions with memberships below 250 have accounted for 60 per cent of the total whilst those with a membership of more than 1,000 decreased to about 12 per cent. Though the number of small unions increased much faster than medium and large unions, their total membership was still very low, 0.7 per cent in 2005.

There are only 23 large unions with a membership size over 5,000 with their total membership accounting for 65 per cent of total union members (Registry of Trade Unions 2005). Seven unions have memberships over 20,000. The largest unions are mainly found in the sectors of community and transport as the unionization rates are highest among employees in community service, including civil servants, teachers, and bus drivers. Most of these large unions are affiliated to the FTU and only a few with the CTU or TUC. Some very large unions, which are independent from union centres, are mainly concentrated in the public service.

Unions by economic sectors

In 2005, both the largest numbers of unions and union membership were representing the community, social and personal services sector: 377 unions with 352,000 members. The transport, storage and communications sector, the next largest, had 111 unions representing 109,000 employees. The sizes of membership of three other sectors, manufacturing, financing, insurance, real estate and business, and wholesale, retail and import/export trades, restaurants and hotels, were very close, being about 50,000. The smallest number of union members was in the electricity, gas and water sector, which is consistent with its low sectoral employment. The top two sectors with highest union density are consistently community, social and personal services and transport, storage and communication (England 1989).

Hong Kong unions are more well established in the public service than in the private sector because the government, following British tradition, behaves as a role model of a 'good employer', voluntarily recognizing unions and civil servants, a group with a long history of activism.

Unions in the transport and communications sector have a long history of industrial activity and their members have been well organized and active in participating in union-sponsored activities and industrial action (England 1989; Chan and Snape 2000). Almost every year, unions in the bus companies organize or threaten to organize industrial action during the annual wage negotiation exercise.[9]

There was an increase in union density in the manufacturing sector, from 6.3 per cent in 1985 to 25.4 per cent in 2004. But in terms of membership size by sector, the increment was found to be insignificant, from 57,000 in 1985 to 59,000 in 2004.

Union centres or federations

Union centres or federations in Hong Kong register either as limited companies or as societies rather than as 'trade unions' because they are not formed for the sake of a specific industrial or occupational group of employees. The most powerful union federations are those formed with memberships cutting across industries, but with similar political or union ideologies, such as the FTU, the TUC, and the CTU. These comparatively well-resourced federations are the *de facto* engines of Hong Kong's labour movement.

The FTU was established in 1948. It is the most important union centre in the history of Hong Kong's union movement. Its motto is 'Advancing with Hong Kong and working with the grassroots' with guiding principles of 'patriotism, solidarity, rights and benefits, welfare, and participation'. By 2005, the FTU had 158 affiliated unions with 282,000 members, accounting for 23 per cent of unions and 43 per cent of union membership in Hong Kong. Its affiliated unions were traditionally in the manufacturing, transport, office work, and retail sectors. It had been successful in organizing new unions in almost every sector since 1985, the year the signing of the Sino-British Declaration on Hong Kong's future sovereignty took place. The FTU's growth rate fell, however, in the early 1990s because of the June Fourth Incident in Beijing and the formation of the CTU. Its membership dropped to below 40 per cent of the aggregate union members in the territory. After 1997, however, the year of the return of Hong Kong's sovereignty to China, the FTU became the 'preferred union centre' due to its close relations with the HKSAR and Chinese governments and membership is rebounding.

The TUC was founded in 1948. During the 1970s and 1980s it possessed a similar number of affiliated unions as the FTU, but gradually fell behind after the 1980s. By 2005, the TUC had only 36 affiliated unions and less than 20,000 members. This represents a loss of half of its affiliated unions and 45 per cent of its members within 20 years. On the whole, this fall in participation was the result of difficulties in recruiting new members and developing leaders from younger generations due to the union centre's long political allegiance to the Nationalists in Taiwan (England 1989; Chiu and Levin 2000). Its main affiliates are still in traditional manufacturing, transport and restaurant sectors.

The CTU was founded in 1990 by Lau Chin-sek and Lee Cheuk-yan, who had served on the Christian Industrial Committee (England 1989), a pressure group. The CTU's core principles are 'solidarity, rice bowl, justice, and democracy' and it attracted many unions which agreed with its promotion of autonomy and pro-democracy stance. In 1990, it had 21 affiliated unions and 74,000 members. The Professional Teachers' Union (PTU), with 47,000 members, also joined the CTU. With aggressive strategies for union organization, the CTU grew steadily in the following two decades. By 2005, it had 68 affiliated unions and over 111,000 members. The CTU attracted professional employees including teachers, social workers, and employees in transport and public utilities. It has been largely unsuccessful in organizing unions in manufacturing because of its short history and is not the preferred federation for civil servants due to its radical political stance and militant approach to handling labour disputes.

Other than these federations, there are also 'independent' unions which are not affiliated with any union centre. Some of the most powerful 'independent' unions are found in the community service and public utilities. The Hong Kong Chinese Civil Servants' Association (CCSA), founded in 1949 for all civil servants, has been the largest registered union in Hong Kong for many years. In 2005, the CCSA had over 82,000 members. Other large 'independent' unions were formed respectively by nurses and the disciplined forces including policemen, immigration officers, and fire-fighters.

What do unions do?

Though there may be some variations in different periods of time, Hong Kong unions in general appear to cluster around three key dimensions of activity: first, job-based unionism – regulating the terms and conditions of jobs at workplace level; second, services unionism – providing services and benefits to members; and third, political unionism – acting as political agents in the interests of labour (England 1989; Snape and Chan 1999).

Job-based unionism has been under-developed in Hong Kong as unions are ineffective at the workplace level (Levin and Chiu 1996). Unions can only serve in a consultative role rather than becoming involved in fully-fledged collective bargaining since the final say on terms of employment resides with management (England 1989). In practice, Hong Kong unions have adopted so-called 'defensive economism', i.e. union participation in workplace disputes mainly in the form of offering post-hoc advice to strikers or representing them in negotiations (Chiu and Levin 2000).

It is rare for unions to touch on issues relating to job control; they mainly focus on matters relating to wages or benefits. In the private sector, the main causes of labour disputes have been employer insolvency, cessation of business or restructuring. Such cases have arisen recently, especially after the Asian Financial Crisis, and unions could only help workers to claim back their wages in arrears. See Table 6.3 for a summary of what Hong Kong unions do.

Hong Kong unions have been active in lobbying the government on labour matters at the territory level, such as the importation of foreign workers, establishment of a government-sponsored retirement scheme, and the introduction of statutory collective bargaining. Some of these problems have been resolved. For example, there has been a tightening of control on the importation of foreign workers and a central provident fund has been established. Union centres still strive hard for a minimum wage scheme and collective bargaining laws. They usually organize street rallies to voice their demands. Another channel is to communicate with the government via the Labour Advisory Board, a tripartite consultative mechanism for elected union representatives and employer representatives, with the Commissioner for Labour as the chairman, to discuss and reach agreement on major employment issues. Historically, however, it has proved difficult to reach consensus on controversial issues, such as minimum wage legislation.

Table 6.3 What do Hong Kong unions do?

Activities	
Extent of collective bargaining[1,2]	Low
Level of collective bargaining[1,2]	
National	Low
Industry	Low
Enterprise	Low
Extent of joint consultation[1,2,3]	Low
Industrial disputes[3]	
Working days lost per 1,000 employees (2005)	0.03 (consistently below 0.50 for past 5 years)
Relative assessment	Low
Degree of state intervention in employment protection	Medium

Sources
1 Hong Kong Institute of Human Resource Management (2004) *Human Resource Management Strategies and Practices Research Report 2004*, Hong Kong Institute of Human Resource Management.
2 Ng S. H. and Chan A. W. (2000) *A Report on the Survey 'Communication and Human Resources: Hong Kong Style'*, Hong Kong: Labour Department and University of Hong Kong.
3 Labour Department (2006) *Labour Department Annual Report 2005*, Hong Kong: Labour Department.

Also, unions, with their supported councillors, express their views on labour policies and put forward their proposals in the Legislative Council. It is not easy to get union proposals passed because business and conservative representatives dominate the Council under the current election system. Elected legislators with union backgrounds however adopt various degrees of collaboration with political parties and their influence cannot be underestimated.

A key role of Hong Kong unions is to participate in the wider political arena. In Legislative Council elections since the 1990s, about one-sixth of the 60 elected councillors were either union leaders or they were endorsed by unions; they won the seats respectively via the geographic and functional constituencies.[10] Unions also participated in the elections for the district councils and the then urban and regional councils. In addition, unions became vocal lobbyists on behalf of labour and social interests, including campaigning against increased bus fares and utility charges, and demanding tax reduction for the middle class. As union leaders have high visibility due to involvement in labour disputes or union-sponsored rallies, they have a high chance of beating ordinary contestants in elections. Thus, Hong Kong's political context was vital in nurturing the development of a politicized labour movement during the long transition period from 1984, the year of signing the joint declaration, to 1997 and immediately after it (Chai 1993; Ng and Rowley 2000).

As mentioned before, the FTU and the TUC were closely related to the political struggle in China. The labour riot of 1967 was attributed in part to FTU influence (England 1989). The political polarization of these two federations severely affected Hong Kong's union movement for many years. Then after the 1990s, the CTU developed rapidly and with close links to local political groups replaced the TUC as the major opponent to the FTU. Hong Kong unions were highly politicized as they showed their political allegiance to various political parties. Instead of the industrial relations context, the direction of their development was greatly influenced by political factors. Unions' recent development in politics is further discussed in the next section.

Last but not the least, Hong Kong unions have contributed significantly in providing welfare services to workers, especially in the hard times of the 1950s and 1960s. The FTU operated schools, clinics and canteens for grass-roots employees and provided cash subsides to sick or unemployed workers. Now, with rising living standards, Hong Kong unions have tried to meet workers' needs by providing discount sales on merchandise, issuing credit cards, offering training courses, organizing recreational activities and trips to China and Taiwan.

With a long history and sufficient resources, the FTU has established the largest network offering employee assistance, with five supermarkets which provide comprehensive retail services of daily goods at lower prices. It started a work education centre in 1990 to offer training courses; set up district offices in 1992 to provide comprehensive community services; and operated a labour service centre in 1995 to help workers with their employment grievances and claims due to injuries at work (FTU 2003). In 2004, the FTU started its service centres in Guangdong to assist those Hong Kong citizens working or studying there. Compared with the FTU, the TUC and CTU offered only limited union services. The TUC organizes social functions and trips to Taiwan. The CTU issues CTU cards to members to get discount sales on electrical appliances and other consumer goods. It has also established the CTU Education Fund to offer training courses to retrain low-skilled workers and to educate them regarding their legal rights in employment. In terms of individual industrial or occupational unions, only a few can provide similar union services, such as the CCSA and the PTU. Overall, unions tend to provide popular services so as to meet members' needs and also attract potential members.

Explaining the development, structure and strategies of trade unions

The vast majority of business establishments in Hong Kong are very small. In 2004, over 98 per cent of the 289,897 establishments employed less than 50 persons; only 93 establishments had 1,000 or more employees and they employed about 290,000 persons.[11] Such small firms adopt flexible employment strategies in order to survive in highly unstable markets. As rates of pay are low, workers need to work long hours. In family businesses, the core workforce is composed of family members and permanent skilled workers whilst unskilled workers are employed on a temporary or contract basis (England 1989). The owner-managers adopt an authoritative leadership style, relying on person-to-person communication; no union activities appear in their establishments.

Most large local business firms have adopted the unitary approach in managing organizations (see Table 6.4), while entrepreneurs have often exhibited a desire to make quick profits without forming any long-term development plan for their business. Other companies, however, behave like benevolent paternalists, providing good fringe benefits to workers and developing an indirect communication network via supervisors. In these situations, personal complaints can reach top management who do not want unions to limit their authoritative power as they believe unions are 'subversive' (England 1989). Some open-minded employers implement human resource management practices, such as performance appraisal systems and two-way communication, but they do not recognize unions. Some US firms in Hong Kong, including IBM and Motorola, adopt a sophisticated HRM approach but reject unions.

Many large public utilities providing monopolized services in energy, transport and telecommunications have adopted a more pluralist approach to employment. They recognize unions and maintain regular dialogue with them. Some have signed collective agreements with unions. For instance, Cable & Wireless (HK)

Table 6.4 Explaining the development, structure and strategy of Hong Kong unions

Political context	
Degrees of liberalization and autonomy (repression, tolerance, support, indifference) Relations with the state (dependent, independent)	Indifference Quite independent
Markets	
Openness (imports + exports as % of GDP)[1] Degree of competition (high, medium or low)	High (21.8% in 2004) High
Financial markets Openness to market financing Ownership (group, institutional, foreign, dispersed)	High Dispersed
Labour markets Demand elasticity (relates to ability of employers to pass on wage increases in prices – high, medium or low)	Medium–high
Employers	
Concentration (top 100 companies as a percentage value of total)[2] Employer organization membership Multinational Unitarist or pluralist perspective	13% (for 2004, excluding civil service) Medium High Mainly unitarist in private sector and pluralist in public sector

Sources
1 Computed based on the table 'GDP by Economic Activity at Constant (2000) Prices', *Hong Kong Annual Digest of Statistics, 2005 edition*, Hong Kong: Census and Statistics Department.
2 Estimated based on the table 'Number of Establishments and Persons Engaged (Other than Those in the Civil Service) by Industry Sector and Size of Establishment', *Hong Kong Annual Digest of Statistics, 2005 edition*, Hong Kong: Census and Statistics Department.

Limited and its union signed procedural and substantive agreements between 1971 and 1988 (Cheung 1992). These companies also formulated sophisticated employment practices including suggestion boxes, attitude surveys, and joint consultative committees to foster labour–management relations (England 1989; Chan and Snape 1996). In the last ten years, after the opening of the market in bus and telecommunications services, these companies have had to downsize to compete with newcomers. Labourmanagement relations deteriorated and employee representatives were not consulted even on major decisions such as redundancies (Chiu and Levin 1996).

On the whole, therefore, most employers are reluctant to establish regular dialogue with union representatives. About 5 per cent of all employees were covered by collective agreements (Yeung 1988) but this figure has decreased with the further relocation of manufacturing plants to elsewhere and recent economic restructuring. Some employers' associations had developed various forms of industrial collective agreements with respective unions in cotton textiles and other traditional industries including furniture making, printing and rattan-wares (England 1989). With the decline of manufacturing, many of them have been insignificant. Only a few large corporations including airlines, bus operators, and telephone companies as well as organizations in public service, recognize unions and adopt collective bargaining. A recent survey revealed only one-tenth of the sample companies conducted meetings with union representatives (Ng and Chan 2000). Also, successive surveys between 1996 and 2004 showed only 2–3 per cent of employers would negotiate with unions on pay determination.[12]

In 2005, 21 employers' associations were registered as 'trade unions' based upon a specific industry under the *Trade Unions Ordinance* (Registry of Trade Unions 2005). For example, the Employers' Federation of Hong Kong claims to be the only employers' organization in Hong Kong that 'focuses on representing employers'' interests on employment matters such as labour legislation and human resource management.[13] It provides guidelines to members on how to handle labour disputes and determine pay adjustments. There are also non-union type employers' associations, mainly from diverse trades, registered officially as either societies or limited companies. They are influential in lobbying the government on public policies affecting the business environment, providing support to members on business development and on employment matters. Typical examples are the Hong Kong General Chamber of Commerce, the Federation of Hong Kong Industries, and the Chinese Manufacturers' Association. Five key employers' associations send their representatives to sit on the statutory Labour Advisory Board.

In the 1980s, unions in Hong Kong continued to grow in number as new unions were formed, mainly in the service sector, especially in the civil service. Such a proliferation of small-sized unions has continued in the past two decades, increasing both the number of unions and the number of small unions as a percentage of the total. In 1986, only about 16 per cent of all unions had 50 members or fewer. Since then the percentage of small unions has increased, reaching 27 per cent in 2005. Such small unions represent an insignificant share of total union membership, and are a result of a changing industrial structure characterized by the relocation of manufacturing plants to mainland China leaving many small firms providing services. The consistent government policy of allowing small unions to form, requiring only a minimum membership of seven, has facilitated the fragmentation of unions in Hong Kong.

Unionization in wholesale, retail and import/export trades, restaurants and hotels has been weak for the past two decades because in these business sectors, firms such as hotels and restaurants have high employee turnover and employees find it difficult to form collective organizations. Recently, unions were formed by employees working in large supermarkets. Union density is still high in the transport industry and in energy companies because they are public utilities with a less competitive market. Employees of these sectors have a long history of unionization and their unions are active in organizing industrial actions for wage bargaining.

Unionization in the community service sector has been high in Hong Kong since the 1980s and represents 'white-collar unionism' involving professionals and quasi-professionals in the social and public sectors (Levin and Jao 1988). These professional employees know how to organize, and they bargain over issues including pay and promotion opportunities. Their union participation rates are very high, about 80 per cent for teachers and 50 per cent for nurses. They have become the spearhead of the union movement in Hong Kong (England 1989; Levin and Chiu 1993). However, employees in the professions (and their unions), due to the nature of their employment, education and occupations, do little to support the general labour movement in Hong Kong (Chan and Snape 1996).

To cope with the rapid changes in Hong Kong's economy and industrial structure, some unions have merged with one another, enlarging their scope to include the new areas of employment growth in the same or related industries. Successful cases of amalgamation of unions are not frequent because amalgamation takes a long time and usually they belong to the same union centre. For instance, FTU-affiliated unions in the garment trade, printing, transportation and civil service have undergone such restructuring (England 1989). Another successful example is CTU's Hong Kong Buildings Management and Security Workers General Union.[14]

In recruiting members, the FTU has adopted an all-inclusive approach, including the provision of retraining opportunities for redundant workers, providing retail discounts and other direct services, and also handling labour disputes and protecting worker interests. The growth in the number of affiliates and their membership size indicate that the FTU has been successful and has moved beyond its blue-collar origins to recruit white-collar employees (Snape and Chan 1997). The FTU, with its wide geographic coverage, a total of 18 district offices, provides comprehensive social and cultural services in addition to labour services.

Having strong relationships with local communities, the FTU is expected to develop further its community-oriented role in Hong Kong (Ng and Ip 2001). As the FTU has been particularly active in providing services, it has unavoidably recruited members who want to take advantage of the benefits of FTU membership, but who are not necessarily committed to the union's ideology. Members of this kind may be inactive in participating in militant action for collective rights. That their membership is accepted however reflects one of the FTU's guiding principles: that the organization act in a 'fair' and 'reasonable' manner in handling labour disputes (Snape and Chan 1997). Unfortunately such a strategy of 'industrial pacifism' may weaken the FTU's effectiveness in workplace representation.

The CTU aims to build an autonomous union centre, which is independent of any influence from political parties or the government, to forcefully represent labour interests with an effective organization in order to safeguard workers' rights. CTU leaders have formulated a three-fold strategy. Firstly they aim to build grass-root support by effectively representing workers' rights. The second strategy is to develop the political consciousness of union leaders and members, and thirdly the CTU aims to make a concrete contribution to the democratic development of Hong Kong (Snape and Chan 1997). They maintain steady growth in affiliates and union membership, especially in the community and transport sectors.

Due to the reality of the political situation, the TUC experienced negative growth in membership recently and it stopped issuing its bulletin, *Hong Kong Labour*. Without additional financial support from Taiwan, the TUC continues to face difficulty in recruiting new members as Hong Kong workers will gradually forget this Taiwanese-based organization. Thus, its future role as a labour advocate in Hong Kong appears very limited.

Owing to the political rivalries among the FTU, the CTU and the TUC, mostly arising from issues related to mainland China and the pace of democratization of Hong Kong, the three union centres seldom cooperate or work together on labour issues. An example of their strained relationship was the repeal of the Employee's Rights to Representation, Consultation and Collective Bargaining Ordinance in 1997. The bill, being proposed by the CTU's Lee Cheuk-yan, gave employees the right to joint consultation and to collective bargaining if they expressed support for a union. It passed in the Legislative Council in June 1997 but the FTU's legislators, with other legislators, agreed that the government should repeal the law, which it did in October 1997.

The slow progress in developing a minimum wage is another example of the result of poor cooperation. The FTU and the CTU have organized separate activities to demand the enactment of minimum wage legislation and standard working hours.[15] These divisions are a reflection of politically-divided unionism that reduces union strength in bargaining with management.

To summarize, Hong Kong employers are free not to recognize unions or establish formal bargaining with unions under the law and thus unions cannot develop strong occupation-based unionism. To survive and grow, unions need to increase their visibility in social and political issues, such as participating in the pro-democracy movement and strengthening the political link with the Chinese government. Though Hong Kong unions have relatively strong political power, their influence on labour and workplace matters is very weak because major union centres do not work together owing to political rivalry. Thus the development of Hong Kong unions is predominately shaped by political rather than industrial or economic factors.

Conclusion

In general, Hong Kong unions have experienced steady growth in membership for the past two decades. Unions in the community and public sector have remained strong and independent, free from political intervention after Hong Kong's transfer of sovereignty to China. Both the ex-Hong Kong government and the SAR government tried to behave as a role-model employer to encourage communication and consultation with public sector employees and their unions. Unions in the private sector, however, continue to be organizationally fragmented and functionally weak when attempting to represent workers and influence their employment conditions. They usually face difficulties in the unionization of the workplace as most employers in the business sector are hostile to unions in Hong Kong.

Though many union leaders have stated that their unions will emphasize activities that relate to employment conditions and the workplace, providing a service rather than participating in politics (Snape and Chan 1999), their success in establishing themselves as independent organizations on whom workers can depend for advocacy has been limited. Without any statutory requirement, most employers are reluctant to recognize unions formally or informally, especially in the private sector (Chiu and Levin 2000). They may either ignore the presence of union members in their enterprise or adopt the employer-sponsored joint consultation approach to exclude unions as employee representation (Chiu and Levin 1996; Snape and Chan 1999).

China's resumption of sovereignty has become one of the key factors shaping the future of Hong Kong's trade unionism. The FTU has become more popular than before as it is the 'politically correct' union centre and more acceptable to the middle class as those employees with views left of centre are dismissed as 'left-wing trouble makers'. This is why the FTU's union membership has increased at a faster rate than the territory's aggregate increment. The federation has a mission to maintain a good balance between its 'representative' role for workers and its 'political' role in maintaining the stability of HKSAR, similar to the state union in China. Though the FTU's pro-government stance might be a liability (Levin 1998), it has successfully repositioned its image to appeal not only to the grass-roots, but also to the middle class, the majority of Hong Kong people, and thus it has become the most popular political organization in Hong Kong.[16] It will continue to exert its political influence, especially adopting a collaborative approach with the patriotic groups in future elections.

The pro-Taiwan TUC has become inactive, especially after the Nationalist Party was defeated twice in Taiwan's presidency elections in the 2000s. Resources are limited and recruitment of union members is ineffective because Taiwan faces an uncertain situation in its political relations with Hong Kong and the Chinese mainland. With the decline of affiliated unions and membership, the TUC will be further marginalized in its role to represent Hong Kong labour.

The CTU, with its pro-democracy stance and militant profile on labour matters, has attracted many unions and members of similar ideologies. It stresses worker representation and protection, but it cannot obtain much support from employers owing to its controversial political image and industrial relations strategy (Snape and Chan 1997). Its future direction is expected to focus on political issues and to cooperate with pro-democracy parties.

With the increasing wealth gap in Hong Kong, unskilled workers need unions to represent them to fight for their interests, but union centres cannot form a united alliance to help them. Such an ideological division in political perspective and union ideology means that Hong Kong's labour movement fits the 'contestatory' type of unionism (Chiu and Levin 2000).

Many labour activists wish for a unified labour organization in Hong Kong to better represent workers. This is, however, unlikely to happen in the near future. Rival union centres should critically review their current policies and consider cooperation with other groups. There is room for union leaders to resolve their differences under changes in local contexts after Hong Kong's return to China. Perhaps, with a more stable political environment, the FTU should re-consider adjusting its strategy of 'industrial pacifism' and actively represent workers at the workplace. It may need to re-adjust to work with pro-democracy groups on common labour issues. The CTU, on the other hand, should not stress democratization and militant activities, but make efforts to give constructive proposals on various labour policies and cooperate with other unions. To conclude, both the FTU and the CTU may need to consider toning down their role as workers' political agents and focus more on representing workers on job-based regulation, otherwise they might lose worker support in the long-run.

Notes

1 Article 5, The Basic Law of Hong Kong Special Administrative Region of the People, Republic of China, 1991.
2 See *Government Structure, Hong Kong: The Facts*, Hong Kong: Information Services Department of the Hong Kong SAR Government, January 2006.
3 See the World Economic Forum *Report for 2006–07* released in September 2006.
4 See tables of Employed Persons by Industry in *Hong Kong Annual Digest of Statistics*, various years (published by the Census and Statistics Department).
5 See tables of Annual Growth rates of GDP Estimates in *Hong Kong Annual Digest of Statistics*, various years.
6 See tables of Employed Persons by Job Hierarchy in *Hong Kong Annual Digest of Statistics*, various years.
7 Commerce, Industry and Technology Bureau, HKSAR Government 'CEPA Impact on the Hong Kong Economy'. Online. Available HTTP <http://www.legco.gov.hk/yr04-05/english/panels/ci/papers/ci0419cb1-1259-3e.pdf> (accessed on 20 August 2006).
8 See tables of unemployment rates in *Hong Kong Annual Digest of Statistics*, various years.
9 See for examples *South China Morning Post* (*SCMP*) 9 June 2003; *Ming Pao* 20 June 2006.
10 Author's analysis on the results of Legislative Council elections of 1998, 2000, and 2004. In both 1998 and 2000 elections, out of 60 seats, union-endorsed candidates won six seats via geographic constituencies and five seats via functional constituencies (including three from Labour, one from Education, and one from Health Services

constituencies); in the 2004 election, candidates with union backgrounds won five seats via geographic and five seats via functional constituencies.
11 See *Hong Kong Annual Digest of Statistics, 2005 edition*.
12 See Hong Kong Institute of Human Resource Management, *Human Resource Management Strategies and Practices in Hong Kong – Research Reports* (1996, 2001, 2004).
13 See the promotion leaflet *Employers' Federation of Hong Kong Membership Application Form*, Hong Kong: Employers' Federation of Hong Kong, September 1996.
14 Author's fieldwork and analysis of *Statistical Reports of Registry of Trade Unions* (1996–2000).
15 See *SCMP* 9 September 2006; *Ming Pao* 10 September 2006.
16 See *SCMP* 25 August 2006. The FTU continued to rank as top political group in a survey by the University of Hong Kong's public opinion programme.

Bibliography

Census and Statistics Department (1992) *1991 Population Census Main Report*, Hong Kong: Census and Statistics Department.

Census and Statistics Department (1996–2005) *Hong Kong Annual Digest of Statistics*: various editions, Hong Kong: Census and Statistics Department.

Census and Statistics Department (2006) *Hong Kong in Figures 2006 Edition*, Hong Kong: Census and Statistics Department.

Census and Statistics Department (2007) *Population Census 2006 Main Report – Volume I*, Hong Kong: Census and Statistics Department.

Chai, B. K. (1993) 'The politicization of unions in Hong Kong', in D. H. McMillen and M. E. DeGolyer (eds) *One Culture, Many Systems: Politics in the Reunification of China*, Hong Kong: Chinese University Press.

Chan, A. W. and Snape, E. (1996) 'No change for fifty years? The development of trade unionism in Hong Kong during the transitional period', *International Journal of Employment Studies*, 4(2): 55–75.

Chan, A. W. and Snape, E. (2000) 'Union weakness in Hong Kong: workplace industrial relations and the federation of trade unions', *Economic and Industrial Democracy*, 21(2): 117–46.

Chan, M. H. Y., Ng, S. H. and Ho, E. Y. Y. (2000) 'Labour and employment', in S. H. Ng and D. Lethbridge (eds) *The Business Environment in Hong Kong*, New York: Oxford University Press.

Cheung P. C. (1992) 'Collective bargaining with the Cable & Wireless (HK) Limited', in E. K. Y. Chen, R. Lansbury, S. Ng and S. Stewart (eds) *Labour–Management Relations in the Asia-Pacific Region*, Hong Kong: University of Hong Kong.

Chiu, S. and Levin, D. A. (1996) 'Prosperity without industrial democracy? Developments in industrial relations in Hong Kong since 1968', *Industrial Relations Journal*, 27(1): 24–37.

Chiu, S. and Levin, D. A. (1999) 'The organization of industrial relations in Hong Kong: economic, political and sociological perspectives', *Organization Studies*, 20(2): 293–321.

Chiu, S. and Levin, D. A. (2000) 'Contestatory unionism: trade unions in the private sector', in S. Chiu and T. L. Lui (eds) *The Dynamics of Social Movement in Hong Kong*, Hong Kong: Hong Kong University Press.

Commissioner for Labour (1990–2002) *Report of the Commissioner for Labour*, Hong Kong: Labour Department.

England, J. (1989) *Industrial Relations and Law in Hong Kong*, 2nd edition, Oxford: Oxford University Press.

England, J. and Rear, J. (1981) *Industrial Relations and Law in Hong Kong*, Hong Kong: Oxford University Press.

FTU (Hong Kong Federation of Trade Unions) (2003) *The FTU's Classic Photo Album* [in Chinese], Hong Kong: Hong Kong Federation of Trade Unions.

Jao, Y. C., Levin, D. A., Ng, S. K. and Sinn, E. (eds) (1988) *Labour Movement in a Changing Society: The Experience of Hong Kong*, Hong Kong: Centre of Asian Studies, University of Hong Kong.

Labour Department (2006) *Labour Department Annual Report 2005*, Hong Kong: Labour Department.

Levin, D. A. (1998) 'A cloudy future for Hong Kong trade unions after handover', *Access China*, 28: 38–41.

Levin, D. A. and Chiu, S. (1993) 'Dependent capitalism, a colonial state, and marginal unions: the case of Hong Kong', in S. Frenkel (ed.) *Organized Labor in the Asia-Pacific Region: A Comparative Study of Trade Unionism in Nine Countries*, New York: ILR Press.

Levin, D. A. and Chiu, S. (1996) 'Prosperity without industrial democracy? Developments in industrial relations in Hong Kong since 1968', *Industrial Relations Journal*, 27(1): 24–37.

Levin, D. A. and Jao, Y. C. (1988) 'Introduction', in Y. C. Jao, D. A. Levin, S. K. Ng and E, Sinn (eds) *Labour Movement in a Changing Society: The Experience of Hong Kong*, Hong Kong: Centre of Asian Studies, University of Hong Kong.

Ng, S. H. (1997) 'Revision to China: implications for labour in Hong Kong', *International Journal of Human Resource Management*, 8(5): 660–76.

Ng, S. H. and Chan, A. W. (2000) *A Report on the Survey 'Communication and Human Resources: Hong Kong Style'*, Hong Kong: Labour Department, HKSAR Government and Chinese Management Centre, University of Hong Kong.

Ng, S. H. and Ip, O. (2001) *Phenomenon of Union Exhaustion in Hong Kong: is There a 'Third Way' for Trade Unionism?* Hong Kong: Chinese Management Centre, University of Hong Kong.

Ng, S. H. and Rowley, C. (2000) 'Globalization and Hong Kong's labour market: the deregulation paradox', *Asia Pacific Business Review*, 6 (3/4): 174–92.

Registrar of Trade Unions (1990–1994) *Annual Departmental Reports*, Hong Kong: Government Printer.

Registry of Trade Unions, Labour Department (1995–2005) *Annual Statistical Reports*, Hong Kong: Labour Department.

Snape, E. and Chan, A. W. (1997) 'Whither Hong Kong's union: autonomous trade unionism or classic dualism?', *British Journal of Industrial Relations*, 35(1): 39–63.

Snape, E. and Chan, A. W. (1999) 'Trade unions: in search of a role', in P. Fosh, A. W. Chan, W. Chow, E. Snape and R. Westwood (eds) *Hong Kong Management and Labour*, London and New York: Routledge.

Turner, H. A., Fosh, P. and Ng, S. (1991) *Between Two Societies: Hong Kong Labour in Transition*, Hong Kong: Centre of Asian Studies, University of Hong Kong.

Wong, T. Y. C. (1994) 'Hong Kong's manufacturing industries: transformation and prospect', in B. K. P. Leung and T. Y. C. Wong (eds) *25 Years of Social and Economic Development in Hong Kong*, Hong Kong: University of Hong Kong.

Yeung, C. (1988) 'Joint consultation, collective bargaining and trade union recognition: status and prospect', in Y. C. Jao, D. A. Levin, S. K. Ng and E, Sinn (eds) *Labour Movement in a Changing Society: The Experience of Hong Kong*, Hong Kong: Centre of Asian Studies, University of Hong Kong.

7   Trade unions in Singapore

Corporatist paternalism

Chris Leggett

Introduction

Singapore has been described as an 'administrative state' (Chan 1975), and its governance as 'the management of compliance' (Wilkinson and Leggett 1985). It is a state whose People's Action Party (PAP) leaders have established a mode of institutional social control – labelled 'bureaucratic authoritarian corporatism' by Deyo (1981) – and proclaimed 'pragmatism' as their party's ideology. Since the 1980s there has been a softening of the exercise of social control. For example, Singapore workers who were *chided* in the early 1980s for 'job hopping' (*Straits Times* 14 September 1981), in the late 1990s were *urged* to become mobile (Ministry of Manpower 1999).

Almost 50 years ago the PAP was elected to government in Singapore and immediately set about regulating industrial relations to meet the requirements for industrialization, an example of its pragmatic approach to governance in the state, including the management of industrial relations. Since then, there have been three transformations – morphological changes in which residual elements of the previous state remain discernible in the new – of Singapore's industrial relations. The first transformation, from 1960 to 1967 was from regulation by colonial administrators (Kerr *et al.* 1960) to the regulation of a plurality of industrial relations parties by the post-colonial PAP government. The second transformation, from 1968 to 1978, was from regulated pluralism to corporatist industrial relations, in which the trade union movement became an adjunct to the government's imperatives for Singapore's economy. The third transformation, from 1979 to 1986, saw a shift to paternalism by the government and the incorporated institutions of industrial relations. Since 1986, there has been a progression (rather than a transformation) from 'industrial relations' towards 'manpower planning' (Leggett 2007). Following Hyman's typology (Gospel, Chapter 2 this volume), with the second transformation, Singapore's trade unions moved away from their confrontational class direction under the colonial regime towards a collaborative social partnership under PAP hegemony, but with market goals stressed as national imperatives.

Each period of morphological change in Singapore's industrial relations had its defining event or events. They were the Industrial Relations Act in 1960, the

Employment Act and the Industrial Relations (Amendment) Act in 1968 and the NTUC's 'Modernisation' seminar in 1969, wage reform from 1979 and the Trade Unions (Amendment) Act of 1982. The changes represent transitional peaks rising above intervening incremental changes and are sufficiently distinguishable from each other to justify their being separate transformations. None of these transformations has involved a wholesale reversion of a previous one, so there has been a cumulative as well as a transformational effect on Singapore's industrial relations.

Singapore's trade unions today are different from those formed and reformed under the colonial authorities in the 1950s, to an extent that raises questions about the essence of trade unionism and requires caution against committing the nominalist fallacy of assuming that institutions with the same name perform the same functions in different countries (Gospel, Chapter 2 this volume). While mindful of the nominalist trap, the author of this chapter adopts an analytical approach developed by Kochan *et al.* (1986) and locates the strategic choices made and initiatives taken to bring about the transformations of Singapore's industrial relations (and thereby its trade unionism) in their historical, political and economic contexts.

Context and history

Political and economic context

Singapore is a tiny (682.7 km^2) island city state with a deep natural harbour positioned at the southern end of the Strait of Malacca through which as much as a quarter of the world's shipping travels. Its immediate neighbours are Malaysia and Indonesia. Ceded to the British by the resident sultan in 1824, its potential had been recognized in 1819 by Sir Stamford Raffles of the British East India Company. From 1826 to 1867, with Penang and Malacca, it formed part of the Straits Settlements governed from India. From1867 to 1941, while it progressed from a coaling station for steam ships to an *entrepot*, it was a British crown colony, a status resumed after the Japanese occupation of 1941 to 1945 was ended.

Amidst rivalry between 'leftists' backed by the Communist Party of Malaya (CPM) and aspirants to a non-communist polity ('moderates'), Singapore achieved a measure of self-government in 1955, and full self-government in 1959 when the PAP, at the time a coalition of leftists and moderates led by Lee Kuan Yew, was elected into office. An eventual schism in the PAP was followed by a rout of the leftists, who had opposed Singapore's joining the Federation of Malaysia in 1963. In the event, differences with Malaysian leaders obliged Singapore to leave the Federation in 1965 and become an independent republic.

The PAP has been returned to office at every general election since 1959 and has overseen the industrialization and economic development of Singapore. The economic crises presented by the separation from Malaysia and the closure of the British military bases in Singapore in the late 1960s, the world oil price hikes of the 1970s and the Asian financial problems of late 1997 each strengthened the PAP's political resolve and reinforced its avowed pragmatism.

Under colonial rule Singapore's population growth was mostly by the immigration of indentured labourers from southern China and, to a lesser extent, from southern India. Ethnic Malays and Chinese from older settlements in the Malay peninsula and archipelago also contributed to population growth. By 2000, Singapore's population had reached 4,017,700 of which 13.9 per cent were Malays, 76.8 per cent Chinese, 7.7 per cent Indians and 1.4 per cent other races (Ministry of Information and the Arts 2001: 49–52). The ethnic, gender, age, intellectual and skills composition of the population have informed public policy in Singapore since 1959. It has been estimated that more than 10 per cent of the labour force since the 1980s has comprised foreign 'guest workers', mostly from southern India, the Philippines and Indonesia. Construction projects in the 1980s brought guest workers from Thailand and Korea, and Malaysians have remained a traditional but declining source of labour.

Singapore has a parliamentary system of government with a separation of powers. Of the five presidents since independence, two had been prominent in the labour movement as National Trades Union Congress (NTUC) secretaries-general; otherwise the presidency is a mainly ceremonial position, but with some powers over the expenditure of the country's reserves. Lee Kuan Yew remained as prime minister until 1990, when he was succeeded by Goh Chok Tong. Since 2004, Lee Hsien Loong, Lee Kwan Yew's elder son, has been prime minister. Lee Kuan Yew remains in the cabinet as a minister mentor and Goh Chok Tong as senior minister. The secretary-general of the NTUC is a member of the cabinet as a minister in the prime minister's office.

Singapore's parliament is elected every five years and the PAP has secured a majority at all except the first election. It comprises mostly elected members from single-member constituencies, but there are some nominated and non-constituency members, and group representation constituencies allow parties to field teams of three to six candidates, one of whom must be from a minority race. The legal system follows the English system except that in 1994 the right of appeal to the Judicial Committee of the Privy Council in London was abolished and trial by jury, limited in 1960, was abolished in 1969. The death penalty and corporal punishment have been retained and the Internal Security Act allows for renewable 'preventive detention' (Woodiwiss 1998: 234).

In 1965, Singapore's per capita gross national product (GNP) was $1,618; in 2004 its gross national income (GNI) was $41,513 (Department of Statistics 2002: 4; Ministry of Trade and Industry 2005: 1). Singapore is an example of rapid industrialization based on receptiveness to multi-national corporate investment and on the building of an infrastructure that has been conducive to the development of a productive workforce (Rodan 1997: 153–6). Two years national service for males serves as discipline training for the labour market and thereby constitutes an integral part of Singapore's human resource management (HRM). Table 7.1 provides a summary of Singapore's economic and political contexts.

Table 7.1 Contextual factors – Singapore

General statistics	
Population (2005)[1]	3.5 million
Area (square kilometres)[2]	682.7
Employment by sector (%) (2003)[3]	
Industry	30.6
Services	68.7
Others	0.7
Urban population (% of total population)	100
GDP per capita (2006)[1]	$29,474 (US)
Income inequality (High, Medium or Low)	Medium
Gini coefficient (2006)[4]	5.2
Real GDP growth (%)[1]	
1986–1995	8.7
1995–2005	5.5
Unemployment (%)	
1986–1995[5]	2.8
1995–20053	2.7
Summary description	
Product market regulation	Medium
Political context (liberal/pluralistic, state unitarist)	State unitarist
Political stability (high, medium or low)	High

Sources
1 Singapore Department of Statistics (http://www.singstat.gov.sg), accessed 30 May 2007.
2 Ministry of Information and the Arts (2001) *Singapore 2001*, Singapore: Ministry of Information and the Arts.
3 Ministry of Manpower (http://www.mom.gov.sg), accessed 30 May 2007.
4 Singapore Angle (http://www.singaporeangle.com), accessed 31 May 2007.
5 Ministry of Labour (annual) *Annual Report*, Singapore: Singapore National Printers.

Between 1960 and 1980, Singapore's GDP growth annually averaged more than 9 per cent (Pang 1982: 10). By the 1970s, unemployment was low and a tight labour market had increased the city-state's dependence on foreign labour. In 1986, a surprise recession caused the economy to shrink, but by 1988 GDP growth was back to positive figures, lasting until 1998 when the Asian economic crisis of 1997 had a temporary negative effect. In recent years GDP growth has varied between 3.1 per cent and 8.8 per cent. The contribution to GDP of manufacturing, construction and utilities has ranged between 26.7 per cent in 1965 and 33.8 per cent in 2004, of services between 70.3 per cent in 1965 and 66.7 per cent in 2001, but never less than 60 per cent (Department of Statistics 2002: 3–4; Ministry of Trade and Industry 2005: 3). Although beset by the prospect of high unemployment in the 1960s, Singapore's unemployment had fallen to 3.4 per cent in 1979 (Department of Statistics 1980: 43). Since 1979, with the exception of 5.7 per cent in 1986, unemployment has not exceeded 5 per cent in any one year, and annually averaged 2.8 per cent between 1986 and 2004 (Ministry of Labour 1994: 14; Ministry of Manpower 2004a: Table 82).

Occupying such a small physical area and offering few natural resources, Singapore has had to rely on human resources, including labour market participation and productivity for its economic growth; and the government has consistently emphasized human resources management as part of its governing strategy. The population of 1,634,000 in 1960 had increased to 4,185,200 in 2003 (Department of Statistics 2004), having been subject at different times over the previous 40 years to procreation incentives and disincentives, and selective immigration. The employed workforce increased from an estimated 490,000 in 1960, when unemployment was 13.5 per cent (Pang 1982: 10), to 2,067,000 in 2004, when unemployment was 3.7 per cent (Ministry of Trade and Industry 2005: 1). As well as developing its human resources, Singapore built on its advantages as an entrepot and established a reputation for efficient administration and stable banking to become an important financial centre. Since the late 1990s, the labour market has become less regulated as the government has encouraged flexibility in keeping with the demands of globalization and increased competition from newer industrializing countries (Ministry of Manpower 2004a: 1).

Trade union history and development

Chinese *hong* (guilds) had been operating in Singapore for more than a century before the Associations Ordinance 1895 for the Straits Settlements was passed. Divided between associations of employers, *Tong Ka*, and of workers, *Sai Ka*, they settled disputes, functioned as friendly-societies and determined terms and conditions of employment for traditional trades and crafts, but not for unskilled industrial labour (Gamba 1962: 2–3). After disassociating themselves from the criminal Chinese secret societies some guilds registered under the colonial administration's Societies Ordinances. Although an employees' guild was registered as early as 1890 (Gamba 1962: 3–6), it was not until 1937 that a significant number were registered (then as mutual aid societies) only to be dissolved during the Japanese occupation, during which Communist Party of Malaya (CPM) cadres and some trade unionists operated underground.

Insistence by the Colonial Office in London and the passing of the Colonial Development and Welfare Act 1940 by the United Kingdom parliament led to the enactment of trade union ordinances in Britain's territories, including Singapore and Malaya in 1940 (Roberts 1964: 3–166). Although these ordinances emulated United Kingdom legislation and embodied immunity from prosecution for a trade union whose 'objects' were 'in restraint of trade', they required union registration, forbade political levies and restricted affiliation. The drafting of the 'objects' of trade unions, such as the 'object' of 'the promotion or organization or financing of strikes', explicitly legitimized confrontation. The CPM had centred its attention on Singapore rather than Malaya because of the greater concentration of trade unions there (Media Masters 2003: 57), and after World War II put its efforts into the organization of labour and the infiltration of unions as front organizations for its political objectives (Media Masters 2003: 121). The communists and other leftists in Singapore operated through large general associations, such as the General Labour Union (GLU), which in 1946 formed a Pan-Malayan Federation of Trade Unions that included the Singapore Federation of Trade Unions (SFTU). Among the leftists detained by the British authorities was C. V. Devan Nair, who later abandoned his leftist credentials to mobilize the Singapore labour movement for the PAP government's second transformation of Singapore's industrial relations – from colonial authority to regulated pluralism.

By 1947, assisted by the British trade union advisor, some independent unions had been registered, but by this time the CPM's political strategy of promoting strikes through the SFTU was becoming less and less effective (Turnbull 1989: 228–9). A non-communist Singapore Trades Union Congress (STUC) was established in 1951, but gained little support. Between 1955 and 1959, the two Labour Front governments that preceded the PAP government were dogged by industrial unrest, in spite of a Criminal Law (Temporary Provisions) Ordinance 1955 that made industrial action unlawful in some essential services and required a statutory period of notice in others (Ordinance 26 of 1955).

The inclusion of leftists enabled the PAP to win the support of vernacular-speaking union leaders and success in the 1959 election for the first full self-government (Pang 1981: 484). The partial self-government from 1955 had unsuccessfully tried to manage political and industrial unrest while the incoming PAP government immediately set about transforming industrial relations in line with its programme of rapid industrialization. In 1960, the Industrial Relations Ordinance standardized collective bargaining, centralized conciliation in the Ministry of Labour and established judicial Industrial Arbitration Courts (IACs). Amendments to the Trade Disputes Ordinance in 1960 (Ordinance 19) extended illegality to sympathy strikes, strikes aimed at pressuring the government and those inconveniencing the public. Subsequent amendments to the Trade Unions Ordinance (Ordinance 22) in the 1960s extended the regulation of trade unions, while a split in the PAP, ostensibly over whether or not to form part of the Malaysian Federation, was mirrored in the labour movement. The NTUC was established as a protégé of the PAP purged of its leftists, and it soon eclipsed the leftist's Singapore Association of Trade Unions (National Trades Union Congress 1970: 225–8).

The demise of the leftists de-politicized the labour movement but did not prevent confrontational stances, although in effect confrontational trade unionism ended in 1966 after an unofficial strike by the Public Daily Rated Cleansing Workers' Union (PDRCWU), an affiliate of the Public Daily Rated Employees' Unions Federation (PDREUF), was made unlawful by virtue of the government having referred the dispute to the IAC. The PDREUF and the PDRCWU were deregistered. Singapore's prime minister at the time, Lee Kuan Yew, has described this confrontation with his government as a turning point in Singapore's industrial history (Lee 2000: 106–7).

Between the end of the Japanese occupation in1946 and Singapore's exiting the Malaysian Federation in 1965, trade union membership increased from 18,673 to

157,050, peaking at 189,032 in 1962 with a density increasing to an estimated 56 per cent by 1967 (National Trades Union Congress 1970: 231). In 1964, there were 55 NTUC affiliates, and in 1965, 57, a jump from 65 to 73 per cent of organized workers. Of the affiliates, the Amalgamated Union of Public Employees (AUPE) in 1963 recorded 21,000 members and the Singapore Manual and Mercantile Workers' Union (SMMWU) 16,000. Most trade unions, however, organized less than 1,000 members and about 15 'house' unions each less than 100.

In 1965, following differences between the PAP leaders and the political elite in Malaya, Singapore left the Federation of Malaysia. This event and the impending closure of the British military base, a major employer of Singapore labour, prompted the government to legislate to ensure that Singapore's industrial relations would not be a deterrent to multi-national corporate investment. The Employment Act 1968 consolidated and extended the existing substantive rules to complement the mainly procedural rules set out in the Industrial Relations Ordinance 1960 and, together with the Industrial Relations (Amendment) Act 1968, severely curtailed the scope and substance of collective bargaining, particularly in officially designated 'pioneer' industries. The 1968 legislation was the prelude to the transformation of Singapore's industrial relations from regulated pluralism to a corporatist mode of regulation.

The NTUC had little choice but to define a new direction for its affiliates (National Trades Union Congress 1970), i.e. towards the provision of consumer cooperatives and educational services, and representation on a range of public corporations and associated bodies. From then for almost a decade the NTUC leaders reiterated the need for wages to trail productivity growth. To this end, in 1972, the government established a tripartite National Wages Council (NWC). Such was the NWC's authority – derived from its tripartite representation – that its annual recommendations were adopted by most of the private as well as the public sector.

The reduction in industrial action in Singapore during the second transformation of industrial relations was due to the Ministry of Labour's 'preventive mediation', to it being unlawful when the IAC had cognizance of a trade dispute, and to the Industrial Affairs Council of the NTUC reviewing affiliates' grievances with the aim of finding a peaceful resolution (National Trades Union Congress 1976: 33). In spite of these measures, a non-NTUC house union called a strike at Metal Box in 1977. By making unlawful demands, i.e. that the personnel manager be dismissed, the strikers forfeited rights to mediation and the union was dissolved. This was the last strike for nearly nine years and it became reasonable to claim that 'a legal strike in Singapore is virtually impossible without the tacit consent of the government' (Wilkinson and Leggett 1985: 12).

The limitations on the scope of collective bargaining contained in the 1968 legislation started a decline in trade union membership. Growth had been by recruitment to 'omnibus' unions, general unions for workers in the 'pioneer industries' upon which rapid industrialization was based. The Pioneer Industries Employees' Union (PIEU) had been registered in 1963 but the Singapore Industrial Labour Organisation (SILO) was only registered in 1970. Together with the

AUPE they came to organize almost 50 per cent of NTUC membership (Ministry of Labour 1977).

The third transformation of Singapore's industrial relations was labelled by the NTUC *Progress into the 80's* (National Trades Union Congress 1980). Half of Singapore's GDP growth in the 1970s was due to labour force expansion, and the ratio of capital and efficiency to labour inputs had fallen, so the government initiated a transition of Singapore's economy from a labour-intensive, low technology, low value-added one to a more capital-intensive, high technology, high value-added one (Lim 1979; Lim, C. Y. 1980; Goh, C. T. 1980; Goh, K. S. 1980; Howe 1980; Lee 1980; Wong 1983: 264–5).

In this endeavour four strategic initiatives directly affecting trade unions were taken. In 1978, the NTUC amended its constitution to allow non-elected cadre delegates to participate in policy-making (National Trades Union Congress 1985b: 30) and a 'wage correction' policy was implemented through the NWC (Lim 1979; Lim 1980). Meanwhile the NTUC restructured its 'omnibus' unions into 'industry-wide' ones (Ong 1980) and then some of these, and others, into 'house' (enterprise) unions (*Straits Times* 27 July 1984; Leggett 1987, 1988). Trade union restructuring broke up the power bases of some prominent 'old guard' organizers and was partly a response by a government committed to the election to office in the NTUC of a 'new guard' of technocrats. The rationale for 'house' unions was that they contributed to increasing productivity by linking workers more closely with the enterprises by which they were employed. Finally, the Trade Unions Act was amended (Act 28 of 1982) to redefine the 'purposes' of trade unions to include the achievement of productivity.

Although membership densities in the new house unions tended to be higher than those in the former branches from which they had been formed, it was not sufficient to offset an overall decline that had begun again in 1979. By 1985, 70 of the 85 registered unions were NTUC affiliates but organized less than 186,000 workers (National Trades Union Congress 1985a: 70).

From 1987 to 1997, Singapore's industrial relations were not so much transformed as prepared for increasing globalization. Prominent issues were the need for a more flexible wage system, the membership, leadership and representation of Singapore's trade unions, and the quality of the industrial relations institutions. After 1997, with weakened economic prospects, the Singapore government strategically progressed employment relations towards 'manpower planning' and away from 'industrial relations'. The Ministry of Labour was renamed the Ministry of Manpower (MoM) with a mission '[t]o develop a globally competitive workforce and foster a highly favourable workplace to achieve sustainable economic growth for the well-being of Singaporeans' (Ministry of Manpower 2001: 2).

For its part, the NTUC had opened the Singapore Institute of Labour Studies (SILS) to upgrade its officials' qualifications and had endeavoured to increase the representation of women in its senior echelons (Tan 1995: 78–9). However, membership remained a problem as it failed to keep pace with employment growth, in spite of the introduction of 'general branch' unions to recruit in non-unionized firms and of lifelong and portable membership.

Union types and structure

Singapore's unions have had a mixed structure (classified by the former Ministry of Labour as 'omnibus', 'industry-wide', 'craft/occupational', and 'house') reflecting colonial politics and the rapidity of industrialization. Until the late 1970s the ascendancy of the NTUC to become an encompassing peak body (Visser 1990; Gospel, Chapter 2 this volume) was more important than structural changes. In 1968, 110 unions, of which nearly 75 per cent were affiliated to the NTUC, had organized 125,518 workers, or 33 per cent of employed persons; in 1969, membership was down to 120,053 or 30 per cent of employed persons. But between 1972 and 1979 trade union membership and the NTUC's portion of that membership increased annually until they reached 249,710 and 95.5 per cent, respectively. The NTUC's association with the NWC, along with the organizing prowess of NTUC officials in the pioneer industries, may have contributed to the reversal of its membership decline. However, union density in 1979 was still only around 25 per cent (Ministry of Labour Annual).

In the 1980s, planned restructuring was integral to industrial relations transformation. In 1986, the two, by then residual, omnibus unions were dissolved and another house union was registered. This was the only type of union registered for a few years after 1986: one in 1987, two in 1988 and three in 1989, all NTUC affiliates (Ministry of Labour Annual). Non-NTUC unions had only represented 5 per cent of unionized employees in 1980 (Ministry of Labour 1980: 10). However, one of them, Singapore Airline Pilots' Association (SIAPA) flouted the prevailing non-confrontational norms by taking unauthorized industrial action, and the officers of some NTUC unions, notably the Singapore Air Transport Union (SATU) resisted, albeit unsuccessfully, the NTUC's insistence that they break up into house unions. By 1998, the NTUC's share of union membership exceeded 99 per cent, and continues to do so.

In the 1990s, the NTUC abandoned the promotion of house unions, its secretary-general reasoning that they had not functioned as well as enterprise unions had in Japan because Singapore companies were too small and could not include executives and other professionals who might have strengthened their leadership (Lee 2000: 113). To overcome the deficiencies of size the NTUC restructured some of its affiliates through amalgamation. By 2003, of the 68 registered trade unions 27 had less than a 1,000 members, 41 had more than 1,000, and 13 had more than 10,000, compared with five with more than 10,000 in 1993 (Ministry of Manpower 2004b: 131). Table 7.2 provides an overall statistical and summary description of Singapore's trade unions.

What do unions do?

It is difficult to assess the role of Singapore's trade unions in collective bargaining because of the constraints placed on the process and substance by the Employment Act and the Industrial Relations (Amendment) Act of 1968. Collective agreements must be in the public interest and are made between a

Table 7.2 Singaporean trade unions

General statistics	
Number of unions,	
1986[1]	83
2005[2]	68
Number of union members	
1986[1]	200,613
2005[2]	450,004
Union density (%)	
1986[1]	17.5
2005[2]	19.9

Summary description	
Union type	
Main	Political
Secondary	Economic/market
(Economic/market, political, other)	
Union structure	
Main	Mixed
Secondary	Mixed
(Occupational, industrial, general, enterprise)	
Unity of peak organization (high, medium or low)	High
State control of unions (high, medium or low)	High
Involvement in collective bargaining (high, medium or low)	Low–medium

Sources
1 Ministry of Labour (1986) *Annual Report 1986*, Singapore: Singapore National Printers.
2 Department of Statistics, http://www.singstat.gov.sg (accessed 31 May 2007).

single employer and a trade union. They are then reviewed and certified by the IAC. It is not lawful for a trade union to raise for collective bargaining issues of hiring, firing, job assignment, promotion and transfer. For workers in pioneer industries and other designated categories, terms and conditions of employment cannot exceed the minima set out in Part IV of the Employment Act. Collective bargaining is also constrained by the NTUC's compliance with NWC recommendations. Thus it is not possible to claim that collective bargaining is the central activity for most of Singapore's trade unions. Table 7.3 illustrates what Singapore's trade unions do.

Of Singapore's 69 trade unions in 2007, 63 were affiliated to the NTUC and organized over 99 per cent of employed persons. Their activities are defined by the transformations that have taken place in Singapore's industrial relations, so that, with a few exceptions, they ceased to be adversarial in the 1970s and the NTUC unions expanded their service and welfare functions, especially through consumer cooperatives and by the establishment of the Singapore Labour Foundation (SLF) in 1977. The transformation of industrial relations begun in 1979 has progressed towards what is now labelled 'manpower planning' and qualified as a 'social

Table 7.3 What do Singaporean unions do?

Activities	
Extent of collective bargaining (high, medium or low)[1]	Low
Level of collective bargaining (high, medium or low)	
National	Medium
Industry	Low
Enterprise	High
Extent of joint consultation (high, medium or low)[1]	Medium
Industrial disputes	
Working days lost per 1,000 employees (2005)[2]	Zero
Relative assessment (high, medium or low)	Low
Degree of state intervention in employment protection (high, medium or low)	Medium

Sources
1 Leggett, C. (2007).
2 Ministry of Manpower, (http://www.mom.gov.sg), accessed 30 May 2007.

partnership' in Singapore. Unionized disputes continue to occur – 163 in 2005 (Ministry of Manpower 2007) – but are mostly resolved by conciliation.

Its leaders claim Singapore's NTUC to be a grass roots organization, but some members of its Central Executive Committee were not members of branch unions (Pang 1981: 491). In the 1970s, the NTUC became a 'transmission belt' (Pravda and Ruble 1987) for conveying the government's workforce imperatives. The Modernization seminar of 1969 that became the NTUC's manifesto for the transformation of Singapore's industrial relations from regulated pluralism to corporatism (National Trades Union Congress 1970) had requested the government to accept a code of management–labour relations for the achievement of high norms of productivity, and in 1974 the NTUC's secretary-general advised trade unions that wage increases must be related to productivity growth. In 1975, the NTUC set up its own Productivity Services Unit while continuing to hold seminars and conferences promoting productivity consciousness (National Trades Union Congress 1970: 241, 1985b: 6–15).

The NTUC progressed beyond the transmission belt role in the 1980s and 1990s to become what its leaders describe as engaged in a social partnership with government and employers, to anticipate the human resource requirements ('manpower planning') of the Singapore economy. In the twenty-first century, government is represented more proactively by MoM than it was by the former Ministry of Labour. Institutionally, the tripartite partnership of government, unions and employers is not an equilateral one, qualified as it is by the 'symbiotic' relationship between the PAP and the NTUC and by the pervasive influence of the main employers' association, the Singapore National Employers Federation (SNEF), deriving from its multi-national composition.

The PAP–NTUC symbiosis has endured for longer than other partnership arrangements in the industrializing countries of Southeast and East Asia. When, in the 1980s, the Japanese model was regarded as exemplary, rapport was between its enterprise unions and the employer, at the enterprise rather than the national level. Korea's official national union federation was more of a government tool than a partner, and, since 1987, has been rivalled by an independent federation at both national and workplace levels. Similarly, Malaysia, Taiwan, Hong Kong and Thailand have experienced both pro-government and oppositional trade unions. However, these unions have not been able to play such a formative role in national labour policies as has Singapore's NTUC.

The SNEF, on the other hand, has a shorter history, it having been formed, at the suggestion of the then Minister of Labour from a merger of associations in 1980. Today, however, it is the key employers' body in national manpower planning. The SNEF's policies are made by its 17-member council comprising senior executives of member companies who reflect the multi-national corporate structure of much employment in Singapore. Its industrial relations policies are formulated by a panel of human resource practitioners and the chairpersons of each industry group.

Explaining the development, structure and strategies of trade unions

All three transformations of Singapore's industrial relations have been a response to the imperatives of a competitive global context, and the character of trade unionism has been largely determined by compliance with these imperatives. This is underscored by the following extract from an account written during the third transformation, from corporatism to corporatist paternalism:

> While restructuring the economy is presented by the government as imperative and technological change as inevitable and irresistible if Singapore is to remain competitive in an increasingly hostile world economic environment, the requirements of labour as a human resource cannot be fully understood within an economic frame of reference. Rather, the initiatives for upgrading human and industrial relations in Singapore need to be studied in the light of the city-state's unique social and political context. Human resource management in Singapore, therefore, comprises two analytically distinct but interdependent areas of public policy initiative. One ensures the provision of the appropriate quality of human resources to the economy. The other concerns the management of compliance of human resources, i.e., the workforce, with the imperatives defined for it by the PAP government. Both entail the upgrading of human and industrial relations.
>
> (Wilkinson and Leggett 1985: 10)

Figure 7.1 illustrates the strategic initiatives of trade unions that have contributed to the transformation of Singapore's trade unionism.

Such autonomy as Singapore workers might have exercised in their industrial lives before 1969 has diminished because decisions on labour matters are taken

Colonial Authority to 1960	Regulated Pluralism to 1968	Corporatism to 1979	Corporatist Paternalism to 1998	'Manpower Planning' after 1997
Strategic choices made by trade union leaders				
Labour Fronts	SATU and NTUC	NTUC	NTUC	NTUC
⟶	⟶	⟶	⟶	⟶
From the challenge to authority through labour unrest. From confrontational bargaining.	To identification with Barisan Socialis (SATU) or with the PAP (NTUC).	To the abandonment of confrontational bargaining in favour of cooperatives and social welfare provision.	To strengthening the NTUC leadership with technocrats. To restructure unions along industry and enterprise lines.	To the engagement with MoM and SNEF To increase workforce mobility and promote lifelong learning.

Figure 7.1 The transformations of Singaporean trade unionism

by NTUC technocrats in symbiosis with the PAP and social partnership with the SNEF. The current manpower planning policy with its objective of constructing an employment system more sensitive to variable performance has to some extent deregulated the labour market, but the PAP government's successful management of financial crises may have reinforced the tendency of Singaporeans to rank social stability as more important than personal liberty (Mauzy and Milne 2002: 197).

The third transformation of Singapore's industrial relations – from corporatism to corporatist paternalism – has progressed towards a comprehensive national HRM labelled and institutionalized as 'manpower planning' and conceptualized as 'Human Capital Management' (Ministry of Trade and Industry 2003: 174). Except for notional genuflections towards the grass roots heritage, the progression relieves the NTUC trade unions of any resonance with their traditions. Restructuring and redefinition in the early 1980s formalized what had begun at the grass roots level after the government's successful confrontation with the public daily-rated workers in 1966 and confirmed by the demise of the Metal Box Union in 1977. By the end of the 1990s, the NTUC was well placed to accommodate the social partnership role with the employers and the government.

The NTUC's manifesto for the progression to manpower planning, *NTUC 21*, was produced two years before MoM's *Manpower 21* and in the same year as the employers' *SNEF 21* (Singapore National Employers' Federation 1997). *NTUC 21* identified five pillars for the labour movement in the twenty-first century: 'Enhance Employability for Life'; 'Strengthen Competitiveness'; 'Build Healthy Body, Healthy Mind'; 'Care More'; 'Develop a Stronger Labour Movement' (National Trades Union Congress 1997). The last pillar, expressed as an imperative in *Manpower 21*, reflects the perennial concern with the shrinking union membership base of the NTUC, affecting its capacity to deliver as a social partner in national manpower planning (Ministry of Manpower 1999: 48).

Of the 41 recommendations in the government's *Manpower 21*, 33 require MoM to take the lead, and one each the Ministries of Trade and Industry, Finance, Education and Environment, but involving MoM. The lead partners with MoM, i.e., the NTUC and the SNEF, have responsibilities for three manpower planning strategies: lifelong learning and employability, the transformation of the workplace, and redefining partnerships. For lifelong learning and employability they are required to: '[c]ontinue to provide support for workforce development programs targeted at older and less educated workers, and for developing manpower for strategic industries'. Their responsibilities within the transformation of the work environment are to: '[p]romote best HR [Human Resource] practices by developing national recognition awards for companies with exemplary HR practices and organizing HR conferences'. The roles of the SNEF and NTUC, together with MoM, in redefining partnerships, have been to organize the annual Manpower Summit and 'Introduce a Labour Management Partnership Programme to support joint labour–management initiatives' (Ministry of Manpower 1999: 52–8).

While the Chambers of Commerce and the Singapore Manufacturers' Federation (SMF) are represented on the NWC, the SNEF is the key industrial relations body representing employers in national manpower planning. However, it is only indirectly that employers have influenced trade union strategy and structure. The PAP government is sensitive to the requirements of the multinational companies that invest in Singapore and in the early 1980s, employers' complaints of worker tardiness led to NTUC and government action to remedy the perceived faults (Lim 1979; Lim, C.Y. 1980: 5–13; *Straits Times* 14 September 1981; Cheah 1988: 272–5). With regard to union structure, it was an SNEF-sponsored report that recommended the emulation of productivity exemplar Japan by making house unionism the preferred structure, which it remained for almost two decades.

SNEF 21 listed its strategies for the new millennium as: pursue productivity to build strong companies for growth; stay competitive by improving the cost structure of businesses; win workers through corporate bonding programmes, and equip them with skills to keep pace with changes; create more high value-added jobs; cultivate corporate citizenship (Tan 2004: 119). The issues considered by the SNEF in 2000 and 2001 are much the same as those that are the concern of MoM and the NTUC, but with the SNEF's greater concentration on labour costs, especially the NWC's annual wage guidelines, the level of employers' superannuation contributions and the retirement age (Singapore National Employers' Federation 1991, 2001). Like the government and the unions SNEF's industrial relations role is largely determined by its commitment to their tripartism.

Apart from the involvement of these industrial relations institutions in manpower planning there is little in the recommendations of Manpower 21 that relates to the industrial relations of the past except for MoM's responsibilities for occupational health and safety, workmen's compensation, and amendments to the Employment Act for greater flexibility. Collective bargaining was already curtailed in scope and depth by the 1968 legislation and the NTUC deliberates in secret with government and SNEF officials in the NWC to ensure that wage increases are commensurate with productivity gains.

Neither the PAP–NTUC symbiosis nor the social partnership sits easily with the model of the parties as 'actors' making rules in an 'industrial relations system' as conceptualized by Dunlop (1958). Because it builds on Dunlop's model by dividing the activities of management, labour and government into three tiers (at the top of strategic decision taking; in the middle of the functions of collective bargaining and personnel policy; at the bottom of policy implementation) the strategic choice model of Kochan *et al.* (1986) might offer a more useful explanatory framework for the industrial relations of Singapore (Leggett 2007), especially as the PAP government takes the strategic initiatives. Table 7.4 summarizes the political and market contexts in which the trade unions implement the PAP government's strategic initiatives.

The economic outcome of the role of Singapore's trade unionism, it has been claimed, is the economic growth that has 'resulted in enormous benefits to workers in all sectors':

> Singapore workers [since the early 1970s] rarely felt the bite of unemployment, which for most of the 1980s and 1990s remained well under four percent, and enjoyed a broad range of social benefits. Today, workers are able to purchase housing at low cost, medical benefits are widely available, and social insurance programs include workers' compensation, unemployment insurance, and retirement benefits.
>
> (US Department of State 2003: 1)

Table 7.4 Explaining Singaporean trade union development, structure and strategy

Political context	
Degrees of liberalization and autonomy	
(repression, tolerance, support, indifference)	Repression/support
Relations with the State (dependent, independent)	Dependent
Markets	
Openness (Imports + Exports as % of GDP)[1]	High
Degree of competition1 (high, medium or low)	High
Financial markets	
Openness to market financing	High
Ownership (group, institutional, foreign, dispersed)	Foreign
Labour markets	
Demand elasticity (relates to ability of employers to pass on increases in prices – high, medium or low)	Low
Employers	
Concentration (top 100 companies as percentage value of total)	High
Employer organization membership (high, medium or low)	Medium
Multinational (high, medium or low)	High
Unitarist or pluralist perspective	Unitarist

Source: 1 GlobalEDGE, Michigan State University, (http://globaledge.msu.edu) accessed 31 May 2007.

While some benefits are directly provided by trade unions and the SLF, the point being made above is that it is the incorporation of trade unions into the wider planning of Singapore's development – social and economic – as outlined above that has produced the benefits.

Conclusions

This chapter has placed its analysis of Singapore's trade unions in the context of the government's strategic choices initiated by the transformations of the city state's industrial relations. The pluralism inherited from colonial Singapore has been displaced by regulation and corporatism with the NTUC, the key institution for achieving the compliance of labour with the government's economic imperatives. Through its symbiotic relationship with the PAP, the NTUC serves as the mouthpiece for organized labour at all levels of government as well as a conduit for carrying government policy to the workforce. Since 1979, its leadership has been technocratic rather than charismatic or populist and its governance oligarchic (although democratic in form).

Because this chapter has applied the strategic choice approach (Kochan *et al.* 1986) a qualification may be in order. The qualification echoes an earlier criticism of the original systems model (Dunlop 1958), i.e., the reference to 'actors' rather than 'people' (Banks 1974: 13). It is that 'such a model does little more than list the parties to industrial relations and their interactions', i.e., it is not a significant improvement on the systems approach as an explanatory device, 'its actors being disembodied managements and unions (with workers and the state not really figuring as active participants)' (Edwards 1995: 19–20). The significance of this criticism for this study is that, *prima facie*, in Singapore the state is the strategic driver of industrial relations with workers seemingly 'disembodied' by the exclusive authority of the NTUC – to an extent that the NTUC since the 1980s has sought to balance technocrats with 'grass roots' leaders to re-embody Singapore workers (Vasil 1989: 168–9; *Straits Times* 5 May 1991).

For the future, the NTUC's membership remains a problem if it is to fulfil the social partnership role required of it by manpower planning. Unless the NTUC affiliates organize a greater proportion of Singapore workers than they do now, the legitimacy of their role as representatives of labour will remain somewhat tenuous. The trade union membership problem is not confined to Singapore, where it is partly a result of labour market restructuring and, possibly, the perception of workers that trade unions are irrelevant with regard to the determination of their terms and conditions of employment. There is a discernible convergence here of trade unionism in industrialized countries, but a diversity in the ways national peak union bodies deal with it. Singapore has responded to global market conditions since the 1960s, industrializing as it did through dependence on multinational corporate investment. Its trade unions were required to accommodate to this approach to development and consequently their leaders in the NTUC and government are highly sensitive to the increased pace of globalization and the challenge of insuring the appropriateness of the directions of workplace change.

Thus the substantive, procedural and political effects of trade unions as outlined by Gospel (Chapter 2 this volume) have invariably taken an opposite direction in Singapore to those in other industrialized countries. For example, their effect on wages has been dictated by the assessments of productivity growth rather than by a direct concern with social and economic fairness. Singapore's trade unions invoked social partnership and political stability, sometimes in different guises, as being in the interests of their members earlier than their invocation in some advanced industrialized countries.

Bibliography

Banks, J. A. (1974) *Trade Unionism,* London: Collier-Macmillan.

Chan, H. C. (1975) 'Politics in an administrative state: where has the politics gone?', in C. M. Seah (ed.) *Trends in Singapore*, Singapore: Singapore University Press.

Cheah, H. B. (1988) 'Labour in transition: the case of Singapore', *Labour and Industry*, 1(2): 258–86.

Chua, B. H. (1995) *Communitarian Ideology and Democracy in Singapore*, London: Routledge.

Department of Statistics (annual) *Yearbook of Statistics Singapore*, Singapore: Singapore National Printers.

Deyo, F. (1981) *Dependent Development and Industrial Order: An Asian Case Study*, New York: Praeger.

Dunlop, J. T. (1958) *Industrial Relations Systems*, New York: Holt, Rinehart and Winston.

Edwards, P. K. (1995) 'The employment relationship', in P. K. Edwards (ed.) *Industrial Relations: Theory and Practice in Britain*, Oxford: Blackwell.

Gamba, C. (1962) *Trade Unionism in Malaya*, Singapore: Eastern Universities Press.

Goh, C. T. (1980) 'The Singapore Economy – progress into the 80s', in National Trades Union Congress (ed.) *Progress into the 80s*, Paper presented at the NTUC seminar on progress into the 80's, 6–10 November 1979, Singapore: SILO Coop Printing.

Goh, K. S. (1980) 'Prospects of the labour movement in Singapore in the 1980's', in National Trades Union Congress (ed.) *Progress into the 80s*, Paper presented at the NTUC seminar on progress into the 80's, 6–10 November 1979, Singapore: SILO Coop Printing.

Howe, Y. C. (1980) 'Industrialisation in the 1980s', in National Trades Union Congress (ed.) *Progress into the 80s*, Paper presented at the NTUC seminar on progress into the 80's, 6–10 November 1979, Singapore: SILO Coop Printing.

Kerr, C., Dunlop, J. T., Harbison, F. H. and Myers, C. A. (1960) *Industrialism and Industrial Man*, Cambridge, MA: Harvard University Press.

Kochan, T. A., Katz, H. C. and McKersie, R. B (1986) *The Transformation of American Industrial Relations*, New York: Basic Books.

Lee, C. M. (1980) 'The second phase of industrialisation and its implications on productivity for workers and managers', in National Trades Union Congress (ed) *Progress into the 80s*, Paper presented at the NTUC seminar on progress into the 80's, 6–10 November 1979, Singapore: SILO Coop Printing.

Lee, K. Y. (2000) *From Third World to First: The Singapore Story: 1965–2000: Memoirs of Lee Kuan Yew*, Singapore: Times Editions.

Leggett, C. (1987)'The Japanization of Singapore's trade unions', paper presented at the Cardiff Business School conference on the Japanization of British industry, Cardiff, 17–18 September.

Leggett, C. (1988) 'Industrial relations and enterprise unionism in Singapore', *Labour and Industry*, 1(2): 242–57.

Leggett, C. (2007) 'From industrial relations to manpower planning: the transformations of Singapore's industrial relations', *International Journal of Human Resource Management*, 18(4): 642–64.

Lim, C. O. (1980) *Work and Excel for an Even Better Quality of Life: NTUC's Position Paper*, Singapore: SILO Coop Printing.

Lim, C. Y. (1979) Press Release by Lim Chong Yah, Chairman of the National Wages Council, 12 June 1979 (Mimeograph).

Lim, C. Y. (1980) 'Economic restructuring in Singapore', in National Trades Union Congress (ed.) *Progress into the 80s*, Paper presented at the NTUC seminar on progress into the 80's, 6–10 November 1979, Singapore: SILO Coop Printing.

Mauzy, D. K. and Milne, R. S. (2002) *Singapore Politics under the People's Action Party*, London: Routledge.

Media Masters (2003) *Alias Chin Peng*, Singapore: Media Masters.

Ministry of Information and the Arts (2001) *Singapore 2001*, Singapore: Ministry of Information and the Arts.

Ministry of Labour (annual) *Annual Report,* Singapore: Singapore National Printers.

Ministry of Labour (1994) *Report on the Labour Force Survey of Singapore 1994*, Singapore, Singapore National Printers.

Ministry of Manpower (1999) *Manpower 21: Vision of a Talent Capital*, Singapore: Singapore National Printers.

Ministry of Manpower (2001) *Human Capital: Ministry of Manpower Annual Report 2001*, Singapore: MoM Corporate Communications Department.

Ministry of Manpower (2004a) *Report on the Labour Force Survey in Singapore 2004*, Singapore, Singapore National Printers.

Ministry of Manpower (2004b) *Tripartite Taskforce Report on Wage Restructuring*, Singapore: Singapore National Printers.

Ministry of Manpower (2007) Online. Available HTTP: <http://www.mom.gov.sg> (accessed 30 May 2007).

Ministry of Trade and Industry (2003) *New Challenges, Fresh Goals – Towards a Dynamic Global City*, Singapore: Singapore National Printers

Ministry of Trade and Industry (2004) *Economic Survey of Singapore 2004*, Singapore: Singapore National Printers.

Ministry of Trade and Industry (2005) *Economic Survey of Singapore*, Singapore: Singapore National Printers.

National Productivity Board (1981) *Report of the Committee of Productivity*, Singapore: National Productivity Board.

National Trades Union Congress (1970) *Why Labour Must Go Modern: The NTUC Case for a Modernized Labour Movement*, Singapore: National Trades Union Congress.

National Trades Union Congress (1976) *Tomorrow: The Peril and the Promise*, Secretary-General's report to the 2nd triennial delegates' conference of the NTUC, Singapore: National Trades Union Congress.

National Trades Union Congress (1980) *Progress into the 80s*, Paper presented at the NTUC seminar on progress into the 80's, 6–10 November 1979, Singapore: SILO Coop Printing.

National Trades Union Congress (1985a) *Secretary General's Report to the Fourth Triennial Delegates' Conference*, Singapore: National Trades Union Congress.

National Trades Union Congress (1985b) *Chronology of Trade Union Development in Singapore, 1940–1984,* Singapore: National Trades Union Congress (mimeograph).

National Trades Union Congress (1997) *NTUC 21*, Singapore: National Trades Union Congress.

Ong, Y. H. (1980) 'Future directions of the Singapore labour movement', in National Trades Union Congress (ed) *Progress into the 80s*, Paper presented at the NTUC seminar on progress into the 80's, 6–10 November 1979, Singapore: SILO Coop Printing.

Pang, E. F. (1981) 'Singapore', in A. Blum (ed) *International Handbook of Industrial Relations: Contemporary Developments and Research*, Westport, CT: Greenwood Press.

Pang, E. F. (1982) *Education, Manpower and Development in Singapore*, Singapore, Singapore University Press.

Pravda, A. and Ruble, B. A. (eds) (1987) *Trade Unions in Communist States*, London: Allen and Unwin.

Roberts, B. (1964) *Labour in the Tropical Territories of the Commonwealth*, London: London School of Economics and Political Science/G. Bell and Sons.

Rodan, G. (1997) 'Singapore: economic diversification and social divisions', in G. Rodan, K. Hewison and R. Robinson (eds) *The Political Economy of South-East Asia: An Introduction*, Melbourne: Oxford University Press.

Singapore National Employers' Federation (1991) *Annual Report,* Singapore: Singapore National Employers' Federation.

Singapore National Employers' Federation (1997) *SNEF 21,* Singapore: Singapore National Employers' Federation.

Singapore National Employers' Federation (2001) *Annual Report,* Singapore: Singapore National Employers' Federation.

Tan, C. H. (1995) *Labour–Management Relations in Singapore*, Singapore: Prentice Hall.

Tan, C. H. (2004) *Employment Relations in Singapore*, Singapore: Prentice Hall.

Turnbull, M. (1989) *A History of Singapore 1819–1988,* Oxford: Oxford University Press.

US Department of State (2003) *Labour Rights Report: Singapore.* Online. Available HTTP: <http://www.dol.gov/ilab/media/reports> (accessed 30 May 2007).

Vasil, R. K. (1989) 'Trade unions', in K. S. Sandhu and P. Wheatley (eds) *Management of Success: the Moulding of Modern Singapore*, Singapore: Institute of Southeast Asian Studies.

Visser, J. (1990) *In Search of Inclusive Unionism*, Deventer: Kluwer.

Wilkinson, B. and Leggett, C. (1985) 'Human and industrial relations in Singapore: the management of compliance', *Euro-Asia Business Review*, 4(3): 9–15.

Wong, E. S. (1983) 'Industrial relations in Singapore: challenge for the 1980s', in Institute of Southeast Asian Studies (ed) *Southeast Asian Affairs 1983*, Aldershot: Gower.

Woodiwiss, A. (1998) *Globalisation, Human Rights and Labour Law in Pacific Asia*, Cambridge: Cambridge University Press.

8 Trade unions in Malaysia

Complexity of a state-employer system

Nagiah Ramasamy and Chris Rowley

Introduction

The Malaysian trade union movement faces a number of challenges, notably from neo-liberal policies and changing structures of employment. Unions often accuse employers of over-emphasizing profits, the return on equity and earnings per share, at the expense of the welfare and dignity of employees. Unions, which are constrained particularly by legislative controls, have also accused the state of being pro-capitalist and seeing unions as a threat to investments. Those on the management side believe unions are out to destroy free competition. As noted by Leap (1995), neither statement is entirely accurate, although each contains some elements of truth.

This chapter analyses trade unionism in Malaysia and the Malaysian industrial relations (IR) system. It covers the contextual and historical issues, the evolution of trade union development in Malaysia, union types and structure, unions' external relationship with the state, business and society, the major activities of unions, union development and strategies in terms of confronting pressures from political changes, economic uncertainties and competition under market forces. Finally, the chapter concludes by illustrating the possible future of the union movement in Malaysia.

Context and history

Malaysia has a population of 26.64 million, of whom 63 per cent are urban-based (Table 8.1). Employment (in percentages) in the different industrial sectors has changed over time: with declines in the primary sector from 20.4 in 1995 to 15.08 by 2005 and in the secondary sector from 31.91 to 29.42, but with growth in the tertiary sector from 47.69 to 55.5 (Department of Statistics 2006a: 23, 2006b: 185). This shift has clearly affected union membership. Union density dropped from 9.3 per cent in 1990 (MHR 1991) to 7.8 per cent in 2004 (Department of Statistics 2006a, 2006b). Average membership per trade union also dipped from 1,945 in 1982 to 1,296 in 2003.

With high political stability (against a back-drop of numerous labour and trade union legislative controls), unemployment has declined and real gross domestic product (GDP) has increased steadily since the 1997 Asian Financial Crisis. However, inequalities, as measured by the Gini coefficient, have worsened from 0.442 in 1990 to 0.462 in 2004 (NMP 2006). Other contextual factors are listed in Table 8.1.

In any discussion of trade unionism, it is important to understand the contextual issues surrounding them, such as history and the roles played by the various 'actors' in the IR system. This requires examining unionism from a historical

Table 8.1 Contextual factors – Malaysia

General statistics	
Population[1] (2006)	26.64 million
Area (square kilometres)[2]	329.8 thousand

Employment proportion in (%) (2005)[3]
  Primary (agriculture, fishing and mining & quarrying)
  Secondary (manufacturing, construction & electricity,
  gas & water supply)
  Tertiary
	15.08
	29.42
	55.50

Urban population (% of total population)[4]	63.0
GDP per capita (interim)[3] (2005)	$4,867 (US)
Income inequality Gini coefficient[4] (2004)	Medium 0.4620

Real GDP growth (%)
  1990–1995[6]
  1996–2000[6]
  2001–2004[6]; 2005[1]
  2005[1]
	9.38
	4.98
	4.48
	5.2

Unemployment (%)
  1986–1995[5]
  1996–2005[5]
  2005[3]
	5.38
	3.24
	3.50

Summary description	
Product market regulation (1998)	Medium
Political context: the system of regime	Constitutional monarchy, Parliamentary democracy
Political stability	High

Sources
1 Department of Statistics, 'Key Statistics' (http://www.statistics.gov.my, accessed 26 June 2006).
2 Department of Statistics (2005) *Yearbook of Statistics 2005*, Malaysia, November.
3 Department of Statistics (2006a) *The Malaysian Economy in Brief*, Malaysia, May.
4 NMP (2006) *9th Malaysia Plan 2006–2010*, Government of Malaysia, Kuala Lumpur.
5 Department of Statistics (2006b) *Malaysia Economic Statistics – Time Series 2005*, Malaysia, February.
6 Treasury, Ministry of Finance Malaysia, GDP 1990–2004 in 1987 constant prices (updated as at December 2005), http://www.treasury.gov.my.

Note
RM3.697 = US$1, as at 11 August 2006.

perspective and understanding the role of legislation and executive action influencing regulations.

Colonial government and the Emergencies

Malaysian IR is largely a post-1945 development and shaped by legislation and executive action (Wu 1982; Anantaraman 1997). The colonial government, the First National Emergency (1948–60), the Second National Emergency (1964–67) and the Third Emergency (1969–71), all influenced Malaysian IR. Emergency provisions in the Malaysian constitution allow the government to rule without recourse to Parliament and elections, if considered necessary.

The precedent for a pattern of direct and a high degree of state intervention in IR, and in particular, the activities of organized labour, was initiated by the British colonial government in 1948 (Peetz and Todd 2001). The government banned the Communist Party of Malaya and many Communist-led unions, and declared the First Emergency in 1948. During this period, there was not much scope for unionism because British employers were able to exert considerable and successful pressure against moves to organize workers. Tunku Abdul Rahman, soon after becoming the first prime minister of the newly independent Malaya in 1957, announced that the growth of healthy trade unionism 'is being encouraged by Government to provide bargaining power to union members for the ultimate purpose of safeguarding their interest and well-being' (Josey 1958: 1).

The Second Emergency, during the Indonesian Confrontation beginning in 1964, came about because Indonesia disapproved of the merger of the Federation of Malaya with Sabah and Sarawak. Following the Confrontation (when Indonesia landed forces on coastal areas of Peninsular Malaya, with armed incursions into Sabah and Sarawak), the Second Emergency was declared in September 1964.

The Third Emergency began in 1969 during the Kuala Lumpur racial riots (Anantaraman 1997). In their aftermath, Tunku Abdul Rahman's successor, Tun Abdul Razak, offered an affirmative action-oriented New Economic Policy (NEP). In line with measures to encourage labour-intensive, export-oriented industrialization, the government pushed through some harsh labour legislation. However, it also declared May Day a public holiday, encouraged trade unions to go into business, awarded a banking licence to set up the *Bank Buruh* (Labour Bank) and formulated a Code of Conduct for Industrial Harmony, encouraging tripartism involving the government, employers and unions (Jomo and Todd 1994).

Subsequent prime ministers, and in particular Dr Mahathir Mohamad, have not been liberal in their policies towards unions (Wu 1982; Jomo 1995). While there does not appear to be any major shift in IR policies under the current government of Prime Minister Abdullah Badawi, his government does project itself as more transparent. It should be kept in mind that while many restrictions on unions exist, as Wu (2006: 120) points out, Malaysia is not a liberal democracy in the Western tradition, but a developing country striving for rapid economic growth against a backdrop of conflicting ethnic interests, and with a past that includes Communist infiltration of organized labour, insurrection and racial riots.

Malaysian union history in brief

The main stages in Malaysian union history, argues Wad (1988), can also be labelled by the dominant union structure. These are *General Unionism*, from the 1920s to the defeat of the Communist trade union movement in 1947–8 and *Industrial Unionism* from 1948 until the 1980s. Dr Mahathir Mohamad's Look East Policy, including emulating the success of Japanese management and IR practices, saw the prospect of unions being replaced by in-house unions or *Enterprise Unionism*.

After independence, Malaysia adopted an import substitution industrialization (ISI) strategy. During this period, IR reflected the system inherited from the British, with legislation providing for collective bargaining and minimum standards, while the focus of government policy was to contain conflict in the interests of economic development (Kuruvilla and Arudsothy 1995). The first phase of ISI, from 1957 to 1963, focused on infrastructure and rural development, with industrialization left to the private sector. In the second phase of ISI, up to 1970, the state emerged as a leading investor, motivated by the NEP that promised the economic advancement of ethnic Malays relative to ethnic Chinese and Indians (Kuruvilla and Arudsothy 1995; Spinanger 1986).

The shift to export-oriented industrialization (EOI) occurred in the 1970s, following the enactment of policies to attract foreign direct investment (FDI) into the electronics sector. A range of financial, fiscal, regulatory and infrastructure incentives, coupled with low-cost labour, resulted in the attraction of foreign capital to the electronics and electrical goods sectors (Spinanger 1986; Salih *et al.* 1987; Rowley and Bhopal 2005a, 2005b, 2006). In the late 1980s, given the influence of rapid technological change, globalization of products and markets, increased competition from other low-cost Asian exporters and a labour shortage arising from the inflow of foreign firms, the government articulated a second-stage EOI strategy. This focused on attraction of more technology-intensive FDI in electronics and electrical goods and textiles, for example. As Malaysia's transformation from the low-cost EOI to a more advanced EOI was characterized by exports of more technology-intensive products (Kuruvilla 1996a), people-management techniques were based increasingly on the development of skills with high pay and employee involvement in a non-union environment (Rasiah 1994).

Overall, the general increase in union membership between 1995 and 2005 has not kept pace with employment expansion. In fact, 2002 saw the highest number of union members, 811,472, which declined to 800,951 by 2005 (see Table 8.2). As Kuruvilla (1996b) notes, this situation is a reflection of numerous unions but with few members. A greater degree of union density would not only provide trade unions with legitimacy, influence, strength and confidence when tackling problems but also enhance bargaining power. With the continuing decline in trade union density, the labour movement has not had a significant voice at either national or local levels and current developments seem to signify a weakening of their influence.

Table 8.2 Malaysian trade unions

General statistics	
Number of unions	
1990[1]	446
2005[2]	603
Number of union members	
1990[1]	658,499
2005[2]	800,951
Union density (%)	
1990[1]	9.35
2005[2,3]	7.97
private/public, male/female	
Level of collective bargaining	Low
Summary description	
Union type	Economic/market-oriented
Union structure	Enterprise unionism (since the 1980s) Industrial unionism (up to late 1980s) Political unionism (during the communist-controlled era of 1930s/1940s)
Unity of peak organizations	Medium
State control of unions	High

Sources
1 MHR (1991) *Labour Indicators 1990*, Malaysia, December.
2 MHR (2006) 'Statistical Summary of Labour and Human Resource: Department of Trade Unions', (http://www.mohr.gov.my/mohr_key.php, accessed 30 June 2006). Figures are for January to September 2005.
3 Department of Statistics (2006a) *The Malaysian Economy in Brief*, Malaysia, May (800,951 union members/10,043,700 workers).

Gengadharan (1990) states that many employees remain outside unions after recognition to avoid the payment of union subscriptions knowing full well that the union will negotiate collective agreements for its members and thereby benefit them as well. In the Malaysian context, there is no 'closed shop' policy. The *Industrial Relations Act* 1967 (IRA) prevents workers from being forced to join a union. Furthermore, the IRA makes collective agreements binding on all workers of the undertaking whether or not they are members of the union which negotiated the agreement and whether or not they joined the undertaking subsequent to the date of the agreement. The 'free-rider' problem, therefore, poses an issue for membership as a means of achieving instrumental goals.

Unionization rates among women workers in Malaysia have been lower than among men. The percentage of female unionists increased slowly from 21 per cent in 1952 to almost 40 per cent by 2003. However, this does not reflect increased female participation in the labour force as a whole. Jomo and Todd (1994: 31) provide a number of explanations for this gender bias: male domination of unions; society's disapproval of female involvement in organizations outside the home because of patriarchal values; and union failure to address major issues confronting women, such as childcare, harassment and discrimination.

Union types and structure

Martin's (1989: 113) typology of union movements is based on three distinctive positions that trade unions may occupy in relation to a state or to a political party. Trade unions may be dominated by the state (*ancillary* position); they may dominate it (*surrogate* position); or they may neither dominate nor be dominated (*autonomous* position). A union may be said to be in an ancillary position when major union bodies are characteristically subordinate or subservient to either a political party or the state, or both. In the case of the surrogate position, unions dominate the party or the state. This domination may ultimately take the form of union bodies acting in place of party or state by displaying qualities, espousing purposes and discharging functions normally associated with parties or states.

The autonomous position does not necessarily imply complete independence of parties and state, rather, it is better seen as being intermediate between the ancillary and surrogate positions. In this position, unions are neither clearly subservient to, nor clearly dominant over, either party or state. These three positions, given that there are three nominally distinct organizations involved, yield five categories, that is, party-ancillary, state-ancillary, party-surrogate, state-surrogate and autonomous. It would appear that in Malaysia, where a state employer dominated IR system exists (Kuruvilla and Venkataratnam 1996), the state-ancillary position is the most appropriate classification.

As stated by Todd and Peetz (2001), overall Malaysia's IR remains firmly within a 'control' rather than a 'commitment' framework. Malaysian unions are generally small, fragmented and regional. This is due largely to the strict requirements of the *Trade Union Act* 1959 (TUA), and in particular the manner in which a union is defined as:

> Any association or combination of workmen or employers … whose place of work is in West Malaysia, Sabah or Sarawak … within any particular establishment, trade, occupation or industry or within similar trades, occupations or industries …

The implication is that membership is limited to any one of the three geographical regions, that is, workers in Peninsular Malaysia may only join a trade union all of whose members work in Peninsular Malaysia, and the same applies to workers in Sabah and in Sarawak.

Further, the law has ensured that unions remain fragmented in their respective establishments, trades, occupations or industries. Therefore, unions of a general nature cannot be formed except in a particular establishment. The Director General of Trade Unions (DGTU), therefore, has very wide powers in respect of the registration of unions via ascertaining similarity of trades, occupations or industries. This has far-reaching consequences. One of the most important examples is that employees in the electronics industry may not be represented by the union of electrical workers as in the opinion of the DGTU the electronics industry is not similar to the electrical industry (Rowley and Bhopal 2006).

The rights of workers and employers under the IRA include the right to form, assist in the formation of or join a union and participate in its lawful activities. The union can represent its members in disputes as long as they are employees. However, certain categories of public officers are not eligible to join or be a member of a union. These include members of the police, prison service, armed forces and public officers engaged in a confidential or security capacity. Public officers holding any post in the managerial and professional group may unionize if they are so allowed in writing by the Chief Secretary to the government. This further emphasizes the extent of executive control over unionization in the public sector. The DGTU has the discretion not only to register a union or not, but also to cancel or withdraw the certificate of registration issued to a union under several circumstances, and may order suspension of union branches.

Unions can be classified under the following categories: private sector employees' unions, public sector employees' unions, unions in statutory bodies and local authorities, and employers' unions. Unions in the private sector can be further classified as either national or in-house (enterprise) unions. While national unions attempt to cover all workers in the same trade, occupation or industry, the same employer employs all members in in-house unions (enterprise unions).

Membership of the Malaysian Trades Union Congress (MTUC) consists of unions of employees in various trades, occupations and industries. Accordingly, it does not qualify for registration as a union under the Act. It is registered as a society under the *Societies Act* 1966, although it seems to have received *de facto* acceptance as the national representative of employees in IR matters (Wu 2006; Maimunah 2003). The MTUC, whose membership comprises both private and public sector unions, represents workers on tripartite bodies such as the National Labour Advisory Council (NLAC) and the Employees Provident Fund Board. It is affiliated to the International Confederation of Free Trade Unions. Individual unions can also be affiliated to international federations, for example, the Public Services Union is affiliated to the Public Sector International Federation.

Collective bargaining can take place between a single employer and a trade union or between a group of employers and a union. Multi-employer bargaining is found where employer's associations exist, for example, the Malayan Commercial Banks Association, which represents many of the larger banks, bargains with the National Union of Bank Employees (NUBE), which represents non-executive bank employees. According to Maimunah (2003: 175), in terms of numbers of workers covered, multi-employer bargaining is more significant, although the majority of agreements are made between unions and a single employer.

When different groups of employees in the company belong to separate unions, then employers carry out bargaining with these different unions. For example, many banks bargain not only with NUBE, but also with the Association of Bank Officers Malaysia. Malaysian Airlines negotiates with four unions, namely the Malaysian Airlines Employees Union, Peninsular Malaysia for non-executive graded staff, the Malaysian Airlines Executive Officers Union, Sabah, the Airlines Workers Union, Sarawak, and the Malaysian Airlines Executive Staff Association (Maimunah 2003: 175)

What do unions do?

The main services that unions provide for members are bargaining and representation. Collective bargaining provides a means for unions to defend and improve members' welfare through better, safer and healthier working conditions. Maimunah (2003: 163) explains that in Malaysia collective bargaining mostly focuses on economic issues. It could be expanded to include a host of other areas relating to the welfare of workers, especially in the areas of safety and productivity schemes. The outcomes of collective bargaining provide a measure of job security, status, self-respect, better working conditions and greater control of their working lives (Wu 2006: 145).

Unions offer legal representation if their members have problems at work. They may also consider and decide upon strikes, lockouts and similar industrial action affecting members. Unions also offer advice on labour disputes, protect against unfair labour practices such as unlawful dismissals, provide advice and training for laid-off workers and promote social and educational welfare. The NUBE (2006) organizes family days and activities such as various tournaments for members. Further, it provides for personal accident insurance cover and a retirement fund. In addition to this, it plays an active role in creating awareness in regard to broader issues such as social protection, the outsourcing of jobs and the privatization of water. However, very few unions have the resources and capability that the NUBE has, such as using the internet to reach out to its members. Its e-bulletins are informative and serve to inform members of current activities, issues and injustices, and generally promote the interests of the union and its members.

All collective agreements, which must specify the duration of the agreement, which cannot be less than three years, have to be taken cognizance of[1] by the Industrial Court, that is, recognized as a binding, valid document enforceable by it. Such agreements are deemed to be an award and become binding on the parties and on workers who are employed or subsequently employed in the undertaking to which the agreement relates, regardless of whether they are members of the union or not (Section 17, IRA). The Industrial Court could refuse to recognize agreements that were unfavourable to national economic development interests. In 1991, some 379 collective agreements were taken cognizance of. Only in 1995 and 1997 did the number go slightly beyond 400. Since 2004, there has been a noticeable decline in the number of collective agreements taken cognizance of, from 369 in 2003 to 263 in 2005 (figures provided by the Industrial Court Department, 20 July 2006). Other aspects of collective bargaining are indicated in Table 8.3.

Administrative controls limit the right to strike. Once conciliation or mediation proceedings commence strikes should stop. Furthermore, bargaining on matters

Table 8.3 What do Malaysian trade unions do?

Activities	
Extent of collective bargaining[1]	Low
Level of collective bargaining[1] National Industry Enterprise	 Low Low–medium High
Extent of joint consultation[1] (High, medium or low)	Medium
Industrial disputes Working days lost per 1,000 employees (2004) Relative assessment (high, medium or low)	 < 1 Low(3 strikes occurred involving 279 employees leading to 3,262 'Mandays' lost, in 2004)[1]
Degree of state intervention in employment protection	Medium
Income inequality – Gini coefficient (2004)[2]	Medium (0.4620)

Sources
1 MHR (2006) 'Statistical Summary of Labour and Human Resource: Industrial Relations Department', (http://www.mohr.gov.my/mohr_key.php , accessed 30 June 2006).
2 NMP (2006) *9th Malaysia Plan 2006–2010*, Government of Malaysia, Kuala Lumpur.

deemed managerial prerogatives are not allowed by legislation, thus ensuring that disputes regarding these subjects do not result in conflict. There were only four reported strikes in 2002 (involving 506 workers and 1,638 workdays lost) and three in 2004 (involving 279 workers and 3,262 workdays lost) (MHR 2006).

Ayadurai (in Leong 1991: 96) attributes the weakness of the labour movement to 'the incompetence of the labour leaders … the fear or hostility … of employers to unions, … and the attitude or policies of the government' which since 1980 has become more unsympathetic, if not hostile, towards workers' organizations. This might have been due to the policy to industrialize the country and the need for a more docile labour force. Jomo (1994: 141) is critical of both the MTUC and Congress of Unions of Employees in the Public and Civil Services (CUEPACS) for having failed to launch effective action against government measures that seriously weakened labour's position. Many attempts were made to reunite the MTUC and CUEPACS into a single national centre, but these attempts, argues Jomo (1994), were undermined, largely by personal interests and ambitions.

Leadership crisis between factions in unions and in the national labour centre have led to observations that such divisiveness could lead to them being ignored by the government (Fernandez 1993: 18). Some of the MTUC's major weaknesses are the absence of a sound research centre run by professionals, the inability to settle differences (within and outside the organization) and even smug optimism, notes Fernandez (1997). Allegations of misappropriation of funds by union leaders do not put the union movement in a positive light among members and the regulatory authorities (see, for example, *The Sun* 2003; Selvarani and Abas 2004).

Explaining the development, structure and strategies of trade unions

Governments, states Windmuller (1987: 121):

> [perceive] their primary responsibility to be the protection of the freedom of the market place and the sanctity of the individual contract of employment and as long as they considered trade unions to be a major threat to both, the purpose of intervention by the public authorities was the suppression, or at the least the tight containment, of unions.

In Malaysia, where unions are tightly regulated, collective objectives are undermined by the state-employer system of IR where labour market flexibility, productivity, individual rights and economic objectives are promoted. The TUA does not allow employees of political parties to hold office or be employed by a union. According to the then Minister for Labour and Manpower, political unionism 'can only lead to wide divisions within the trade union movement and prejudice its effectiveness in pursuing trade union objectives' (ILO 1980: 286).

In the 1990 general elections, the MTUC took a controversial move by fielding its own candidates. This led the government to approve the formation of a new labour front for trade unions called the Malaysian Labour Organization (MLO) in July 1990 (Anantaraman 1997: 48–9). However, in May 1996 the MLO disbanded and its member union re-affiliated with the MTUC. This came about when Zainal Rampak, former president of MTUC, who also had a long-standing attachment to the opposition, joined UMNO (United Malays National Organization – the dominant partner in the government since Independence) (Bhopal 2001).

Legislation regulates the collective bargaining process and restricts the role of Malaysian unions in collective bargaining. The IRA, for example, prohibits the inclusion of items deemed managerial prerogatives – employment, termination due to redundancy or reorganization, promotion, transfer and the allocation of duties – in a union's proposal for a collective agreement, in effect pointing towards managerial unilateralism. In addition, the *Promotion of Investments Act* (1986) prohibits workers in 'pioneer' industries from negotiating working conditions more favourable than the minimum standards embodied in the *Employment Act* 1955 (EA). This means that there is little reason to form unions in many companies that have such pioneer status. The government, by providing minimum legal requirements in matters such as annual, sick and maternity leaves, social security and health and safety, further minimizes the incentive to form unions.

Furthermore, provisions on collective bargaining in the IRA (as amended in 1980) do not apply to any government service, service of any statutory authority or any worker employed by the government or statutory authority. Therefore, public sector employees are excluded from collective bargaining even though Malaysia ratified the International Labour Organization (ILO) Convention No. 98 on the Right to Organize and Collective Bargaining in 1961. The government, based on recommendations made by salary commissions set up from time to time, determines salaries unilaterally (Shatsari and Kamal 2006). These restrictions prevent many workers from benefiting from collective agreements.

One of the four categories of principles and rights related to the eight core ILO Conventions is the freedom of association and right to collective bargaining. The conventions in this category are Convention 87 (Freedom of Association and Protection of the Right to Organize Convention 1948) and Convention 98 (Right to Organize and Collective Bargaining Convention 1949). Convention No. 87 states that all workers' and employers' organizations have the right to draw up their constitutions and rules, to elect their representatives in full freedom, to organize their administration, to organize their activities and to formulate their programmes. The failure by the government to ratify this convention is seen as a denial of the freedom of association, and had profound effects on the drafting of the TUA. The government has discouraged any form of external interference in its IR matters. Restrictions on the freedoms of movement, speech and association include those under the *Sedition Act* (1948), the *Police Act* (1967), the *Printing Presses and Publications Act* (1984), the *Societies Act* (1966) and the *Universities and University and Colleges Act* (1975). See Table 8.4.

The IRA states that members, once organized, must seek recognition from the employer, who in turn must give a reply within 21 days from the day of claim. Rajasekaran (2002) argues that the entire process could take more than a year, during which employees are harassed, victimized and even dismissed. Fernandez (1996) adds that by the time recognition is given the original number of members could be drastically reduced, even to less than half, as many would have left the company or lost interest in the whole process of unionization.

The TUA regulates unions and union federations *per se* and it defines trade unions, delineates their membership, prescribes their registration and describes their rights and responsibilities. The TUA, the state's principal means of control over organized labour, applies throughout Malaysia; to both public and private sectors. To regulate the birth and growth of unions the DGTU is armed with discretionary, arbitrary and far-reaching powers. Under Section 2(2) of the TUA the power of the DGTU 'can be exercised by him not only in registering a new union but also in determining who is competent to be recognized as the representative union'. Furthermore, failure to obtain a registration certificate or rejection of an application by the DGTU will make the organization an illegal organization. The DGTU also has sweeping powers to deregister an existing union if it is considered to have contravened its own rules or objects or failed to comply with the statutory requirements under the Act; and to prefer a new union to an existing one, if satisfied that the new one would serve the interest of the workers.

Finality clauses, that is, clauses in statutes that seek to restrict the jurisdiction of the courts to review decisions made by non-judicial and administrative authorities, are common in the TUA and IRA. The discretionary powers conferred on the DGTU are subject to appeal only to the relevant Minister whose decision is final. While the exercise of such discretion is subject to judicial review, it is difficult for the court to intervene when such discretion is conferred using phrases like 'is satisfied' or 'in the opinion of'.

Table 8.4 Explaining Malaysian trade union development, structure and strategy

Political context	
Degrees of liberalization and autonomy	Repressed
Relations with the State	Independent
Product markets	
Openness (imports + exports as % of GDP)[1]	198% (High)
Degree of competition[2]	High
Financial markets	
Openness to market financing[3]	Low
Ownership[4] (group/family, institutional, foreign, dispersed)	Substantially family and state-owned
Labour markets[3] – demand elasticity	Medium
	Demand is greater than supply in both low-skilled, labour-intensive occupations and highly skilled jobs
Employers	
Concentration (top 100 companies as % value of total)[5]	47.61% (Medium)
Employer organization membership	Low
Multinational	Low
Unitarist or pluralist perspective	Increasingly unitarist management approach

Sources:
1 Dept of Statistics (2006c), http://www.statistics.gov.my/english/frameset_keystats.php, accessed 26 June 2006.
2 Mohamed, A. (2005) Drivers of competitiveness in Malaysia, Australia Malaysia Free Trade Agreement, Conference Proceedings, Melbourne, Australia, Available: http://www.apec.org.au/event_list2.asp?type=conf.
3 Miles, M. A., Holmes, K. R. and O'Grady, M. A. (2006) *Index of Economic Freedom*, Heritage Foundation and Dow Jones.
4 Claessens, S., Djankov, S. and Lang, L. H. P. (1999), 'Who controls East Asian corporations - and the implications for legal reform', Public Policy for the Private Sector, Note No. 195, World Bank Group – Finance, Private Sector, and Infrastructure Network, September.
5 KLSE (2006) Top 100 companies (http://www.klse.com.my/website/bm/market_information/ftse_bm_indices/Total market capitalization: RM747 billion (as at 5 October 2006) http://www.klse.com.my/website/bm/market_information/market_statistics/equities/downloads/keyindicators.pdf.

The MTUC (2004) has highlighted numerous inconsistencies in the decisions made by the DGTU. The Non-Metallic Mineral Products Manufacturing Employees Union (NMEU) case is an example. While the previous DGTU allowed the NMEU to represent employees of Taiko Bleaching Earth Sdn. Bhd. (which not only produces the same products as that of Syarikat Premier Bleaching Earth Sdn. Bhd., but also owns Premier Bleaching), the DGTU ruled that NMEU cannot represent employees of Syarikat Premier Bleaching Earth Sdn. Bhd. The DGTU also ruled that the National Union of Petroleum and Chemical Industry Workers (NUPCIW) cannot represent employees of Shin-etsu Polymer Sdn. Bhd, whereas the previous DGTU ruled that another company producing exactly same products can be represented by NUPCIW.

The formation of a national union for the electronics sector is a long-standing issue dating back to the early 1970s. It was only in 1988 that the government relented and allowed electronic workers to form in-house unions as opposed to a national union. The Minister of Human Resources, Fong Chan Onn, was quoted as saying that the government would continue to impose a ban on a national union for workers in the electronics sector, and that it has always been government policy to only allow the establishment of in-house unions for the electronics sector (Malaysiakini 2001). The inception of the government's in-house union policy in 1983 came in the wake of the government's Look East Policy.

In furtherance of 'Malaysia Incorporated', the government officially encouraged 'in-house' or enterprise unions instead of the existing national or (in the case of textiles and clothing) regional/state wide unions. Quality control circles, as well as several other Japanese IR institutions were encouraged, while selected workers – mainly those employed in the recently established heavy industries – were sent for brief training and exposure stints in Japan and, to a lesser extent, South Korea (Jomo 1995). Under the Look East Policy enterprise unionism was regarded as perhaps the key factor behind the Japanese miracle and worthy of being copied.

There are a few large in-house unions. The Malaysian Airlines Employees Union, for example, has some 7,000 members and two of the largest unions in Malaysia are in-house unions, that is, the Telekom Bhd Employees Union and the Tenaga Nasional Employees Union (Maimunah 2003: 139). However, the number of employees in most Malaysian companies is so small that most in-house unions are relatively ineffective, argues Jomo (1995: 189). Maimunah (1996) notes that the Malaysian Employers Federation (MEF) foresaw as early as 1982 that in-house union leaders would be more amenable during collective bargaining sessions.

The number of employer associations has remained unchanged at a low 14 since 2001. Membership in the associations has increased from 550 in 2001 to 644 in September 2005 (Department of Trade Unions 2006; Wu 2006: 11). This appears to be a positive development for employers in their push for more liberal economic policies. The MEF is the premier private sector employers' representative at national, regional and international levels. Its membership comprises 4,044 individual companies and 14 employer associations (MEF 2006: 30). The MEF is a member of the ASEAN Confederation of Employers and the Confederation of Asia Pacific Employers, whilst at the international level, it is a member of the International Organization of Employers.

Jomo and Todd (1994) and Maimunah (2003) state that tactics used by employers to control the workforce have included indefinitely delaying union recognition applications, victimizing or promoting activists to remove them from the shop floor and forming company-sponsored in-house unions. The problem of recognition, or rather the lack of it, by employers has been a long-standing one, with unionists accusing employers of intentionally delaying recognition while using allegedly unfair practices to dampen unionism in the workplace (*The Star* 1996). In an MTUC survey of union officials in the mid-1970s, some 31 per cent stated that their employers had transferred their active union officials to make it inconvenient and difficult for them to carry out their union activities (MTUC 1976–8: 284).

FDI flows to Malaysia have slowed significantly in recent years. Bank Negara Malaysia Annual Reports (1996–2005) show a sharp drop in FDI from RM18.4 billion in 1996, to RM14.4 billion in 2000 and to RM2.7 billion in 2005 (Shamsuddin 2006). The need to attract FDI brings Malaysia into competition with countries such as China and India for these sorts of investments. Employers argue that to be cost competitive and attract FDI they must lower labour costs, reduce the skills gap and be more proactive in drafting labour legislation that supports the recruitment of foreign labour, the mobility of labour and flexible work schemes.

According to Bhopal (2001), dependency theory argues that multinational enterprises (MNEs) in search of low labour costs and weak labour organization lead to the suppression of trade unionism owing to the dependent states' relative powerless *vis-à-vis* MNEs. This situation is reinforced by inter-state competition to provide an attractive site for inward investments. MNEs, therefore, can reduce trade union bargaining power as they can threaten to shift production to other countries (Hodgkinson and Nyland 2001).

Foreign workers have been brought in legally as well as illegally through contractors from Indonesia, Thailand, Burma, the Philippines, Cambodia, Sri Lanka, India, Nepal and Bangladesh (Navamukundan and Subramaniam 2003: 343). This is a convenient and inexpensive way to obtain labour services, but it is easy to abuse workers' rights through this system. According to Navamukundan (2002), the formal IR system is weakened by the emergence of an informal system controlled by contractors and employers.

Although the real number of foreign workers and the types of employment category in which they are involved in the various economic sectors are difficult to determine, their presence has at least reduced the chronic shortage of labour supply in the country. Many Malaysian employers tend to employ foreign workers because they are willing to accept relatively lower wages with flexible working hours compared with Malaysian workers. Foreign workers, therefore, threaten the local labour market and reduce the bargaining power of locals. In addition, hiring migrant workers relieves employers of a number of legal requirements and employee benefits such as the Employees Provident Fund, Social Security Organization, medical and social benefits. Workers are required to work long hours and are not covered by local labour laws (*The Star* 2002).

Trade unions seem to take dual positions on these issues. On the one hand, the MTUC wants foreign workers to receive the same benefits and payments as local workers and urges the government to take measures against foreign workers' exploitation by unscrupulous agents (Rudnick 1996: 47). On the other hand, unions do not seem to be otherwise actively involved in changing the plight of the foreign workers (Rudnick 1996: 47). Unions fear that by recruiting large numbers of immigrant workers the labour market would be adversely affected. At a national conference on guest workers organized by the union movement in 1994 it was stated that: 'there is no doubt that there is a dampening effect on the general wage increase through the employment of guest workers, as they are generally paid lower wages' (MTUC, in Rudnick 1996: 48).

Datuk Lim Ah Lek, former Minister of Human Resources, stated that the TUA did not give foreign workers rights to union membership (Azman 1995). However, such an argument can be disputed. Since the TUA states that foreigners cannot hold executive positions in trade unions, it can be interpreted that they can become members. Furthermore, the IRA has no provisions to exclude foreigners from collective agreements. However, the reality is that the Immigration Department has placed conditions on foreign workers' permits that effectively bar them from joining trade unions (Wu 2006: 11).

There has been, in any case, a shift in the work environment in Malaysia: more skilled workers, female workers, flexibility in job design and use of information and communication technology (ICT) have brought about new ways of participating in the workforce. Increasingly work, and in particular, knowledge-based jobs, need not be performed in formal working environments. A former president of the MTUC, Zainal (2001), states that teleworking, part-time work and job sharing are increasingly features in Malaysia. Knowledge workers work on highly varied terms and conditions of work and remuneration. Unions, which traditionally draw their collective strength from the standardization of terms and conditions of work through collective agreements, will find the growing individualization of work, particularly in the knowledge work sector, an organizational and leadership challenge.

More and more women are entering the paid workforce. In developing new structures, unions should reflect on how few women take part in discussions on the future of the union movement. Furthermore, the MTUC, as the national labour centre, and unions, will have to re-invent themselves as e-organizations. The union movement must make better use of ICT, which is sorely lacking. ICT would be able to support union membership database systems, websites, websites to support political and corporate campaigns, on-line vocational learning for members, on-line education for officials, delegates and members, communication with members and delegates and on-line surveys and news.

Conclusion

What will a trade union need to look like to address the aspirations of a new generation who could be better known as 'Dr Mahathir's children', that is, those born during his long premiership which focused on development, who are now adults and are in the job market or are already employed? These young workers represent the building blocs of the unions of the future, yet they do not offer a bright picture for unionism in Malaysia. While there are no specific studies on youth participation in unions, research in Australia, New Zealand, North America and Europe shows a decline in youth membership in unions, and in some countries, at an alarming rate. The work attitudes of the new generation of younger workers are different. Their interest is greater in non-work benefits and they are less keen to join the labour movement. The failure to mobilize young people will have greater consequences in the years to come.

Nevertheless, issues such as workers' rights, job security, social protection, career development and productivity growth have to be collectively addressed in a tripartite relationship. Malaysia's dependency on global markets, accompanied by the need to attract foreign investors and keep investments does not seem to augur well for the union movement. It continues to fight an uphill battle in trying to organize the unorganized into a union of their own choosing. While the former Prime Minister saw trade unions as 'superfluous', the outlook for unionism under of the government of Abdullah Ahmad Badawi is still unclear. The fundamental nature of IR in Malaysia's workplaces appears to remain unchanged by Malaysia's economic development drive.

Note

1 These words appear both in legislation and in published material. Examples are provided below.
   Anantaraman, V. (1997) 'The same caution is valid for the parties depositing the concluded agreement with the Registrar of the Court for the purpose of the Court's cognizance. A lapse of three months between the signing of a collective agreement by the parties and the court taking cognizance of the agreement is not common' (p. 96). '… the variation has legal effect only if it has been taken cognizance of by the Industrial Court' (p. 97).
   Section 17(1) of the Industrial Relations Act 1967 'A collective agreement which has been taken cognizance of by the Court shall be deemed to be an award …

Bibliography

Anantaraman, A. (1997) *Malaysian Industrial Relations: Law and Practice*, Serdang: Universiti Putra Malaysia Press.

Azman, A. (1995) 'Lim: adequate laws to protect foreign workers', *New Straits Times*, September 24.

Bhopal, M. (2001) 'Malaysian unions in political crisis: assessing the impact of the Asian contagion', *Asia Pacific Business Review*, 8(2): 73–100.

Claessens, S., Djankov, S. and Lang, L. H. P. (1999) *Who Controls East Asian Corporations – and the Implications for Legal Reform*, Policy Research Working Paper Series, No. 24, Washington, DC: World Bank.

Department of Statistics (2005) *Yearbook of Statistics 2005*, Kuala Lumpur: Department of Statistics.

Department of Statistics (2006a) *The Malaysian Economy in Brief*, Kuala Lumpur: Department of Statistics.

Department of Statistics (2006b) *Malaysia Economic Statistics – Time Series 2005*, Kuala Lumpur: Department of Statistics.

Department of Statistics (2006c) *Key Statistics,* http://www.statistics.gov.my (accessed 26 June 2006).

Department of Trade Unions (2006) *Statistical Summary of Labour and Human Resources*, http://www.mohr.gov.my/mohr_key.php (accessed 30 June 2006).

Fernandez, L. (1993) 'It's hard to stay together', *Sunday Star*, November 7: 18.

Fernandez, L. (1996) 'Unionism's alive but not kicking', *The Star*, December 7: 23.

Fernandez, L. (1997) 'More expected from the MTUC', *The Star*, January 25.

Gengadharan, K. P. (1990) 'Dispute settlement – the Malaysian system', *LAWASIA Second International Seminar on Labour Law Proceedings*, 28–30 September, p. 1.

Hodgkinson, A. and Nyland, C. (2001) 'Space, subjectivity and the investment location decision: the case of Illawarra', *Journal of Industrial Relations*, 43(4): 438–61.

ILO (1980) *Social and Labour Bulletin No. 3*, Geneva: International Labour Organization.

Jomo, K. S. (1994) *U-Turn? Malaysian Economic Development Policy after 1990*, Townsville, QLD: James Cook University.

Jomo, K. S. (1995) 'Capital, the state and labour in Malaysia', in J. Schor and J. You (eds) *Capital, the State and Labour*, Aldershot: United Nations Press.

Jomo, K. S. and Todd, P. (1994) *Trade Unions and the State in Peninsular Malaysia*, Kuala Lumpur: Oxford University Press.

Josey, A. (1958) *Trade Unionism in Malaya*, 2nd edn, Singapore: Donald Moore.

KLSE (2006) *Top 100 Companies*, http://www.klse.com.my/website/bm/market_information/ftse_bm_indices/ (accessed 5 October 2006).

Kuruvilla, S. (1996a) 'National industrialisation strategies and their influence on patterns of HR practices', *Human Resource Management Journal*, 6(3): 22–41.

Kuruvilla, S. (1996b) 'Industrialization strategies and national industrial relations policy in South East Asia: India, Malaysia, Singapore and the Philippines', *Industrial and Labor Relations Review*, 49(4): 635–57.

Kuruvilla, S. and Arudsothy, P. (1995) 'Economic development strategy, government labour policy and firm-level industrial relations practices in Malaysia', in A. Verma, T. A. Kochan and R. Lansbury (eds) *Employment Relations in the Asian Economies*, London: Routledge.

Kuruvilla, S. and Venkataratnam, C. S. (1996) 'Economic development and industrial relations: the case of south and southeast Asia', *Industrial Relations Journal*, 27(1): 9–23.

Leap, T. L. (1995) *Collective Bargaining and Labor Relations*, 2nd edn, Upper Saddle River, NJ: Prentice Hall.

Leong, C. H. (1991) 'Late industrialization along with democratic politics in Malaysia', unpublished doctoral thesis, Harvard University.

Maimunah, A. (1996) *Malaysian Employment Law and Industrial Relations*, Kuala Lumpur: McGraw-Hill.

Maimunah, A. (2003) *Malaysian Industrial Relations and Employment Law*, 4th edn, Kuala Lumpur: McGraw-Hill.

Malaysiakini (2001) 'Ban on national union for electronics workers to stay'. http://www.freeanwar.com/news012001/mk210801.htm (accessed 10 November 2003).

Martin, R. M. (1989) *Trade Unionism: Purposes and Forms*, Oxford: Clarendon Press.

MEF (2006) *Annual Report 2005*, Petaling Jaya, Malaysia: Malaysian Employers Federation.

MHR (1991) *Labour Indicators 1990*, Kuala Lumpur: Ministry of Human Resources.

MHR (2006) *Statistical Summary of Labour and Human Resource*, http://www.mohr.gov.my/mohr_key.php (accessed 30 June 2006).

Miles, M. A., Holmes, K. R. and O'Grady, M. A. (2006) *Index of Economic Freedom*, Washington, DC: Heritage Foundation/Dow Jones.

Mohamed, A. (2005) *Drivers of Competitiveness in Malaysia*, Australia Malaysia Free Trade Agreement – Conference Proceedings, Australian APEC Study Centre, Monash

University, Melbourne, Australia. Available at: http://www.apec.org.au/event_list2. asp?type=conf.

MTUC (1976–8) *Report of the General Council*, Kuala Lumpur: Malaysian Trades Union Congress.

MTUC (1997–8) *Report of the General Council,* Kuala Lumpur: Malaysian Trades Union Congress.

MTUC (2004) *Memorandum to YAB Datuk Seri Abdullah Ahmad Badawi, Prime Minister of Malaysia, on serious problems facing trade unions and workers*, Kuala Lumpur: Malaysian Trade Unions Congress, January 19.

Navamukundan, A. (2002) 'Industrial relations issues and promotion of social dialogue in plantation sector in Malaysia', in A. Sivananthiran and C. S. Venkata Ratnam (eds) *Labour and Social Issues in Plantations in South Asia: Role of Social Dialogue*, New Delhi: South Asia Multidisciplinary Advisory Team-International Labour Organization (ILO-SAAT)/Indian Industrial Relations Association (IIRA).

Navamukundan, A. and Subramaniam, G. (2003) 'Decent work in agriculture in Malaysia', in D. P. A. Naidu and A. Navamukundan (eds) *Decent Work in Agriculture in Asia*, Bangkok: International Labour Office.

NMP (2006) *9th Malaysia Plan 2006–2010*, Putrajaya: Economic Planning Unit, Prime Minister's Department.

NUBE (National Union of Bank Employees) (2006) *History*, http://www.nube.org.my/ history.asp (accessed 20 October 2006).

Peetz, D. and Todd, P. (2001) 'Otherwise you're on your own: unions and bargaining in Malaysian banking', *International Journal of Manpower*, 22(4): 333–49.

Rajasekaran, G. (2002) 'Impact of globalization on workers and trade unions', paper presented to the MTUC/LO Norway National Workshop on Globalization and its Impact on Workers in Malaysia, Petaling Jaya, 16–17 September.

Rasiah, R. (1994) 'Flexible production systems and local machine tool subcontracting: electronics transnationals in Malaysia', *Cambridge Journal of Economics*, 18(3): 279–98.

Rowley, C. and Bhopal, M. (2005a) 'The role of ethnicity in employment relations', *Asian Pacific Journal of Human Resources*, 43(3): 308–31.

Rowley, C. and Bhopal, M. (2005b) 'Ethnicity as a management issue and resource', *Asia Pacific Business Review*, 4(1): 105–33.

Rowley, C. and Bhopal, M. (2006) 'The ethnic factor in state–labour relations: the case of Malaysia', *Capital and Class*, 88: 87–116.

Rudnick, A. (1996) *Foreign Labour in Malaysian Manufacturing: Bangladeshi Workers in the Textile Industry*, Kuala Lumpur: Insan.

Salih, K., Young, M. and Rasiah, R. (1987) *Transnational Capital and Local Conjuncture: the Semiconductor Industry in Penang*, Kuala Lumpur: Malaysian Institute of Economic Research.

Selvarani, P. and Abas, M. (2004) 'Airline's union officials under probe', *Malay Mail*, January 31.

Shamsuddin, B. (2006) 'Impact of globalisation and technical innovation on industrial relations – employer perspective,' paper presented to the Regional Policy Dialogue Workshop on Industrial Relations: Globalization, Regional Integration and Technical Innovation, Kuala Lumpur, 11–15 September.

Shatsari, R. S. and Kamal, H. H. (2006) 'The right to collective bargaining in Malaysia in the context of ILO standards', *Asian Journal of Comparative Law*, 1(1): 1–20.

Spinanger, D. (1986) *Industrialisation Policies and Regional Economic Development in Malaysia,* Singapore: Oxford University Press.

Star, The (1996) 'MTUC wants speedy recognition', December 17.

Star, The (2002) 'Don't interfere in our affairs, Zainal tells MEF', March 4.

Sun, The (2002) 'Bank employees picket: 1,000 union members defy human resources minister' November 22.

Sun, The (2003) 'NUBE may face legal action, says Fong', August 12.

Todd, P. and Peetz, D. (2001) 'Malaysian industrial relations at century's turn: vision 2020 or a spectre of the past?' *International Journal of Human Resource Management,* 12(8): 1365–82.

Treasury (2005) *GDP 1990–2004 in Constant Prices.* Online. Available at: http://www. treasury.gov.my (accessed 10 June 2006).

Wad, P. (1988) 'The Japanization of the Malaysian trade union movement', in R. Southall (ed.) *Trade Unions and the New Industrialization of the Third World*, London: Zed Books.

Windmuller, J. (1987) 'Comparative study of methods and practices', in J. Windmuller (ed.) *Collective Bargaining in Industrialized Market Economies: A Reappraisal*, Geneva: International Labour Organization, pp. 3–161.

Wu, M. A. (1982) *Industrial Relations Law of Malaysia*, Kuala Lumpur: Longman.

Wu, M. A. (2006) *Industrial Relations Law of Malaysia*, 3rd edn, Kuala Lumpur: Longman.

Zainal, R. (2001) 'Employment concerns of the future', *Business Times*, June 21.

9 Trade unions in China

In search of a new role in the 'harmonious society'

Malcolm Warner

Introduction

Trade unions in the People's Republic of China (PRC) today have come a long way from their early days but their history still conditions their responses to events and they still live in the shadow of the Chinese Communist Party (CCP). Yet China is changing dramatically, as its apparently breathtaking economic growth continues to truly transform the society.

In this chapter, we will consider the past, present and future direction of trade unions in the Chinese workplace as a *country case-study*, so that we can compare it with that of unions in Asia and elsewhere. We will thereby address what they have in common with other unions around the world, especially in Asia, as well as where they are different, even singular. The treatment will be historical, analytical and comparative.

This chapter will tackle the following *key* questions regarding these themes, as raised in Chapter 2: how have Chinese trade unions organized themselves to represent and defend their members' and economic, political and social interests? What are the main roles of trade unions in China? What impacts have trade unions had on workers, enterprises and business in general? And how can we best explain the development path of China's trade union movement?

In order to tackle these themes, this chapter present the following sections: Section 1 looks at the introductory questions as above; Section 2 looks at the contextual and historical issues, not withstanding the underpinning theoretical approach on different types of unionisms, the evolution of trade union development in the PRC given its changes in economic and political environments, and an overview of union membership. Section 3 scrutinizes union types and structure, their external relationship with the state, business/market and society in general as whole and their interactions with each other. Section 4 presents the key activities of trade unions, such as their involvement in collective bargaining, legal enactment, social benefits and so on. Section 5 attempts to explain the development, structure and strategies of contemporary Chinese unions in terms of coping with political change, economic uncertainty and competition in the market economy. The last section sums up the possible future of unions in China and the implications for theory as well as policy consideration.

The study of trade unions in China remains problematic. The role of unions in socialist economies in general has always been a difficult issue to deal with (see Ruble 1981; Ng and Warner 1998; Clarke 2005). Since they were deemed not to be autonomous nor able to 'bargain' freely, they were also seen as appendages of the state, for example.[1] But in many ways, they are clearly recognizable as unions, as will be seen from the data presented in this chapter. In terms of the Webbs' classic definition of unions (Webb and Webb 1894) for instance, the existence of Chinese unions as a 'continuous association' of workers is clear; in Child *et al.*'s (1973) schema, these organizations have both the 'representative' as well as 'administrative' functions found in unions; again, in Hyman's (2001) terms, they can be seen as incorporating the following models: (1) labour market actors; (2) vehicles of anti-capitalist mobilization; (3) agents of social integration, and so on; so, the Chinese unions, like counterparts elsewhere, may have multiple, often conflicting roles, for example accommodating to market forces but also attempting to do the best for their members' interests.

Context and history

Trade unions are a relatively recent institution in China's long historical narrative (Ng and Warner 1998). After all, China has had the longest continuous existence of any nation-state in the world. Such a tradition is often used to explain what is held to be quintessentially 'Chinese' in cultural terms (see Child and Warner 2003; Warner 2003). The nation has had a long Imperial history that extended from 221 BC right up to the beginning of the twentieth century, when the Republican Revolution of 1911 took place and later the Communist 'Liberation' occurred in 1949. Since then, the present regime has enjoyed over half a century of rule, punctuated by both stability and turmoil. The death of Mao Zedong in 1976 ended what one might call the 'formative' phase of 'Red' China. After a short interregnum, Deng Xiaoping, formerly called a 'capitalist-roader', became the Paramount Leader. He launched a new era of economic reforms in 1978, with pragmatic slogans that dramatically changed economic life and with it, management–labour relations, such as 'it doesn't matter if the cat is black or white, so long as it catches mice' and 'to get rich is beautiful'.[2]

From the 1950s onwards, the Soviet-inspired state-owned enterprises (SOEs) had been *de rigueur* in China, with their distinctive 'iron rice bowl' (*tian fan wan*) cradle-to-grave employment system and relatively egalitarian wage system (see Warner 1995). Once hired, workers had jobs for life; dismissals were rare. One old adage was 'the managers pretended to pay us and we pretended to work'. The 1960s even appeared to put 'worker-power' further to the fore in the throes of the Cultural Revolution, yet the experimentation eventually fizzled out (see Perry 1993).

The next phase of change came after Deng Xiaoping's economic reforms were introduced in the late 1970s, with the Four Modernizations (*sige xiandaihua*) and the Open Door (*kaifang*) policies that set out to transform a wide range of hide-bound institutions which set about learning how to be more efficient from the

West and Japan (see Child and Heavens 1999; Child 2000). Even so, afraid of a Polish *Solidarity*-style reaction (Wilson 1990), Deng tried to sweeten the pill of reform by encouraging a new kind of workers' committee (see Ng and Warner 1998), even as he was creating a 'nascent' labour-market that heralded the demise of the 'iron rice bowl'. Finally in 1992, managers were allowed to 'manage', to 'hire and fire' and so on (see Child 2000). Deng's economic reforms or variations thereof continue to the present day.

Over 1.3 billion people now live in the People's Republic. Its economy currently accounts for close to one-eighth of world output in purchasing power parity (PPP) terms; the gross domestic product (GDP) per capita/PPP was US$6,800 at the end of 2005 and still rising (see Table 9.1). By 2006, the Chinese economy was on track for historically high levels of economic performance. Entry into the World Trade Organization (WTO) in 2001 gave a boost to the critical economic indicators. The new decade witnessed very high annual rates of growth in GDP, culminating in the early 2000s, when it rose to around 9 per cent in the official statistics and industrial production grew almost half as much again.[3] Foreign direct investment

Table 9.1 Contextual factors – China

General statistics	
Population (2005)	1.3 billion
Area (square kilometres)	9.6 million

Employment proportion in:
   Primary
   Secondary
   Tertiary
	
	50
	23
	27

Urban population (% of total population)	376 m
GDP per capita (2005)	US$6,800 [PPP]

Growth rates (%)
   Average for 1985–95
   Average for 1995–2005
	
	10.1
	8.6

Unemployment (%) [official rate]:
   1985–1995
   1995–2005
	
	2.3
	4.6

Summary description	
Openness and degree of competition: International trade (import + export) as % of GDP World Bank regulation index	 31 + 34 Rank 93
Political context: System of regime Political stability	 Changing from top-down 'Party-State hegemony' in the direction of 'Party-guided pluralism'

Source: State Statistical Bureau (2005) *China Labour Statistics Yearbook*, Beijing: State Statistical Bureau.

(FDI) flooded into the economy. Chinese exports burgeoned; foreign exchange reserves were flourishing at the end of 2005. Over 30 per cent of world GDP growth (in PPP terms) has been attributed to China's economic surge.

The pace of rapid growth was achieved however at a high cost internally, with rising job losses, especially in the state-owned sector, letting go many in the urban labour force, particularly older workers and a disproportionately high number of women workers in industries such as textiles. Unemployment jumped to over 4.5 per cent officially (China Statistical Bureau 2005a) but probably was at least double this in reality (see Lee and Warner 2007).

The *Gini coefficient* has veered in the direction of greater inequality (around 0.45[4] – see Table 9.2), probably becoming one of the most unequal in East Asia, which seems odd for a country officially calling itself 'socialist' (Khan and Riskin 2005). Wage income also grew at a slower rate than overall income. This change was due to the worsening urban employment situation. Employment in urban China fell by more than 9 per cent. The demise of the 'iron rice bowl' (*tie fan wan*) system, of 'jobs for life' and the in-house welfare state for state sector workers, constituted a 'sea-change' in the Chinese way of managing people. The evolution of a nascent labour market changed both institutions and behaviour (see Warner 2005). There have been rapid increases in private, foreign, joint-stock enterprise and self-employment categories, but these have not been fast enough to offset the fall in state and collective enterprises jobs on a per capita basis (Khan and Riskin 2005: 369).

Trade unions in China have long been an established institution set up to defend workers' interests. Yet they are historically a relatively recent phenomenon

Table 9.2 Trade unions in China

General statistics	
Number of unions (end of 2005)	15 national industrial unions in single federation
Number of union members (end of 2005)	c. 140m
Union density (end of 2005)	M
Level of collective bargaining	L
Summary description	
Main union type	State/Party dominated federation
Main union structure	ACFTU – only union permitted
Extent of unity of peak organization	Changed from H to M
State control of unions	H
Involvement in collective bargaining	L

Source: State Statistical Bureau (2005) *China Labour Statistics Yearbook*, Beijing: State Statistical Bureau.

Notes
H – high, M – medium, L – low.

and did not appear in their present guise until the early 1920s, after the First World War had run its course. The Chinese Communist Party (CCP) was first on the scene, in 1921. The All-China Federation of Trade Unions (ACFTU) was founded a little later, in May 1925, making it now an octogenarian, as an organization to 'represent' the Chinese 'working-class', mainly in a few industrialized centres and the major sea-ports, like Canton (now Guangzhou) and Shanghai.

The ACFTU was soon suppressed by the Nationalist authorities and went underground in 1927, when the Communists and Nationalists were locked in open inter-factional conflict. The organization was to surface after the Second World War and in 1948 it assembled its Sixth National Congress. In 1949 it was institutionalized as the nation's trade union fulcrum after the 1949 'Liberation' (Harper 1969; Hearn 1977), with the *Trade Union Law* of 1950, updated at the Seventh National People's Congress in 1992 and amended at the Ninth National People's Congress in 2001.

The ACFTU is the world's largest national trade union body in terms of its formal membership numbers, although some say much of its adherence is 'on paper' only.[5] By the mid-1980s, the ACFTU membership exceeded 80 million workers, covering some 15 national industrial unions, over 22,000 local trade union organizations and more than 460,000 enterprise unions, employing around 300,000 full-time union officials. By 1990, there were over 89 million members, in 15 national industrial unions, 30 provincial or municipal union councils and more than 560,000 grassroots trade union organizations. By the end of the millennium, the size of the membership stood at over 133 million, while the number of grassroots trade unions registered some 1.7 million. By its eightieth anniversary, at the end of 2004, the ACFTU was said to have around 137 million members, covering 1.93 million enterprises; by 2005, it had over 140 million (see Table 9.3). Of the total members, 46 million were to be found in state-owned enterprises, accounting for 45 per cent of the workforce; those in the private sector numbered 55 million, making up 54 per cent. On a note of caution, it is worth noting that Chinese official statistics are often unreliable and it is hard to gain impartial confirmation of the numbers and percentages cited above.

Table 9.3 What do trade unions do in China?

Extent of collective bargaining	L
Level of collective bargaining	Industry and enterprise levels
Extent of joint consultation	L
Strikes, working days lost per 1,000 employed	L
Degree of state intervention in employment protection	H
Income inequality	M (Gini coefficient = 0.45)

Source: State Statistical Bureau (2005) *China Labour Statistics Yearbook*, Beijing: State Statistical Bureau.

Notes
H – high, M – medium, L – low.

Union types and structure

Chinese trade unions do not follow conventional union models such as those that characterize Western economies; they are more akin to the ones that evolved in communist states in the last (twentieth) century (Ruble 1981). The latter were 'top-down' organizations that were under the hegemony of the Party. The ACFTU, as noted above, falls into this category, again albeit 'with Chinese characteristics' (see Ng and Warner 1998). Since the original Soviet stereotype has now largely been effaced, the main Leninist 'transmission-belt' unions that remain are to be found in residual 'hard-line' communist regimes such as Cuba and North Korea. 'Soft-line' and 'transitional' economies such as China and Vietnam have reformed their organizational structures and regulatory regimes for their unions, but the latter it must be said still do not approach their Western counterparts as independent workers' organizations (see Warner *et al.* 2005).

The ACFTU is in effect an 'organ of the State' and has been since 1949. There is only one union allowed by the Party and that is the ACFTU (see Table 9.4). *The Trade Union Law* of 1950 enshrined its monopoly. This piece of labour legislation survived almost intact until 1992, when a new version was enacted, and more broadly until 1994 when a new portmanteau *Labour Law* was approved, functional in the following year. The amendment of the *Trade Union Law* in 2001 reasserted the organizational control of the ACFTU by the Party (Article 4). This consolidated the ban on any trade union independent of the ACFTU structure (Articles 10 and 11).

The main official goal of the amendment to the 1994/5 law was to boost the legal status of ACFTU. The 2001 legislation entrenches the position of the ACFTU as the sole legal representative of workers and employees in enterprises. It also consolidates the legal rights of ACFTU over its assets and revenues. This underscores the reality that the ACFTU is not a 'workers' organization' but a 'quasi-state body', and that any other representative labour organizations outside the ACFTU are legally prohibited from forming. At the same time, the 1994/5 *Labour Law* also placed the emerging labour-market at its heart, legalizing individual and collective contracts, dismissals and other workforce management practices, with the ACFTU wielding oversight (Warner 1996).

Adversarial v. cooperative

The ACFTU is basically a 'cooperative' institution, as it continues to be an appendage of the Communist Party. Although there are no independent unions in China, there has been a move in recent years to comply, on paper at least, with International Labour Organization (ILO) practice and thus move to a convergence of sorts (see Howell 2006). Commentators have sometimes noted that China may possibly be slowly moving towards Western practice; but most observers would agree that this change has largely been one of degree. Workers in China have and continue to confront their employers about conditions when pressed hard enough, but this is not a response always organized or supported by the union.

Table 9.4 Explaining Chinese trade union development, structure and strategy

Political context of degrees of liberalization and autonomy	
	The society is evolving from top-down 'Party-State hegemony' in the direction of 'Party-guided pluralism'. The attitude towards the union movement has changed from Leninist 'transmission-belt' to post-Deng 'longer leash'. But Party politics still influence union movement substantially.
Economic context	
Product markets Financial markets Labour market	H trade as % of GDP H degree of competition M level of openness to market financing H level of state ownership M level of foreign ownership M level of institutional ownership Supply is larger than demand in low-skills occupations, with downsizing and unemployment as SOEs decline. Demand is larger than supply in high-skills positions.
Employer context	
Organization – top 100 as % of total Employer organization membership Multinational Unitarist vs. Pluralist	 H L–M M Majority have 'unitarist' management approach.

Source: State Statistical Bureau (2005) *China Labour Statistics Yearbook*, Beijing: State Statistical Bureau.

Notes
H – high, M – medium, L – low.

Unions now have to cope with a vast range of new business owners, foreign and domestic. There has been a flowering of new ownership-structures such as joint ventures (JVs) and privately-owned enterprises (POEs). One manifestation of these changes has been the move to individual and collective contracts, of which the latter may be said to approximate to collective bargaining and therefore may raise the prospect of adversarial relations (Ng and Warner 1998). There is little evidence, however, of much resembling a Western-style approach, although in some cases the innovation represents a surrogate for bargaining of sorts.[6] In 2006, there was a move to a new *Labour Contract Law*, greatly opposed by foreign employers in multinationals that have invested in China, more of which later.

Democratic v. oligarchic

Where Chinese trade unions follow the Soviet format (see Ruble 1981), they claim democratic and representative status, as the Constitution implies (see above). In reality, they are plainly oligarchic, as many observers of the phenomenon will testify (Chan 2001). Whether the recent attempt to introduce greater grassroots influence by more open elections has achieved much is debatable. A recent working paper (Howell 2006) sets out to examine this attempt to open up elections in the ACFTU, ponder its significance for reforming the ACFTU, bettering workers' conditions and the implications for wider processes of governance in China. The paper's author starts by outlining the pressures on the ACFTU to reform its organizational structures, modes of operation, and interest-representation and the steps taken to address these issues. Three major challenges, the paper continues, facing the proponents of direct elections in the trade union structure are: the issue of resistance at all levels; the need to make clearer the identity and interests of the union; and the growing power of both domestic and foreign capital. Despite these challenges, however, there is:

> also some room for optimism. The changes within the trade union, and in particular the direct elections, are not isolated events, unique to the trade union. They are part of a more general attempted shift in China towards a more inclusionary process of governance.
>
> (Howell 2006: 25)

Chinese trade unions apply the twin organizational principles of having leadership on industrial lines, as well as recruiting on a locality basis. There are currently 31 federations of trade unions all told, based respectively on provinces, autonomous regions and municipalities directly under the control of the Central ACFTU government and 10 national industrial unions in industries such as construction, defence, communications, manufacturing, aviation and banking.

Organization in the Chinese workplace is thus complex. It is more bureaucratic than in the capitalist West and its form is neither a result of either mere custom and practice on the one hand nor collective negotiation on the other. Workplace organization is highly politicized.

What do unions do?

The ACFTU had not pursued collective bargaining historically; in Leninist terms such a move would have smacked of 'economism', yet at certain points in times Chinese unions have followed this road (see Perry 1993). But its mission over the decades has been more 'holistic'. Article 6 of the *Trade Union Law* reads as follows:

> The basic duties and functions of trade unions are to safeguard the legitimate rights and interests of workers and staff members. While protecting the

overall interests of the entire Chinese people, trade unions shall represent and safeguard the legitimate rights and interests of workers and staff members. Trade unions shall coordinate labor relations and safeguard the rights and interests enjoyed in work by the workers and staff members of enterprises through consultation at an equal footing and the collective contract system.

(*Trade Union Law*, amended 2001)

In Russia as well as China, the incidence of the signing of 'collective agreements' is seen as an indicator of the effectiveness of both local and regional trade union organizations (see Ashwin and Clarke 2002; Clarke 2005). But such collective bargaining in both countries is still characterized:

by a high degree of formalism, collective agreements rarely providing any benefits not already accorded to the labour force and often illegally providing conditions inferior to those already provided by the law … . Moreover, while the trade union leadership encouraged primary organizations to play a more active role, at the same time it discouraged them from taking any effective action to support such a role, for fear that overt conflict would undermine the political role of the trade union as the institution that guarantees social peace.

(Clarke 2005: 27)

In China, the ACFTU has in its turn introduced 'collective contracts' but whether these may be considered as agents of genuine collective bargaining is moot, as noted above (see Ng and Warner 1998). Thus, at best, the trade union leadership is seen as transmitting contradictory messages to the organization's base.

The upshot is that workers' protests continue to be articulated largely outside and often against the traditional trade unions. In China, the number of wild-cat strikes (at least recorded officially) runs into tens of thousands nationally, over 78,000 recorded protest 'incidents' to the end of 2005. One observer has gone as far as to say that:

when some of these workers do show the courage to organize, sometimes in tens of thousands, they never go to the ACFTU. This has most recently been shown when over 80,000 petroleum and metal workers staged mass street-demonstrations in Daqing and Liaoyang, in the northeast, in March and April, 2002. Instead the protesters declare their actions, which sometimes last for weeks, to be spontaneous outbreaks without any leadership or organization. On occasion, protesters have tried to organize independent unions or alternative bodies to represent their demands. A most recent example of this is the two month-long struggle waged by 50,000 workers from the Daqing Oilfield who formed their own union body.

(Leung 2002: 1)

In spite of its constrained role in Chinese society, the ACFTU has contributed to a raft of new legislation over the past 20 years to deal with the changing situation of workers (see Ding *et al.* 2002). This has included the 1992 *Law on the Protection of Women's Rights and Interests in the Workplace*, the introduction of the *Labour Law* in 1994/5, and the revision of the *Trade Union Law* in 2001.

On 20 March 2006, the National People's Congress (NPC) released a draft *Labour Contract Law of the People's Republic of China* and asked for comments from the general public. The draft law, aimed at supplementing the existing labour law, was scheduled for deliberation by the NPC in 2006 but this was to be delayed (*China Daily*, 27 December 2006: 1).

On 30 June 2007, however, a new *Labour Contract Law* was enacted by the Standing Committee of the NPC. The law hopes to create a 'harmonious society' (*hexie shehui*) now the new catchword of the present leadership (See Quarterly Chronicle and Documentation 2007: 261ff) and be more inclusive, particularly of those on the boundaries of present jurisdiction, like migrant workers (Gill 2006: 3). Although at the time of writing the full implications of the new law are unclear, it does require employers to provide written contracts to all workers, restricts the use of temporary labour and makes it harder to lay off employees. The new law is scheduled to come into effect in early 2008, as is a new mediation law (*New York Times*, 30 June 2007; *The Economist*, 28 July 2007).

The role of the unions in achieving economic outcomes for their members is a contentious issue, since during the years of the 'command economy' (at least up to the 1978 reforms) the share of income allocated to wages was decided by central planning via a nationally applicable wage-grade system. Since Deng's reforms, however, especially after 1992, workers' incomes have been decided more in relation to productivity, mainly through a complex wage system including group-based bonuses. Since the move to a more market-based economy, wages have become decidedly less egalitarian, as can be seen from the change in the Gini coefficient referred to earlier. Clearly, the progress of reform in the state-owned and collective enterprises and the rapid growth of private, foreign and mixed ownership enterprises has made the structure of wages quite unequal, with the pressure of market forces shaping these trends (Khan and Riskin 2005). These changes may be seen as the continuation of a longer-term trend: the first is the growth of wage inequality driven by the differential rates of growth of labour productivity across industries; the second underlying process is that of growing inter-province income inequality (Woo and Ren 2002). It is precisely in these sectors that the ACFTU has been traditionally less prominent, although claiming to have made up some ground in membership in recent years.

A number of government policy responses in recent years have however contributed to the highest growth in per capita annual net income of rural households (2,936 yuan) since 1997, registering a real increase of 6.8 per cent after price factors are deducted (China Statistical Bureau 2005b). Agriculture, however, is for the most part not unionized in China. Government initiatives are a major factor that has increased job availability in the rural sector (see Lee and Warner 2004), while adoption of the 'great western development strategy' has led to a large increase in infrastructure investment in the regions. Governments and departments at all levels have been conscientiously carrying out policies concerning employment (see Wei 1998); and the liberalization of the *hukou* residence-based permit system has facilitated a great deal of *de facto* movement of labour out of rural areas.

The non-economic dimension, the ACFTU might argue, may be as important, as far as unions nationally having a say on a wide range of wider policy issues, such the number of hours worked, national days off and holiday time and so on, as well as in better working conditions. In addition, other outcomes often spoken of may include the provision of training, encouraging worker participation in business decisions, profit sharing schemes, and workers' involvement in the ownership of enterprises. Unions are also encouraged (at least in theory) to actively promote the introduction of modern management systems in firms.

Unions have, however, frequently been seen by their critics as having a poor reputation (see Chan 2001), as just conforming to the official ACFTU line and merely attending to residual duties such as organizing sports and leisure activities at plant level for workers in many SOEs. The union at a national level however often plays a role in government mobilization campaigns, as it did, in a recent example, in the case of the SARS epidemic. In April 2003, the ACFTU urged that trade unions 'do whatever it takes to curb the spread of the deadly disease, popularize prevention knowledge, care for medical workers and assist the government in its effort to combat SARS' (ACFTU 2003: 1). Meanwhile, the ACFTU did commit 3.7 million yuan (about US$4.5million) to local trade unions and medical workers to help prevent the SARS outbreak.

Explaining the development, structure and strategies of trade unions

Chinese trade unions have long been organized to represent workers in ways based on the bedrock Chinese version of Marxist-Leninism, suggestively dubbed Confucian-Leninism by one leading scholar (Pye 1990). The most frequently used explanation of how unions are organized in this context is through the use of the Leninist 'transmission belt' model, linking the Party at the top down to the working class at the base. As the Principles of the ACFTU set out: 'The Chinese trade unions are mass organizations of the Chinese working class led by the Communist Party of China and formed by the workers and staff members on a voluntary basis' (ACFTU 1998: 1). As in other former and current communist regimes, trade unions were considered a symbolic institution that legitimized the 'dictatorship of the proletariat' in terms of its ideological, political and sociological dimensions. Chinese trade unions still do perform a wide range of roles, both representative and administrative (see Child *et al.* 1973).

Since so many economic, social and political activities are dependent on the state in communist countries, the role of the unions is often said to be confined to residuals. The ACFTU has in its turn been a reliable arm of the Party and has done its bidding. It was largely devoted to the mobilization of the urban proletariat, as and when the CCP wished. From the early days of the communist regime on, its role was to boost the regime's legitimacy in the workplace. Any hope it had for any significant autonomous or dissident political stance was quickly stifled.

It is often said that Chinese unions organized not much more than dance parties and sports events by the 1980s (see Ng and Warner 1998). In the 1980s, the present writer was told by workers that if they had a grievance they went to see their manager rather than the union. But the ACFTU had large funds to spend on their vast spectrum of welfare activities and generously provided services for workers, in addition to those provided by their work-unit (*danwei*). But they also often acted as 'police' in the workplace for the authorities in terms of monitoring women workers' fertility cycles at factory level *vis-à-vis* the 'one-child' policy. More recently, their activities have been seen as those of a 'middle-man', acting to facilitate the implementation of labour legislation enacted to enable the market-led form of socialism to work. In the new tripartite China, the ACFTU is considered to represent the workers; the employers' equivalent the Chinese Enterprise Directors' Association (CEDA) speaks for the bosses; and the Ministry of Labour is the figurehead for the state, simulating the tripartite requirements of International Labour Organization (ILO) protocols the country had signed. This indicates perhaps the beginning of the formation of integral players for a form of collective bargaining, albeit 'with Chinese characteristics' as noted earlier (Warner and Ng 1999).

The trajectory of Chinese trade unions since the 1920s may be best seen in the context of China's modernization from a rural to an industrial economy; as agricultural labourers became less proportionately prominent and urban workers grew in number, there was fertile ground for unionization. When the ACFTU was initially established, China was then a largely agricultural country, with a modicum of industrialization in the main cities. The labour force was largely composed of peasants, on which Mao Zedong built his revolution rather than the industrial proletariat as posited by Marx and Lenin, even in 1949 when the 'liberation' took place. During the first decades of the new People's Republic, the industrial base was limited and the proletariat was a small percentage of the Chinese labour force as a whole, but it eventually grew to a dominant role in the economy through industrial weight, even if the peasantry was numerically superior (Ng and Warner 1998). The ACFTU became, as it were, the representative organ of the new 'masters', the *avant-garde* of the working class.

A historical explanation of how Chinese trade unions developed would highlight the 'top-down' legacy of the older Confucian tradition and the newer twentieth-century Leninist one, modified by its more recent evolution, as noted earlier. Both coincide to produce the hierarchical model that we currently find. There is a corresponding institutional and organizational inertia that often permeates Chinese society in general and its labour movement in particular.

Political liberalization and autonomy has thus lagged behind the very rapid rate of economic change. The lack of any significant degree of liberalization and autonomy reflect not only historical influences, but also the very nature of the Party's hegemony, in spite of possible moves in recent years in the direction of a 'civil society' as some claim (see Ogden 2000). Nonetheless, China today is a very different place from what it was in the Maoist years. The PRC has an unprecedented level of GDP per capita, even more if calculated in PPP terms, if with greater economic and social inequality; it is also moving towards a more open regime, with high mobile phone and internet usage, albeit censored in part; it furthermore has a more educated and trained citizenry, if apparently passive politically. Even so, there is only one – still hegemonic – political party, the CCP, and only one – still dominant – trade union, the ACFTU.

The economic context in which the extension of the market has taken place has been one of reform and diversification, as responses to globalization (see Chiu and Frenkel 2000). Before 1978, the PRC was a closed economy; after that date, Deng's open-door policy exposed China to foreign 'know-how', in a repetition of events in the nineteenth century. Students were soon sent abroad in large numbers to assimilate new ideas and skills, although only a modest proportion returned. New ways of running its economy and enterprises filtered in, as well as ways of coping with the labour concomitants of these market-driven forces. In 2001, China entered the WTO and opened up its markets.

China is different from many other countries in Asia. For almost three decades, the state was the main industrial employer. After the economic reforms were launched in 1978, the SOEs became less dominant as we have seen and the non-state sector more visible. There is now a private sector, with both foreign owners and domestic ones. But there are no employers' federations as known in West, except possible surrogate bodies as we have seen and overseas firms' entities like Chambers of Commerce, such as the American one, the AmCham.

Conclusions

The future of unionism in the PRC is unclear and fraught with ambiguities. While the nation has adapted to the economic reforms launched by Deng in 1978, it has not yet fully conceptualized its role in the new globalized economy with which China is confronted and the resultant internal pressures released by the 'Open Door' policy.

Convergences and divergences

There are continuing convergences and divergences between trade unions in China and those in the outside world. As noted earlier, China may be seen as very slowly moving towards Western practice, although this change has largely been superficial. It is clear that in the 'workers' state', whether inside or outside the union context, conflicts of interest have grown between employees and their employers, even in the paternalistic SOEs, and these continue to this day. Increasingly, convergences with the West relate to adapting to globalization and the market forces unleashed by this process. The signing of ILO conventions, entering the WTO, and attempting to comply with the requirements of these organizations are also reflected in current adaptations, most of which have been eclectic and are not systematic.

Nonetheless, China has tried to observe the ILO and WTO commitments it has made, often in the letter, if not always in the spirit, of the agreements. It has attempted to set up a sort of tripartite IR system as in say, the European Union (EU); it has launched a surrogate for collective bargaining; it implemented the *Labour Law* of 1994/5; and the latest *Labour Contract Law* of 2007/8 is another step forward. There is also talk of greater union democracy, but progress has been limited (see Howell 2006).

Yet divergences with the West remain more characteristic of Chinese unions than convergences. Employee relations have been reformed 'with Chinese characteristics' as the phrase goes and the term human resources management (*renli ziyuan guanli*) is now often used (if perhaps a little too inexactly) (see Zhu and Warner 2003; Warner 2005). But the right to strike is still officially unlawful; independent unions are suppressed; and internal union dissent is largely discouraged, in spite of the 'longer leash' being offered to the ACFTU (Howell 2006).

New models

To answer the general question raised in the start of this chapter about how the Chinese union movement might fit into Hyman's (2001) three models, we can see that there is no easy answer. Although the ACFTU has in the past advanced the notion of 'class struggle', this is less and less the case. Today, as noted earlier, the 'harmonious society' (*hexie shehui*) has become the official Party line, even as market forces that disadvantage workers become ever more powerful. The unions in the PRC have adopted more market-oriented strategies with an emphasis on social integration, in a model that looks a lot like that found in Taiwan, as Zhu notes in Chapter 5, this volume (see also Zhu *et al.* 2000; Zhu and Warner 2001).

It is a very different trade union model from that found either in Europe, where trade unions are regarded as agents of social integration and emphasize a social partnership in a constrained capitalist economy; or in the United States, where trade unions behave as labour market actors in one that is less constrained (see Hyman 2001: 3). Trade unionism in China begins to look like a synthesis of both roles, neither of which fares well in the Chinese context given that the workplace is managed in a relatively unitary style (see Table 9.4), and unions are afraid of companies closing down their sites in the PRC and are therefore likely to be more cooperative with management. Such challenges confront the union movement and their routine activities not only in China but also in other Asian countries and elsewhere (Zhu *et al.* 2007). Hence, academics in the industrial relations field continually have to rethink their projections of the future development and patterns of union movements in an increasingly globalized world economy.

A possible change in the model of Chinese trade unionism might be to move in the direction of the Japanese one, with 'one-party' political governance *de facto*, in tandem with a more 'differentiated' trade union representative body like *Rengo* (see Chapter 3) if still under a 'guided' umbrella-federation. But it is still early days *vis-à-vis* such developments and an incremental change on the present *status quo* may be all we see in the next few years.

Notes

1 There are no sources we are aware of that argue the contrary case regarding this lack of independence of Chinese trade unions.
2 Deng's pragmatism and its implications for Chinese management is well documented in a number of books on Chinese management, including Child (2000) and Warner (1995).
3 Even the SARS epidemic of 2003 which led to a short-term fall in GDP of around 0.5 per cent failed to deter the onward surge in growth in the subsequent years, although the World Bank recently revised its estimates of aggregate Chinese GDP by 40 per cent.
4 The coefficient had been as low as 0.20 during the highpoint of Maoism in the 1960s.
5 By this we mean that with a virtual 'check-off' system, ACFTU membership was almost compulsory in the SOEs, with densities of the upper 90 per cent in these enterprises.
6 'Hard' evidence of Western-style collective bargaining in China is very hard to find but 'weak' cases may be found.

Bibliography

ACFTU (All-China Federation of Trade Unions) (2003) *ACFTU News*, 4: 1. Online. Available HTTP: <http://www.acftu.org.cn/0304.htm> (accessed 25 July 2005).

ACFTU (1998) *Constitution*, Beijing: All-China Federation of Trade Unions.

Ashwin, S. and Clarke, S. (2002) *Russian Trade Unions and Industrial Relations in Transition*, Basingstoke and New York: Palgrave.

Chan, A. (2001) *China's Workers Under Assault*, Armonk, NY: M. E. Sharpe.

Child, J. (2000) 'Management and organizations in China: key trends and issues', in J.T. Li, A. S. Tsui and E. Weldon (eds) *Management and Organizations in the Chinese Context*, Basingstoke: Macmillan.

Child, J. and Heavens, S. (1999) ' Managing corporate networks from America to China', in M. Warner (ed.) *China's Managerial Revolution*, London: Frank Cass.

Child, J. and Warner, M. (2003) 'Culture and management in China', in M. Warner (ed.) *Culture and Management in Asia*, London: RoutledgeCurzon.

Child, J., Loveridge, R. and Warner, M. (1973) 'Towards an organizational study of trade unions', *Sociology*, 7(1): 71–91.

China Statistical Bureau (2005a) *National Bureau of Statistics Annual Survey*, Beijing: CSB. Online. Available HTTP: <http://www.stats.gov.cn/english/indicators/index.htm> (accessed 12 August 2005).

China Statistical Bureau (2005b) *Statistical Communique of the People's Republic of China on the 2004 National Economic and Social Development*. Online. Available HTTP: <http://www.stats.gov.cn.> (accessed 12 September 2005).

Chiu, S. W. K. and Frenkel, S. J. (2000) *Globalization and Industrial Relations and Human Resources Change in China*, Bangkok: ILO Regional Office for Asia and the Pacific.

Clarke, S. (2005) 'Post-socialist trade unions: China and Russia', *Industrial Relations Journal*, 36(1): 2–18.

Ding, D. Z., Goodall, K. and Warner, M. (2002). 'The impact of economic reform on the role of trade unions in Chinese enterprises', *International Journal of Human Resource Management*, 13(3): 431–49.

Economist, The (2007) 'Red Flag', 28 July, p.74.

Gill, C. (2006) 'Come the revolution', *The Guardian*, 24 June: 3.

Harper, P. (1969) 'The party and the unions in communist China', *China Quarterly*, 37: 84–119.

Hearn, J. M. (1977) 'W(h)ither the trade unions in China?', *Journal of Industrial Relations*, 19(3): 158–72.

Howell, J. (2006) 'New democratic trends in China? Reforming the All-China Federation of Trade Unions', Working Paper 263, Institute of Development Studies, University of Sussex, April.

Hyman, R. (2001) *Understanding European Trade Unionism*, London: Sage.

Khan, A. R. K. and Riskin, C. (2005) 'China's household income and its distribution, 1995 and 2002', *China Quarterly*, 182: 356–84.

Lee, G. O. M and Warner, M. (2004) 'The Shanghai re-employment model: from local experiment to nation-wide labour market policy', *China Quarterly*, 177: 174–89.

Lee, G. O. M and Warner, M. (2007) *Unemployment in China: Economy, Human Resources and Labour Markets*, London and New York: Routledge.

Leung, T. (2002) 'ACFTU and union organizing', *China Labour Bulletin*, 26 April: 1.

Ng, S. H. and Warner, M. (1998) *China's Trade Unions and Management*, New York: St Martin's Press.

Ogden, S. (2000) 'China's developing civil society: interest groups, trade unions and associational pluralism', in M. Warner (ed.) *Changing Workplace Relations in the Chinese Economy*, New York: St Martin's Press.

Perry, E. J. (1993) *Shanghai on Strike: The Politics of Chinese Labor*, Stanford, CA: Stanford University Press.

People's Republic of China (1951; revised 1992) *Trade Union Law*, Beijing: State Publishing House.

People's Republic of China (1994–5) *Labour Law*, Beijing: State Publishing House.

Pye, L. (1990) 'China: erratic state, frustrated society', *Foreign Affairs*, 69(4): 1–15.

Quarterly Chronicle and Documentation (2007) *The China Quarterly*, 189, 232–85.

Ruble, B. (1981) *Soviet Trade Unions: their development in the 1970s*, Cambridge: Cambridge University Press.

Warner, M. (1995) *The Management of Human Resources in Chinese Industry*, New York: St Martin's Press.

Warner, M. (1996) 'Chinese enterprise reform, human resources and the 1994 *Labour Law*', *International Journal of Human Resource Management*, 7(4): 779–96.

Warner, M. (ed.) (2003) *Culture and Management in Asia*, London and New York: Routledge.

Warner, M. (ed.) (2005) *Human Resource Management in China Revisited*, London and New York: Routledge.

Warner, M. and Ng, S. H. (1999) 'Collective contracts in Chinese enterprises: a new brand of collective bargaining under market socialism', *British Journal of Industrial Relations*, 32(2): 295–314.

Warner, M., Edwards V., Polonsky, G., Pucko, D. and Zhu, Y. (2005) *Management in Transitional Economies: from the Berlin Wall to the Great Wall of China*, London and New York: Routledge.

Webb, S. and Webb, B. (1894) *The History of British Trade Unionism*, London: Longman Green.

Wei, M. (1998) 'ACFTU proposes solutions for the reemployment of laid-off workers', *Chinese Trade Unions*, June: 5–6.

Wilson, J. L. (1990) 'The Polish lesson: China and Poland 1989–1990', *Studies in Comparative Communism*, XIII(3/4): 259–79.

Woo, T. W and Ren, R. (2002) *Employment, Wages and Income Inequality in the Internationalization of China's Economy*, Geneva: International Labour Office.

Zhu, Y. and Warner, M. (2001) 'Taiwan business strategies *vis-à-vis* the Asian financial crisis', *Asia Pacific Business Review*, 7(3): 139–56.

Zhu, Y. and Warner, M. (2003) 'HRM in Asia', in A. W. Harzing and J. V. Ruysseveldt (eds) *International Human Resource Management*, London: Sage.

Zhu, Y., Chen, I. and Warner, M. (2000) 'HRM in Taiwan: an empirical case study', *Human Resource Management Journal*, 10(4): 32–44.

Zhu, Y., Warner, M., and Rowley C. (2007) 'Human resource management with 'Asian' characteristics: a hybrid people-management system in East Asia', *International Journal of Human Resource Management*, 18(5): 745–68.

10 Trade unions in India

From politics of fragmentation to politics of expansion and integration?

K. R. Shyam Sundar

Introduction

Trade unions are social organizations which seek to protect and promote economic and non-economic interests of workers both at the workplace and in the larger society. Trade unions in India owing to their colonial origins built close ties with political parties. This continued even after political independence. State regulation of the industrial relations system (IRS) and labour market has contributed to politicization of IRS. Unions were initially organized on the principles of industrial unionism (i.e. organizing workers in a number of firms in an industry in a region irrespective of their occupations or skills), especially in traditional industries like textiles, though plant level unions are becoming increasingly more prominent.

A model of political unionism has dominated in India for quite some time. Centralized political unionism used predominantly 'political' methods to secure benefits to their members. The use of industrial action was often dictated by 'political' considerations – strikes take place to embarrass the party in power, demonstrate the political power of unions, to bring the attention of the government to the dispute so that it could be referred to compulsory adjudication by the obliging government. The dominance of political unions has been challenged by the rise of enterprise unions in recent decades. On the other hand, the liberalization, privatization and globalization (LPG) model adopted in India, as well as labour flexibility measures adopted by employers, and declining formal sector jobs are providing challenges to unions, which are, in fact, providing opportunities to restructure the union movement. Trade unions are trying to move away from their politics of fragmentation and sectionalism to consolidate and expand the union movement.

This story of unions in India is told in five sections in this chapter. Section 2 covers historical and contextual issues, such as the broad features of the political and economic systems, the evolution and growth of unions, and an overview of union membership. Section 3 identifies union types and structures and their relationship with the state. Section 4 seeks answers to the question, 'what do unions do?' Section 5 explains the development, structure and strategies of unions in confronting the challenges that have arisen due to changes in the system.

Finally, the chapter concludes by outlining the challenges faced by unions and evaluates unions' responses to them.

Context and history

India was under colonial rule by Britain for over 200 years and attained political independence on 15 August 1947. Colonial rule impacted heavily on all the sub-systems of the social system. The federal–democratic–pluralistic model of polity adopted in India assured the fundamental right to form unions and freedom of industrial action subject to legal regulation. India has ratified only five of the eight core conventions of the International Labour Organization (ILO); but the constitutional guarantees and the liberal–pluralist legal framework uphold the principles contained in the core conventions and India's record in respecting the principles of freedom of association is certainly better than that in other countries in Asia (Venkata Ratnam 2006).

India, unlike its neighbours in South Asia, enjoys political stability; though with the dawn of coalition politics, governmental stability[1] has weakened. The average tenure of the elected government has declined since 1989. The colonial state, operating on *laissez-faire* principles, did not attempt to promote industrial development; and industrial growth during the first half of the twentieth century was sluggish (Kohli 2005: 250). Table 10.1 summarizes the economic and political context in India.

India preferred the state-led, planned, import-substituting industrialization model (Kohli 2005: 263) to usher in speedy economic progress. Export pessimism, discouragement of foreign capital (though domestic savings and capital formation were low) and import substitution policies limited international trade and capital flows and offered protection to domestic industries. The failure of the public sector, poor performance by the industrial sector since the mid-1960s, and inefficiencies associated with a closed economy led to an economic reform process in the early 1980s (Kohli 1989). The balance of payment crisis in 1991 and the consequent conditional structural adjustment loan from the IMF led to the intensification of the reform process in the 1990s. Liberalization of the industrial sector, limited but persistent attempts at privatization (via the disinvestment route), and the opening up of the economy reflected the dominance of the logic of competition.

Though industrialization began in the mid-nineteenth century (Kohli 2005: 248), the labour movement was characterized by only stray organizing efforts and sporadic strikes until the early twentieth century. The Madras Labour Union was the first labour organization formed (in 1918) on the lines of a modern trade union. Subsequent to Mahatma Gandhi's intervention in a bonus dispute in the textile industry in Ahmedabad, the Textile Labour Association (TLA) was formed in 1920. The All India Trade Union Congress (AITUC) was formed in 1920 primarily to fulfil the need for nominating employer representatives in the tripartite delegation to the ILO. The Indian National Congress played an important role in establishing the AITUC. There developed a mutually beneficial relationship between the working class and the Congress Party. The union movement provided the critical

Table 10.1 Contextual factors – India

General statistics	
Population[1] (2004)	1080 million
Area (square kilometres)[2]	3287.2 thousand
Employment by sector (%)[3] (2002)	
Agriculture	60
Industry	18
Services	22
Urban population (% of total population)[4] (2001)	27.78
GNI per capita[1] (2004)	$620 (US)
Income inequality (high, medium or low)	Medium
Gini coefficient[1] (1999–2000)	32.9
Real GDP growth[5] (%)	
1980–1990	5.8
1991–2004	5.6
Unemployment rate[6] (on current daily status basis)	
1983	8.28
1987–1988	6.09
1999–2000	7.32

Summary description	
Product market regulation (1998)	Low
Political context (liberal/pluralistic, state unitarist [communist, non-communist])	Liberal/pluralistic
Political stability[7]	High
Governmental stability[7]	Medium–High

Sources
1 2006 World Development Indicators, Table 1.1, World Bank, Washington, DC.
2 Statistical Abstract India 2003, Table 1.1, Central Statistical Organization, Government of India.
3 Papola (2005: 10–11).
4 http://www.censusindia_net/results/rudist.html (accessed 19 July 2006).
5 Kohli (2006, Table 1).
6 Deshpande et al (2004, Table 2.7).
7 Chakrabarty (2006: 212, 230).

mass to mount opposition to British control; political parties lent their status and organizational leadership to unions and resolution of industrial disputes.

The colonial government passed the *Trade Unions Act* in 1926 which legalized unions and contributed to their growth. The conflicts between factions within the AITUC on various events and issues (such as cooperation with the Royal Commission) created rifts in the AITUC and led to formation of splinter organizations, such as the National Trade Union Federation (NTUF) by moderates in 1930 and the Red Trade Union Congress (RTUC) by communists in 1931. The RTUC returned to the AITUC in 1935 and NTUF in 1940. During the Second World War (in 1942) the Congress leaders in the AITUC were jailed for opposing the British government's war effort and asking Britain to quit India. In their absence, the communists took control of the organization. The Congress faction found working with the communists increasingly difficult as the differences of opinion and views from day-to-day matters to policy issues became unbridgeable and formed its own labour wing, the Indian National TUC (INTUC) in 1947.

The Congress Party checked the growth of communist unions with the aid of its (un)official labour wing, the INTUC, and blunted the class character of the union movement in India. With the Congress Party's patronage (as alleged by other unions and several scholars, see for example Hiro 1976; Rudolph and Rudolph 1987), the INTUC soon grew powerful. The union movement witnessed a series of splits owing to ideological differences between communists, socialists and radicals, however. The socialists walked out of the AITUC to form Hind Mazdoor Panchayat (HMP) which soon became Hind Mazdoor Sabha (HMS) after M. N. Roy's Indian Federation of Labour merged with HMP. The revolutionary socialists and non-communist Marxist groups walked out of HMS to form the United Trade Union Congress (UTUC). The latter witnessed a split and UTUC (Lenin-Sarani) was formed. George Fernandes and his supporters walked out of HMS and formed HMP in 1962. The Jan Sangh (now BJP), fired by Hindutva ideology, established Bharatiya Mazdoor Sangh (BMS) in 1955. The split in the Communist Party of India (CPI) in 1964 (see Sen 1997: 395) led to the formation of the Centre of Indian Trade Unions (CITU) in 1970 by CPI (Marxist). The split in the Congress party engineered by Indira Gandhi in 1969 led to a rift in INTUC; the TLA withdrew from INTUC as it found that after the split in the National Congress INTUC was deviating from Gandhian principles and was joining hands with the communist union AITUC (Sharma 1982: 161). The TLA was instrumental in forming the National Labour Organization (NLO) in January 1972. The split in the Congress (I) party in May 1999 caused by Sharad Pawar led to further splits in INTUC, significantly in Bombay. Meanwhile, the regional political parties like Dravida Munnetra Kazhagham (DMK) in Tamil Nadu, and Shiv Sena in Maharashtra formed their labour wings (in 1970 and 1966 respectively), riding on primordial loyalties like regional parochialism and linguistic identity.

The number of central trade union organizations (CTUOs) increased from 3 in 1947 to 11 by 1974 and to 17 presently. According to the recent data available (though controversial) on verified membership of 12 CTUOs (as on 31 December 1989), the BMS recorded the highest membership (3.1 million), followed by the erstwhile leader INTUC (2.7 million), CITU (1.8 million) and HMS (1.5 million) (http://www.bms.org.in/htm/trade_unions.htm, accessed on 3 August 2006). The regional trade unions such as the DMK party's union and Shiv Sena party's union have significant following in Tamil Nadu and Maharashtra, respectively.

The multiplicity of CTUOs resulted in an 'involuted' union movement (Rudolph and Rudolph 1987). This has caused concern even to the CTUOs. It was realized that multiplicity, especially along political lines, created disunity which was exploited by employers (Pandhe 2005). Unity moves have been taking place for a long time with limited success. The failure of a move to merge the HMS and AITUC in recent times is a significant pointer to the unbridgeable gaps between the CTUOs. However, there have been some attempts in building common fronts for struggle. They are sector-specific (e.g. public sector) or issue-oriented (see Shyam Sundar 2003b for more details on unity moves). The CTUOs in India, engaged as they were in organizing workers in the formal or organized sector, neglected certain sections of the Indian workforce, such as informal sector workers and women workers. They have, however, begun to organize informal sector workers in recent times (see Shyam Sundar 2003a for details).

The *Trade Unions Act* 1926 as amended in 2001 requires a minimum of 100 or 10 per cent of workers in an establishment, whichever is less (subject to a minimum of seven workers) to form trade unions. Registration of unions under the Act is voluntary, so not all unions that exist in India register under the Act. The registered unions are required to submit annual returns to the state labour departments, which keep a record of the number of union members and the nature of the union. For inexplicable reasons many registered unions do not submit annual returns or submit them late. The proportion of registered unions not submitting returns has increased substantially over the years (see Shyam Sundar 1999b, 2006). The state labour departments are supposed to compile what information they receive and send it to the Labour Bureau (the central statistical office for compiling and publishing statistics on industrial relations). In the last two decades, however, the state labour departments have not been sending the compiled information to the Labour Bureau. The compiled information on trade unions presented in the statistical publications of the Labour Bureau (like Indian Labour Statistics) therefore suffer from problems of validity and reliability. The union membership data in India has been *unusable* since the early 1980s (see Shyam Sundar 1999b).

The degree of unionism estimate is small (4 to 5 per cent) if the denominator is non-agricultural employment which also includes the unorganized sector, and is somewhat high (22–23 per cent, Table 10.2) if formal sector employment is used (see Deshpande 1984: 30; ILO 1997: 238; Visser 2003: 385). Though the degree of unionism is low in India, the concentration of union membership is high in critical sectors like banking, insurance, railways, postal services, ports, telecoms and power. The manufacturing sector accounted for 40 per cent, the transport sector just over 25 per cent, the finance and insurance sector a little less than 10 per cent of membership of unions in 1978, the last date for which information about unions was reasonably credible (Table 10.2) (see Deshpande 1984). Though the aggregate union density is low (largely owing to the predominance of the non-unionizable informal sector), concentration of unionism in important and critical industries/sectors gives it significant economic and political power. These institutional features peculiar to India highlight the fact that the degree of unionism is an inadequate indicator of union power.

Two features of unionism deserve mention here: union concentration and the poor representation of vulnerable workers. Unionism covers only a small portion of the workforce in the economy, primarily due to the presence of a large informal sector which is largely non-unionized. Even in the formal sector, unions are concentrated in a few states and in selected industries, such as the public sector. They are centred in large establishments, among men, and among permanent

Table 10.2 Trade unions in India

General statistics		
Number of estimated registered unions[1]		
1990	52,016	
2000	66,056	
Number of union members (thousands)		
1990–1992 (average)	6,288	
1998–2000	6,359	
Union density[3] (%)	A[2]	B[2]
1990–1992	23.29	5.03
1998–2000	22.65	4.33

Summary description[4]	
Union type	
Main	Political
Secondary	Economic
(economic/market, political, other)	
Union structure	
Main	Industrial
Secondary	Enterprise
(occupational, industrial, general, enterprise)	
Unity of peak organizations (high, medium or low)	Low
State control of unions (high, medium or low)	Low
Involvement in collective bargaining (high, medium or low)	Medium

Sources

1 *Indian Labour Year Book*, 1996, 2004; *Trade Unions in India 2000*, Labour Bureau, Shimla.

2 (A) Members of union submitting returns as percent of employment in organized sector (employment data from Economic Survey, 1996–7, 2005–6, Government of India, Ministry of Finance). (B) Members of union submitting returns as percent of non-agricultural workforce (employment on current daily status for 1999–2000 from Planning Commission Reports on Labour and Employment, New Delhi, Academic Foundation, 2002.

3 Venkata Ratnam (1997: 9).

4 Ramaswamy (1999, 2004).

workers (see contributions in Davala 1992; Deshpande *et al.* 2004: 126; Venkata Ratnam 1997). Women account for a small share of total membership (estimated at between 15 and 25 per cent in the 1990s). Unionism is insignificant in the informal sector,[2] small enterprises, and among women and flexible job holders.

The union density in many countries is said to have exhibited an 'inverted V pattern' and union membership has been declining despite renewal efforts (Kaufman 2006). Macro data being difficult to find and verify, it is impossible to say with certainty whether union density in India has declined or not. There are reasons to believe that union density has fallen in the post-liberalization period. Membership decline was admitted by some union leaders in the textile industry in Coimbatore and the knitwear industry in Tiruppur in Tamil Nadu (Gurumurthy 2006; Vijayabaskar 2006: 67). Some foreign researchers noted a decline in union density (using official national data despite its poor quality) between the mid-

1980s and mid-1990s and later (e.g. Betcherman *et al.* 2001: Table 2; Visser 2000: Annex 1, 2003: 381).

However, the number of registered unions increased from 36,507 in 1980 (see Shyam Sundar 1999b: Table 1) to around 52,016 in 1990 and to 66,056 in 2000. We can see that the increase in the number of registered unions in the 1980s is higher than that in the 1990s. Thus, their rate of growth has slowed down in the 1990s (2.42 per cent) as compared with that in the 1980s (3.60 per cent).

Regional data lends some support to the union decline view.[3] New union formation shows a decline in union growth in Maharashtra during 1991–2003 (Shyam Sundar 2006), in Uttar Pradesh during 1991–2004 (*Uttar Pradesh Statistical Diary*, various years) and in West Bengal during 1995–2004 (data in Banerjee 2006: 69). The number of registered unions in Andhra Pradesh declined from 14,561 in 2000 to 11,268 in 2005 (Reddy 2006: Table 5.6).

Labour market factors (such as a decline in employment in the organized sector by 1.2 million between 1997 and 2003, increasing employment of flexible categories of workers like contract and casual workers, an increase in employment in non-unionizable sectors like information technology, and a decline of union-conducive industries like textiles), political factors (like the withdrawal of state support to unions), and organizational factors (like the 'saturation' of unions in the organized sector) could explain the decline in unionism in India.

Union type and structure

Craft[4] and general unions are not prominent in India, as the country 'by-passed the merchant–craftsman stage of capitalism and went straight from agriculture to factory stage of production' (Sturmthal cited in Sharma 1982: 195). Unions were organized on the principle of industrial unionism in India; it is a dominant organizational form (Ramaswamy 2004: 54). There are two variants of industrial unionism: the region-cum-industry unions (e.g., unions of textile, plantation workers in a city or district) and national industrial unions (e.g., unions in banking, transport, ports and docks, steel, insurance industries).

A secondary type of unions in India is 'enterprise' or 'plant' unions, though organized on the principle of industrial unionism. Enterprise unions arose due to the failure of political unionism (see Bhattacherjee 1987; Ramaswamy 1988). The growth of enterprise unions has been noted by many (see Davala 1992; Ramaswamy 1988). The distinct feature of these unions is that they shun wider alliances and affiliations with political parties and concentrate on plant level issues. They enjoy greater unity and genuine dues-paying membership. But they lack ideological bases and are sectional in nature which weakens their power (Ramaswamy 2004; Sengupta 1993). To overcome this, some unions tried to form 'firm-level federations' (embracing unions in all units in India). There was even an attempt to form a National Convention of Unaffiliated Union Federation (see TUSC 2000).

Though the political unionism model is facing a serious challenge from enterprise unions, it still plays a dominant role in the policy making arena. Trade unions in India have a long and established association with political parties and political unionism has been a dominant feature of the union movement in India for several reasons. Party sponsorship of unions, splits and factions in unions because of party politics, strong links between party and union policies, leaders exchange programmes between parties and unions, the political objectives of unions, political considerations determining strategies and actions (say strikes) of unions, the relationship between union activity and political elections, the political commitment of leadership and members, the reward mechanism for union leaders (top positions in political parties or government ministries or awards or positions in consultative bodies) are some of the features of unionism in India that qualify it to be described as political unionism (see also Chatterjee 1980). The common refrain of commentators has been to decry political unionism in India. But it is argued that while unions could stop being mere adjuncts of political parties, they cannot escape politics (see e.g. AITUC 1996; Ramaswamy 1999). Table 10.2 summarises the structure of India's unions.

The strong ties between political parties and unions have ensured that unions do not often take a stance or indulge in protest actions that would embarrass the political parties; this trait becomes stronger when the party to which the union is connected is in power. The INTUC or BMS often remains antagonistic or opposes the struggle of other unions in order not to embarrass its political ally in power (see Shyam Sundar 2003b: 716–17 for details).

Unions in India do not, however, operate as a part of the state apparatus or as 'transmission belts' of state policies. The competitive pressures in the pluralistic union movement are too great; rival unions would capitalize on the failures of state-patronized unions and create advantages for themselves in the situation.

Unions enjoy a significant measure of independence from the state and the political parties respect the differing stance of unions. The high incidence of industrial conflict in the system, national level agitations on policy issues like labour rights by *all* unions, and conflicts between the ruling party and its labour wing strongly indicate independent attitudes among the unions in India (see Bhattacherjee 2001; Shyam Sundar 2005a), which are to a great extent independent of the state. While as labour wings of the political parties they are subject to some control, in recent times they have differed significantly from the party line on labour issues.

Conflict with employers is still the dominant union strategy in India, in spite of scholars and firms advocating cooperation and industrial peace in the face of an economic environment of intense global competition. Cooperation is also held to be a realistic policy in these times of union retreat. An adversarial stance has, however, always been the defining principle of industrial relations in India.

Employers and unions have never learned to compromise or accommodate one another. India has been amongst the top five strike-prone countries in the world for the last three decades (see Shyam Sundar 1999a). They eschewed an adversarial stance only during crisis or times of war (Sharma 1982). Since the mid-1970s, an employer offensive in the form of lockouts has increased (Sengupta 1993).

What do unions do?

Unions in India adopt a variety of methods in order to achieve their goals, the important ones being collective bargaining, direct action, political action and legal enactment to secure monetary and non-monetary benefits to workers. There are two views on the role of unions. The 'monopoly view' accuses unions of acting like monopolies to raise wages above market level and introducing distortions and inefficiencies. The 'voice model' takes a benevolent view of trade unions (see Freeman and Medoff 1991 for an exposition of and evidence on the two views). This perspective argues that unions contribute to efficiency of firms by providing 'voice' mechanisms like grievance procedure. See Table 10.3 for a summary of what Indian unions do.

The standard criticism of IRS in India has been that the state regulated system gives secondary place to collective bargaining and the compulsory state intervention system does not encourage collective bargaining. But collective bargaining gradually developed mainly owing to failure of state regulation (see Ramaswamy 1988; Shyam Sundar 2005b). The large size of the unorganized sector (93 per cent of the total workforce, see Venkata Ratnam 2006: 6) and the dominance of government employment in the organized sector means that the extent of collective bargaining is low (less than 2 per cent of the total workforce or 30 per cent of the formal sector workforce, Venkata Ratnam 2006: 198). Collective bargaining is absent in the former and nominal in the latter.

There are three tiers in the bargaining structure in India. The dominance of industry-wide unionism and wage boards and the tribunal system of wage determination contribute to wage determination at the industry level in traditional

Table 10.3 What do Indian trade unions do?

Activities	
Extent of collective bargaining[1]	Low
Level of collective bargaining[2]	
National	Medium
Industry	Medium
Enterprise	High
Extent of joint consultation	Low
Industrial disputes Workdays lost per 1,000 employees in organized sector[3] (2001–2003)	983
Degree of state intervention in employment protection[4]	High

Sources
1 Venkata Ratnam (2006: 191).
2 Visser (2000, Annex 2).
3 Industrial disputes data for 2001 from *Indian Labour Year Book*, 2004 (ibid.) for 2002, 2003, http://Labourbureau.nic.in/idtab.htm (accessed 7 August 2006); employment data from Economic Survey, 2005–6, Table 3.3.
4 India was ranked 116 among 155 countries on the criteria of 'hiring and firing', see *Doing Business 2006 Survey*, World Economic Forum, http://www.doingbusiness.org (accessed 4 June 2006).

industries like cotton and jute textiles, and plantations. National/sectoral bargaining takes place in industries like coal, steel, ports and docks, banks, insurance. The bargaining is between a single employer body (say the Indian Banks' Association for banks), the administrative ministry from the government where necessary and major industry-wide union federations. The third tier is decentralized firm or plant level bargaining, which takes place mostly in the private sector. Decentralized bargaining may either take place at the plant level or embrace all plants of a firm wherever they are located throughout the country (multi-unit bargaining). The average duration of agreement in the private sector was 3–4 years in the 1990s (see Venkata Ratnam 2003). The public sector agreements were for five years and in some cases even ten years in the 1990s (e.g., in ports and docks).

Some important trends can be discerned in collective bargaining. Employers are increasingly emphasizing productivity and wage revisions often accompany demands for productivity increases, even in the public sector (see Guha 2000; Venkata Ratnam 2003). There is a definite trend towards the decentralization of collective bargaining. Where industry-wide bargaining has been taking place, as in banking, employers have indicated a preference for decentralized bargaining as the latter would reflect firm-level realities; but the trade unions resist this, realizing that their bargaining power would be weakened.

Quantitative studies on the economic effects of unions in India are conducted at two levels, macro (using secondary data) and micro (using primary data). Real wage rises and slow employment growth, especially in the 1980s, was attributed to the role of unions[5] and tough employment protection laws (see Nagaraj 1994 for a good review of the monopoly view of unions). The monopoly view did not go uncontested. Nagaraj (1994) and Shyam Sundar (2005a) provide a review of these studies. It was shown that the rise in wages was not disproportionate and the wage rise could be explained by an increase in workdays per worker and productivity. It was also shown that union power as measured by strikes in fact declined while lockouts increased.

The monopoly view of unionism lost ammunition in the 1990s as union power declined and real wage growth slowed (Goldar 2003). Unions could not change the functional distribution of national income that saw the redistribution of income from capital to labour (Brahmananda 1993; Dadi cited in Deshpande 1984: 10). The relative share of wages either remained constant in the early period or it showed a 'mild downward trend' and that of the profits increased (Brahmananda 1993).

Some economists have noted the existence of wage differential between the organized and unorganized sectors and this obviously generated concern over the distribution issue (Brahmananda 1993; Deshpande 1984; Rudolph and Rudolph 1987). The principal blame for the 'undeservedly high wages' of organized labour fell on trade unions and the institutionalization of wage protecting mechanisms like cost of living allowance and bonuses.[6] Thus, trade unions in India are often accused of creating 'islands of prosperity' amidst widespread poverty. The burden of changes in the functional distribution noted above fell on the workers in the unorganized sector as they are least protected (Brahmananda 1993).

The micro-level studies in general found that unionized workers earned more than non-unionized workers (see Deshpande *et al.* 1998; Mahalingam cited in Deshpande 1984). Unionized workers *perceived* that unions definitely increased their wages (Ramjas 1993: 122). The union wage premium varied: 10 per cent (Mahalingam), 8 and 14 per cent (for skilled and unskilled workers respectively (Deshpande *et al.* 1998). Bhattacherjee (1987) argues that 'plant level based' unions secured significantly higher wages and bonus benefits to workers than did political unions. Deshpande *et al.* (1998: 145) stressed the egalitarian role of unions by showing that the wage premium enjoyed by skilled male workers over the unskilled was less in unionized than in non-unionized firms.

Some micro-level studies show that unions positively affected working conditions, safety measures, reduced quit rates, raised workers' morale and bettered promotion prospects of unionized workers; they provided support to the 'voice' model of unionism (see Ramjas 1993; Shyam Sundar 1998). Bhattacherjee's (1993) econometric analysis of agreements in Bombay shows that enterprise unions delivered a fairer grade structure than the affiliated unions because enterprise unions operated at the plant level and were more concerned with issues at the point of production.

Unions used the tripartite consultative institutions (such as the Indian Labour Conference, National or State Labour Advisory Boards) effectively to build a base for the enactment of labour laws and to construct principles for policies for implementation both at macro (by the government) and micro (by private sector employers) levels. Workers in the organized sector enjoy rights like employment security, the right to strike, bonuses, and social security. The unions played an important role in establishing and protecting these rights: many of the labour protests in the 1990s were centred on protecting these rights of workers.

The political-organizational theories of strikes point out that though objective factors like real wage decline may warrant worker protests, unions are necessary to transform discontent into work stoppages (see Shyam Sundar 1998). The association between the two cannot be predicted *a priori* because while higher union power can cause conflicts, greater organizational strength (via strike threats) may result in compromise and reduce the probability of conflicts. There is support for both hypotheses. Aggregate data analysis found a positive relationship between the degree of unionism and workdays lost (Deshpande 1984; Bean and Holden 1992); but unionism became insignificant when an instrumental variable technique was used in the latter study. Disaggregated studies using industry level data found a negative relationship between unionism and strike activity (Bharadwaj and Mathur 1970; Saha and Pan 1994). Organized labour was responsible for many of the workdays lost during the 1960s and 1970s (see Saha and Pan 1994), while the incidence of lockouts has increased since then (see Shyam Sundar 2004a). Strike frequency declined steeply but workdays lost due to strikes showed spurts in the 1990s (Shyam Sundar 2003b).

Trade unions and efficiency of firms

Employers argue that unions, by obstructing employment of flexible categories of workers, not only impede the economic efficiency of firms but also reduce the creation of jobs. There is evidence that employers achieved numerical flexibility to some extent in the 1990s despite restrictive laws and unions (see Deshpande *et al.* 2004; Kuruvilla and Erickson 2000: 30; Venkata Ratnam 2003). Studies of collective agreements show instances where unions have agreed to reductions in manpower, higher workload, increased productivity, and flexibility in work norms and redeployment (Venakata Ratnam 2003; Guha 2000). There is some evidence to support the classic view of the Webbs that unions make dynamic contributions to the firm's efficiency. Deshpande *et al.* (2004) found that unionized firms were more likely to introduce changes in technology, extend product range and effect improvements in the quality of the product (see Deshpande *et al.* 2004: Table 4.27).

Infrequency of union elections, 'managed' elections, regular 're-election' of leaders, absence of strike ballots, non-ratification of agreements by members, and low participation of leaders and members in union organizational matters could be taken to indicate low levels of union democracy in India (see Modi *et al.* 1995 and studies mentioned therein; Ramaswamy 1988; Sharma 1982). It has been argued that union democracy is weak due to political unionism (Sengupta 1993) as leadership is remotely connected to the rank and file and is often insensitive to members' demands. Charismatic leaders (like Datta Samant) who rose to prominence because of the frustration of workers with political unions have done little to promote union democracy (see Ramaswamy 2004: 70–1).

Three agencies can ensure union democracy: government, employers and members. The government can ensure democracy through a legal framework. Central trade union law in India does not provide a mechanism for the recognition of unions and there is no consensus on the method of determining the actual existence of a union. The INTUC prefers 'membership verification' and others prefer the 'secret ballot'. Ballots for union election and strike conduct do not exist in India. Employers and the government prefer strike ballots on the ground that many strikes are imposed on unwilling members. But employers are not crusaders of union democracy; they prefer assertive leaders as the latter ensure the implementation of agreements.

It is important to recognize that union members in India have devised their own ways of ensuring that their voices are heard. There have been instances when the rank and file asserted itself and ousted negligent leadership or effectively challenged ideologically deviant leadership (Ramaswamy 1999; Venkata Ratnam 2006). It may be noted here that some significant strikes like the Simpson strike in Madras in the early 1970s and the Bombay textile strike during 1982–3 occurred primarily because of discontent arising out of the undemocratic functioning of existing unions. Currently there is growing consciousness among workers and they look for leadership who understand their problems and can provide solutions. The rank and file have become assertive in the affairs of the unions and they frequently displace union leaders when the latter do not deliver results (Ramaswamy 1988, 2004).

Explaining the development, structure and strategies of trade unions

The industrial relations system in general and union movement in particular has in many ways been a continuation of the colonial model. Close association between unions and political parties, workers' dependence on 'outside' leadership, 'political' functions of strikes, splits in the union movement, union rivalries, unity moves and leader assertiveness are features of the colonial model of union movement that continues to be relevant even today.

State intervention was preferred to bipartism for managing IRS in post-colonial India. Trade unions accepted state intervention and relied mainly on political methods and legal enactment to secure benefits to their members. The ruling party could use interventionist institutions like conciliation machinery to further the interests of their labour wings or those of their allies (see Shyam Sundar 1998). Leadership with political connections matter in a state-regulated system and workers preferred them. Employers could use their political links to achieve favourable settlements. What mattered in such a system was 'access to government'. Thus, the 'politics' of industrial relations dominated the industrial dimension and 'political unionism' grew out of these forces and in turn fed them. The compulsory adjudication system favoured unions and their political methods.

Two major strikes, that of public sector workers in Bangalore in 1980–1 and the Bombay textile workers' strike in 1982–3 redefined the IRS in India. The strikers failed as a result of state intervention or the lack of it. The state–labour coalition ended. Employer militancy began its ascendancy. Around that time economic reform measures began to be introduced (see Kohli 1989; Kumar 2005). The 'politics of economic growth' gradually began to give prominence to markets, support employers and tame unions. There was transition from state regulation to collective bargaining and ascendancy of enterprise unionism in IRS. Bargained agreements reflect market forces and pressures more closely than adjudication awards. The structure of the union movement changed. The labour regime showed a shift from centralized union settings where unions played a role in national politics to a decentralized regime where unions shunned political links. Decentralization of bargaining complemented the market process.

The government intensified the reform process in the product market in the 1990s. The reforms led to greater competition in the product market. Competition reduced 'rents' for unions and employers. It reduced the capacity of firms to pass on the wage increases to consumers. The responsibility for employment generation and industrial development was shifted from the state to the private sector. This had implications for unions and collective bargaining. The state redefined its labour market and industrial relations policies in the public sector: it imposed a freeze on recruitment, imposed a longer period of wage agreement, and shed surplus workers via voluntary retirement schemes.

The labour market strategy of employers was to cut labour costs and employ flexible labour. The managerial strategies in response to increased competition included reduction in core labour and expansion of peripheral categories of workers, reduction in employment via voluntary or coercive methods, a shift of production to non-union areas, sub-contracting work, prolonged lockouts and closures (see Ramaswamy 2004). Globalization enhanced the bargaining power of employers, *vis-à-vis* unions. Relatively greater mobility of capital, elastic labour demand, and huge reserves of unemployed and informal workers considerably weakened the power of unions. The state's role changed from active intervention in IRS and support for unions to withdrawal and indifference. Indeed, the state–business coalition, according to union leaders, became stronger (see Kuruvilla and Erickson 2000).

Employers' associations differed over economic issues like the role of foreign capital; but they were united in calling for labour reforms (see Kohli 1989, 2006). Multinational presence in India is low but slowly rising (Kumar 2005: 1463). Foreign investors have considerable influence over economic and labour policies. They, along with domestic employers, are demanding reform of the labour market and the IRS. Though the central government has been keen to introduce labour reforms, it is not because of union protests and the political costs associated with the reforms. Judiciary consistent with changed times has delivered several judgements that have curtailed established labour rights (restrictions on *bandhs*,[7] the right to strike, for example, see Shyam Sundar 2004b; Venakata Ratnam 2006: 267). Table 10.4 explains the development of trade unions in India.

Trade unions faced with adverse circumstances have adopted strategies that have included broad-basing the labour movement, forging alliances with other social groups like farmers, students and youth (e.g., the formation of the National Platform of Mass Organizations) and initiating unity moves. They have devised a number of strategies like nation-wide struggles and political action to stall the government's moves to introduce labour reforms and dilute their hard-won rights. Most importantly, the political unions have realized the negative implications of party control of and influence over union affairs (see for example AITUC 1996, 1997). The 1990s have witnessed a number of mass struggles waged on many occasions on a common front by the CTUOs. The unions have realized the need to consolidate in order to fight against neo-liberal policies. They have also realized the need to organize the informal type workers and workers in the informal sector. The CTUOs have certainly moved away from 'politics of fragmentation' to 'politics of consolidation and expansion'.

Conclusion

The institutions of the state, such as the government and judiciary, have not been supportive of unionism in recent times. The market and political powers of employers have increased. Employer offensives against unionism as a result have increased. The LPG model has weakened union power. The post-reform era witnessed efforts to dilute their hard-won rights such as the right to strike

Table 10.4 Explaining Indian trade union development, structure and strategy

Political context	
Degree of liberalization and autonomy	Indifference
Relations with the state	Independent
Markets	
Openness (imports + exports as % of GDP) 2004–5[1]	28.9 (Low)
Degree of competition	High
Financial markets Openness to market financing[2] Ownership[3]	 Medium Family
Labour market Employment elasticity with respect to real output[4] for 1994–2000 Demand elasticity	 Low Low
Employers	
Concentration[(a), 5]	High
Employer organization membership[6]	
Private sector	Low
Public sector	High
Multinationals[(b), 7]	Low
Unitarist or pluralist perspective	Pluralistic

Sources
1 Economic Survey (2005–6, Table 6.3).
2 NSEI (2005: 5–6).
3 Allen *et al.* (2006, Table 2.2).
4 Deshpande et al. (2004, Table 2.2)
5 CMIE (2005: 303).
6 Venkata Ratnam (2001: 34).
7 Kumar (2005: 1463).

Notes
(a) Based on per capita share of top 50 business houses in gross sales of non-financial private sector in 2004–5.
(b) Foreign direct investment as percentage of gross fixed capital formation.

and employment security. Trade unions have so far successfully thwarted the government's efforts to introduce labour flexibility measures and privatize central public enterprises. But these efforts by the government constitute permanent challenges to unions.

There are three organizational challenges for unions: consolidation, penetration and expansion, and integration. Specifically, the union movement must fight to: remain independent of political parties and yet be able to pursue political methods to achieve union objectives; effect mergers of like-minded union organizations; find suitable methods and organizational structures to organize the unorganized; and integrate parallel worker and non-worker organizations to create a social movement. While political unionism suffers from too much politics, enterprise unionism devoid of politics is not the answer. It is important to realize that unions need political action to achieve their objectives and tackle systemic issues like labour reforms.

There are two organizational tendencies that give hope: consolidation and expansion. The union movement is slowly shifting from the politics of fragmentation to the politics of consolidation and expansion. Political unions have shown significant interest in organizing workers in the informal sector. The union movement has devised new strategies like union solidarity, social movement unionism, review of political unionism, promotion of worker ownership, and massive national protests. There are indications of a convergence in the union movement: women and informal type workers are increasingly brought within the fold of unions; central federations are forging unity moves; and unaffiliated unions are attempting to form national forums. There are some positive signs in the union movement: increasing worker consciousness, a greater role for worker activists, inclusive membership, and stress on union democracy, for example. The dialectics of social and economic change are that the very forces that weaken social institutions provide the basis for restructuring and reorienting them. The challenges as well as scope for union renewal are enormous.

Acknowledgement

I wish to thank Dr L. K. Deshpande and Dr E. A. Ramaswamy for useful discussions which enhanced my understanding of unions in India.

Notes

1 Political scientists make a distinction between political and governmental stability. The former means stability of a political regime (say democracy) and the constitutional framework; barring the internal emergency period (1975–7), India enjoyed political stability (Chakrabarty 2006). Governmental stability is indicated by average tenure of the elected government.
2 The terms 'unorganized sector' and 'informal sector' are used interchangeably. The organized sector covers establishments employing 10 or more employees. It is well nigh impossible to define the unorganized sector owing to its vastness and diversity. It is usually taken to be the residual of the organized sector (see SNCL 2002).
3 State level data used by others also shows evidence of union decline (see Kuruvilla *et al.* 2002: 445).
4 Craft unions are found in some industries like railways, aviation, textiles (e.g. Pilots' Guild, TLA).
5 Most early studies found insignificant or weak correlation between unionism variables and money wages/earnings (Chatterjee 1980; Deshpande 1984 and studies cited therein). The explanation was that union influence on wages is *indirect* in the sense that unions play an important role in influencing wages in two ways: institutionalization of wage-protecting mechanisms like linkage between wages and cost of living index and establishment of institutions like wage boards, industrial tribunals and labour law (see Chatterjee 1980).

6 Union struggles led to institutionalization of the bonus payment. [It is a *right* of workers to get a bonus and a minimum bonus of 8.33 per cent is payable even in loss-making units (Sharma 1982: 147).]

7 A 'bandh' is a political form of protest usually sponsored by political parties. During the bandh all forms of activity (shops, offices, factories, transportation, etc.) stop. Though compliance is intended to be voluntary, the sponsors of the bandh use coercion to shut shops, transportation etc. (see <http://en.wikipedia.org/wiki/Bandh> for more details).

Bibliography

All India Trade Union Congress (AITUC) (1996) 'On the problem of trade union unity – a dialogue with Com. Balanandan', *Trade Union Record*, 5 June: 3–6.

All India Trade Union Congress (AITUC) (1997), 'Trade union unity', *Trade Union Record*, 5 June.

Allen, F. *et al.* (2006) *Financing Firms in India*. Online. Available HTTP: <http://www.darden.virginia.edu/em/PDFs/Allen_Franklin.pdf> (accessed 15 July 2006).

Banerjee, D. (2006) 'Labour regulations and industrial development in West Bengal', project report to the European Union.

Bean, R. and Holden, K. (1992) 'Determinants of strikes in India: a quantitative analysis', *Indian Journal of Industrial Relations*, 28(2): 161–8.

Betcherman, G., Luinstra, A., and Ogawa, M. (2001) *Labor Market Regulation: International Experience in Promoting Employment and Social Protection*. Online. Available HTTP: <http://www.siteresources.worldbank.org/SOCIALPROTECTION> (accessed February 2005).

Bharadwaj, V. P., and Mathur, R. S. (1970) 'Inter-industry variation in strike proneness in India 1959–1967', paper presented to the Second World Congress of the International Industrial Relations Association, Geneva, 1–4 September 1970.

Bhattacherjee, D. (1987) 'Union-type effects on bargaining outcomes in Indian manufacturing', *British Journal of Industrial Relations*, 25(2): 247–66.

Bhattacherjee, D. (1993), 'Job classification, grading and union strategy: an empirical analysis of plant-level contracts from greater Bombay', in J. S. Sodhi and S. P. S. Ahluwalia (eds) *Industrial Relations in India: The Coming Decade,* New Delhi: Shri Ram Centre for Industrial Relations and Human Resources.

Bhattacherjee, D. (2001) 'The "New Left", globalization and trade unions in West Bengal: what is to be done?', *Indian Journal of Labour Economics*, 44(3): 447–57.

Brahmananda, P. R. (1993) 'Economic theory and labour economics: 20 percent fortress and 80 percent ocean', in T. S. Papola, P. P. Ghosh and A. N. Sharma (eds) *Labour, Employment and Industrial Relations in India*, Patna: Indian Society of Labour Economics; Delhi: B. R. Publishing Corporation.

CMIE (2005) *Corporate Sector – December*, Mumbai: Center for Monitoring Indian Economy.

Chakrabarty, B. (2006) *Forging Power: Coalition Politics in India*, New Delhi: Oxford University Press.

Chatterjee, R. (1980) *Unions, State and Politics: A Study of Indian Labour Politics*, New Delhi: South Asia Publishers.

Davala, S. (ed.) (1992) *Employment and Unionization in Indian Industry*, New Delhi: Friedrich Ebert Stiftung.

Deshpande, L. K. (1984) *Role of Trade Unions in India*, Bombay: Tata Institute of Social Sciences (mimeograph).

Deshpande, L. K., Sharma, A. N. , Karan, A. K. and Sarkar, S. (2004) *Liberalization and Labour: Labour Flexibility in Indian Manufacturing*, New Delhi: Institute for Human Development.

Deshpande, S., Standing, G. and Deshpande, L. (1998) *Labour Flexibility in a Third World Metropolis*, New Delhi: Indian Society of Labour Economics and Commonwealth Publishers.

Dutt, P. (2006) *Labour Market Outcomes and Trade Reforms: The Case of India*. Online. Available HTTP: <www.arts.ualbarta.ca/~econweb/dutt/India-labour.pdf> (accessed 15 July 2006).

Freeman, R. B. and Medoff, J. L. (1991) *What Do Unions Do?* New Delhi: East-West Press.

Goldar, B. (2003) *Trade Liberalization and Real Wages in Organized Manufacturing Industries in India*. Online. Available HTTP: <http://cegindia.org/dis_bng_63.pdf> (accessed 16 July 2006).

Guha, B. P. (2000) *Wage Movement in Indian Industries: As Reflected in Collective Bargaining Agreements*, Delhi: B. R. Publishing Corporation.

Gurumurthy, G. (2006) 'Trade union power wearing thin – deunionization at textile mills', *Business Line*. Online. Available HTTP: <http://www.thehindubusinessline.com/2004/09/28/stories/2004092801901700.htm> (accessed 5 July 2006).

Hiro, D. (1976) *Inside India Today*, New York: Routledge Kegan Paul.

ILO (1997) *World Labour Report: Industrial Relations, Democracy and Social Stability*, Geneva: International Labour Organization.

Jha, R. (2006) *Reducing Poverty and Inequality in India: Has liberalization helped?* Online. Available HTTP: <http://ideas.repec.org/p/pas/papers/2002-04.html> (accessed 18 July 2006).

Kaufman, B. E. (2006) *The Global Evolution of Industrial Relations: Events, Ideas and the IIRA*, New Delhi: Academic Foundation.

Kohli, A. (1989) 'Politics of economic liberalization in India', *World Development*, 17(3): 305–28.

Kohli, A. (2005) *State-Directed Development: Political Power and Industrialization in the Global Periphery*, Cambridge: Cambridge University Press.

Kohli, A. (2006) 'Politics of economic growth in India, 1980–2005: parts I & II', *Economic and Political Weekly*, 1–7 April: 1251–61 and 8 April: 1361–70.

Kumar, N. (2005) 'Liberalization, foreign direct investment flows and development: Indian experience in the 1990s', *Economic and Political Weekly*, 2 April: 1459–69.

Kuruvilla, S. and Erickson C. L. (2000) 'Change and transformation in Asian industrial relations', *Industrial Relations*, 41: 171–228.

Kuruvilla, S., Das, S., Kwon, H. and Kwon, S. (2002) 'Trade union growth and decline in Asia', *British Journal of Industrial Relations*, 40: 431–61.

Modi, S., Singhal, K. C. and Singh, U. C. (1995) 'Workers' participation in trade unions', *Indian Journal of Industrial Relations*, 31(1): 40–58.

Nagaraj, R. (1994), 'Employment and wages in manufacturing industries: trends, hypothesis and evidence', *Economic and Political Weekly*, 22 January: 177–86.

NSEI (2005) *A Review of the Indian Securities Market, VIII*, Mumbai: National Stock Exchange of India.

Pandhe, M. K. (2005) *Twenty-five Years of CITU*. Online. Available HTTP: <http://citu.org.in/25years.htm> (accessed 4 July 2006).

Papola, T. S. (2005) *Emerging Structure of Indian Economy: Implications of growing inter-sectoral imbalances*, Presidential address to the 88th Annual Conference of the Indian Economic Association, Vishakhapatnam, 25–27 December.

Ramaswamy, E. A. (1977) *The Worker and his Union: A study in south India*, New Delhi: Allied Publishers Private.

Ramaswamy, E. A. (1988) *Worker Consciousness and Trade Union Response*, New Delhi: Oxford University Press.

Ramaswamy, E. A. (1999) *A Question of Balance*, New Delhi: Oxford University Press.

Ramaswamy, E. A. (2004) *Managing Human Resources: A Contemporary Text*, New Delhi: Oxford India Paperbacks.

Ramjas, (1993), 'Unionised workers in the production process: perceptional analysis', in J. S. Sodhi and S. P. S. Ahuluwalia (eds), *Industrial Relations in India: The Coming Decade*, New Delhi: Shri Ram Centre for Industrial Relations and Human Resources.

Reddy, D. N. (2006) 'Labour regulation in Indian industry: a case study of Andhra Pradesh', project report to European Union.

Rudolph, L. I. and Rudolph, S. H. (1987) *In Pursuit of Lakshmi: The Political Economy of the Indian State*, New Delhi: Orient Longman.

Saha, B. and Pan, I. (1994) 'Industrial disputes in India: an empirical analysis', *Economic and Political Weekly*, April 30: 1081–7.

Sen, S. (1997) *Working Class of India: History of Emergence and Movement, 1830–1990*, Calcutta: K. P. Bagchi.

Sengupta, A. K (1993) *Industrial conflict in India (1961–87)*, New Delhi: Friedrich Ebert Stiftung.

Sharma, G. K. (1982) *Labour Movement in India, Its Past and Present: From 1885 to 1980*, New Delhi: Sterling Publishers Private.

Shyam Sundar, K. R. (1996) 'Internal emergency and industrial relations', *Indian Journal of Labour Economics*, 39(4): 1023–40.

Shyam Sundar, K. R. (1998) 'Industrial conflict in Tamil Nadu, 1960–80', unpublished thesis, Mumbai University.

Shyam Sundar, K. R. (1999a) 'Industrial conflict and the institutional framework of the industrial relations system in India', *Management and Change*, 3(1): 53–88.

Shyam Sundar, K. R. (1999b) 'Official data on trade unions: some comments', *Economic and Political Weekly*, 2 October: 2839–41.

Shyam Sundar, K. R. (2003a) 'Organizing the unorganized', *Seminar*, 531: 47–53.

Shyam Sundar, K. R. (2003b) 'Industrial conflicts in India in the reform decade', *Indian Journal of Labour Economics*, 46(4): 703–24.

Shyam Sundar, K. R. (2004a) 'Lockouts in India, 1961–2001', *Economic and Political Weekly*, 25 September: 4377–85.

Shyam Sundar, K. R. (2004b) 'The issue of right to strike', in *Workers and the Right to Strike: Report on four consultations*, New Delhi: Indian Society of Labour Economics/ Institute for Human Development.

Shyam Sundar, K. R. (2005a) 'Labour flexibility debate in India: a comprehensive review and some suggestions', *Economic and Political Weekly*, 28 May–4 June: 2274–85.

Shyam Sundar, K. R. (2005b) 'State in industrial relations system in India: from corporatist to neo-liberal?' *Indian Journal of Labour Economics*, 48(4): 917–37.

Shyam Sundar, K. R. (2006) 'Impact of labour regulation on growth, investment and employment: A study of Maharashtra', project report to European Union.

SNCL (Second National Commission on Labour) (2002) *The Report of the National Commission on Labour, Volume I (Part I)*, New Delhi: Ministry of Labour, Government of India.

TUSC (2000) *To Work Towards Organizing a National Convention of Unaffiliated Unions*, Mumbai: Trade Union Solidarity Committee.

Venkata Ratnam, C. S. (1997) *Indian Industrial Relations: A Report Prepared for the ILO Task Force on Industrial Relations*, Geneva: ILO.

Venkata Ratnam, C. S. (2001) *Globalization and Labour–Management Relations: Dynamics of Change*, New Delhi: Response Books.

Venkata Ratnam, C. S. (2003) *Negotiated Change: Collective bargaining, liberalization and restructuring in India*, New Delhi: Response Books.

Venkata Ratnam, C. S. (2006) *Industrial Relations*, New Delhi: Oxford University Press.

Vijayabaskar, M. (2006) 'Garment industry in India', in G. Joshi (ed.) *Garment Industry in South Asia: Rags or Riches? Competitiveness, Productivity and Job Quality in the Post-MFA Environment*, New Delhi: South Asia Multidisciplinary Advisory Team/ILO.

Visser, J. (2000) *Trends in Unionization and Collective Bargaining*, Geneva: ILO. Online. Available HTTP: <http://www.ilo.org/public/english/bureau/exrel/global/ilopub /tucb. pdf> (accessed 15 July 2006).

Visser, J. (2003) 'Unions and unionism around the world', in J. T. Addison and C. Schnabel (eds) *International Handbook of Trade Unions*, Cheltenham: Edward Elgar.

Wolkinson, B. W. and Dayal, S. (1973) 'Strikes in India's industrial relations system: INTUC's policy and practice', *Indian Journal of Industrial Relations*, 8(3): 431–49.

11 Trade unions in Sri Lanka

Beyond party politics

*Samanthi Gunawardana and
Janaka Biyanwila*

Introduction

Trade unions in Sri Lanka emerged out of the struggle for independence from colonial powers. Older models of trade unionism in developing countries have highlighted trade union links to nationalist movements (Bates 1970), as well their duality of purpose in balancing member interests and the requirements of nation building (Galenson 1958). Of the 1,604 trade unions registered in Sri Lanka (Department of Labor 2005), the majority are close affiliates of ideologically diverse political parties. This modern industrial relations system, shaped by colonial needs to institute a compliant labour subject and mitigate the effect of political pressure, has been described as a 'politicized multi-union model,' typical of South Asia (Kuruvilla and Erickson 2002; Biyanwila 2004; Fernando 1988).

Perspectives on the political role of trade unions (see Gospel, Chapter 2 this volume) can help to give insight into early trade unions in Sri Lanka, where political unionism, supplemented with some collective bargaining, has often proved advantageous. However, political unionism disarmed and undermined union capacities to organize and mobilize, reflecting the point made by Kuruvilla and Mundell (1999: 12) that closeness of political party ties does not correlate to trade unions' level of influence and power of voice. Nevertheless, in Sri Lanka, even party unions have at times asserted their autonomy. In the post-1977 era, however, this perspective needs to be broadened to assess the impact of militarized ethnic identity politics and the role of the state in advancing deregulated labour markets. In this period, Sri Lankan trade unions have acted as both economic and social actors (Hyman 2001), while continuing to retain political linkages to political parties.

The chapter first presents an overview of the political and economic context in which trade unions emerged. From this overview, it is apparent that four historical characteristics have influenced contemporary the nature of Sri Lankan trade unions: (1) political party linkages; (2) the post-colonial emergence of ethno-religious contestation over the nation state; (3) neo-liberal economic reform; and (4) the rise of an authoritarian state. These aspects of the Sri Lankan context shape both the possibilities and limitations for any future trade union trajectory in Sri Lanka. The chapter goes on to explore how trade unions are structured, what unions do, and the challenges ahead for trade unions in Sri Lanka. This chapter is based on research carried out by both authors since 2000 with extended research conducted with ten trade union leaders,[1] and additional archival research in July 2006.

Context and history

Sri Lanka is a multi-ethnic and multi-religious society. The main ethnic groups include Sinhala (86 per cent), Tamil (13 per cent), Hill Country Tamil (6 per cent), Muslim (7 per cent), Bhurgers and Eurasians (0.3 per cent) and Malays (0.3 per cent). While Buddhism (69 per cent) is the dominant religion, it has historically coexisted with Hinduism (16 per cent), Islam (8 per cent), and Christianity (8 per cent) (Department of Census and Statistics 2005a, 2005b).[2] Ethnic categories are often differentiated according to regional identities such as low-country and up-country Sinhalese or Jaffna Tamil and Hill Country Tamil. The anti-colonial struggles in the late 1800s reconstituted this hybridity of hierarchical ethnic, religious, caste and regional identities into a nationalist project. Following independence, this national identity was articulated in terms of a Sinhala Buddhist nationalism[3] (Gunawardena 1996; Moore 1994; Sivanandan 1984).

The history of trade unions in Sri Lanka can be mapped in terms of three distinct phases intertwined with the changing nature of the state. The early trade unions (1893–1930) emerged in urban factories in 1893, while unions among Tamil tea plantation workers formed in the late 1930s (Jayawardena 1972; Biyanwila 2004). Unions combined with anti-colonial movements which included religious agitation against Christianity as it was linked to the imperialist venture. Nevertheless, liberal perspectives of British Labourism influenced the first formal organization of trade unions. The growing union protests led to the introduction of early labour legislation and social welfare reforms (Jayawardena 1972).

The second phase, from 1931 to 1956, following adult franchise in 1930, marked the emergence of the labour movement and a liberal paternalist colonial regime. During this phase, the working class parties radicalized the labour movement and democratized the colonial state. Labour market institutions designed to settle disputes were first introduced under the *Trade Disputes Conciliation Ordinance* of 1931 (Jayawardena 1972). Trade unions were recognized with the introduction of the *Trade Unions Ordinance 14* of 1935. Under this act, a trade union is defined in concurrence to the Webb's original classification of a trade union (Webb and Webb 1894). Freedom of association and right to organize and collectively bargain are embedded in both this act and the post-independence Constitution of the country (Jayawardena 1972).

After independence in 1948, unions were integrated with the main political parties, particularly under the developmental state strategies of 1956–77, which extended protective labour legislation and social welfare. While plantation workers gained franchise in 1931, their disenfranchisement in 1948/9 following independence reinforced union divisions along the lines of ethnic identity politics. Although working class parties countered the assertion Sinhala–Buddhist nationalism, by the mid-1950s the major parties [the Sri Lanka Freedom Party

(SLFP) and the United National Party (UNP)] promoted Sinhala as the official language while subordinating Tamil nationalists' demands (Jayawardena 1985; Uyangoda 2000).

During this time, economic nationalism integrated unions into a new liberal corporatist regime. Unlike the colonial paternalist regime, state intervention in the economy established economic and social rights that expanded the social provision of education, health, employment, and social welfare (Liyanage 1997). The changes also reinforced interlocking union–party leaderships, which increasingly subordinated trade unions to political party interests. By the mid-1970s, the working class parties were in disarray with unions fragmented and increasingly compromised by party politics (Fernando 1988).

Voted in on a platform of change in 1977, the UNP launched the first wave of economic reform by introducing neo-liberal policies promoting flexible labour markets and export-oriented industrialization. The setting up of free trade zones (FTZs) in 1978, and their extension to the whole island in 1992 was a centrepiece of this policy. This reform was later reinforced by World Bank Structural Adjustment Programs in 1980. In addition, the state actively promoted Sinhala–Buddhist nationalism within a 'righteous society', or *Dharmishta samajaya,* discourse (Obeysekere 1984; Manor 1984).

Authoritarian state tendencies began with the new presidential constitution introduced in 1978, which extended wide-ranging interventionist powers to the president overriding parliamentary as well as electoral processes (Moore 1994, 1997a; Stokke 1997). With the enactment of the *Prevention of Terrorism Act* (PTA) in 1979, the state institutionalized political violence which included torture and disappearances (Obeysekere 1984; Amnesty International 1989; Senaratne 1997; AHRC 2006).

Correspondingly, the post-1977 phase in trade unionism illustrated a transition to an authoritarian labour market regime which featured weakening collective bargaining rights and freedom of association. Not only did FTZ factories engage in recruiting a gendered labour force which was seemingly compliant to the needs to capital (Gunawardana 2007), but also enterprises suppressed union formation and activity, while the regular enforcement of the Essential Services Act criminalized union activities. The use of Emergency Regulations, often rationalized as necessary for safeguarding vital national economic interests, continues to be central to restraining freedom of association and collective bargaining (Gunatilaka 2001). The formation of new trade unions was hindered by the promotion of enterprise-bound and management-driven Worker's Councils. These were monitored by the Board of Investments, a statutory body responsible for the administration of the FTZs (Teitelbaum 2007; Gunawardana 2007). The weakening of unions is intertwined with changes in party politics and local governing bodies.

Representative politics in Sri Lanka in the post-1977 period is shaped by state and counter-state violence anchored in grievances along ethnic and class injustices. A key characteristic of this phase has been the near absence of working class parties from representative politics and the lack of an alternative working class programme with mass appeal. Along with increasing self-censorship, the state and private sector media play a critical role in framing political debates which often suppress union and labour movement perspectives (Rathnayake 2000; Fernando 1988).

With protests from below and civil society restrained, the electoral system, in particular the multi-tier institutions of governance – at village, division, district, province and national level – have become sites of intense struggle for entering a complex web of economic and political relations (Uyangoda 1997). Although post-independence Sri Lanka has sustained an active democracy with high voter turn-out at elections, multi-party elections and a layering of local governing bodies, political violence during election times has permeated the electoral system in the post-1977 period (Uyangoda 1997).

The 1983 outbreak of the ongoing ethnic war related to the Tamil youth struggles for recognition and redistribution in the mid-1970s (Uyangoda 2000). The Sri Lankan state has been involved in ongoing conflict with the Liberation Tamil Tigers Elam (LTTE) since 1983, the latter pursuing an armed separatist campaign in the northeast of the island. The ethnic war was amplified for a short violent 'terror' period, during the 1988–9 *Janatha Vimukthi Peramuna* (JVP) insurrection by rural Sinhala youth against state attempts to devolve power to the regions. This insurrection was also fuelled by the growing unemployment and underemployment in rural areas and the articulations of class resentment in terms of ethno-nationalist politics (Senaratne 1997; Uyangoda 2000). The JVP insurrection and the counter-insurrection of 1988–9 claimed around 40,000 lives, involving thousands of 'disappearances', including those involved in trade union activities (Amnesty International 1989; Senaratne 1997; AHRC 2006; Rathnayake 2000).[4] Meanwhile, the on-going war has claimed over 60,000 lives, and the population of refugees (displaced) has fluctuated from half a million to a million at various points in the war (Ganguly 2004). In this context of war, unions are faced with a militarized authoritarian state implicated in a range of human rights violations (Amnesty International 1989; Uyangoda,2000; Obeysekere 1984).

Following 17 years under UNP rule, the SLFP came to power in 1994 in a broad coalition called the People's Alliance (PA), supported by the working class parties, the Communist Party (CP) and the Lanka Sama Samja Party (LSSP), and the labour movement. Although the new coalition enabled some union freedoms, it failed in the peace process and in protecting workers. The UNP returned to power in 2000 and negotiated a ceasefire agreement in 2002 with the LTTE, while renewing market reforms. In response, the SLFP formed a fragile coalition with the Sinhala nationalists' JVP and the newly launched Buddhist monks' party, the *Jathika Hela Urumaya* (JHU – National Sinhala Heritage Party). This new coalition ousted the UNP at the 2004 parliamentary elections, and again during the 2005 presidential elections (Ganguly 2004). Despite the formal ceasefire agreement, the LTTE, as well as the state, engaged in acts of violence. With the escalation of the conflict, the SLFP led the coalition and the opposition UNP moved towards a new power-sharing agreement in October 2006. Outside the party unions in the coalition, most unions remain critical of this new trend towards a 'national government' which has also gained employers' support (Kearney 2006).

Owing to successive cycles of economic reforms emphasizing the liberalization of the economy (Athukorala and Rajapatirana 2000), Sri Lanka is one of the most open economies in the region. In 2006 and 2007, Sri Lanka was ranked 89th using the World Bank Regulation Index (World Bank 2007). Table 11.1 outlines some of the general characteristics of the Sri Lankan economy.

Table 11.1 Contextual factors – Sri Lanka

General statistics	
Population (2005)[1]	19.6
Area (square kilometres)	65,610
Employment by sector[2] (%)	
Agriculture	35
Industry	17
Services	47
Urban population[3] (% of total population)	20
GDP per capita[4]	4,600
Income inequality (high, medium or low)	High
Gini coefficient[5]	0.47
Real GDP growth[6] (%)	
1986–1995	4.4
1995–2005	4.2
Unemployment (%)	
1986–1995[7]	14
1996–2005[8]	9
Summary description	
Openness and degree of competition:	
International trade (import + export) as % of GDP[9]	(835,510 + 628,046) GDP at current market price is 2,407,775
World Bank regulation index	89
Political context (liberal/pluralistic, state unitarist [communist, non-communist])	Pluralistic, however, undermined by the ongoing conflict
Political stability (high, medium or low)	High, however, undermined by the ongoing conflict

Sources
1 World Bank (2006).
2 World Bank (2005b).
3 World Bank (2005b).
4 World Bank (2004).
5 Central Bank (2005).
6 Central Bank (2005).
7 Rama (2003).
8 Central Bank (2005).
9 Department of Census and Statistics (2005).

In comparison with other South Asian countries, Sri Lanka has maintained relatively high per capita GDP levels, improved literacy, nutrition and low fertility rates. The post-independence development state extended access to education, health and social provision, as well as political participation (Lakshman 1997). Yet despite economic growth and a per capita GDP of around US$900 in 2002, poverty rates have remained high. Although poverty in Sri Lanka has declined slightly from 26.1 per cent in 1990–1 to 22.7 in 2002, the poverty rates in the plantations have increased. While poverty in urban and rural areas has declined, poverty in the plantation sector (tea, rubber and coconut) has increased by over 50 per cent during the 1990–2002 period (World Bank 2004: 21). In effect, a significant character of poverty, which is linked with the fall in real wages, is increasing the population of working poor.

The employed population in Sri Lanka has increased from 2.6 million in 1946, to 3.6 million in 1971, to 5.2 million in 1986, to 6.5 million in 2003 (Nanayakkara 2004). During the 1990–2005 period, the labour force participation rates for men ranged from 65 to 67 per cent, while for women it ranged from 30 to 37 per cent (Nanayakkara 2004: 5; Central Bank 2005). The overall unemployment has reduced from around 16 per cent in 1990 to 9 per cent in 2003. However, women and educated youth, particularly those in the 15 to 29 age group, represent a disproportionate share of the unemployed (Nanayakkara 2004: 16–19).

In terms of the changing sectoral division of labour in the post-1977 period, employment in the agricultural sector has marginally declined while manufacturing and services sectors have expanded. In 1977, employment in agriculture accounted for 52 per cent, manufacturing 13 per cent and services 34 per cent. By 2000, employment in agriculture declined to around 35 per cent (2.4 million), while manufacturing increased to 17 per cent and services 47 per cent (World Bank 2004: 87). Within the agricultural sector, a significant share of the labour force is engaged in subsistence agriculture. Rural areas account for 80 per cent of the population and 90 per cent of those in poverty in 2004 (World Bank 2004: 13).

The plantations are the largest organized sector with close to 450,000 workers. Employment in manufacturing increased from around 140,000 in 1977 to over 500,000 in the mid-1990s (World Bank 2004: 6). Export-oriented manufacturing increased from 25 per cent in 1977 to nearly 80 per cent by the mid-1990s, with garments as the main sector (World Bank 2004: 5–6). Women workers formed 88 per cent of total employed (310,530 workers) in the garment sector in 2001 (Board of Investments 2003). Most of them are Sinhala women from rural areas between the ages of 16 and 24, unmarried, and secondary level educated (Rosa 1994; Abeysekere 1997; Caspersz 1998). With limited development of a manufacturing base and linkages with other sectors, most services sector activities are family-based enterprises engaged in retail trade, transport, repair and maintenance, construction, personal and domestic services. Most of this work, characterized by insecure, unprotected and low-wage work, involves women workers.

Although women in Sri Lanka have gained greater access to the public realm than most others in the region, the shift towards privatization and deregulation has directly affected women workers. Women are facing new challenges of accessing public goods, particularly education and health, and public sector jobs, which are increasingly casualized (Abeysekere 1997; Lynch 2002).

Overview of trade union membership

Between 1975 and 2002, the numbers of unionized workers fluctuated between 693,000 and just over 1,500,000. In 2002, around 9.8 per cent of the 6.5 million employed were union members. The Labour Department has limited statistical coverage of trade union membership, with only around 33–37 per cent of all unions submitting annual reports.[5] Trade unions are often reluctant to give details for fear of harassment and victimization (Biyanwila 2004).

Public sector workers are a core segment of the labour movement, with politically independent unions. In 1999, the combined public sector unions (banking, electric utilities, telecommunication, health and education) accounted for nearly 23 per cent of the total membership of reporting unions (Labour Department 2001). The majority of unions are, however, found in large private sector firms which represent around 15–20 per cent of the non-agricultural workforce. The Hill Country Tamil plantation workers represented the largest segment of organized agricultural workers, while urban unions are mostly dominated by services and industrial sector workers. Table 11.2 gives a brief overview of trade union numbers and membership as recorded by the Ministry of Labor Relations and Foreign Employment.

Table 11.2 Sri Lankan trade unions

General statistics	
Number of unions (2004)[1]	1,604
Number of union members (2004)[2]	583,323
Union density (end of 2005)[3] Public Private	23% 77%
Level of collective bargaining	L
Summary description	
Main union type	Political unions; party unions; politicized multi-union model
Main union structure	Centralized, bureaucratic, male dominated
Extent of unity of peak organization	Low
State control of unions	Low
Involvement in collective bargaining	Low

Sources
1 Department of Labor, Trade Unions (2005).
2 Department of Labor, Trade Unions (2005).
3 Department of Labor, Trade Unions (2005).

Women workers represent a significant proportion of unionized workers, particularly in sectors with high densities of women workers. The largest segment of organized women workers are in the plantations followed by education and health sectors. While women often take up leadership positions at the grassroots level, they are largely absent from the executive leadership level. Many trade unions report that they have set quotas for women in leadership; however recruiting and retaining the women in these positions has proved problematic (discussed in the following section). Nevertheless, new worker organizations in the FTZs, mostly based on young women workers, depict new tendencies of more democratic unions with a younger generation of leaders (Rosa 1994: 79; Abeysekere 1997; Caspersz 1998; Gunawardana 2007).

The nature of unions, types and structure

Workers are generally organized along sectoral/industrial unions; tea plantation workers represent the main organized sector. The membership of plantation unions is mainly drawn from the Hill Country Tamil community and their strategies are intertwined with cultural struggles for recognition (Kandasamy 2002). Within the public sector, unions are mostly formed on the basis of occupational identities. While enterprise unionism is the preferred strategy promoted by employers, the main political parties maintain their general unions.

The emergence of working class parties in the 1930s was central to a deepening of class consciousness and the class politics of trade unions. The working class parties emerged prior to the consolidation of the main bourgeois liberal parties (UNP 1946, SLFP 1951). A unique ideological orientation of working class parties in Sri Lanka is the influence of Trotskyism, which emphasized the realm of internationalist politics in shaping domestic class struggles (Amarasinghe 1998: 240). The LSSP was the leading working class party with the greatest popular support until the early 1970s. However, with the outbreak of the 1971 JVP insurrection and the counter-insurrection of the state, the LSSP and the CP (Communist Party) lost their legitimacy and their capacities.

Radical gains aimed at expanding democratic labour market institutions and state social provision also ended in 1977, with neo-liberal policies promoting flexible labour markets (Liyanage 1997). Recognizing the limits of dominant party unions, radical Christian and women's organizations working with non-organized workers emerged through early struggles in the 1980s. In particular, a handful of women workers in NGOs have maintained an active involvement in the FTZs, organizing mostly women workers (Rosa 1994; Abeysekere 1997).

As the dominant union strategy, political unionism has reinforced party control over unions. In narrowing trade unions to institutionalized representative politics, these unions reproduce labour market institutions that restrain workers' capacity to mobilise and build alliances. The two main parties, the UNP and the SLFP, have maintained broad union organizations covering workers in the plantations and the urban sector. In the plantations the dominant union, the CWC (Ceylon Workers Congress) is also a political party representing the Hill Country Tamil community. The SLFP union benefited from the decline of working class party unions in the post-1977 period. However, the SLFP's incapacity to restrain the neo-liberal assault on unions under the 1996–2000 People's Alliance (PA) government illustrated the contradictions of political unionism.

The UNP unions as well as the JVP have been accused of undermining the labour movement, often through violence. While the UNP unions promote business interests, the JVP is focused on its own self-promotion as the 'vanguard' workers' party. The UNP repression of the 1980 July strike, commemorated as Black July, was a historic event, crushing the labour movement (Fernando 1988). It was a decisive, targeted attack on working class parties (CP and LSSP), militant unions and labour militancy.

The working class parties, the LSSP and the CP, have seen their membership rapidly decline since the launch of liberalization in 1977. The CP unions were particularly repressed with a legal ban in the aftermath of the 1983 anti-Tamil pogrom (Fernando 1988). Both the LSSP and the CP unions remain mostly disoriented and impotent. Nevertheless, the *Nawa Sama Samaja Party* (NSSP), an early 1970s splinter group of the LSSP, has unions across diverse sectors and industries and maintains alliances with a range of worker-oriented organizations and social movements, such as the Christian Workers Fellowship and the Free Media Movement, including links with the FTZ labour organization *Niveka* (previously known as *Kalape Ape* or We in the Zone). These parties continue to articulate union struggles in terms of class politics, and sustain loose alliances. The working class party unions are active within the two main union coalitions, the Joint Trade Union Centre (JTUC) and the Joint Plantation Trade Union Centre (JPTUC) which also include powerful independent unions.

Banned after the 1983 July pogrom, the JVP re-emerged with the 1988–89 insurrection which involved attacks against other unionists. After being suppressed by government forces, they reorganized and expanded by engaging in collective action. As a political party that represents counter-movements from below, the JVP articulates a radical agenda that contains a mixture of broadly leftist socialism and Sinhala patriotism (Uyangoda 2000). Under the PA, the JVP reorganized their unions under the Socialist Workers Union (SWU) banner. In 2000, according to union leaders, the JVP consisted of 20 unions in the public sector and two in the private sector, with a total membership of around 60,000 and nearly 1,000 core activists.

The main party-independent unions are clerical and professional unions which are mostly in the public sector. These include administrative and skilled workers (CMU – Ceylon Mercantile Union; CBEU – Ceylon Bank Employees Union; UPTO – Union of Postal and Telecommunications Officer; CESU – Ceylon Estate Staff Union), doctors (GMOA – Government Medical Officers Association); and nurses (PSUNU – Public Service United Nurses Union). Although expressing mostly occupational interests, these unions have engaged in collective action, highlighting issues of wages, working conditions, privatization, emergency regulations and the devolution of state powers to regions. Particularly among party-independent unions new union strategies are encouraging union–community relations. Generally these unions are led by relatively progressive leaders within the CMU (private sector clerical workers), CBEU (banks), UPTO (post and telecom), GNOA (nurses) and FTZWU (free trade zone workers). These union–community alliances are often temporary and issue-based, so that deepening these alliances into structured, long-term alliances remains problematic.

Union integration within formal labour market institutions, as the 'industrial wing' of the political parties, has reinforced bureaucratic modes of organization (Lambert 2002; Biyanwila 2004). In their practical orientation towards representative politics, the bureaucratic unions have encouraged oligarchic union leaders with limited interests in building alliances with other unions or civil society networks. By avoiding contentious collective action or adversarial positions, these bureaucratic union forms often create consent to ethno-nationalist state strategies.

Although cooperative business unionism is promoted and encouraged by the state, employers and some international labour NGOs, such as the Friedrich Ebert Stiftung (FES) and the American Centre for International Labour Solidarity (ACILS), most unions are positioned in an adversarial role. Nevertheless, the dominant unions are rooted in patriarchal bureaucratic modes of organizing workers and increasingly avoid contentious movement politics. While reproducing a small network of male union leaders that interact with employers and the state, these structures continue to limit the initiatives of the members and new leaders. The narrow occupational and workplace focus of unions also restrains alliances with the majority of unorganized workers. Nevertheless, the enclaves of democratic unions with an orientation towards building alliances are engaging in collective action, revitalizing union identities as civil society actors.

In terms of labour internationalism, a few Sri Lankan unions maintain links with the WFTU (World Federation of Trade Unions) and the ICFTU (International Confederation of Free Trade Unions). As the main international unions, the ICFTU and GUFs (Global Union Federations) often engage in promoting union rights and raising awareness (ICFTU 2006). Along with the International Labor Organization (ILO), other international labour institutes, particularly the FES and the ACILS, continue to assist unions, primarily focusing on institutional reform and representative politics, often avoiding contentious movement politics and local–global collective action.

While maintaining links with old labour internationalism, some unions are also discovering new alliances. These alliances involve international labour NGOs or activist networks which include the Transnational Information Exchange (TIE Asia), the Asia Pacific Workers Solidarity Links (APWSL), Women Working Worldwide (WWW), and the Southern Initiative on Globalization and Trade Union Rights (SIGTUR) (Marcus and Brehaut 2003). In promoting new forms of worker solidarity within and among unions, these new strategies, mostly initiated by garment workers (FTZWU), are aimed at mobilizing workers and engaging in collective action (Rosa 1994; Biyanwila 2004).

In contesting authoritarian labour regimes, democratic unions are gradually gaining momentum among party independent unions and a few labour NGOs

(Lambert 2002; Biyanwila 2004). Recognizing a range of interconnected goals with multiple sites of struggle, the democratic unions are led by a new generation of leaders committed to building solidarity in order to engage in collective action (Lambert 2002). Holding union leaders and officials accountable to the members, these democratic unions prioritize members' initiatives and encourage forms of participatory democracy (Biyanwila 2004).

Women workers continue to be actively involved in labour struggles, contesting enduring patriarchal structures within and outside unions (Jayawardena 1986). In building women workers' organizations there is an enduring socialist feminist tradition in Sri Lanka (Jayawardena 1986: 135). These tendencies emerged with the formation of the *Kantha Handa* (Voice of Women) in 1978, initiated by a core group of mostly middle-class women. In subsequent years, several other socialist feminist groups formed, and among them were the Women's Liberation Movement in Ja-Ela and the Progressive Women's Forum, linked with a radical Christian development organization (Biyanwila 2004). Both of these organizations were instrumental in launching women workers' organizations around the free trade zones and promoting independent democratic unions (Jayakody and Goonetilake 1988; Rosa 1994).

Yet the number of women in traditional trade union leadership positions remains low. Union leaders have expressed gender-based concerns, centred on the low number of women in leadership positions, gender training and general enforcement of labour laws in women-dominated sectors such as apparel. Even in progressive independent unions such as the Bank Employees Union , only 6 per cent of the large 500 member central committee are women.

Some of the larger unions have quotas and reservations for women office bearers and central committee membership. For example, the Joint Plantation Trade Union Centre has quotas of 30 and 35 per cent representation respectively on their central committee, while the Tamil Teachers Association reserve the positions of co-vice president and co-general secretary for women, as well as having one-third of the central committee positions reserved for women.

However, this does not guarantee that these quotas are filled. Trade union leaders express the difficulties of involving women in trade union leadership and other activities owing to what almost all refer to as 'cultural reasons'. Even the most committed and politically-minded women, according to the leaders, withdraw from union activities after marriage. In essence, what these leaders are articulating is the triple burden women face at home, work and with trade union activities, where childcare and household duties take priority. In addition, women cannot participate in activities that involve culturally 'disrespectable' activities such as staying overnight at training camps or staying at meetings late into the evening.

The trade unions, such as the FTZWU, interviewed for this chapter reported providing training for women workers, including training aimed explicitly at developing leadership capabilities. These programmes are usually run with the assistance of labour organizations such as the FES and the American Solidarity Centre. Some unions also encourage training in alternative livelihood programmes for women. However, much more needs to be developed to include women in trade union activities.

What do unions do?

Sri Lankan trade unions have engaged in collective bargaining and legal enactment (Webb and Webb 1894, 1897 in Gospel, Chapter 2 this volume). Importantly, they have also asserted their role as civil society actors within the labour movement, particularly during the anti-colonial, nationalist movements.

The two major areas of industrial relations that unions in Sri Lanka have focused upon are salary and wage matters and opposition to economic liberalization policies encompassing labour law reform. In relation to the former, unions have agitated for wage rises in line with cost of living rises, the payment of gratuity and retirement entitlements, and in some sectors, such as the garment sector, a living wage. For example, the Apparel-industry Labour Rights Movement (ALaRM) encompasses diverse trade unions such as the Free Trade Zone Workers Union, JSS and the National Workers Congress. In relation to the latter, in 2003 trade unions assembled with NGOs and other people's movements to form the Alliance for the Protection of Natural Resources and Human Rights. This alliance mobilized against the IMF Poverty Reduction Strategy Paper, which promoted policies deepening economic, social and environmental crises in the country. Besides protesting the lack of civil society consultation in the development of the proposals, the alliance opposed the 'second generation' economic liberalization policies such as labour law reform, privatization and agricultural reform. Despite the protests, the International Monetary Fund (IMF) suggested reforms were introduced by amending the *Termination of Employment and Workmen Act*, *Industrial Disputes Act*, *Industrial Disputes-Hearing and Determination Proceedings Act*, and *Employment of Women, Young Persons and Children Act*. The reforms, however, were modified or limited to some extent owing to union pressure.

In lobbying for change or protesting against proposed changes, public sector unions must appeal to ministers. Regardless of the sector, almost all unions continue to attempt to use political or personal connections to key ministers in gaining concessions. These may be in the form of informal or semi-formal meetings, or structured formal processes such as dialogue with ministerial committees or through the tripartite National Labor Advisory Council. This also reveals the nature of labour market institutions as dispute-settlement mechanisms. Unions often utilize the conciliation and arbitration offered through national labour law, by taking disputes to the labour tribunals. However, this is often a lengthy and costly process for workers. Recent amendments to the *Industrial Disputes Act* (2003) have addressed the backlog of cases waiting to be heard or solved.

Trade unions continue to engage with other trade unions around key issues of national importance and with unions in the global arena. The formation of the National Association for Trade Union Research and Education (NATURE) was intended to present united policy positions to the general public. However, the dominance of party unions continues to restrain union solidarity. While certain unions are beginning to forge links with labour-focused NGOs, a number of older leaders avoid them, arguing that some NGOs were apolitical and could not engage in representing workers. They were suspicious of NGO motives and questioned their legitimacy as representatives of the working class. This reluctance to encourage links with other activist NGOs also reflects the narrowing of union strategies to a legalistic collective bargaining focus.

With regard to collective bargaining agreements, older independent trade unions such as the CMU and the CBEU were party to the most CAs made between 2000 and July 2006. The relatively new JVP Inter-Company trade union has also been successful in securing a number of CAs with employers; they have the second largest number of CAs after the CMU. In this period, the Ceylon Estates Staff Union and the United Tea, Rubber and Local Produce Workers' Union were also well represented in the number of CAs. In a handful of cases, a number of trade unions jointly entered into a CA with one employer. It should be noted that almost all sectors outside the public sector are represented, and a number of CAs are with the Employers Federation of Ceylon, a representative peak body association. Table 11.3 illustrates that Sri Lankan trade unions also engage in collective bargaining, albeit in an uneven manner.

In terms of collective action, Sri Lankan trade unions organize strikes, work-to-rule activity, and picketing. Since 2000, the number of strikes has fallen from an average of 144 per year in the 1990s to an average of 94 per year. The number of days lost went from 293,519 in 1995 to 81,100 in 2004 (Department of Labor 2005). However, it must be noted that strike action which can happen without unions, such as wildcat strikes in Sri Lanka's FTZ (see Rosa 1994), and lockouts are absent from official statistics.

A number of employers, most notably in the BOI (Board of Investments) sector, set up workers' councils to allow for consultation and grievance handling. There is little research into the scope of these councils. However, research suggests that in the FTZ sector, workers councils limit their operations to discussions

Table 11.3 What do Sri Lankan trade unions do?

Extent of collective bargaining	L
Level of collective bargaining	National – L Industry – M Enterprise – H
Extent of joint consultation	L
Strikes, working days lost per 1,000 employed	15.48[1]
Degree of state intervention in employment protection	M
Income inequality (Gini coefficient)	0.47[2]

Sources
1 Department of Labor (2005) *Sri Lanka Labor Gazette. Colombo.* Vol. 56, No. 1 Ministry of Labor.
2 Department of Census & Statistics (2006) *Household Income and Expenditure Survey 2005 Summary Findings.* Colombo. Accessed at http://www.statistics.gov.lk/HIES/HIES%202005/HIES_2005_Buletin.pdf (12 January 2007).

over welfare matters and working hours, rather than wages and other conditions (Gunawardana 2007).

Explaining the development, structure and strategies of trade unions

It is clear that the trajectory of union development in Sri Lanka was influenced by anti-colonialist struggle, trends in social justice and Labourism in Britain, while Trotskyism was a key factor in the intellectual orientation of unionism in the mid-twentieth century. Nationalism and ethnic politics have been significant in shaping the strategic orientation of unions. An authoritarian state promoting employer interests as well as Sinhala–Buddhist nationalism continue to demobilize and de-legitimize unions – as well as other facets of civil society – while restraining workers' capacities to organize. More recently, following a series of worker protests in August 2006, the state re-enacted Emergency Regulations banning strikes and other industrial action in workplaces connected with international trade, including ports (Kearney 2006). The advent of neo-liberal economic reform has also had a great impact on the development of trade unions in Sri Lanka, particularly for those workers and workplaces falling under the jurisdiction of the BOI.

Political interdependence has continued to be a key characteristic of trade unionism in Sri Lanka well into the twenty-first century. The integration of trade unions within state and political parties extended worker rights; however it also strengthened bureaucratic unions that have restrained their capacity for engaging in collective action. Independent, but politically aligned unions tend to work towards the interests of the party rather than working class interests, and this weakened the movement. While there are some democratically based unions in operation, there is no convergence towards the wholesale adoption of this model, with the political party orientation of trade unions unlikely to change.

However, in interviews, trade union leaders, even those aligned to political parties, reported that such affiliations resulted in a weakening and fragmenting of worker solidarity on the shop floor. The subordination of unions to party politics not only restricts union control but also promotes competition among unions where rival unions would 'poach' members from one another. Different unions compete for workers in the same workplace and thus undermine unity. At other times, workers have swapped allegiance when different political parties are in power, intensifying the rivalry between unions. Furthermore, when certain political parties have declined in influence, so has their union.

Employers' behaviours and attitudes, as well as those of workers, have been important in shaping the development, structure and strategies of trade unions. Encouraged by the post-1977 liberalization strategies, the employers in Sri Lanka have promoted authoritarian labour regimes, undermining workers' capacities to unionize. The business and the political elite have increasingly converged in promoting markets, as well as ethno-nationalist notions of nationhood (Moore 1997a, 1997b). By positioning the private sector as the 'engine of growth', the World Bank and International Monetary Fund policies promoting international competitiveness have overlapped with interests of global capital (World Bank 2004). The subordination of unions to employer interests was set in motion with the early promotion of FTZs in 1978 along with the new presidential constitution. Even under the PA government (1994–2000), the employers campaigned against the proposed Workers' Charter, which was made into an amendment to the *Industrial Disputes Act* in December 1999.

Historically, the private sector in Sri Lanka has been shaped by mercantilist and monopolist practices of colonial capitalism driven by tea plantations. The indigenous capitalists were mostly higher caste Sinhala (graphite and liquor trading) and Tamil (plantations) mercantile capitalists. They were faced with key sectors of the economy controlled by the British (the plantations, agency houses, banks and foreign trade), Indian merchants (foreign trade and wholesale trade) and Muslim and Chettiars (retail trade and money-lending) (Jayawardena 1984: 54–5). The rise of Sinhala–Buddhist nationalist projects is a key feature of the competition among Sinhala and Tamil capitalists over limited avenues for capital accumulation. In the post-independence period, particularly during the 1956–77 closed economy period, statist interventions reinforced the positioning of the upper caste Sinhala capitalists (Moore 1997a). These ethnic and caste dynamics of the private sector were heightened with open economy policies. Accordingly, most Sri Lankan companies, including those listed in the stock market, are controlled by individuals, families or by a small number of senior executives (Moore 1997a: 361).

While the new corporate private sector articulates a modernizing agenda, this modernity is grounded in restraining worker rights. The orientation of the employers is illustrated by the recent dismantling of the *Termination of Employment of Workmen (Special Provisions) Act* (TEWA), which was introduced in the early 1970s in order to institutionalize dispute settlement mechanisms and protect workers from unfair dismissal. The UNP government introduced changes to the TEWA in January 2002, increasing employers' authority to 'hire and fire'. According to a 1998 IMF report, the TEWA 'may have a negative impact on the work ethic and productivity, and firms seem to prefer overtime, subcontracting, and casual or contract labour over hiring more permanent staff'.[6] In effect, international finance institutions continue to play a key role in reinforcing employer hostility towards unions (ICFTU 2006). Table 11.4 provides a broad overview of the operating environment for employers and some general characteristics.

The main business associations – the Employers' Federation of Ceylon and the Ceylon Chamber of Commerce – along with the BOI, maintain an antagonistic position towards unions. In a policy climate of promoting non-unionized workplaces to attract international investors, the discourse of social partnership and 'social clause' emerged in the mid-1990s under the PA government. The 'social clause', also referred to as transnational company 'codes of conduct', promotes the enforcement of ILO Core Conventions, covering issues such as health and safety, forced labour, fair wages, minimum age of employment and hours of work. Some unions (FTZWU) have used code-based strategies for communication and information exchange through activist networks to engage in local worker struggles. The form of self-regulation of employers represented by the 'codes of conduct' remains ineffective, and reflects the uneven and selective application of national labour legislation (Hensman 2000).

The challenges unions face relate to both internal and external factors. One of the major challenges perceived by trade union leaders is how to attract new members, particularly among the youth, and retain them. In relation to the former, plantation trade unions report that young people are afraid of employer harassment, regardless of occupational status. Among some private sector unions, there exist issues surrounding ways to communicate the relevance of trade unions to younger workers, particularly with the changing character and aspirations of the working class over the past 10 to 15 years. Indeed, there is a case to be made that political unionism fails to respond to the on-going changes occurring in economies, societies and cultures, making them socially weak (see Candland 2001: 84 for India comparison).

From the union leaders' perspectives, once members have been recruited, retaining them is a difficult task. Workers often leave the union or become inactive

Table 11.4 Explaining the Sri Lankan trade union development, structure, and strategy

Political context	
Degrees of liberalization and autonomy (repression, tolerance, support, indifference) Relations with the State (dependent, independent)	Tolerance, some repression (on-going war)
	Independent, however most have strong political party ties
Markets	
Openness (imports + exports as % of GDP)	45.6[1]
Degree of competition (high, medium or low)	Medium
Financial markets Openness to market financing Ownership (group, institutional, foreign, dispersed)	Medium Institutional investors, with some foreign
Labour markets Demand elasticity (relates to ability of employers to pass on wage increases in prices – high, medium or low)	Low–Medium
Employer context: Organization – top 100 as % of total Employer organization membership Multinational Unitarist vs. pluralist	NA H H Majority Unitarist Management Approach

Source
1 World Bank (2007) 'Doing business in South Asia 2007'. Online. Available HTTP: <http://web.worldbank.org/WBSITE/EXTERNAL/COUNTRIES/SOUTHASIAEXT/0,,contentMDK:21217344~pagePK:146736~piPK:146830~theSitePK:223547,00.html> (accessed 1 March 2007).

following certain union campaigns and victories. Concern about the lack of commitment of union members is common across all sectors except the plantation and banking sectors, which maintain high levels of union density. In addition, union leaders report that the welfare activities sustained by some of the unions are being co-opted by NGOs and employers implementing 'soft' HRM practices.

The main external challenge is seen to be neo-liberal globalization, involving the pressure to attract international investment by extending deregulated flexible labour markets, which has the effect of weakening existing labour rights. Trade union leaders argue that this is associated with the dismantling of national labour laws to the detriment of workers. They also report that a recent increase in contract and outsourced labour contracts had made labour organizing and representation complicated, as they found it difficult to access workers and ensure continuity in membership. Where workers were organized, they faced multiple forms of employer harassment.

A major challenge facing the trade union movement in Sri Lanka is the non-implementation of labour laws by employers and their non-enforcement by the state. This also extends to the public sector, where the lack of dispute-settlement mechanisms often drains valuable union resources. Arguing that it was time consuming and unreliable to depend on ministerial decisions, these unions have asserted the need for formal structures to assist in the creation of an equitable and efficient dispute-settlement process. However, the state's capacities are restrained by the ongoing ethnic war, which is a serious external constraint on trade union activity. Some unions, such as the Tamil Teachers Association, have expressed the difficulties of working under 'high security' settings where territories and identities are contested, while other unions explained how anti-terror legislation is periodically enacted to 'crush' the union movement.

Despite the challenges, trade union leaders believe that unions still have popular appeal and a vital role to play in the future of Sri Lanka. They see opportunities for revitalizing unions, particularly in certain sectors. In sectors such as the garment industry where there is a tight labour market or in the plantations where there is a semi-captive labour force, there is capacity to organize successfully. Although the informal sector is a key area to expand unions, this has not been seriously attempted. Nevertheless, by asserting union autonomy from political parties, unions have an opportunity to build alliances and to expand and regain their role as civil society actors.

Conclusions

This chapter has examined the historical development of trade unions, current trajectories and challenges facing trade unions. We have argued that the character of trade unions, and their struggles in Sri Lanka can be understood by examining wider societal contexts such as the struggle to end colonialism, the contestation over the nation-state and economic reform. The type of action taken by trade unions and their structures can be understood by examining political party linkages and the changing role of the state; the latter is particularly salient in the post-1977 period.

Trade unions have played an important part in Sri Lanka's political and social landscape and the political unionism model which emerged out of the colonial economy and with anti-colonial struggles remains at the core of the trade union movement in Sri Lanka. While this model has limitations, it has not precluded unions from taking action against the party line, as during times of proposed privatization, economic and labour market reform. Trade unions have had an impact on the wellbeing of their members through the securing of wage increases and other conditions. Although these conditions have been eroded, some unions are building alliances, both locally and globally, and strengthening their capacities to engage in collective action, expressing tactics of society-oriented unions (see Hyman 2001).

Notes

1 The authors would like to acknowledge the assistance of Bala Tampoe, T. M. R. Rasseedin, Jayaratne Maliyagoda, Palitha Athukorale, S. Saravanapavanathan, Anton Marcus, Lesile Devendra, M. R. Shah, Vasantha Samarasinghe, Linus Jayatillake, Mr Piyadasa and Mr Moheedin. We would like to thank Mr Rassedin in particular for facilitating contact with others.
2 With the outbreak of the ethnic war in 1983, the North and East provinces have been excluded from Census figures. After the 1981 Census, the next Census was in 2001, which covered only 18 out of 25 districts.
3 Sinhala ethnic identity as a hegemonic construct emerged towards the thirteenth century, although the Sinhala–Buddhist legends of origin dates back 2,500 years. See Gunawardena (1996) for a substantive discussion on contestations over collective history and identity politics in Sri Lanka.
4 See 'Forced disappearances in Sri Lanka constitute a crime against humanity' http://www.disappearances.org/mainfile.php/articles_srilanka/ (accessed January 2006).
5 The Trade Union section of the Labour Department has maintained reporting systems that were designed in the late 1960s. The internal systems of data collection and categorization are often incompatible with standard labour force categories published by the Department of Census and Statistics. There is a lack of gender disaggregated data and there is little initiative to update the division. Similarly, the Labour Department library is limited on trade union resources and there is no systematic effort towards trade union documentation. The *Sri Lankan Labour Gazette*, published by the Labour Ministry, is generally limited on trade union statistics as well as contemporary literature on trade unions and industrial relations. Also see Kelly, T. F. (1993) *Labour and the Number Racket – An Assessment of Labour Market Information in Sri Lanka*. Employment Series No. 12, IPS: Colombo.
6 IMF staff country report on labour markets 98/118; annex on 'The need for labour market reform' pages 54–9.

Bibliography

Abeysekere, S. (ed.) (1997) *A Review of Free Trade Zones in Sri Lanka*, Colombo: Dabindu Collective.

AHRC (2006) 'Sri Lanka: The Situation of Human Rights 2006'. Accessed at <http://material.ahrchk.net/hrreport/2006/SriLanka2006.pdf> (November 2006).

Amarasinghe, Y. R. (1998) *Revolutionary Idealism and Parliamentary Politics – A Study of Trotskyism in Sri Lanka*, Colombo: Social Scientist's Association.

Amnesty International (1989) *Political Killings in Southern Sri Lanka: On the Brink of Civil War*, London: AI Publications.

Asian Development Bank, South Asia Regional Department and Regional and Sustainable Development Department (2004) *Sri Lanka: Country Gender Assessment.* Online. Available HTTP: <http://www.adb.org/Documents/Reports/Country-Gender-Assessments/sri.asp> (accessed 23 October 2005).

Asian Human Rights Commission (2003) *Massacres in Asia: Sri Lanka: Bindunuwewa Massacre.* Online. Available HTTP: <http://massacres.ahrchk,net/bindunuwewa /index.php> (accessed 20 February 2006)..

Athukorala, P. C. and Rajapatirana, S. (2000) 'Liberalisation and industrial transformation: lessons from the Sri Lankan experience', *Economic Development and Cultural Change*, 48(3): 200.

Bates, R. (1970) 'Approaches to the study of unions and development', *Industrial Relations*, 9: 365–78.

Biyanwila, J. (2004) 'Trade unions in Sri Lanka under globalisation: reinventing worker solidarity', unpublished dissertation, University of Western Australia.

Board of Investments (2003) *Sri Lankan Apparels – An Overview.* Online. Available HTTP <http://www.boisrilanka.org/portal/index.phtml?catId=6&newsId=371> (accessed 15 January 2006).

Candland, C. (2001) 'The cost of incorporation: labor institutions, industrial restructuring, and new trade union strategies in India and Pakistan', in C. Candland and R. Sil (eds) *The Politics of Labor in a Global Age*, Oxford: Oxford University Press.

Caspersz, D. (1998) 'Difficulties in organising FTZ workers in Sri Lanka', in M. Hess (ed.) *Labour Organisation and Development: Case Studies*, ANU (Canberra): NCDS Asia Pacific Press.

Central Bank of Sri Lanka (2005) *Central Bank of Sri Lanka Annual Report*, Colombo: Central Bank of Sri Lanka.

Department of Census and Statistics (2005a) *Summary of Household Statistics.* Online. Available HTTP: <http://www.statistics.gov.lk/HIES%202005/HIES_2005_Buletin.pdf> (accessed 15 January 2006).

Department of Census and Statistics (2005b) *Statistics Abstract: Chapter II Population.* <http://www.statistics.gov.lk/Abstract_2006/Pages/chap2.htm>.

Department of Census and Statistics (2006) *Household Income and Expenditure Survey 2005 Summary Findings.* Colombo. Accessed at <http://www.statistics.gov.lk/HIES/HIES%202005/HIES_2005_Buletin.pdf> (accessed 12 January 2007).

Department of Labor (1992–2000) *Annual Administration Reports. Trade Union Division*, Colombo: Ministry of Labor.

Department of Labor (2001) *Annual Administration Report. Trade Union Division*, Colombo: Ministry of Labor

Department of Labor (2005) *Sri Lanka Labor Gazette. Colombo*, Vol. 56, No. 1. Colombo: Ministry of Labor.

Fernando, L. (1988) 'The challenge of the open economy: trade unionism in Sri Lanka', in R. Southall (ed.) *Trade Unions and the New Industrialisation of the Third World*, London: Zed Books.

Galenson, W. (ed.) (1958) *Labor and Economic Development*, New York: Wiley.

Ganguly, R. (2004) 'Sri Lanka's ethnic conflict: at a crossroad between peace and war', *Third World Quarterly*, 25(5): 903–18.

Gunatilaka, R. (2001) 'Freedom of association and collective bargaining in Sri Lanka: progress and prospects', paper presented at ILO National Convention on Implementation of Conventions, 87 and 98, Colombo.

Gunawardena, R. A. L. H. (1996) *Historiography in a Time of Ethnic Conflict*, Colombo: Social Scientists Association.

Gunawardana, S. (2007) 'Struggle, Perseverance and organization in Sri Lanka's export processing zones', in K. Bronbenbrenner (ed.) *Global Unions: Challenging Transnational Capital Through Cross-Border Campaigns*, Ithaca, NY: Cornell University Press.

Hensman, R. (2000) 'World trade and worker's rights: to link or not to link', *Pravada*, 6(6): 23–30

Hyman, R. (2001) *Understanding European Trade Unionism: Between Market, Class and Society*, London: George Allen & Unwin.

ICFTU (International Confederation of Free Trade Unions) (2006) 'Sri Lanka: Unions overcome barriers to organising in export processing zones'. Online. Available HTTP: <www.icftu.org> (accessed 24 September 2006).

Jayakody, S. and Goonetilake, S. (1988) 'Industrial action by women workers in Sri Lanka: The Polytex Garment Workers', in N. Heyzer (ed.) *Daughters in Industry: Work, Skill and Consciousness of Women Workers in Asia*, Kuala Lumpur: Asian and Pacific Development Centre.

Jayawardena, K. (1972) *The Rise of the Labour Movement in Ceylon*, Durham, NC: Duke University Pres.

Jayawardena, K. (1984) 'Class formation and communalism', *Race & Class*, 26: 51–62.

Jayawardena, K. (1985) *Ethnic and Class Conflict in Sri Lanka: Some Aspects of Sinhala Buddhist Consciousness over the Past 100 Years*, Colombo: Sanjiva Books.

Jayawardena, K. (1986) *Feminism and Nationalism in the Third World*, London: Zed Books.

Jayawardena, K. (1987) 'Ethnic conflict in Sri Lanka and regional security'. Online. Available HTTP <http://www.infolanka.com/org/srilanka/issues/kumari.html> (accessed 15 December 2005).

Jensen, C. S. (2006) 'Trade unionism: Differences and similarities – a comparative view on Europe, USA and Asia', *Journal of Industrial Relations*, 48: 159–81.

Kandasamy, M. (2002) *The Struggles Continues …: Women's Leadership in Plantation Trade Unions in Sri Lanka*, Kandy, Sri Lanka: ISD Publications.

Kearney, N. (2006) 'Government of Sri Lanka asked to explain scope of sweeping new emergency regulations'. Online. Available HTTP: <http://www.itglwf.org> (International Textile, Garment and Leather Workers' Federation).

Kuruvilla, S. and Erickson, C. L. (2002) 'Change and transformation in Asian industrial relations', *Industrial Relations*, 41(2): 171–227.

Kuruvilla, S. and Mundell, B. (eds) (1999) *Colonialism, Nationalism, and the Institutionalisation of Industrial Relations in the Developing World*, Monographs in Organizational Behaviour and Industrial Relations 25, Stamford, CT: JAI Press.

Lakshman, W. D. (ed.) (1997) *Dilemmas of Development: Fifty Years of Economic Change in Sri Lanka*, Colombo: Sri Lanka Association of Economists.

Lambert, R. (2002) 'Labour movement renewal in the era of globalisation: Union responses in the South', in J. Harrod and R. O'Brien (eds) *Theory and Strategy of Organised Labour in the Global Political Economy*, London: Routledge.

Liyanage, S. (1997) 'The state, state capital and capitalistic development', in W. D. Lakshman (ed.) (1997) *Dilemmas of Development: Fifty Years of Economic Change in Sri Lanka*, Colombo: Sri Lanka Association of Economists.

Lynch, C. (2002) 'The politics of White women's underwear in Sri Lanka's open economy', *Social Politics*, Spring.

Manor, J. (ed.) (1984) *Sri Lanka in Change and Crisis*, New York: St Martin's Press.

Marcus, A. and Brehaut, M. (2003) 'Sri Lanka: Busting Jaqalanka', in AMRC Asian Labour Update. Online. Available HTTP: <www.amrc.org.hk/4808.htm> (accessed 5 October 2005).

Moore, M. (1994) 'Guided democracy in Sri Lanka: the electoral dimension', *Journal of Commonwealth and Comparative Politics*, 32(1): 1–30.

Moore, M. (1997a) 'The identity of capitalists and the legitimacy of capitalists: Sri Lanka since Independence', *Development and Change*, 28: 331–6.

Moore, M. (1997b) 'Leading the Left to the Right: populist coalitions and economic reform', *World Development*, 25(7): 1009–28.

Munck, R. (1988) *The New International Labour Studies: An Introduction*, London: Zed Books.

Nanayakkara, A. G. W. (2004) *Employment and Unemployment in Sri Lanka – Trends Issues and Options*, Colombo: Department of Census and Statistics Sri Lanka.

Obeyesekere, G. (1984) 'The origins and institutionalisation of political violence', in M. James (ed.) *Sri Lanka in Change and Crisis*, New York: St Martin's Press.

Rama, M. (2003). 'The Sri Lankan unemployment problem revisited', *Review of Economic Development*, 7(3): 510–25.

Rathnayake, M. (2000) 'Freedom of expression and the media', in *Sri Lanka: State of Human Rights 2000*, Colombo: Law and Society Trust.

Rosa, K. (1994) 'The conditions and organisational activities of women in free trade zones: Malaysia, Philippines and Sri Lanka, 1970–1990', in S. Rowbotham and S. Mitter (eds) *Dignity and Daily Bread: New Forms of Economic Organising Among Poor Women in the Third World and the First*, London: Routledge.

Senaratne, J. P. (1997) *Political Violence in Sri Lanka, 1977–1990: Riots, Insurrections, Counterinsurgencies, Foreign Intervention*, Sri Lanka Studies series, Amsterdam: VU University Press.

Sivanandan, S. (1984) 'Racism and the politics of underdevelopment', *Race and Class*, 26: 1–37.

Stokke, K. (1997) 'Authoritarianism in the age of market liberalism in Sri Lanka', *Antippode*, 29(4): 437–55.

Teitelbaum, E. (2007) 'Can a developing democracy benefit from labour repression? Evidence from Sri Lanka', *Journal of Development Studies*, 48 (5): 830–5.

Uyangoda, J. (1997) 'Local bodies as domains of localized power', *Pravada* 5(1): 5–10.

Uyangoda, J. (2000) 'Post-independence social movements', in W. D. Lakshman and C. A. Tisdaell (eds) *Sri Lanka's Development since Independence: Socio-Economic Perspectives and Analysis*, New York: Nova Science Publishers.

Waterman, P. (1993) 'Social movement unionism: a new model for a new world order', *Review*, 16 (3): 76–81.

Waterman, P. (1998) *Globalisation, Social Movements and the New Internationalisms*, London and New York: Mansell/Continuum.

Webb, S. and Webb, B. (1894) *The History of Trade Unionism*, London: Longmans.

Wijayaraatam, K. (2002). 'Industrial Disputes Act' in Ministry of Employment and Labor, Sri Lanka, *Understanding Labor Law*, 2nd edition, Colombo: Sri Lanka Ministry of Employment and Labor.

World Bank (2004) *Sri Lanka Development Policy Review*, Colombo: World Bank.

World Bank (2005a) 'Attaining Millennium development goals in Sri Lanka: how likely and what will it take to reduce poverty, child mortality and malnutrition and to increase school enrolment and completion?' Online. Available HTTP: <http://www-wds.worldbank.org/servlet/WDS_IBank_Servlet?pcont=details&eid=0001600 16_20050630090640> (accessed 11 March 2006).

World Bank (2005b) *Sri Lanka Data Profile* <http://devdata.worldbank.org/external/CPProfile.asp?PTYPE=CP&CCODE=LKA> (accessed 15 January 2007).

World Bank (2006) 'Sri Lanka at a glance'. Online. Available HTTP: <http://devdata.worldbank.org/AAG/lka_aag.pdf> (accessed 20 May 2007).

World Bank (2007) 'Doing business in South Asia 2007'. Online. Available HTTP: <http://web.worldbank.org/WBSITE/EXTERNAL/COUNTRIES/SOUTHASIAEXT/0,,contentMDK:21217344~pagePK:146736~piPK:146830~theSitePK:223547,00.html> (accessed March 2007).

12 Trade unions in Vietnam

From socialism to market socialism

Vincent Edwards and Anh Phan

Introduction

Trade unions in Vietnam have been experiencing substantial change since the adoption of the *doi moi* policy of economic reform in the mid-1980s. Up till then the trade unions were conceived and functioned as a 'transmission belt' (Kornai 1992) of the ruling communist party in the context of a socialist planned economy. *Doi moi*, however, changed the institutional context in which companies and consequently the trade unions operated. Small private enterprise became an increasingly important employer as did foreign companies that operated in Vietnam (Williams 1992; Quang 2001; Warner *et al*. 2005). At the same time state-owned enterprises were rationalized and subjected to privatization (equitization, as it is known in Vietnam).

The trade unions therefore have had to come to terms with the new circumstances (Zhu and Fahey 1999; 2000). This chapter will explore the development, role and activities of Vietnamese trade unions through the lens of Hyman's (2001) 'eternal triangle' of market, class and society (see Chapter 2). A study of the Vietnamese trade unions is therefore a study of response to change and the influence of globalization. Such a study may provide insights into trade union relevance and adaptability in a changing world which have implications beyond Vietnam, as well as testing the applicability to Vietnam of Hyman's framework.

Historically Vietnamese trade unions have been a mass organization representing workers' interests and closely linked to the ruling party. In a largely agricultural society such as Vietnam, state employees and trade union members represent only a small proportion of total employees and are concentrated in certain sectors, and have been most active in the state sector, i.e. among employees paid by the state. These included employees of state-owned enterprises (SOEs) and employees of state organizations such as the public administration, education system and health services.

The Vietnamese trade union movement can be considered 'encompassive' (Visser 1990). Trade union activity is determined by the Vietnam General Confederation of Labour (VGCL) which has traditionally incorporated both industrial and locality-based trade unions. The main role of the trade union is to 'function as the representative to protect the rights and interests of workers and employees' (VietnamNet 2006). However, there has been a shift from locality-based to occupation-based trade unions, with industrial unions dominant in the state sector and professional and occupational unions prevalent in the private sector (Zhu and Fahey 1999).

Traditionally, the trade unions undertook a range of functions in addition to representing the interests of their members. They acted as agents of the ruling party, organized and distributed welfare, took part in state organizations in the decision-making process and mobilized workers to achieve production targets. To a large degree, trade unions have been perceived as being, on the one hand, an extension of the ruling party and, on the other hand, as being predominantly concerned with members' welfare. One respondent commented that her role as trade union representative had been mostly taken up by lending a sympathetic ear to members' personal problems, visiting former employees and organizing events, what Chan and Nørlund (1999: 205) have described as 'the human touch for bureaucratic institutions'. Trade unions have also regarded themselves as owners of the enterprise and assumed a mediating role in reconciling differences of interest between managers and workers (Zhu 1998). Relating these roles to Hyman's (2001) 'eternal triangle', Vietnamese trade unions have tended to operate on the class–society side of the triangle.

Formally, according to Article 10 of the 1992 Constitution of the Socialist Republic of Vietnam, the role of the trade unions is described as follows:

> The trade unions, being the socio-political organization of the working class and the labouring people, in cooperation with government agencies, economic and social entities, take care of and safeguard the rights and interests of cadres, workers, employees and other labouring people; participate in State administration and social management, in the control and supervision of the State agencies, economic and social entities; educate cadres, workers, employees and other labouring people to do their utmost for national construction and defence.

More recently, trade unions have been concerned with recruiting members and safeguarding their interests outside of the growing non-state sectors, that is, among domestic and foreign private enterprises. This is a particularly important task as employment in SOEs has fallen (Dollar 1999; Rondinelli and Litvack 1999). A number of press articles have extolled the benefits of unions in private enterprises and praised bosses who work constructively with the union. Even in private companies the annual employer–employee congress is considered a significant and formal event.

Whilst it is difficult to assess the impact of the trade unions, it is nevertheless possible to indicate areas where the trade unions have influenced workers and the economy. Although Vietnam is a low-wage economy and many enterprises ignore or adopt a cavalier attitude to health and safety issues (Chan and Nørlund 1999; Wang 2005), one could argue that the situation might be even worse were it not for the presence of trade unions. Trade unions, moreover, 'formalize' worker dissatisfaction with employment conditions and provide a channel for their resolution.

Trade unions also have the legal right, according to the 1994 Labour Code (amended in 2002), to have a presence in all companies. Trade unions are therefore present in all types of companies: state-owned, private and foreign-owned. The problematic nature of this presence, especially in foreign-invested and foreign-owned companies, will be addressed later.

At the level of the economy it could be argued that trade unions represent a constraint on employer discretion, increase costs and act as a disincentive to foreign investors, many of whom come from countries with weak trade unions (Dixon 2000).

All in all, the trade unions are having to develop a more distinctive role as the Vietnamese economy has opened up to market forces and foreign investment. The traditional role as party transmission belt has had to be reviewed as new forces have entered the economic arena. The closed socialist system in which all organizations strove to achieve the same social, political and economic goals has given way to a situation in which competing interests, for example, between the state and foreign companies and between employers and employees, are brought out into the open. The trade unions thus have to face the difficult task of supporting the ruling party and representing their members' interests, a task which often resembles squaring the circle.

Context and history

The development of Vietnamese trade unions needs to be understood within the broader context of Vietnamese history. In brief, Vietnamese history can be viewed as a process of safeguarding Vietnamese national identity against the threat of foreign powers. Between the eleventh and thirteenth centuries, Vietnam successfully resisted incorporation in the Chinese Empire, and remained an independent state until the mid-nineteenth century when it was absorbed piece by piece into the French Empire. The origins of the Vietnamese trade unions can be traced back to the early twentieth century when most industrial activity in Vietnam was controlled by French nationals. Vietnam has always been a predominantly agricultural society. Under French colonial rule there was an expansion of commercial and industrial activities, for example, rubber plantations. Vietnamese also travelled overseas to work and study and some participated in the local trade unions. The beginnings of trade union activity in Vietnam began around 1920. There was some trade union activity in Saigon in the early 1920s and the so-called Red Federation of Trade Unions was formed in 1929 in Hanoi. This event was followed by the founding of the Communist Party of Indochina in 1930 (Vien 2004).

Trade union activity was closely linked to the struggle for national independence throughout the first half of the twentieth century, and thus became closely linked with nationalist, socialist and communist ideas. The close link between trade union and ruling party was institutionalized with the establishment of the Democratic Republic of Vietnam (North Vietnam) in 1945 and the creation of the Fatherland

Front which comprised a number of mass organizations. French rule came to an end in 1954. However, instead of a unified Vietnam, the country was divided into a socialist North Vietnam and an anti-communist South Vietnam, the latter supported mainly by the United States. The struggle for national reunification came to an end in 1975 when North Vietnam took control of and incorporated the South.

The nature of trade union involvement was strongly influenced by its links with communist ideas and the Vietnamese Communist Party led by Ho Chi Minh (1890–1969). The Vietnamese trade unions thus bore many of the hallmarks of trade unions in other socialist countries. The close link between party and trade unions became manifest in the person of Nguyen Van Linh (1915–98), the promulgator of *doi moi,* who at different times held the post of General Secretary of the Communist Party (1986–91) and Chairman of the Trade Unions (1976–80).

In South Vietnam, trade unions adopted an adversarial stance towards capital and the government, and trade union activities were often physically repressed (Chan and Nørlund 1999). Following reunification of North and South Vietnam in 1976, the system prevalent in the North was adopted throughout the country. The activities of trade unions are enshrined in the 1992 Constitution and the 1994 Labour Code.

The period following reunification was marked by severe economic problems, including major food shortages. These problems led to a review of economic policy and the announcement in 1986 of the policy of economic renovation (*doi moi*). Reforms affected a broad range of areas, including agriculture, internal and foreign trade, prices, central planning, taxation, banking, monetary policy and privatization (equitization) of SOEs.

Doi moi encouraged rapid and widespread growth (Fforde and de Vylder 1996; Rondinelli and Litvack 1999). This growth included the expansion in the number of small private businesses which contributed both to output growth and to employment. Vietnam thus became one of the booming economies of South East Asia and, contrary to many expectations, was robust enough to withstand to a considerable degree the impact of the 1997 Asian economic crisis. See Table 12.1 for an outline of the contextual factors in Vietnam.

In the period since 1986 Vietnam has undergone a profound transformation. Whilst the political system has remained largely unchanged, there have been major changes in the economy and society. With regard to the economy, state control of industry and agriculture has given way, in part, to private ownership, market forces and the entry of foreign companies. The state-owned sector, although with a declining share of employment, still retains its pre-eminent economic position in terms of output (Griffin 1998). Overall, Vietnam has become a more open society with greater employment and business opportunities.

At the same time, labour has become more vulnerable to exploitation and Tuyen (1999) highlights the increased precariousness of female employment in sectors such as textiles, garments and food processing. Collins (2005) has also argued that, along with job opportunities, *doi moi* has led to higher unemployment and

Table 12.1 Contextual factors – Vietnam

General statistics	
Population1 (2005 est.)	83.5 million
Area (square kilometres)[1]	329.5 thousand

Employment by sector (%)[1] (2004 est.)
  Agriculture
  Industry and services
	
	63.0
	37.0

Urban population (% of total population)[2] (2003)	25.8
GDP per capita (PPP)[1] (2004 est.)	US$2,700
Income inequality (high, medium or low) Gini coefficient[3] (2003)	Medium 0.37

Real GDP growth (%)
  1986–1995[4]
  1996–2005[5]
	
	7.1
	6.3

Unemployment (%)[5]
  1986–1995
  1996–2004
	
	N/A
	6.17

Summary description	
Product market regulation (1998)	Medium–High
Political context (liberal/pluralistic, state unitarist [communist, non-communist])	State unitarist (communist)
Political stability (high, medium or low)	High

Sources
1 GlobalEDGE, Michigan State University <http://globaledge.msu.edu/ibrd/CountryStats.asp> (accessed 29 September 2006).
2 Calculated from <http://www.ngocentre.org.vn> (accessed 26 September 2006).
3 <http://hdr.undp.org> (accessed 26 September 2006).
4 World Bank (1996) *World Development Report: From Plan to Market, Executive Summary*, World Bank: Washington, DC.
5 Calculated from <http://www.vvg-vietnam.com> (accessed 10 October 2006).

greater job insecurity, as female employment has shifted from SOEs to domestic private enterprises (DPEs).

A distinctive feature of the Vietnamese trade union context, however, is that Vietnam is a predominantly agricultural country with a small industrial sector, although the post-1945 industrialization of North Vietnam has allowed the trade unions to expand their industrial base. At the same time the establishment of a socialist society permitted the trade unions to recruit members amongst employees of the state organizations. As a consequence, state-owned enterprises and state organizations have become the mainstay of the trade unions.

However, one of the results of *doi moi* has been to rationalize SOEs, reducing numbers of employees and union members (Khan 1998; Dollar 1999; Rondinelli and Litvack 1999). As privately owned companies (both domestic and foreign) have expanded, however, new sites have been created in which the trade unions can establish branches. This process has been supported by legislation such as the 1994 Labour Code (revised in 2002) which places considerable responsibility on employers to recognize and facilitate the work of trade unions. Although membership is not compulsory, there is an expectation of membership and members pay 2 per cent of wages as union dues.

Decades of colonial occupation and war have, essentially, given way to a period of national consolidation and rebuilding. Nevertheless Vietnam remains one of the world's poorest countries and the economic reforms have increased the gap between rich and poor. One of the key aims of the government has indeed been to increase prosperity for the benefit of all and this remains one of its greatest challenges.

Union types and structure

As there is no one reliable data source for trade union statistics, data have been drawn from a number of sources, including the Vietnamese General Confederation of Labour (VGCL), International Labour Organization (ILO), Friedrich Ebert Stiftung (Singapore) and the Fair Labor Association. In spite of data inconsistency, a number of general facts and trends can be identified.

The VGCL comprises 20 national industrial unions and 64 provincial and municipal federations of labour. There are both national industrial unions and unions organizing particular occupations and professions. All unions operate under the umbrella of the VGCL. As of June 2006 there were 81,781 trade union branches. Total union membership was calculated at over 5.4 million. The largest industrial union is the Vietnam National Union of Industrial Workers with some 375,000 members. See Table 12.2 for a summary of trade unions in Vietnam.

Trade union density is highest in SOEs and the state apparatus (at least 90 per cent). Union density falls to around 50 per cent in private companies. Trade union membership is therefore concentrated in the state-controlled sectors (82 per cent of total membership), with only 7 per cent of members in domestic private enterprises, 2.5 per cent in foreign-invested companies and 1.3 per cent in the cooperative sector.

In recent years employment in the state-controlled sector, especially SOEs, has fallen and this has impacted on the composition of membership. The trade unions have therefore had to become more active in establishing branches in private companies and recruiting members there. Nevertheless, many private companies have no union representation.

The Vietnamese trade unions retain their traditional identity of political class organizations in that they are still associated closely with the ruling party and are viewed primarily as an organization of the working class. However, the unions are also having to come to terms with the changing economic context, in particular the expanding private sector. Whilst historically unions worked hand-in-hand with the ruling party, they now have to deal with private employers and directors of equitized companies (former SOEs). The nature of the trade unions is thus

Table 12.2 Vietnamese trade unions

General statistics	
Number of unions[1]	
1990	N/A
2006	81,781
Number of union members[1]	
1990	N/A
2006	5.4 million
Union density (%)	
1990	N/A
2005[2]	9.82

Summary description	
Union type	
Main	Political
Secondary	Economic/market
(economic/market, political, other)	
Union structure	
Main	Enterprise
Secondary	Industrial, occupational
(occupational, industrial, general, enterprise)	
Unity of peak organization (high, medium or low)	High
State control of unions (high, medium or low)	High
Involvement in collective bargaining (high, medium or low)	Medium

Sources
1 <http://www.congdoanvn.org.vn/ >(accessed 28 November 2006).
2 <http://www.fesspore.org> (accessed 10 October 2006).

also having to reflect business and market circumstances. While industrial unions are dominant in the state sector, occupational and professional unions tend to be active in the private sector (Zhu and Fahey 1999). It could thus be argued that the dimension of the market in Hyman's (2001) framework is exerting an increasing influence on the identity and activities of Vietnamese trade unions.

Since its establishment in 1946, the Vietnam Federation of Trade Unions (VFTU) has acted as an agent of the ruling party and the state. However, the changing nature of the state and economy are also influencing what trade unions do and how they do it. In 1988, at the Sixth Trade Union Congress, the VFTU changed its name to VGCL and declared a degree of independence from the Communist Party and the state. Vietnam has been described as a weak state (Masina 2006) which has sought consensus in policy making and has been basically pragmatic (rather than purely ideological) in its approach. One feature of this pragmatism, influenced by the long-lasting war economy, has been a willingness to allow a greater degree of decentralization compared with China (Warner *et al.* 2005). Furthermore, the policy of attracting foreign direct investment (FDI) has transformed the industrial landscape, introducing players with interests that have not always conformed with those of the ruling party. The Communist Party may therefore be forced to give trade unions greater independence if they are to be effective in representing and safeguarding workers' interests (another of the party's aims) (Masina 2006). There is some evidence to suggest that the trade unions have had some success in achieving this goal.

The trade unions have traditionally been cooperative institutions which have striven for conflict avoidance and resolution. They have been regarded as one of the 'four pillars' of the enterprise, together with the Communist Party, Youth Organization and management. Trade unions have not regarded their function as entering into adversarial disputes with 'management'. Such an approach is both typical of socialist ideology and conforms with Vietnamese cultural values of harmony and homogeneity (Zhu and Fahey 1999; Zhu 2003).

This tradition of cooperation persists in much recent legislation which is concerned with conflict resolution (Vietnam Economy 2006). Recently great concern has been expressed about the rise in unofficial disputes, including strikes. At the same time criticisms have been made that trade unions are too close to private employers and that trade unions in private companies often behave as if they have been incorporated in the company structure (Tuyen 1999; Wang 2005).

Historically, the trade unions have been subservient to the Communist Party and implementers of party policy. Trade union officials are generally also Party members, though party membership is not compulsory. Trade union organization has been highly centralized and hierarchical. Local branches report to the union at municipal or provincial level. These in turn report to the national union, with the VGCL as the capstone organization.

All enterprises with at least 10 permanent employees are legally bound to have and support union representation. Members belong to one of about 82,000 basic organizations which report to either 623 district-level organizations or 436 local organizations of the industry unions. These in turn report to the provincial and city federation or national industry union respectively. About one-quarter of overall union membership is represented by the 20 national industry unions.

Trade unions, in spite of legal requirements, have met with some difficulties in organizing in private companies and, in some instances, for example, in industrial zones, employers have sought to circumvent legal requirements by employing workers only on temporary or short-term contracts.

What do unions do?

The trade unions are increasingly regarding themselves as mediators between capital and labour rather than 'transmission belts' of the ruling party. The right to collective bargaining is written in the Labour Code. According to Fairlabor (2004), collective agreements have been signed with 56 per cent of SOEs, 36 per cent of foreign-invested enterprises (FIEs) and 20 per cent of DPEs. However, there is considerable criticism of collective agreements as they are not always discussed with the workforce or their union representatives. In practice, this means that collective agreements are actually imposed on the company's employees.

The weakness of collective agreements is evidenced by the number of unofficial strikes, which have become a source of concern for official bodies. The ILO reported 212 strikes (both legally sanctioned and wildcat) between 1995 and 2000 in Ho Chi Minh City alone (ILO 2003). According to Clarke's (2006: 345) detailed study of strikes in Vietnam, there were 978 officially reported strikes between 1995 and 2005. Unofficial strikes tend to be tolerated by the authorities and the trade unions generally intervene to resolve any dispute (Clarke 2006; Lee 2006). Wang (2005) has commented that strikes can be regarded as instruments of the government's pro-labour policies. There is, moreover, a system approved in law to resolve disputes. This system involves both internal procedures and external courts, although the court system has yet to be comprehensively developed. See Table 12.3 for a summary of what Vietnamese trade unions do.

There is consequently an inherent tension between the trade unions' aim of representing workers' interests and workers' rights enshrined in legislation on the one hand and the viewpoints and actions of employees on the other hand. One reason for this tension is that the state authorities, including the trade unions, are seeking to meet, at least in a circumscribed way, the needs of both capital and labour.

There is substantial legal enactment, with a number of pieces of legislation relating to the role of the trade unions and employment. The most significant are the Constitution of 1992, the Labour Code of 1994 (amended in 2002), the 1990 Law on Trade Unions and Decree No 196-CP of 1994 which make explicit the drafting and implementation of collective agreements. Legislation gives trade unions a strong position in the economic sphere. Although the trade unions' main role is seen as representing the rights of workers and employees, this role extends beyond narrow trade union issues. As reported in VietnamNet (2006) on the occasion of the 2006 Tenth Party Congress:

> Strengthening and promoting the role of the working class and the Trade Unions is to ensure a successful implementation of national industrialization

Table 12.3 What do Vietnamese trade unions do?

Activities	
Extent of collective bargaining (high, medium or low)	Medium
Level of collective bargaining (high, medium or low)	
National	Low
Industry	Low
Enterprise	High
Extent of joint consultation (high, medium or low)	Low
Industrial disputes	
Working days lost per 1,000 employees (2003)	N/A
Relative assessment (high, medium or low)	Low
Degree of state intervention in employment protection (high, medium or low)	Medium

and modernization. Actually, this is to build strong social establishments for the Party and State, thus helping to create a strong political system 'of the people, by the people and for the people'.

(VietNamNet 2006)

It is by no means easy to assess the economic impact of trade unions, either on their members or more generally. It could be argued that the overall organization of industrial relations, for example, collective agreements and the conciliation process, has created a structured approach for employment relations. This structure has provided clarity for both employers and employees and has contributed to overall economic growth by attracting foreign investors and supporting domestic firms.

Specifically, although wages are set by state bodies, the trade unions are part of the decision-making process and can therefore articulate the interests of their members at the highest level. A similar argument applies to working conditions as trade unions are in a strong position to influence legislation affecting terms and conditions of employment and working conditions. In summary, one could argue that wages would be lower and working conditions worse, if it were not for the presence and influence of the trade unions.

There are of course a number of counter-arguments. First, trade unions are relatively weak (in spite of state and party support and legislation), compared with employers. Moreover, trade unions are often regarded as part of the management structure. Historically, the trade union was one of the four pillars of the enterprise and hence closely linked to management and the enterprise decision-making process. Even in FIEs and DPEs trade union representatives are often seen as 'incorporated' in the firm's management structure, with trade union officials nominated and supported by the company. Moreover, company money is used to run activities for members. In this way private firms have been able to mitigate union influence.

Similarly, some companies do not pay the stipulated minimum wage (Wang 2005; Vietnam Economy 2006). They do this either blatantly or by classifying workers so that they do not qualify for the minimum wage. This appears to be a particular problem in export processing zones (EPZs) where the majority of employees in a firm may be put on temporary contracts so that they are not entitled to the benefits of employment legislation. Disputes related to the level and payment of wages and other benefits are often the cause of unofficial actions (Fairlabor 2004).

With regard to working conditions, the monitoring of conditions and the implementation of legislation is weak because the responsible body lacks adequate resources. Greater pressure is exerted on the issue of working conditions by codes of conduct demanded by Western buyers. Western codes of conduct, however, do not seem to increase the influence of the trade unions (Wang 2005). Nevertheless, other studies have indicated that the trade unions have improved their ability to defend workers' rights, especially in FIEs (Chan and Nørlund 1999; Dixon 2000).

Traditionally, the role of the trade unions extended beyond the workplace and this continues to be the case, albeit in a diminished form. Some of the traditional welfare functions of the unions have been taken over by the Ministry of Labour, Invalids and Social Affairs (MOLISA), although the unions and MOLISA work closely together. Trade unions have been given a broader, societal role by the 1992 Constitution.

Explaining the development, structure and strategies of trade unions

The Vietnamese trade union movement developed in close collaboration with the movement for national liberation and has thus been closely allied with the political parties fighting to re-establish an independent Vietnam. In practice this meant that since the establishment of the Democratic Republic of Vietnam in 1945 the trade unions were one of the mass organizations of the ruling party and at the company level one of the four pillars of the enterprise. The core notion that trade unions should be present in all companies (above a certain minimum size) has been retained under *doi moi*.

The rapid pace of change in the economy has not been matched, however, by change in the political sphere, although there is a certain degree of greater political openness. Trade unions have been encouraged to develop a more independent role in representing workers' interests and the state continues to support workers' rights. In fact, the state's insistence on supporting employees has been regarded as a factor inhibiting foreign investment in Vietnam. Notwithstanding the many criticisms of the state, both from the left and the right of the political spectrum, the state's policy has succeeded in raising living standards and distributing the benefits to broad sections of the population. However, the opening up of the political context lags far behind the economy. Although employees have a right to strike, trade unions independent of the VGCL are not permitted.

Vietnam now regards itself as a socialist-oriented market economy. Before *doi moi* the economy had many of the features of a socialist economy, relying on the support of China and, from 1978, especially on the former Soviet Union. The reform process was driven by both external and internal forces (Fahey 1997). Vietnam became a full member of the Association of Southeast Asian Nations (ASEAN) in 1995 and became increasingly integrated into the regional and global economy as a low-cost manufacturing base. A main competitor in this regard is China, and Vietnamese labour costs tend to be fixed at a level lower than China's. A key feature of the Vietnamese context is that the state has sought to reap the benefits of globalization, for example, FDI and exports, without sacrificing its ideological commitments to the state sector and workers' rights (Dixon 2000). See Table 12.4 for an overview of trade union development and structure in Vietnam.

With *doi moi* the employer base has become more and more diversified and there are now: state-owned enterprises; former, now equitized, state-owned enterprises; domestic private enterprises; and foreign-invested enterprises. There is also a very substantial small business sector. Vietnam is still a predominantly

Table 12.4 Explaining Vietnamese trade union development, structure and strategy

Political context	
Degrees of liberalization and autonomy (repression, tolerance, support, indifference)	Support
Relations with the state (dependent, independent)	Dependent

Markets	
Openness (imports + exports as % of GDP)[1]	128 (High)
Degree of competition (high, medium or low)	Medium
Financial markets	
Openness to market financing	Low
Ownership (group, institutional, foreign, dispersed)	Dispersed
Labour markets	
Demand elasticity (relates to ability of employers to pass on wage increases in prices (high, medium or low)	Medium

Employers	
Concentration (top 100 companies as a percentage value of total)	
Employer organization membership (high, medium or low)	Medium
Multinational (high, medium or low)	Low
Unitarist or pluralist perspective	Pluralist

Source
1 <http://hdr.undp.org/statistics/data/countries.cfm> (accessed 26 September 2006).

agricultural country although SOEs are still significant in terms of output and their contribution to gross domestic product (GDP). The small business sector plays a significant role in generating employment at a time when employment in SOEs is declining. All types of enterprise are now clearly driven by profitability. Employers' organizations, the primary one being the Vietnam Chamber of Commerce and Industry, exist; and, although the state has attempted to incorporate them into its policy-making structures, these have responded by articulating the demands of their own members (Masina 2006).

Conclusions

Trade unions seem to have a secure future in Vietnam so long as they continue to enjoy state and party support and the political system does not change fundamentally. The trade unions are, however, experiencing difficulties in adapting to a socialist market economy in the context of globalization. There is also evidence of limited employee support for trade unions (in spite of high participation rates) and a willingness for employees to take direct and spontaneous action in the case of disputes.

Vietnamese trade unions still bear a closer resemblance to socialist mass organizations than trade unions in advanced economies. The unions have signed some but not all ILO conventions and even though strikes are possible, there are no independent unions. Although there has been considerable borrowing from the

Chinese experience, this has been adapted to Vietnamese circumstances (Warner *et al.* 2005). This divergence is manifested, in particular, in the greater role of and state support for trade unions, as noted by Chan and Nørlund (1999) and Lee (2006). This reflects the general Vietnamese approach to reforms:

> Despite the proliferation of foreign models and some pressure from allies, the timing and sequence of Vietnamese reforms, in particular, appear to have been drawn primarily from Vietnamese experience.
>
> (St John 2006: 193)

The ruling party has nevertheless granted the trade unions greater discretion and a kind of collective bargaining system is in operation in many companies. The state and unions have, moreover, been tolerant of illegal strikes and have intervened to resolve disputes. In spite of this greater tolerance, trade union activities remain within the ambit of the state rather than divorced from it.

The trade union system has been changing from a traditional socialist system. Indications of this change have included the assertion of greater union independence, the drive to recruit members from domestic and foreign privately owned companies, permission to establish international contacts and the right to strike. Furthermore, the state has continued to assert its commitment to the maintenance of workers' rights. At the same time many features of the traditional system still remain such as the hierarchical union structure, its close relationship to the Communist Party and the generally cooperative approach to industrial relations (IR). The model of industrial relations which is emerging bears little resemblance to other IR models and could be regarded, in line with other aspects of the reform process, as fundamentally Vietnamese.

In terms of Hyman's (2001) 'eternal triangle' Vietnamese trade unions are still strongly positioned along the class–society axis, although the influence of class and society has weakened somewhat. More importantly, the impact of the market since *doi moi* has intensified. Vietnamese trade unions therefore need to respond increasingly to market forces. As Hyman (2001: 4) has noted: 'In practice, union identities and ideologies are normally located *within* the triangle'. It could be argued that in the Vietnamese case the trade unions have moved away, if only a little, from the class–society side and have positioned themselves more deeply within the triangle.

The trade union movement in Vietnam faces a number of key issues and challenges, including the need to:

- establish its role in a socialist market economy, both politically and socially, and overcome the low expectations workers have of trade unions
- retain core members
- expand membership in FIEs and DPEs
- improve its capability to monitor working conditions
- become more representative of members' interests
- establish stronger international links and adopt international norms.

First, trade unions need to establish their role in the socialist market economy which has evolved since the launching of *doi moi*. Socialism allowed trade unions only to be part of the party–state system and did not permit unions to have an independent and/or opposition role. Although the trade unions have achieved some distancing from the Communist Party since 1988, their *modus operandi* has not changed to any great extent. They are still close to the Communist Party and, as evidenced by the number of unofficial strikes, insufficiently close to ordinary employees. In order to achieve a genuine leadership role among ordinary employees, trade unions need to overcome the low employee expectations which have been formed over the past 60 years, as well as move further away from the Party.

Second, the trade unions need to retain their core membership in the state sector as this sector remains the most significant with regard to output and GDP. State enterprises, however, are experiencing job losses and changes in working practices, and the unions will consequently need to demonstrate that they are able to stand up for the interests of their members.

Authors such as Tuyen (1999) and Wang (2005) have argued that the trade unions have not been effective in monitoring working conditions and protecting their members, although this view is not universally accepted (see, for example, Chan and Nørlund 1999). The trade unions must, moreover, expand their membership in the private sector that has expanded under *doi moi*. The significance of the private sector lies especially in its ability to generate jobs and therefore presents the trade unions with a considerable challenge. While job creation is essential for Vietnam's continuing development and prosperity, the trade unions need to ensure that workers do not lose out in the process of growing the economy.

In addition to coverage of all the sectors of the economy, the unions need to improve the effectiveness of their presence. Whereas traditionally trade unions have been criticized as being mere transmission belts of the aims and interests of the party–state, nowadays one of the criticisms of unions in the private sector is that they are too close to employers and fail to represent workers' interests. Unions, therefore, need an identity that distinguishes them clearly from employers and the state. Such a development will require better educated and trained officers and although there is already international support for cadre development, the quality and effectiveness of education and training provided by the Trade Union College needs to be improved. The extent to which unions will be permitted to develop a distinctive and independent identity will depend ultimately, however, on the situation in the broader political context.

Without doubt, the unions need to improve their capability to monitor working conditions. It is widely recognized that working conditions are poor (Tuyen 1999; Zhu and Fahey 1999; Wang 2005) and the state organs lack the capacity to undertake effective monitoring. The trade unions, moreover, have failed to seize the opportunity of raising their profile in FIEs, even when codes of conduct have been invoked by interest groups based largely in the advanced countries in order to improve the conditions of Vietnamese workers.

One of the consequences of *doi moi* has been to integrate Vietnam more strongly into the regional and global economy and the trade unions have developed relationships with trade unions in countries such as Australia, Denmark and Italy which have substantial experience of independent trade unions and operating under globalization. The Vietnamese trade unions have also been supported by the ILO, even though Vietnam has as yet ratified only four of the eight core ILO conventions. The trade unions need to develop strong international links and a greater awareness of international standards in order to provide stronger protection for their members.

As mentioned previously, a key issue is the development of the political context. Since the launching of *doi moi*, the economy and society in general have changed far more than the political system. Dixon and Kilgour (2002) have argued that the Vietnamese government is committed more to the interests of workers than to those of capital. It is certainly true that the Vietnamese state has attempted to control the impact of globalization and impose its own terms and conditions (Masina 2006). As St John (2006: 144) has commented in regard to international pressure from institutions such as the International Monetary Fund and the World Bank in the late 1990s:

> official support for reform continued to be tempered by the Party's concern for retention of political control.

Unless and until this dilemma is solved, it is unlikely that Vietnamese trade unions, notwithstanding the increasing pressure of market forces, will become more similar to trade unions in the advanced economies.

References

Chan, A. and Nørlund, I. (1999) 'Vietnamese and Chinese labour regimes: on the road to divergence', in A. Chan, B. J. T. Kerkvliet and J. Unger (eds) *Transforming Asian Socialiam*, St Leonards: Allen and Unwin.

Clarke, S. (2006) 'The changing character of strikes in Vietnam', *Post-Communist Economies*, 18(3): 345–61.

Collins, N. (2005) 'Economic reform and unemployment in Vietnam', in J. Benson and Y. Zhu (eds) *Unemployment in Asia*, London: Routledge.

Dixon, C. (2000) 'State versus capital: the regulation of the Vietnamese foreign sector', *Singapore Journal of Tropical Geography*, 21(3): 279–94.

Dixon, C. and Kilgour, A. (2002) 'State, capital, and resistance to globalisation in the Vietnamese transitional economy', *Environment and Planning A*, 34: 599–618.

Dollar, D. (1999) 'The transformation of Vietnam's economy: sustaining growth in the 21st century', in J. Litvack and D. Rondinelli (eds) *Market Reform in Vietnam: Building Institutions for Development*, Westport, CT: Quorum Books.

Fahey, S. (1997) 'Vietnam and the "third way": the nature of socio-economic transition', *Tijdschrift voor Economische en Sociale Geografie*, 88(5): 469–80.

Fairlabor (2004) 'Freedom of Association in Vietnam', http://www.fairlabor.org/2004report/freedom/vietnam.html (accessed 2 February 2006).

Fforde, A. and de Vylder, S. (1996) *From Plan to Market: The Economic Transition in Vietnam*, Boulder, CO: Westview Press.

Griffin, K. (ed.) (1998) *Economic Reform in Vietnam*, Basingstoke: Macmillan Press.

Hyman, R. (2001) *Understanding European Trade Unionism: Between Market, Class and Society*, London: Sage.

ILO (2003) 'ILO and Viet Nam Launch New Initiative to Improve Industrial Relations and Promote Economic Development', http://www.ilo.org/public/english/region/asro/bangkok/public/releases/yr2003/pr0301.htm (accessed 22 February 2006).

Khan, A. R. (1998) 'Integration into the global economy', in K. Griffin (ed.) *Economic Reform in Vietnam*, Basingstoke: MacmMillan Press.

Kornai, J. (1992) *The Socialist System: The Political Economy of Communism*, Princeton, NJ: Princeton University Press.

Lee, C.-H. (2006) 'Recent industrial relations developments in China and Viet Nam: The transformation of industrial relations in East Asian transition economies', *Journal of Industrial Relations*, 48(3): 415–29.

Masina, P. (2006) *Vietnam's Development Strategies*, London: Routledge.

Quang, T. (ed.) (2001) *Vietnam: Gearing up for Integration*, Pathum Thani: SAV-SOM Joint Publishing.

Rondinelli, D. and Litvack, J. (1999) 'Economic reform, social progress, and institutional development: A framework for assessing Vietnam's transition', in J. Litvack and D. Rondinelli (eds) *Market Reform in Vietmnam, Building Institutions for Development,* Westport, CT: Quorum Books, pp. 1–30.

St John, R. B. (2006) *Revolution, Reform and Regionalism in Southeast Asia: Cambodia, Laos and Vietnam*, London: Routledge.

Tuyen, N. T. (1999) 'Transitional economy, technological change and women's employment: The case of Vietnam', *Gender, Technology and Development*, 3(1): 43–64.

Vien, N. K. (2004) *Viet Nam: A Long History*, 6th edn, Hanoi: Gioi Publishers.

Vietnam Economy (2006) 'Labour Code essential for solving disputes', http://www.vneconomy.com.vn/eng/index.php?param=article&catid=09&id=44059a0806e9c1 (accessed 22 March 2006).

VietnamNet Bridge (2006) 'The working class and trade union of Vietnam in the new period'. Online. Available HTTP: <http://english.vietnamnet.vn/social/2006/05/566279/> (accessed 9 August 2006). (The original source, *Nhan Dan*, is the official newspaper of the Communist Party in Vietnam.)

Visser, J. (1990) *In Search of Inclusive Unionism*, Deventer: Kluwer.

Wang, H.-Z. (2005) 'Asian transnational corporations and labor rights: Vietnamese trade unions in Taiwan-invested companies', *Journal of Business Ethics*, 56: 43–53.

Warner, M., Edwards, V., Polonsky, G., Pučko, D. and Zhu, Y. (2005) *Management in Transitional Economies: From the Berlin Wall to the Great Wall of China*, London: RoutledgeCurzon.

Williams, M. C. (1992) *Vietnam at the Crossroads*, London: Pinter.

Zhu, Y. (1998) 'The challenges and opportunities for the trade union movement in the transition era: two socialist market economies, China and Vietnam'. Online. Available http://www.ilo.org/public/english/bureau/inst/project/network/netresp/zhu.htm (accessed 22 January 2003).

Zhu, Y. (2003) 'Culture and management in Vietnam', in M. Warner (ed.) *Culture and Management in Asia*, London: RoutledgeCurzon.

Zhu, Y. and Fahey, S. (1999) 'The impact of economic reform on industrial labour relations in China and Vietnam', *Post-Communist Economies*, 11(2): 173–92.

Zhu, Y. and Fahey, S. (2000) 'The challenges and opportunities for the trade union movement in the transition era: two socialist market economies, China and Vietnam', *Asia Pacific Business Review*, 6 (3–4): 282–99.

13 Trade unions in Thailand

Declining strength and influence

Vimolwan Yukongdi

Introduction

In the last two decades, Thailand has been transformed into an export-oriented, industrializing nation. External challenges arising from the impact of globalization, economic restructuring, the liberalization of the financial market, and deregulation of labour markets in Thailand have weakened the trade unions' position and capacity over these years. It was not until the economic crisis in 1997, however, that massive layoffs of workers exposed the inadequacies of the country's social protection scheme and the weakness of trade unions when a large number of workers, particularly those in the informal sector, received little protection. Unemployment insurance was non-existent. Moreover, trade unions could not offer much protection for workers mainly because these organizations lacked resources. Thailand has one of the lowest rates of unionization in the world (World Bank 2000), and hence, offers an interesting case study of trade unions.

This chapter seeks to address the following questions: How do trade unions organize themselves? What kind of activities are trade unions involved in? What are the strategies adopted by trade unions? The chapter begins by tracing the emergence of trade unions within the historical, political, economic, and legal context of Thailand. Following this discussion, the types and structure of unions and the activities in which they engage will be examined. The outcomes and effectiveness of trade unions, and their current condition will be explained. The chapter concludes by discussing the challenges and future prospects for trade unions in Thailand.

Context and history

Thailand has seen a period of great economic change in the past two decades. During the period, 1985–95, Thailand's average GDP growth rate was hovering around 9 per cent per annum (BOT 2006), one of the fastest growing economies in the world. Following the economic crisis in 1997, GDP dropped in 1998 then grew at 4.4 per cent in 1999 (International Bank for Reconstruction and Development and World Bank 1998, 1999). After the decline in the global economy in 2001 and the September 11 terrorist events, the economy slowed down and GDP growth declined from 4.4 per cent in 1999 to 2.2 per cent in 2001 (BOT 2006). The economy revived and continued to grow from 5.3 per cent in 2002 to 4.5 per cent in 2005 (BOT 2006). The unemployment rate was low (around 1 per cent during 1994–6, Labour Force Survey round 3, NSO 2006d) in times of economic prosperity. Table 13.1 summarizes the economic, demographic and political context in Thailand.

Thailand has been a constitutional monarchy since 1932. The most recent and arguably most liberal constitution is the Constitution of the Kingdom of Thailand 1997, which was developed based on input from a wide range of interested parties. Of particular relevance to labour, the Constitution provides Thai citizens with the right to associate and establish collective organizations. However, in practice, many laws and regulations are argued to be in conflict with the Constitution and have been criticized for disadvantaging workers (Brown *et al.* 2002). For instance, the 1998 *Labour Protection Act* provides workers with the right to paid leave for education and training, as long as the leave does not have a negative impact on business operations. It has been argued that this provision tends to favour employers and offers them the opportunity to prevent employees from exercising their right to take leave for such purposes. Others have observed that the hierarchical structure of the laws is extremely complex and that only employers can afford lawyers to determine which particular regulation, act, or law applies in different situations (Thanachaisethavut 2000). Hence, in practice, some of the laws and regulations are somewhat inconsistent with the provisions in the 1997 Constitution, and may place workers in a disadvantaged position. In the same vein, some have observed that the government made a strategic move by introducing the system of tripartite committees to the 1975 *Labour Relations Act* with the aim of controlling and curtailing the bargaining power of trade unions (Laungaramsri 2005). Thus, labour laws enacted in the past and government policy towards trade unions have restricted the development and growth of trade unions in Thailand.

Politically, the relationship between trade unions and the government has been unstable and lacks security. Over various periods, the military-led governments have taken on significant political roles, and during these periods the Constitution has become non-existent or has been ignored (Brown *et al.* 2002). A similar situation can be observed in 2006–7 under the military-appointed government which bans public gatherings, effectively rendering strikes unlawful. The government's suppression of organized labour following military coups in the past is yet another factor that has hindered the development of trade unions.

Economic activity has influenced the pattern of industrial relations in Thailand over different periods. For instance, during the economic crisis in 1997, employers took the opportunity to sack workers, particularly those who were older and earning higher incomes. Many of these workers were trade union members (Thanachaisethavut 2001). During this time, it became quite evident that trade unions lacked the strength to represent workers effectively. In addition, the use of cheap and uneducated labour for comparative advantage by foreign investors tended to promote weak trade unions and unorganized labour. Furthermore, the

Table 13.1 Contextual factors – Thailand

General statistics	
Population (million, 2006)[1]	62.42
Size of the territory[2]	513,115 square km
Employment by sector (% of GDP)[3]:	
Agriculture, forestry and fishing	10.7
Industry	44.6
Construction	3.1
Manufacturing	35.1
Services	44.7
Urban population[4]	22.73
GDP per capita (2004)[5]	US$8090
Growth rates:	
Average for 1985–95[6]	9.0%
Average for 1995–2005[6]	3.4%
Unemployment:	
Average for 1985–95[7]	2.0%
Average for 1995–2005[8]	1.8%

Summary description	
Openness and degree of competition[9]: (based on index of regulatory burden)	Low
Political context	
System of regime[10]	Constitutional monarchy
Political stability[9] (based on index of enabling environment)	Low

Sources

1 Bank of Thailand (2006) Thailand's Key Economic Indicators. Online. Available HTTP: <http://www.bot.or.th/bothomepage/databank/econdata/Thai_Key/Thai_KeyE.asp> (accessed 28 November 2006).

2 Ministry of Foreign Affairs (2007) 'Kingdom of Thailand'. Online. Available HTTP: <http://www.mfa.go.th/web/14.php> (accessed 30 March 2007).

3 *The Economist* (2007a) Country briefings: Thailand. Online. Available HTTP: <http://www.economist.com/countries/Thailand/profile.cfm?folder=Profile%2DEconomic%20Structure> (accessed 30 March 2007)

4 Mahidol Population Gazette (2007) Population of Thailand, 2007 (Vol. 16), Institute for Population and Social Research, Mahidol University. Online. Available HTTP: <http://www.ipsr.mahidol.ac.th/content/Publication/GAZETTE.HTM> (accessed 24 May 2007).

5 Human Development Indicator (2006) Human development index: GDP per capita (PPP US$) (HDI). Online. Available HTTP: <http://hdr.undp.org/hdr2006/statistics/indicators/5.html> (accessed 20 December 2006).

6 Bank of Thailand (2006) Thailand's Key Economic Indicators. Online. Available HTTP: <http://www.bot.or.th/bothomepage/databank/econdata/Thai_Key/Thai_KeyE.asp> (accessed 28 November 2006).

7 Labour Force Survey (1980–2001), average calculated for years 1985, 1988–95.

8 National Statistical Office Thailand (NSO) (2006) Online. Available HTTP: <http://web.nso.go.th/eng/en/stat/lfs_e/lfse.htm> (accessed 23 March 2007).

9 Hafeez, S. (2003) 'The efficacy of regulation in developing countries'. United Nations. Online. Available HTTP: <http://unpan1.un.org/intradoc/groups/public/documents/un/unpan008713.pdf> (accessed 30 March 2007). Thailand ranked 22nd on regulatory burden index and last on enabling environment index (*n*=30 countries). Singapore ranked first on both indices.

10 *The Economist* (2007b) Country briefings: Thailand. Online. Available HTTP: <http://www.economist.com/countries/Thailand/profile.cfm?folder=Profile%2DPolitical%20Structure> (accessed 28 March 2007).

government's policy of privatizing state-owned enterprises had a negative impact on overall union strength (Lawler and Suttawet 2000). In addition, employers have resorted to various tactics to restrict trade union activities, such as dismissal of union leaders, shutting down factories where strong trade unions existed, subcontracting and casualization of labour (Laungaramsri 2005). The government has also been supportive of employers who pursued strategies to hamper union growth and weaken their strength in the bargaining process (Brown *et al.* 2002).

The influence of religion and culture promotes less social activism among the Thais. Over 90 per cent of the population are professed Buddhists (UNESCAP 2000). According to Buddhist doctrine (Theravada Buddhism), individuals accept their current situation which is believed to be a consequence of what they have done in a past life (Lawler and Suttawet 2000). Hence, it would be difficult to change the current situation, a belief which promotes more passive behaviour and greater acceptance of the status quo. Another aspect of Thai culture which can lead to greater acceptance of inequality is that Thailand is a hierarchical society that is characterized by large power distance between employers and subordinates (Komin 1990). Thus, in the organizational setting, there is a tendency for workers to accept inequality in power and to defer to authority figures. These cultural characteristics are not compatible with the concept of participative decision making or activities that strive to reduce inequality, such as worker's participation in union activities.

With respect to the population and labour force, Thailand recorded 62.42 million people in 2006 (BOT 2006). The labour force of 36.1 million comprised 35.5 million employed persons, while 0.6 million were unemployed (NSO 2006a). Among the employed, there were 3.02 million government employees (8.5 per cent), 13.1 million private employees (36.7 per cent), 11.2 million self-employed workers (31.6 per cent), 7.05 million unpaid family workers (19.8 per cent), 56,000 members of producer's cooperatives (0.2 per cent), and 1.1 million employers (3.2 per cent) (NSO 2006b).

Generally, workers in the formal sector include government employees, state enterprise employees, private employees and employers in the non-agriculture sector. The informal sector includes employees in small establishments employing up to five workers, the self-employed, and unpaid family workers, many of whom are female. In general, formal sector workers receive higher pay and are protected by labour protection laws, as well as other forms of social security programmes (Chandoevwit 2004). In 2006, the self-employed included 11.2 million workers and 7 million unpaid family workers, representing 31.6 per cent, and 19.8 per cent, respectively, of the total employed workers (NSO 2006c). Workers in the informal sector are not protected by the *Labour Protection Act* and the *Social Security Act* (Chandoevwit 2004). Consequently, they earn lower wages and often work in poor conditions. Recently, labour protection has been extended to include homeworkers (2004), and agricultural workers (2005), who are employed by small-scale agricultural employers, although labour protection remains relatively limited and is not on par with workers covered by the *Labour Protection Act* 1998 (see Thanachaisethavut and Charoenlert 2006).

Estimates vary, but agricultural workers in Thailand constitute a large proportion of the labour force. In 2006, there were 13.7 million employees in the agricultural sector (NSO 2006c). Others estimate the total number of informal sector workers to be around 20 million or two-thirds of the labour force, which include between 550,000 and 950,000 home-based workers (Laungaramsri 2005). Therefore, the exclusion of informal sector workers from labour protection coverage is another factor argued to be an obstacle to union growth in Thailand (Brown *et al.* 2002).

In terms of union density, the rate of unionization in Thailand is very low relative to that of other developing countries in the region (Chandoevwit 2004). Unions in the public sector are more powerful and larger than those in the private sector (Manusphaibool 1993; Lawler and Suttawet 2000). According to the Labour Force Survey (round 3), 2.9 per cent of employees in the private sector were union members in 1998, while 4.6 per cent of private-sector wage employees had a labour union in their establishment. A survey revealed that in 1999, 2.79 per cent (271,000) of private sector employees were union members out of 9.72 million private sector employees. In contrast, over half of the state enterprise employees, 168,066 (52.6 per cent) were trade union members (Brown *et al.* 2002). The proportion for private sector employees dropped slightly, but increased for state enterprise employees in subsequent years. In 2001, among 11 million private sector employees, only 285,000 (2.58 per cent) were members of trade unions (Charoenloet *et al.* 2004). However, the rate of unionization in the state enterprises was significantly higher. According to the Ministry of Labour, 165,546 employees from a total of 271,645 employees in state enterprises (60.94 per cent) were union members in 2001. The stronger growth of trade unions in state enterprises is believed to be a result of the lack of competitive pressure in this sector and the influence of political factors (Lawler and Suttawet 2000). The low unionization rate in the private sector may be partly due to the lack of protection during the formation of unions and the free rider problem that sees non-union members benefiting from union activity (Chandoevwit 2004).

Overall, the effects of globalization, economic development, politics, labour laws, and deregulation of the labour markets have hampered union growth in Thailand. The extent to which these external forces have influenced the evolution of trade unions in Thailand will be discussed in the following section.

Trade union history and development

Trade unions in Thailand developed after the Second World War (Manusphaibool 1993). In the 1930s, Chinese immigrants provided the key source of wage labour (Phongphaichit and Baker 1995). Following the breakdown of the system of traditional labour practices (the 'phrai' or corvee system), the employment of Chinese immigrants increased as they were cheaper to hire than labour in the corvee system (Wanthana 1982). The 'phrais' or serfs were free to choose their occupation during the Sukhothai period (c. AD 1200–1300) when the system was established. In the Ayuthaya period (c. 1300–1767), phrais were obligated to serve the king and the aristocracy. Serfdom was subsequently abolished in 1903

(Lawler and Suttawet 2000). According to Mabry (1977), Thai labour organizations that emerged during the period 1932–58 comprised mainly shopkeepers, hawkers, rickshaw pullers, as well as other workers who organized themselves and also referred to themselves as trade unions. Other researchers suggest that 'true' trade unions originated in the early 1970s as a consequence of growth in export industries, and the increase in demand for workers in both the private and state enterprises, many of whom began to organize themselves into labour associations that later transformed into trade unions in 1975 (Ativanichayapong 2002).

The modern trade union movement in Thailand can be divided into three phases (Ativanichayapong 2002). During the period 1972–6, the government shifted its strategy from import-substitution to export promotion and encouraged foreign investment (Manusphaibool 1993), a policy which spurred economic growth. The student-led uprising on 14 October 1973 created a relatively politically liberal climate within the country. These two key factors contributed to the growth, increased the role of trade unions and influenced them to pursue objectives that were not limited to defending workers' common interests (i.e., wages and working conditions), but also broad political and social issues. During this period, along with the students, trade unions were able to organize themselves into a powerful social force (Ativanichayapong 2002).

In the second phase of Thailand's trade union history, which extended from 1977 to 1990, the economy grew rapidly following the government's export promotion strategy. In addition, on the political front, following the October 1976 coup, political stability increased. During this period, trade unions emphasized particular interests of the workers, such as the revision of labour laws, including social security laws, and focused less on broad political and social issues. State enterprise unions were relatively more successful than private enterprise unions, which were concerned with raising minimum wages, employment contracts, and social security law. There was also competition among the national labour unions, and as a consequence the trade union movement began to fragment (Ativanichayapong 2002).

During the third phase, from 1991 to 2002, the country experienced rapid economic expansion until the economic crisis in 1997. Following a coup in 1991 and the subsequent constitutional reform movement, trade unions shifted their concerns from wage to non-wage issues because job security became a high priority. After the economic crisis, unemployment increased, particularly in the private sector due to the closure of firms. Trade unions became interested in non-wage issues, including occupational safety, health and environmental protection, the enforcement of social security law (particularly the section relating to unemployment benefits), workers' child care centres; and also campaigned against the privatization of state enterprises (Ativanichayapong 2002).

The government, however, pursued policies in line with the IMF's structural-reform programme which involved the privatization of state enterprises. During this period, state enterprise employees demanded an increase in salaries and protested against the government's privatization policies. These movements were viewed unfavourably by the public and raised debates among academics concerning the role of trade unions. Some academics argued that trade unions should be more concerned about broader social issues and not limit their interest to defending wage levels for the benefit of their members (Samukkethum 1996). Unfavourable opinion and debate about trade union activity weakened the unions, and their bargaining power for raising wages and protecting job security for employees was diluted (Ativanichayapong 2002).

In more recent years, the positive influence of the trade union movement on the position of workers can be felt among the labour force. Thai workers have experienced an improvement in their status, particularly in terms of wages and social welfare relative to workers in the previous decade. However, the status of trade unions as a social force today has declined as they generally have less bargaining power than they did in the past (Charoenloet *et al.* 2004) due to the effects of globalization and deregulation of the labour markets (Lawler and Suttawet 2000).

Union types and structure

In the 1970s, the Thai government issued a decree that workers should not join unions with workers from other provinces or from establishments that differed in terms of working conditions. This policy has hindered the establishment of larger union bodies, promoted enterprise unionism, and the emergence of competing labour councils rather than a single peak organization (Lawler and Suttawet 2000). Thus, trade unions that have developed tend to be weak and fragmented.

Trade unions in Thailand fall into two main categories: formal labour organizations and 'loose' coordination centres (Charoenloet *et al.* 2004). Formal labour organizations, which must be registered with the Ministry of Labour, include labour union councils, labour union federations, state enterprise labour unions, and private enterprise labour unions. A labour union can be established in an organization or in the same industry, but must have a minimum of 10 employees. Two labour unions in the same industry can form a labour federation. A labour council is an organization of trade unions at the national level and must include at least 15 labour unions or labour federations. See Table 13.2 for an overview of trade unions in Thailand.

In 2003, there were 46 state enterprise labour unions, 1,256 private enterprise labour unions, 19 labour union federations, and nine labour union councils. The nine national labour union councils consist of the Labour Congress of Thailand, National Free Labour Union Congress, National Congress of Thai Labour, Thai Trade Union Congress, Thailand Council of Industrial Labour, National Labour Congress, National Congress of Private Employees of Thailand, Confederation of Thai Labour, and Labour Congress Centre for Labour Unions of Thailand (Charoenloet *et al.* 2004). In practice, these multiple labour congresses compete against one another, a situation which contributes to the weakness of the labour movement in Thailand.

Two important points need to be raised regarding the number of unions and the right to establish unions. First, the number of officially registered unions

Table 13.2 Thai trade unions

General statistics	
Number of unions (2003)[1]	46 state enterprise labour unions 1,256 private enterprise labour unions
Number of union members (2001)[1]	450,546 (285,000 in private enterprises; 165,546 in state enterprises)
Union density (2001)[1]	2.58% (private enterprises) 60.94% (state enterprises)
Level of collective bargaining	Low
Summary description	
Main union type	Economic
Union structure 　Main 　Secondary	 Enterprise Industrial
Extent of unity of peak organisation	Low
State control of unions	Medium–High
Involvement in collective bargaining	Low

Source
1 Charoenloet *et al.* (2004).

should be interpreted with caution because in the late 1980s and 1990s, trade unions were formed in response to inter-union competition for seats on tripartite labour bodies. Regardless of the size of membership, each union could cast one vote in elections. Hence, some 'paper unions' existed in name only even if they were legally registered. Some have suggested that only about half of officially registered unions are actually active (Brown *et al.* 2002). Second, according to the law, a minimum of 10 employees are required to establish a trade union. This implies that workers who are employed in establishments with less than 10 employees cannot form unions or join unions. This number was estimated to be around 800,000 in 2000 (Brown *et al.* 2002), which is another obstruction in the law which inhibits the growth of unions.

The second category of labour organizations is the 'loose' coordination centre. These organizations are formed by union leaders who work in the same industry or industrial area/zone. These centres are not registered with any government agency, and some operate as networks and include labour-related, non-government organizations (NGOs) as members. Industrial-based and area-based coordination centres of trade unions that have been active in the trade union movement include the: Omnoi – Omyai Area Group of Unions, Prapadang Area Group of Unions, Rangsit Area and Vicinity Group of Unions, Nawanakorn Group of Unions, Easter Region Group of Unions, Berla Industry Group of Unions, Phuket Province Group of Unions, Saraburi Area Group of Unions, Central and Bangna-Trad Group of Unions, State Enterprise Workers' Relations Confederation (SERC), and Confederation of Thai Electrical Appliances, Electronic, Automobile, and Metal Workers (TEAM) (Charoenloet *et al.* 2004). Loose coordination centres have emerged in response to national labour union councils' ineffectiveness in protecting workers' interests.

More recently, a new network was formed, the Thai Labour Solidarity Committee, which represents an alliance of formal labour organizations, coordination centres, and labour-related NGOs. In addition to these labour organizations, the Women Workers' Unity Group is another coordination centre that consists of female unionists and staff of labour-related NGOs. The Group concentrates on women workers' issues (Charoenloet *et al.* 2004).

Employer organizations have, in general, played a limited role in the industrial relations system. The Employers' Confederation of Thailand, which was established in 1976 under the *Labour Relations Act* 1975, represents private sector employers in Thailand. The Employers' Confederation of Thailand is the principal employer organization at the national level. It provides services to its members such as business consultancy, training and development programmes, scholarships and overseas training, and networking with international agencies (ECOT 2007). The role of the Employers' Confederation has been limited to providing educational and training services to its members. No significant collective bargaining has taken place at the national level (Manusphaibool 1993). Most of the collective bargaining takes place between individual employers and their workforce at the enterprise level (Brown *et al.* 2002).

Employers are also represented by the Thai Chamber of Commerce and Board of Trade of Thailand, Pan Group-Shoe Manufacturers in Thailand, Thai Garment Manufacturers Association (TGMA), Thai Chamber of Commerce, and the Federation of Thai Industries (Thai Labour Campaign 2007). These organizations have not been established for industrial relations purposes. However, they take part in nominating representatives of employers to serve on the Wage Committee, Workmen Compensation Fund Committee, and the Labour Relations Committee (Manusphaibool 1993).

Attempts have been made by multinational companies in Thailand to suppress unions. These organizations have imported newer strategies for union suppression that are highly effective. Among the strategies adopted by Thai employers to oppose unions are: discharging union supporters, using armed force, and cooperating with government officials to restrict union activities or ban the formation of unions (Lawler and Suttawet 2000). In addition, as noted earlier, employers also employ other tactics, such as dismissing union leaders, shutting down factories with a strong union, subcontracting, and supporting casual employment (Laungaramsri 2005).

With respect to labour laws, the Ministry of Labour in Thailand was established in 1993, following the uprising against military dictatorship in May 1992 (Charoenloet *et al.* 2004). The Ministry of Labour oversees the administration and enforcement of labour policy, law and regulations; develops labour skills; creates job; and promotes labour relations (ILO 2007).

Thailand's first labour protection act was enacted in 1975 (Chandoevwit 2004). The *Labour Relations Act* (1975) contains provisions for changing and modifying conditions of employment, procedures for settling labour disputes, employers' and employees' rights to establish labour associations and labour unions. In 1998, the labour protection law was amended. The amended act, *Labour Protection Act* 1998, prescribes the minimum standard practices in terms of general labour force utilization, women workers, child labour, remuneration, holidays and leave, working hours, minimum wages, occupational safety, severance pay, employee welfare funds and punishment, as well as other regulations (Chandoevwit 2004; Ministry of Labour 2006b). However, the *Labour Protection Act* 1998 excludes government officials and state enterprise employees, employees in the agricultural sector and home-based workers (Chandoevwit 2004).

As noted earlier, home-based workers and agricultural workers (only in small-scale establishments) now have limited labour protection under the Ministerial Regulations on Labour Protection for Homeworkers 2004 and Labour Protection for Agricultural Workers 2005, which extend the protection of section 22 of the *Labour Protection Act* 1998 (ILO 2005). However, it should be noted that there is no reference to the legal right to form unions or join unions. Effectively, this implies that 3.02 million government employees (NSO 2006b) and 13.7 million employees in agriculture (NSO 2006c), representing 46 per cent of the labour force in 2006, or nearly half of the labour force, cannot join unions or possess the legal right to form unions (Brown *et al.* 2002)

It should be pointed out that public servants and state enterprise employees are covered by the *Civil Service Act* 1992, Office of the Civil Service Commission (ADB/OECD 2007), and *State Enterprise Labour Relations Act B.E. 2543* (2000), respectively. Following the military coup in February 1991, state enterprise employees who were originally covered under the *Labour Relations Act* 1975, were excluded from the coverage and not permitted to form trade unions (Charoenloet *et al.* 2004). The *State Enterprise Labour Relations Act B.E. 2543* (2000) establishes the right to collective bargaining, the procedures for changing or modifying the Conditions of Employment, settlement of labour disputes, the formation of the State Enterprise Labour Union and State Enterprise Labour Relations Committee, and the compulsory establishment of the Labour Relations Affair Committee (Ministry of Labour 2006b). But state enterprise employees have not been granted the right to strike (Ministry of Labour 2006c).

The social welfare of workers is covered by the *Social Security Act B.E. 2533* (1990) and *Workmen's Compensation Act B.E. 2537* (1994). The *Social Security Act* was adopted in 1990 (Chandoevwit 2004). The Social Security Scheme in Thailand operates in accordance with the *Social Security Act B.E. 2533*, and its Amendments B.E. 2537 and B.E. 2542. The scheme provides financial assistance to the worker or to the next of kin in the event of non-work related sickness, non-work related disability or maternity, as well as death from non-work related causes (Chayasriwong 2001).

The benefits for work-related sickness, loss of organs, invalidity and death are covered by the *Workmen's Compensation Fund B.E. 2537* (1994) for workers employed in enterprises with one or more employees. Following the economic crisis in 1997, the Child Allowance and Old Age Pension Scheme was established for private sector employees in 1998. The *Social Security Act* covers insured workers who are in the 15–60 age group in establishments with one or more employees. Previously, social security coverage was limited to establishments with at least 10 employees, a factor which possibly hampered unionization, but coverage was extended in 2002 to include enterprises with one or more employees (Chandoevwit 2004).

The lack of unemployment insurance for laid-off employees (many of whom were union members) following the economic crisis in 1997 prompted the government to establish an unemployment insurance programme in 2004 (see Yukongdi 2005). The World Bank reported that during the crisis, many employers failed to pay compensation to laid-off employees as stipulated by law (Brown *et al.* 2002). This issue was subsequently pursued by workers, unions and non-government organizations and resolved by the establishment of the programme.

A royal decree in 2003 established an unemployment benefits fund with contributions starting in January 2004 (Charoensuthipan 2003). Unemployment benefits are available to employees who have been dismissed from work and to those who resign on a voluntary basis. Insured persons who are eligible are those who have contributed to the fund for at least six months over a 15-month period prior to their job loss or interruption to their earnings (Chandoevwit 2004). Laid-off workers receive 50 per cent of their wages for 180 days. Employees who resign voluntarily can choose to receive either 50 per cent of their wage for a period of 90 days, or 30 per cent for 180 days. Workers must also register with the Ministry of Labour's employment office (Charoensuthipan 2003). The extension of social security coverage and the availability of unemployment insurance represent some success and progress for workers, trade unions, and non-government organizations that campaigned for these benefits following the 1997 economic crisis.

What do unions do?

Trade unions offer seminars and training programmes, organize tours and social events, provide legal advice, and loans through cooperatives to union members (FES 2005). They are involved in collective bargaining processes, industrial action, the setting of wages, occupational health and safety issues, and in more recent years, women workers' issues. See Table 13.3 for an overview of union activities in Thailand.

Table 13.3 What do Thai trade unions do?

Extent of collective bargaining	Low
Level of collective bargaining	Enterprise level
Extent of joint consultation	Low
Strikes, working days lost per 1,000 employed	Low
Degree of state intervention in employment protection	Low–Medium
Income inequality	High

The settlement of labour disputes is covered by the *Labour Relations Act* 1975 (LRA 1975). Labour disputes may arise in a situation when one party makes a demand upon another, but negotiation does not occur between the parties within a specific time period, or when negotiation has commenced, but fails (LRA 1975, section 21). The process of collective bargaining begins when a demand is made to change the conditions of employment by one party. The demand must be submitted in written form to the other party. Representatives (i.e., a director, shareholder, partner, or regular employee, or a committee member of relevant employers' association or employers' federation) for negotiation must also be specified if a demand is made by the employer.

If a demand is made by the employees, the names of employee representatives must be provided as well as the signatures of at least 15 per cent of the total workforce in the enterprise. But in unionized workplaces, unions are permitted to submit their demand on behalf of employees without the names and signatures of employees. In addition, in workplaces where union members exceed 20 per cent of the workforce, employers must recognize the union as the bargaining agent. Negotiations must begin within three days after the other party has acknowledged receipt of the written demand. The other party must also nominate up to seven representatives and up to two advisors may be appointed by either party (LRA 1975, sections 13–17).

There is no time limit to reach an agreement once negotiation commences. During the course of the negotiation, however, strikes and lockouts are prohibited by law, while employers are not permitted to terminate or transfer the position of the employees' representatives. If an agreement is reached by the parties, a written agreement must be signed by the parties and registered within 15 days with the Labour Registrar's Office. The agreement which provides details of the new conditions of employment must be publicly displayed by the employer for at least 30 days. The duration of the collective agreement must not exceed three years, and if the period is not specified, the agreement is enforceable for a period of one year. Collective bargaining has been quite effective for settling labour disputes in workplaces in Thailand (Manusphaibool 1993).

In the event that either party fails to negotiate within the three-day period or the negotiation breaks down as either party fails to reach an agreement, then the labour dispute must be settled through compulsory conciliation. A conciliation officer from the Labour Department, who takes on an advisory role, must be notified and the dispute must be settled within five days. If this process fails, then the parties may resort to industrial action or agree to proceed with voluntary arbitration (LRA 1975, sections 26–29). Voluntary arbitration may also take place after a strike or lockout has occurred. During the voluntary arbitration process, the parties agree to appoint three arbitrators to settle the dispute, and are prohibited from entering into a strike or lockout. The award made by the arbitrators is legally binding. In Thailand, voluntary arbitration has rarely been used (Manusphaibool 1993).

State enterprises are covered by the *State Enterprise Labour Relations Act* 2000 and labour disputes must be submitted to the Labour Relations Committee for settlement by compulsory arbitration (*State Enterprise Labour Relations Act*

2000). Employees in the state enterprises operating in essential industries (e.g., oil refineries, railway, telecommunications, electric power generation, water supply) are precluded from engaging in strikes or lockouts.

During the course of a labour dispute, strikes and lockouts are regarded as lawful but only after the parties have resorted to the conciliation process (LRA 1975, section 35). A 24-hour written notice prior to engaging in industrial action is required to be submitted to the Labour Department by the parties where strikes and lockouts are lawful. Employees and employers engaging in unlawful industrial action can face fines and imprisonment. If the industrial action is legal, officials and members of the unions will not be liable to criminal prosecution (LRA 1975, section 99).

Since the 1980s, the number of strikes has declined to less than 10 a year, while the number of labour cases that have been referred to the Central Labour Court following its establishment has increased on average to over 6,000 each year. During 1985–91, when negotiations failed, employers staged lockouts, the frequency of which was equivalent to or exceeded the number of strikes. In more recent years, a study by the Japan External Trade Organization (JETRO 2006) reports that, on average, there was only one labour strike per year in Thailand from 2003 to 2006, although the statistics covered a limited period from January to March. The decrease in the number of strikes was attributed to the employers' use of joint consultation processes, as well as the increasing role of tripartite bodies in the arbitration of labour disputes (Ativanichayapong 2002).

Prior to 1999, minimum wages in Thailand were determined by a central wage committee. The *Labour Protection Act* 1998 provided for the establishment of a Wage Committee, which is a tripartite committee that represents employer associations, unions and the government, to determine minimum wage rates for different regions (Chandoevwit 2004; Manusphaibool 1993). Wage rates for each province vary as rates are adjusted to allow for cost-of-living differences within each region. The *Labour Protection Act* 1998 provides for a tripartite sub-committee to be established at the provincial level. The committee is then charged with proposing a minimum wage rate for the province (Ativanichayapong 2002).

The minimum wage rate in the Bangkok metropolitan areas (i.e., Nonthaburi, Nakhon Pathom, Pathumthani, Samut Prakan, Samut Sakhon) increased quite rapidly over the period 1991–6, particularly in 1992 when the growth rate reached 15 per cent (Chandoevwit 2004). Following the economic crisis in 1997, minimum wage rates countrywide stagnated (Ativanichayapong 2002). In 2007, the minimum daily wage rate in Bangkok, Nonthaburi, Nakhon Pathom, Pathumthani, Samut Prakan and Samut Sakhon was Baht 191 (approximately US$5), while the rates ranged from Baht 143 to Baht 182 for the other provinces (Ministry of Labour 2006c).

It should be noted that at the provincial level, workers may be members of weak unions or may not have any unions in their workplace, as trade unions tend to be concentrated in the Bangkok metropolitan areas. In workplaces where there are unions and employee representatives serving on the sub-committee for setting minimum wage rates, some of these employee representatives are influenced or dominated by their employers (Ativanichayapong 2002). For example, in 2000, only four provincial sub-committees demanded higher wages for their provinces, while the sub-committees for 44 provinces out of 67 recommended to the Wage Committee that the minimum wage rates of 1998 should be maintained (Ativanichayapong 2002). Similarly, in 2002, the minimum wage rates for 70 provinces stagnated, while those in only six provinces increased. In provinces where there are strong trade unions, the minimum wage rates have increased over the years (Ativanichayapong 2002).

In practice, the official enforcement of minimum wages has been weak and fines are minimal. Minimum wage rates apply to permanent employees who are employed on a full-time basis. Thus, to avoid paying minimum wage rates, employers often hire employees on a temporary or fixed-term basis, or through subcontracting. Subcontracting has been widespread in industries such as garment, textiles, automatic data processing machines and parts, frozen seafood, electronic integrated circuits, and jewellery. Many of the workers in these industries are home-based female workers (Brown *et al.* 2002).

In sum, trade unions have played an active role in recent years during the economic boom in demanding higher wages for workers. However, during the economic crisis, workers were concerned for their job security, and trade unions were less effective in mobilizing collective action to increase wage rates during this period. Furthermore, since 1999 under the new system, which decentralizes the process for setting minimum wage rates, national labour congresses have become less influential in leading the trade union movement in raising wages. In addition, labour costs in Thailand are no longer low relative to China or other South East Asian countries. Trade unions, therefore, encounter many difficulties in bargaining for higher wages, and have shifted their interest to other non-wage issues in more recent times (Ativanichayapong 2002).

Trade unions presently are less powerful than they were in the 1970s. They have become increasingly dependent on NGOs, international solidarity support organizations, as well as academics for support. A small number of labour-related NGOs have been supportive of the trade union movement since the 1980s. These are the Union for Civil Liberty, Arom Pongpangan Foundation, Friends of Women Foundation, Center for Labour Information Service and Training (CLIST), and Thai Labour Campaign (Charoenloet *et al.* 2004).

International organizations or 'solidarity support organizations' that provide assistance to trade unions fall into two categories: those that are non-trade unions and those that are international labour federations with which trade unions in Thailand are affiliated (Charoenloet *et al.* 2004). Examples of the non-trade union international organizations that have supported trade unions in Thailand over the past years include the ILO, Friedrich Ebert Stiftung Foundation, and Asian-American Free Labour Institute (AAFLI, also known as American Center for International Labour Solidarity or ACILS). The second group of international labour federations includes the International Confederation of Free Trade Unions and the World Confederation of Labour, which have members based in Thailand. Also included in the second group are labour union federations in Thailand that are affiliated with the industrial-based Global Union Federations (GUF), such as the International Metal Workers' Federation (IMF), International Textile, Garment and Leather Workers' Federation (ITGLWF), International Transport Workers' Federation (ITF), International Federation of Chemical, Energy, Mine and General Workers' Unions (ICEM), International Federation of Building and Woodworkers (IFBWW), International Federation of Journalists (IFJ), International Union of Food, Agricultural, Hotel, Restaurant, Catering, Tobacco, and Allied Workers' Associations (IUF), Public Services International (PSI), and Union Network International (UNI).

From their qualitative study, Charoenloet *et al.* (2004) suggested that from the unionists' perspective, the Friedrich Ebert Stiftung Foundation and the American Center for International Labour Solidarity have had greater impact than the Global Union Federations on the trade union movement in Thailand. Both the Friedrich Ebert Stiftung Foundation and the American Center for International Labour Solidarity have established a supportive relationship that dates back three decades. Today, the two organizations operate branches in Bangkok that are staffed with Thai employees, unlike the Global Union Federations which have no offices in Thailand. Hence, with a local presence in Bangkok and staff who speak Thai, both the Friedrich Ebert Stiftung Foundation and the American Center for International Labour Solidarity have local knowledge about the situation of trade unions in Thailand and better access to information than the Global Union Federations.

Occupational health and safety campaign

In the past, occupational health and safety issues have received little attention from trade unions compared with labour rights, wages and employment contracts. However, in 1993 occupational health and safety issues began to attract attention from trade unions and the general public as a result of a number of cases of occupational illnesses and industrial accidents. In the 1990s, many of the workers who worked in textile and electronics factories suffered from lung diseases and lead poisoning (Ativanichayapong 2002). In 1993, the country's worse factory fire, the Kader Fire, killed 188 workers and injured 350 (Charoenloet 2000).

The subsequent labour campaign was led by a coalition of trade unions, NGOs and academics. The campaign demanded fair compensation for the families of the deceased and the injured. In 1994, the coalition established an ad hoc committee on occupational health and safety, the Campaign Committee for Workers' Health and Safety, which consisted of representatives from 13 organizations including trade unions, NGOs, and university-based organizations (Ativanichayapong 2002). The labour campaign was successful and led the government to designate 10 May as National Health and Safety Day in Thailand.

In more recent years, NGOs have taken over from trade unions in leading the social movements in Thailand. NGOs pursue broad objectives and currently allocate their resources to solving social problems, such as those relating to rural development, women workers, child labour, human rights, AIDS, and ecology.

Explaining the development, structure and strategies of trade unions

Trade unions are a product of the country's history, politics, economic development, and the globalization process. This section explains why trade unions in Thailand are enterprise-based, generally weak and fragmented. A summary is presented in Table 13.4.

First, on the political front, trade unions have experienced government suppression, recurring setbacks brought about by military coups and constitutional reforms. Following the military coup in 1991, the powerful state-enterprise unions, which strongly opposed privatization, were removed from coverage under the *Labour Relations Act* 1975 and stripped of their right to strike under new legislation (Charoenloet *et al.* 2004). The government regarded union activities as hampering economic growth and state-enterprise unions were not popular as they were perceived to be self-serving rather than interested in the general workers' interests. The labour movement derived strength principally from state-enterprise unions. As a consequence, the private sector unions, which were fragmented, became even weaker as state-enterprise unions had been their source of power and resources. During this period, the military government enacted legislation which permitted a labour congress to be formed by a small number of unions. This led to the establishment of not one, but several labour congresses, increasing conflicts in the labour movement (Lawler and Suttawet 2000).

Second, during the economic expansion in the 1970s, the Thai government was reluctant to grant full legal rights to workers to join unions with workers from other provinces or from other establishments that had different working conditions. Thus, unions in Thailand tend to be enterprise-based, small and weak.

Table 13.4 Explaining Thai trade union development, structure and strategy

Political context *Degrees of liberalization and autonomy*	*Repression and some degree of tolerance*
Markets Product markets	
Openness	Low
Degree of competition	High
Financial markets	
Openness to market financing	Low
Ownership	Dispersed
Labour markets	Surplus of unskilled workers Shortages of skilled workers
Employer context	
Organization – top 100 as % of total	Medium
Employer organization membership	Low
Multinational	Medium
Unitarist vs. pluralist perspective	Unitarist

Furthermore, there are currently nine labour councils (Charoenloet *et al.* 2004) that compete with one another for seats on tripartite labour bodies (Brown *et al.* 2002). As a single, strong peak labour congress does not exist, this leads to greater competition and disunity among labour organizations.

Third, due to competitive pressure as a result of globalization, organizations are employing strategies to suppress unions or avoid unionization (i.e., dismissing union leaders, closing down plants) as discussed previously. Some of these tactics, which have proved quite effective, have been introduced by multinational companies as part of injecting more advanced HRM systems into their subsidiaries in Thailand (Lawler and Suttawet 2000).

Trade unions will need to pursue strategies to cope with the challenges brought about by globalization and deregulation of the labour market. Already weak and fragmented, they will become increasingly less influential unless they are able to extend their membership to cover workers in the informal industrial sector, which includes a larger number of home-based workers and workers under subcontract than those in the formal factory system. Labour campaigns over the past decade have not been organized independently by trade unions, but have been led by trade unions' alliances with labour-related NGOs. Trade unions will need to develop collaborative relationships with other organizations that support social movements and workers' interests. The establishment of a coalition with other organizations could strengthen the bargaining power of trade unions, but trade unions have to take on the leadership role in these labour campaigns rather than a supportive role if they are to be regarded as strong and viable organizations able to represent the workforce.

Conclusion

Trade unions in Thailand remain weak and fragmented. State enterprise unions which were very strong up until 1991 were disbanded by the military government and currently have been stripped of the right to strike. In the private sector, the national trade union movement lacks unity while trade unions are small in size. Overall, trade unions have lost the strength and the bargaining power they possessed prior to the economic crisis in 1997 when a large number of workers in the formal sector were laid off, many of whom were union members.

In recent times, home-based workers in the informal sector, as well as migrant workers from Burma, Laos and Cambodia (Ministry of Labour 2006a), have been hired to replace permanent employees. These informal sector employees accept lower wages and poorer working conditions. Most of the informal sector workers are not covered by the Labour Protection Act 1998 and cannot join unions. Hence, the number of formal sector workers who constitute the power base of trade unions is shrinking, while the number of workers in the informal sector is increasing significantly. New forms of employment, such as subcontracting in the formal factory system, as well as the increase in employment of casual workers to replace permanent workers, have served to further weaken the power base of trade unions in recent years. The future of trade unions' status and role in Thailand will depend on how well they can increase their power base and collaborate with other social movements.

References

ADB/OECD (Asian Development Bank and Organisation for Economic Cooperation and Development) (2007) *ADB/OECD Anti-Corruption Initiative for Asia-Pacific – Country Report – Thailand*. Online. Available HTTP: <http://www1.oecd.org/daf/ASIAcom/pdf/str_thailand.pdf> (accessed 3 January 2007).

Ativanichayapong, N. (2002) 'Trade unions and the workers' collective action in Thailand: an articulation of social movement unionism and economic unionism, 1972–2002', unpublished thesis, Chulalongkorn University.

BOT (Bank of Thailand) (2006) *Thailand's Key Economic Indicators*. Online. Available HTTP: <http://www.bot.or.th/bothomepage/databank/econdata/Thai_Key/Thai_KeyE.asp> (accessed 28 November 2006).

Brown, A., Thanachaisethavut, B. and Hewison, K. (2002) 'Labour relations and regulation in Thailand: theory and practice', working paper no. 27, University of Hong Kong.

Chandoevwit, W. (2004) 'Labour market issues in Thailand', unpublished paper, Thailand Development Research Institute.

Charoenloet, V. (2000*) Women Workers and the Development of Social Movement Trade Union*. Online. Available HTTP: <orpheus.ucsd.edu/las/studies/pdfs/Voravidh.PDF> (accessed 15 October 2006).

Charoenloet, V., Ativanichayapong, N. and Wanabriboon, P. (2004) *The Impact of Trade Union Solidarity Support Organisations in Thailand 1993–2002*, Bangkok: Chulalongkorn University Political Economy Study Center. Online. Available HTTP: <http://www.fes-thailand.org/Impact%20Study%20(1).pdf> (accessed 20 August 2006).

Charoensuthipan, P. (2003) 'Fund will operate from next January'. Online. Available HTTP: <http://www.thailabour.org/news/03022701.html> (accessed 14 September 2007).

Chayasriwong, S. (2001) 'Feasibility of the Thailand unemployment insurance social system', paper presented at the KLI-FES-ILO seminar on the role of employment/ unemployment insurance under the new economic environment, n.p. Korea, 12–13 September.

ECOT (Employers' Confederation of Thailand) (2007) *About ECOT*. Online. Available HTTP: <http://www.ecot.or.th/about%20us.html> (accessed 11 January 2007).

FES (Friedrich Ebert Stiftung) (2005) *Country Analysis: Thailand*. Online. Available HTTP: <http://www.fesspore.org/pdf/Trade%20union/year%202005/thailand.pdf> (accessed 20 November 2006).

International Bank for Reconstruction and Development and World Bank (1998) *World Development Indicators*, Washington, DC: International Bank for Reconstruction and Development/World Bank.

International Bank for Reconstruction and Development and World Bank (1999) *World Development Indicators*, Washington, DC: International Bank for Reconstruction and Development/World Bank.

ILO (International Labour Organisation) (2005) 'Minister opens discussion on extending protection to millions of informal economy workers'. Online. Available HTTP: <http://www.ilo.org/public/english/ region/asro/bangkok/public/releases/yr2005/pr05_18.htm> (accessed 20 January 2007).

ILO (International Labour Organisation) (2007*) Ministry of Labour and Social Welfare – Thailand.* Online. Available HTTP: <http://www.ilo.org/public/english/employment/gems/eeo/law/thailand/inst_mls.htm> (accessed 3 January 2007).

JETRO (Japan External Trade Organisations) (2006*) Comparative Survey of the Labor Environment in ASEAN, China, India,* n.p. JETRO Overseas Research Department.

Komin, S. (1990) 'Culture and work-related values in Thai organisations', *International Journal of Psychology*, 25: 681–704.

(LRA) (*Labour Relations Act B.E. 2518*) (1975) Online. Available HTTP: <http://www.mol.go.th/ download/laborlaw/labourRelation2518_en.pdf> (accessed 6 August 2006).

Laungaramsri, P. (2005) 'Homeworkers in Thailand: an assessment', paper submitted to Friedrich Ebert Stiftung. Online. Available HTTP: <www.fes-thailand.org/articles/Homeworkers%20in%20Thailand.doc> (accessed on 28 February 2007).

Lawler, J. J. and Suttawet, C. (2000) 'Labour unions, globalization and deregulation in Thailand', *Asia Pacific Business Review*, 6(3–4): 214–38.

Mabry, D. B. (1977). 'The Thai labour movement', *Asian Survey*, 17(110): 931–51.

Manusphaibool, S. (1993) 'Thailand', in S. J. Deery and R. J. Mitchell (eds) *Labour Law and Industrial Relations in Asia*, Melbourne: Longman Cheshire.

Ministry of Labour (2006a) 'ILO raps migrant labour protection'. Online. Available HTTP: <http://eng.mol.go.th/related_newsdec1206.html> (accessed 7 October 2006).

Ministry of Labour (2006b) *Labour Law.* Online. Available HTTP: <http://eng.mol.go.th/law_labour.html> (accessed 7 October 2006).

Ministry of Labour (2006c) *Minimum Daily Wage Rates* [in Thai]. Online. Available HTTP: <http://www.mol.go.th/statistic_01.html> (accessed 7 October 2006).

NSO (National Statistical Office Thailand) (2006a) *Table 1 Population by Labor Force Status for Whole Kingdom: 2001–2005.* Online. Available HTTP: <http://www.nso.go.th/eng/stat/lfs_e/lfse-tab1.xls> (accessed 4 November 2006).

NSO (National Statistical Office Thailand) (2006b) *Table 4 Employed Persons by Work Status for Whole Kingdom: 2001–2005.* Online. Available HTTP: <http://www.nso.go.th/eng/stat/lfs_e/lfse-tab4.xls> (accessed 8 October 2006).

NSO (National Statistical Office Thailand) (2006c) *Table 2 Employed Persons by Industry for Whole Kingdom: 2001–2005.* Online. Available HTTP: <http://www.nso.go.th/eng/stat/lfs_e/lfse-tab2.xls> (accessed 8 October 2006).

NSO (National Statistical Office Thailand) (2006d). *Table 8 Employed Persons by Labor Force Status and Sex: 1988–2006.* Online. Available HTTP: <http://www.nso.go.th/eng/stat/lfs_e/lfse-tab8.xls> (accessed 8 October 2006).

Phongphaichit, P. and Baker, C. (1995) *Thailand: Economy and Politics*, New York: Oxford University Press.

Samukkethum, S. (1996) 'Trade unions and ideology' [in Thai], in S. Piriyarangsan and P. Phongpaichit (eds) *Consciousness and Ideology: Political Parties and Democratic Movement in Thailand*, Bangkok: Chulalongkorn University and Friedrich Ebert Stiftung.

State Enterprise Labour Relations Act B.E. 2543 (2000). Online. Available HTTP: <http://www.mol.go.th/download/laborlaw/labourStateRelation2000_en.pdf> (accessed 6 August 2006).

Thai Labour Campaign (2007) *Labour Links.* Online. Available HTTP: <http://www.thailabour.org/links.html> (accessed 12 January 2007).

Thanachaisethavut, B. (2000) *Problems of Labour Law Enforcement in Thailand* [in Thai], Bangkok: Arom Pongpa-ngan Foundation.

Thanachaisethavut, B. (2001) 'Danger: the crisis of the labour relations system', in B. Thanachaisethavut (ed.) *Toward Reforming Labour Relations Law*, Bangkok: Arom Pongpa-ngan Foundation.

Thanachaisethavut, B. and Charoenlert, V. (2006) 'Extending labour protection to the informal economy in Thailand', in D. Tajgman (ed.) *Extending Labour Laws to All Workers: Promoting Decent Work in the Informal Economy in Cambodia, Thailand, and Mongolia*, Bangkok: International Labour Organization.

UNESCAP (2000) *Report on the State of Women in Urban Local Government: Thailand.* United Nations Economic and Social Commission for Asia and the Pacific. Online. Available HTTP: <www.unescap.org/huset/women/reports/thailand.pdf> (accessed 10 January 2007).

Wanthana, S. (1982) 'The evolution of Thai working class in two centuries' [in Thai], *Thammasat University Journal*, 11(1): 140–65.

World Bank (2000) *Thailand Social Monitor: Thai Workers and the Crisis*, Bangkok: World Bank/National Statistical Office.

Yukongdi, V. (2005) 'Unemployment in Thailand: social issues, challenges and opportunities', in Y. Zhu and J. Benson (eds) *Unemployment in Asia: Organizational and Institutional Relationships*, London: RoutledgeCurzon.

14 Trade unions in Indonesia

From state incorporation to market orientation

Joe Isaac and Sari Sitalaksmi

Introduction

Trade unions in most countries rely on facilitative legislation for their existence, for the economic power they can exert on employers through collective bargaining, and for the collective voice they can command in political matters directly or indirectly. This is also true of contemporary trade unionism in Indonesia. While such legislation is necessary for an effective trade union movement, it may not be a sufficient condition. The state of the economy, the way unions are organized, the competence of their leaders at all levels, the extent of grassroots commitment, their political affiliations and entanglements, and the form of government under which they operate and its attitude to unionism – all these can affect the capacity of unions to meet traditional trade union objectives to improve the pay and conditions of workers.

The history of trade unions in Indonesia shows the operation of these factors to varying degrees in their stages of development from colonial rule to the establishment of the Republic in 1945 and the developments since then. We see here a succession of the main character of unionism from revolutionary/political to statist/incorporatist and, more recently, to market or business, overlaid formally with the cloak of *pancasila*, a Sanskrit word encapsulating the idea of a sort of social partnership. The word translates as 'five principles': belief in the one and only God, humanitarianism, nationalism, consultative democracy, and social justice.

The various trade union models discussed in Howard Gospel's chapter (Chapter 2, this volume) are to be found in the short history of trade unions in Indonesia. The details of this history and the questions they raise will be developed in what follows. Although this chapter will focus on trade union developments since 1998, immediately following the Asian crisis, an understanding of later developments calls for a brief historical context dealing with the changing forms of government, the changing fortunes of the economy and earlier union developments. The chapter then proceeds to deal with developments since 1998 – the new labour laws, the formation of new trade union bodies and their effect on the structure of trade unions and their function at the different levels, employer associations, the minimum wage, and the incidence of strikes.

The discussion of these issues provides the basis for dealing with the following questions and an evaluation of the future prospects for trade unions. How has democratic government since 1998 affected the growth and development of trade unions? How have international institutions assisted Indonesian trade unions? What are the characteristics of the labour laws; how have they affected the growth, structure and what trade unions do? To what extent have unions been involved in political activities? How has the state of the economy affected trade union achievements? What are the likely prospects for unionism in the foreseeable future?

Context and history

Formerly the Netherlands East Indies, the Republic of Indonesia, was proclaimed in 1945 with the end of Japanese occupation. It was recognised by the United Nations in 1949. The leader of the independence movement, Soekarno, became its first President. He was succeeded by President Soeharto following a military coup in 1967. Soeharto's military dictatorship, the *New Order* he instituted and the strong economic growth which accompanied it, came to an end in 1998 amidst the Asian economic crisis which hit Indonesia hard. Since then, the *New Order* has given way to *Reformasi*, and Indonesia has been ruled by democratic governments with important consequences for trade unionism.

Table 14.1 provides elements of the contextual scene relevant to the discussion in this chapter. It is necessary to add that geographically, Indonesia is an archipelago of over 17,000 islands, and that, although the majority of the population is Muslim, the country is multicultural and multiethnic.

On the test of economic growth alone, the three decades under President Soeharto's *New Order* were a golden age. High economic growth was fed initially in the 1970s by an oil boom, and later by the emergence of a rapidly expanding export-oriented manufacturing sector that was accompanied by an expansion of the construction and services sector and foreign direct investment. In the period 1968–96, the economy grew at an annual average rate of 7 per cent, and as shown in Table 14.1, the growth rate averaged 7.9 per cent in the period 1988–95. All this ended with the onset of the Asian Crisis in mid-1997. The GDP growth rate fell to an average of 2.9 per cent in 1995–2005, while the unemployment rate rose substantially. Inflation rose from under 7 per cent in 1997 to over 58 per cent in 1998, falling progressively in the years that followed to about 10 per cent in 2005; while foreign direct investment, which had been US$5–6b in 1996–7, fell to negative figures and did not recover until 2005, according to the Asian Development Bank key indicators.

It is important to note that the informal sector makes up some 60 per cent of the labour force, based on figures supplied to the International Labour Organization by the Ministry of Manpower for February 2006. This high figure is typical of less-developed countries and includes a relatively high level of unemployment, under-employment, self-employment and low productivity, where people are generally at the lower end of the income scale. As will be noted later, the prospect

Table 14.1 Contextual factors – Indonesia

General statistics	
Population (2006)[1]	222 million
Area (square kilometres)[2]	1.9 million
Employment by sector (%) (2005)[3] Agriculture Industry Services	44 13 43
Urban population (% of total population) (2004)[4]	47
GDP per capita (2005)[5]	$1,300
Income inequality (high, medium or low) Gini coefficient (2002)[4]	Medium 34.3
Real GDP growth (%)[3] 1988–1995 1995–2005	7.9 2.9
Unemployment (%)[3] 1986–1995 1996–2004 2005–2006*	3.3 7.1 10.7
Summary description	
Product market regulation (1998)	Not available
Political context (liberal/pluralistic, state unitarist [communist, non-communist])	Liberal/pluralistic
Political stability (high, medium or low)	Medium

Sources
1 Statistics Indonesia (2006).
2 Statistics Indonesia (2004).
3 ADB Key Indicators (2006).
4 Human Development Report 2006, UNDP.
5 World Development Indicators 2006, World Bank.

Note
*The first bi-annual survey was held in 2005 and hence the 2005 figure represents the six-months from August 2004.

of unionization depends on the size of the formal workforce, which in turn depends on the rate of economic development.

The Asian Crisis and its consequences for Indonesia are well covered in the literature. For our purposes, it is sufficient to note the changed economic environment reflected in statistical indicators. Recovery has been slow and lacking in confidence. Nine years after the Crisis, Indonesia's fundamental economic indicators have begun to show improvement, but remain susceptible to both domestic and international shocks. It has been hampered by an unstable political climate arising from a succession of short-term presidents – four in the course of six years – in a new democracy under the present incumbent, Susilo Bambang Yudoyono, and from the ravages of tsunamis and earthquakes.

Union types and structure

The association between trade unions and political parties is not unusual. In most countries, the survival and development of trade unions in the face of employer hostility, has depended on legislative protection and regulation, and hence on political support. However, the nature and strength of this association may vary greatly. In Indonesia, at least until recently, the objectives of trade unions were somewhat mixed. Under Dutch colonial rule, traditional union objectives were marginal to advancing the cause for independence, despite severe repression from the colonial rulers (Suwarno and Elliott 2000). Not surprisingly, this form of 'political unionism' is not mentioned by Howard Gospel's discussion of unionism in advanced countries but is not unusual in colonial countries (Ford 2005: 198).

Moreover, the union movement was polarized between Marxist and non-Marxist unions, thus splitting the movement on political ideological lines. The years following independence, the Soekarno years, saw a rapid growth in unions, most with political affiliations of which SOBSI (Central Organization of All-Indonesian Workers), a Marxist-based union formed in 1947 and linked to the PKI (Indonesian Communist Party), was the largest. However, this link brought it into conflict with the army which took an active and repressive hand against strikes (Hadiz 1997: 172).

Despite these ambiguities, the growth of unionism in this period was accompanied by constitutional and legislative provisions far exceeding those of many developed countries.[1] Thus, the Constitution guaranteed the right to join trade unions and the right to strike, while subsequent legislation provided the framework for these rights in terms of freedom of association and assembly, prohibition of interference in union activity, and the right to bargain collectively (Caraway 2004: 32). Discrimination was prohibited, and there was provision for all lay-offs and dismissals to be approved by tripartite dispute resolution committees, as well as generous termination payments. The government ratified the ILO's Convention 98 (the Right to Organize and Collective Bargaining) as early as 1957.

However, practice did not live up to these lofty provisions. The unions, in particular the largest union body SOBSI, were embroiled in the civil and political conflicts of the times. For this, they were punished when the *New Order* under Soeharto came into being in 1967. Soeharto did not revoke the Soekarno legislative instruments but effectively over-ruled them by executive decrees, backed, as in the early Soekarno years, by military intervention. The *Pancasila* doctrine enshrined in the Constitution and intended in the early years of independence to promote national unity as a concept of social and economic partnership, was subverted to justifying government control of unions, the imprisonment of union leaders and a restriction of workers' rights, including the right to strike (Suwarno and Elliott 2000: 130; Quinn 2003: 13). SOBSI was banned and effective monopoly was given to the government-sponsored union federation, the All Indonesia Labour Federation (FBSI). There was no room for independent unions. All remaining unions had to join this body, the leadership of which was made up of retired civil servants, military officers and politicians (Quinn 2003: 13), while in some cases, workers' representatives at plant level were men with military backgrounds who also functioned as personnel managers (Hadiz 1998: 116). FBSI went through several name changes and restructuring, engineered by the government in the face of labour unrest (Hadiz 1998: 114) and became the SPSI (All-Indonesia Workers' Union) in 1985. Ten years later, it was further renamed the FSPSI to emphasize its federation (*federasi*) status. For the whole of the Soeharto period, essentially one big union, the tool of the government, formally 'represented' labour. The army, acting effectively as an independent political force in its longstanding hostility to unions, assisted this process. However, all this did not stem labour unrest. Economic development was accompanied by the growth of an urban-based industrial workforce, more educated than their parents and less able than in earlier times to return to the village and agriculture; and with aspirations for improved pay and conditions (Hadiz 1997: 255).

From one point of view, the repressive actions of the Soeharto government did not drastically change the industrial relations situation in practice. Soeharto government decrees ensured that the Soekarno legislative instruments were simply sidelined. Union power was wielded at the behest of the government to assist its economic development programme. Leaving aside questions of equity and accepted trade union rights, it is arguable that the Soeharto authoritarian decrees allowed economic development to proceed faster and that, as a dividend to workers, or more likely, in the face of increasing worker unrest, the regime legislated substantial real minimum wage increases during the 1980s when the average annual real minimum wage for Jakarta rose on average by 4.7 per cent (Manning 1997: 118). However, much of this increase did not materialize for many because of large-scale retrenchments and rampant inflation, while hundreds of firms were able to obtain exemption from the minimum wage increase on grounds of economic difficulties and others simply ignored workers' legal entitlements (Hadiz 1998: 110, 118).

International influences

The resulting major strikes, imprisonment of union leaders, violence and military intervention drew international attention to the repressive nature of Indonesian industrial relations. In response to the complaint of the ICFTU to the ILO in 1994 on the denial of workers' rights, the ILO's Committee on Freedom of Association advised the government to remove restrictions on union registration and rights. The government, by regulation, made the meaningless concession of allowing company unions (SBTPs) to be established provided they affiliated with the SPSI within two years. These unions could hardly be regarded as independent. By 1997, some 1,200 of these unions had been formed, many by the companies themselves (Quinn 2003: 15).

In an attempt to meet international criticism and to resolve the contradiction between the Soekarno laws and the Soeharto decrees and regulations, the *Manpower Act* of 1997 was passed at the onset of the Asian financial crisis.

However, this was not to labour's advantage and contained a number of repressive provisions against workers' rights (Caraway 2004: 34). The ILO's Committee of Experts on the Application of Conventions and Recommendations, examining the application of Convention 98, which had been ratified by Indonesia as far back as 1957, was not impressed. It 'observed with deep concern that the discrepancies between the Convention on the one hand, and the legislation and national practice on the other, have continued for many years' (Quinn 2003: 33). For the ILO, this was strong language indeed. It could not be ignored indefinitely, especially as industrial disputes and tensions were not being contained despite the repressive laws. A troubled industrial relations climate could have an adverse effect on the flow of foreign investment on which the country's economic development depended. In the circumstances, the operation of the *Manpower Act* 1997 was deferred and finally abandoned in 2002 (Quinn 2003: 16). It was replaced by legislation, formulated with the guidance of the ILO, as part of the post-1998 labour reform process in the post-Soeharto *Reformasi* era.

It is interesting to note that while genuine trade unionism was suppressed under Soeharto, local community-based labour-oriented non-government organizations (NGOs) engaged in promoting workers' education, cooperatives, training programmes and discussion groups over which the government had little control, were effectively taking the place of unions. These groups, led mainly by middle-class activists outside the labour movement (Ford 2001: 103), strengthened workers' 'class' identity and gave them a sense of unity and purpose, and frequently enabled coordinated strikes to take place (Hadiz 1997: 137–8). Those with international funding links were in a position to apply pressure on the government on human rights issues in which workers rights featured (Ford 2001: 106). They also sponsored informal work groups at the enterprise level, some of which went on to establish enterprise and regional unions following the demise of the *New Order* (Ford 2001: 111–12). However, they retired from being substitute unions when the law reforms after 1998 restored traditional union rights and enabled trade unions to be formed and to function under legal protection.

Post-1998 developments

A number of coherent and wide-ranging legislative instruments followed, the first of which was the *Trade Union Act No.21/2000*, effectively incorporating Conventions 87 and 98. It provides that unions, federations and confederations shall be 'free, open, independent, democratic and responsible', able to engage in collective bargaining and the settlement of industrial disputes, and defend the rights and interests of their members, including civil servants.

Earlier experience with registration requirements in which unions were effectively prevented from securing registration, led the Act to require a simple notification and recording of their establishment. Although under the Soeharto regime '*Pancasila* industrial relations' had been subverted by the government because it regarded strikes as un-Indonesian (Hadiz 1998: 113), Article 2 of the Act specifies that trade unions accept *Pancasila* 'as the state ideology and the

Unitary State of the Republic of Indonesia', inferring that the freely determined statutory basis of trade unions must be consistent with this provision. This seems to be analogous to Gospel's reference to the influence of the Catholic Church in giving trade unionism a moral and ideological force. In 2002, the Minister of Manpower at the time, Jacob Nuwa Wea, who was also chairman of Konfederasi Serikat Pekerja Seluruh Indonesia (KSPSI), sought unsuccessfully to have the word *pancasila* substituted by 'harmonious, dynamic and equal' industrial relations (*Kompas*, 2 March 2002).

The second piece of labour legislation was the *Manpower Act (No. 13/2003)*, originally introduced as the Manpower Development and Protection Bill. The preamble of this Act states the object of building a society 'in which there shall be welfare, justice and prosperity based on equity both materially and spiritually with the *Pancasila* and the 1945 Constitution at its foundation'. It also refers to the important role of workers, their training and their fundamental rights in national development. The Act regulates a wide range of issues in considerable detail, ranging from working conditions within companies such as working hours and outsourcing to national issues such as the determination of minimum wage.

Although the *Manpower Act* and what may be regarded as its 'safety net' provisions had been formulated with the cooperation of the main employers' association (APINDO) and representatives of six union federations, for different reasons, connected with women's rights, severance pay, outsourcing, child labour, strikes, lockouts, many employers and unions were unhappy with the Act (*Kompas*, 25 February 2007: 27).

In particular, mention should be made of a ministerial decree known as KEP-150 which had been introduced in 2000. The decree included dismissals and severance pay provisions so as to give greater employment security to workers and to make the retrenchment of workers more expensive for employers. Employers facing difficulty in attracting investment at a time of declining employment in the formal sector, especially in manufacturing (Manning and Roesad 2006: Table 4), strenuously objected to KEP-150. Compared with its South-East Asian competitors, Indonesia was among the most rigid in its employment requirements (Manning and Roesad 2006: Table 5); and the government relented to pressure from employers and amended the Act in their favour (KEP-78/2001; Kelly 2002: 39). This would provide greater flexibility and less worker protection, especially in relation to outsourcing and short-term contracts, while severance pay and long-service entitlements were to be reduced (Manning and Roesad 2006: 166). The revised provisions of the decree were incorporated into the *Manpower Act*. There was also pressure for a lowering of the minimum wage standard.

However, these changes in labour conditions gave rise to a series of large-scale strikes and demonstrations. A union, Aspec Indonesia, challenged the constitutionality of the Act before a special Constitutional Court. Although the Act was upheld, the Court struck out a provision relating to an employer's right to automatic dismissal of a worker for serious 'violation', requiring the employer to prove any violation first (*Gatra*, 10 April 2006). Rounds of talks called by the government came to nought. Violence accompanying the 2006 May Day rally finally led the government to concede to union demands by withdrawing the amendments favouring greater workforce flexibility.

The third major piece of labour legislation was the *Industrial Disputes Settlement Act (No.2/2004)*. Although legislation providing procedures for dispute settlement has existed for some time (Act No. 22 of 1957 and Act No. 12 of 1964), they had not been effective, partly because of the lack of trust in the fairness of the procedure, ministerial interference, work overload, and confidence in the composition of the Labour Dispute Settlement Committees (Quinn 2003: 21). There were modifications through decrees, but generally grievances were allowed to fester and protest strikes tended to occur frequently (Kelly 2002: 39). To deal with these and other difficulties, the ILO engaged in discussion with the government on drafting the Act to deal with the settlement of industrial disputes.

This Act effectively replaces earlier Acts on the subject. It distinguishes between industrial disputes on rights, interest, termination, and between unions in one company (Art. 2). Disputes are initially required to be resolved through bi-partite negotiations. Should this fail, a mediator would engage in conciliation and if necessary arbitration, with ultimate recourse to the Courts for resolution. In the first instance, the matter may be taken to the Industrial Relations Court in the District Court (Art. 14, 88), which is subject to further appeal to the Supreme Court (Art. 113). Should the matter go to the courts, the process will no doubt involve delays and high costs.

At this point, it is appropriate to say something about employer associations in Indonesia. The main employer association concerned with industrial relations was established in 1952, and renamed Asosiasi Pengusaha Indonesia (APINDO) in 1985. It is affiliated with the Chamber of Commerce. In earlier times, the spate of labour laws and decrees were generally in the employers' interest, and those not in favour of employers could be ignored by them with impunity. Moreover, until 2001, APINDO could not be considered to be representative solely of employer interests, having on its Board members from ministries of Manpower and Industry and Trade as well as retired company managers (Mizuno 2005: 194). However, a combination of factors, including the new climate of legislative reform favourable to unions and workers, the implications of KEP-150 on employment flexibility, and the sharp rise in the minimum wage at a time economic recession, goaded employers into new leadership and greater unity, making it a more credible organization in dealing with the government (Caraway 2004: 39).

The transition from the repressive Soeharto regime to the permissive environment created by the new labour laws resulted in a rapid growth of unions as reflected in the number of federations. These grew progressively from 1 in 1997 to 90 in 2006 (ILO Jakarta, based on figures supplied by Ministry of Manpower). This growth extended beyond the growth of the traditional area of unionism – private sector blue collar – to white collar unions and to the public sector (Ford 2000: 6). The main characteristics of Indonesian trade unions are shown in Table 14.2.

The most recent figures for trade union federations (national unions) and enterprise level unions (also known as branches/locals/working units) are shown in Table 14.3.

Table 14.2 Indonesian trade unions

General statistics	
Number of unions[1]	
1990	1
2004	88
Number of union members	
1990	Not available
2005	3.4m
Union density (%)[1,2]	
1990	Not available
2005	6–7 (of formal sector)
Summary description	
Union type	
Main	Economic/market
Secondary	
(economic/market, political, other)	
Union structure	
Main	Occupational
Secondary	Enterprise
(occupational, industrial, general, enterprise)	
Unity of peak organizations (high, medium or low)	Medium
State control of unions (high, medium or low)	Low
Involvement in collective bargaining (high, medium or low)	Low

Sources
1 Directorate General of Industrial Relations (2006a), Ministry of Manpower. These refer to federations or national unions each with numerous branches at the enterprise level as shown in Table 8.3.
2 Ms Asaneca Colowai, ILO Jakarta Office.

Table 14.3 Membership of Indonesian trade unions 2006

No.	Name of trade union peak body (Confederation)	No. of federations	No. of enterprise unions	Members
1	KSPSI	16	6,122	1,657,244
2	KSPI	10	1,101	793,874
3	KSBSI	11	1,307	227,806
4	National Federation of Trade Unions	3	833	269,509
5	Non-confederation of Trade Union Federation	50	1,677	403,714
6	Non-federation Trade Union	–	1,237	305,959
	TOTAL	90	11,444	3,388,597

Source: ILO Jakarta, based on statistics supplied by the Ministry of Manpower.

In 1998, a number of unions broke away from FSPSI, the existing peak union body or confederation, which once again restructured itself in 2002. The breakaway unions formed the smaller 'reformasi group' KSPI (Indonesian Trade Union Congress). In addition, the communist-led SBSI, which had been banned by Soeharto, came back to life. These were to be the main peak bodies known as confederations – FSPSI, KSPI and SBSI – although many small confederations developed; while hundreds of independent unions and enterprise unions came into being, frequently with more than one union per enterprise.

All this was consistent with the terms of the *Trade Union Act* but it was financially a drain on union resources and created the potential for union rivalry and collective bargaining difficulties. International trade union bodies, which were giving financial assistance and advice to Indonesian unions, were also concerned at the proliferation of unions and encouraged them to consolidate (Kelly 2002: 21). Thus, while the employers could speak through a single collective voice, the trade unions were fragmented and lacked a central body (Quinn 2003: 9); although, as discussed later, on certain issues such as the minimum wage, the main confederations have tended to act jointly. This fragmentation also creates problems of proper representation in tripartite advisory bodies (Kelly 2002: 23).

In terms of their composition, most unions are best described as 'occupational unions' in that a variety of skills are included within enterprise unions, and hence in the national unions to which they are affiliated. However, there are a small number of industry-based unions that are not affiliated with any confederation, of which banking and finance (FOKUBA) and plantation unions (FSPBUN) are examples.

Although there is no doubt that union membership has risen greatly in the post-Soeharto years, estimates of the size of union membership vary from year to year and must be taken with considerable reservation. Quinn (2003: 36), for example, at one time suggested that union membership might have been 8.3 million in 2002. Since the labour force in the formal sector was about 40–50 million, this would make for a union density of 16–20 per cent in that sector. This is a highly doubtful estimate, a point conceded by Quinn (2003: 26). Other estimates for 1999 put the density at around 3 per cent (Quinn 2003: 26). Tables 14.2 and 14.3 show union membership to be 3.4 million. Assuming that the size of the formal workforce is 40–50 million of the total workforce (106 million), union density in the formal sector would at the most be 6–7 per cent.

Table 14.3 shows the concentration of federations and membership in the first three confederations. During the Soeharto era, KSPSI was initially set up as the only government-sanctioned trade union body known as SPSI (All Indonesian Trade Unions). It therefore had strong political affiliation with the ruling Golkar (Golongan Karya) party, although this is no longer so (Interview with Sutanto Suwarno, January 2007). The KSPI (Indonesian Trade Union Congress) is the second largest confederation in Indonesia and it is affiliated with the International Confederation of Free Trade Unions. (See Figure 14.1 regarding the organizational structure of KSPSI.)

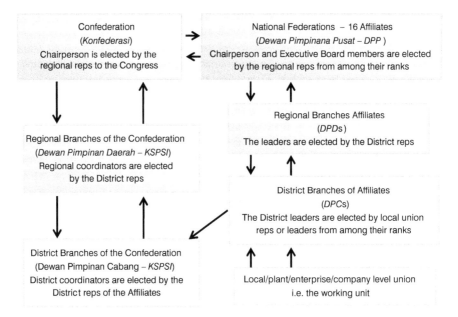

Figure 14.1 Flow diagram of KSPSI's organizational structure (Source: diagram supplied by Aseneca Colowai, ILO Jakarta.

The KSBSI (Confederation of Indonesian Prosperity Trade Union) is a union revived in 1992 from the suppressed SBSI during the Soeharto era and is the third largest national trade union centre. Political figures such as Abdurahman Wahid (who became the fourth president) and Rahmawati Soekarnoputri (sister of Megawati Soekarnoputri, the fifth president) were among those involved in its establishment. It is affiliated internationally with the World Confederation of Labour (www.ksbsi.org).

In the post-Soeharto years, union officials established a number of political parties to contest elections but apart from the National Labour Party (PBN) established in 1999 by SBSI's leader Muchtar Pakpahan to which KSBSI is affiliated, the others did not survive. Although an unusual case, it is of interest that the president of FSIPSI, Mr Jacob Nuwa Wea, was for some years Minister of Manpower and Transmigration in the Megawati government; and in 2002, Pakpahan formed the Partai Buruh Sosial Demokrat (PBSD) which is expected to contest the 2009 election.

However, unionists generally seem reluctant to establish links with existing political parties (Ford 2005: 202) and the value of political connections to unions is difficult to assess. Union leaders appear to be ambivalent about political affiliations partly because of their differing political views, and partly remembering the pre-Soeharto years of divisive political unionism followed by the co-option of unions during the Soeharto period (Ford AIRAANZ 2005: 200). It is fair to assume that the passing of the three Acts discussed provide the basis for improvements in pay and conditions, making it less necessary for unions to be tied to political parties so long as they are able to apply pressures in other ways.

Despite the provisions of the *Trade Union Act*, intimidatory practices by employers, including resort to police and military personnel, have put obstacles in the way of union development (Quinn 2003: 26). The issue of discrimination by employers against trade unionists has been taken to the ILO Committee on Freedom of Association and its report is pending.

What do unions do?[2]

From the statements of trade union leaders, from their contributions to the formulation of the new labour laws, and from their rule books, it is clear what the present generation of Indonesian trade unions seek to do – to engage in collective bargaining, to obtain favourable terms of employment for workers, to be able to process worker grievances effectively, to secure a growing membership, and to influence the government to enact terms favourable to these objectives. On this basis, Indonesian trade unionism is best regarded as essentially 'business' or 'market' unionism, to use Gospel's terms. A summary of the activities of unions is shown in Table 14.4.

The structure of unions and the Acts under which they operate effectively determine the activities of unions at the different levels. We have distinguished the three levels as branch/local/plant/enterprise, national/federation and confederation/peak body. In some of the larger unions, there is also a regional level of branches/locals, as was shown in the flow-diagram of the largest confederation (see Figure 14.1).

Collective bargaining, grievance processing and membership recruitment are undertaken by the union branch/local union at the plant or enterprise level. If the union is established at the plant level only, it becomes, in effect, the national union. Union operations are orchestrated by shop stewards or, where membership

Table 14.4 What do Indonesian trade unions do?

Activities	
Extent of collective bargaining (high, medium or low)	Low
Level of collective bargaining (high, medium or low)	
National	Low
Industry	Low
Enterprise	High
Extent of joint consultation (high, medium or low)	Low
Industrial disputes	
Working days lost per 1,000 employees per annum (2003)	< 1
Relative assessment (high, medium or low)	Low
Degree of state intervention in employment protection (high, medium or low)	Medium–High

Source: Ministry of Manpower.

is large, by the chairperson, secretary or treasurer of the branch. Shop stewards are responsible for recruiting members, being in touch with them, collecting dues, and being generally available to communicate any shop floor problems affecting workers with management. The *Trade Union Act* requires a membership of at least 10 for a union to be registered at the plant level. This requirement has resulted in a proliferation of a large number of small union branches, several of which may operate in an enterprise.

To prevent such a situation from giving rise to a multiplicity of agreements binding an employer, the *Manpower Act* prescribes that only one collective agreement can operate in an enterprise. If there is only one union in the enterprise and if it has more than 50 per cent of the total number of workers, then that union has the right to represent the workers in that enterprise. If the union does not have the membership of the majority of workers, but the majority of workers approve of an agreement, it can still represent the workers. If there is more than one union in the enterprise, the one with the membership of the majority of the workers has the right to negotiate the collective agreement. If no union has a majority membership, the unions may form a coalition, provided the coalition has a majority membership of the workers.

The low density of union membership referred to earlier reflects the weakness of unions at this level where recruitment takes place. This obviously limits the incidence of collective bargaining and grievance processing. Compared with multi-employer bargaining, enterprise bargaining is a costly process for unions, and it is not surprising that a large proportion of small and medium-sized businesses escape collective bargaining. In a survey of companies (Quinn 2003: 35) with more than 25 employees in 2002, it was found that only 14 per cent were covered by registered collective agreements; while the terms of employment of 55 per cent were covered by enterprise/company regulations registered with the Ministry of Manpower or, in other words, they were determined unilaterally by the employers. The rest, 35 per cent, did not register the terms of employment of their workers, presumably also determined unilaterally by employers. Recent figures show that the number of company regulations remained at four times the number of company agreements between 2001 and 2006.

There are no legal sanctions against employers who refuse to bargain or do not do so in good faith. Effective application of these laws in a country new to them calls for education and training of the leaders of the stakeholders at various levels. To this end, the ILO, sometimes in conjunction with funds supplied by other countries – Japan, the Netherlands, the USA, France, the UK – has carried out a running programme of technical assistance (Quinn 2003: 59–60).

The regional branches assist their union at the enterprise level by way of advice or more direct assistance, particularly where the branches are very small and the union is inadequately represented. This level of activity occurs mainly in the larger federations where the union at the enterprise level is ineffectual, a common feature at this level of the union hierarchy.

Union organizations at the national or federation level, assist the lower levels with advice whenever needed. They communicate industrial relations information and developments, and organize education and training sessions from time to time. Where branches are involved with a number of firms in a particular sector, provided the matter is on a small scale, the national union may intervene to coordinate grievance action and collective bargaining.

The main function of the confederation or peak level is to formulate union policy and strategy, and to engage in political dialogue with the government, singly or in conjunction with other confederations. Discussions on legislation, the minimum wage and other matters affecting industrial relations take place at this level. Organizations at peak level are better equipped to handle national issues, using international links for advice and assistance. In some cases, where major sector-specific issues are in dispute with employers, the confederation may step in to provide stronger leadership than might be available at the regional level in resolving a dispute, often using government leverage and protest marches of workers in the process.

In practice, this has proved to be the industrial and political driving force of the trade union movement. What unions lower down can do depends in large measure on what can be achieved politically at the higher level. However, this force is weakened by the lack of unity of the peak unions on many issues.

Nonetheless, the peak trade union bodies play an important part in the determination of minimum wages (MWs) by applying political pressure on the government. As mentioned above, the history of MWs in Indonesia goes back to the Soeharto years in the 1970s. At first, coverage was limited to the construction industry but by the 1980s, MWs were fixed for various provinces. However, adjustments were irregular and compliance was patchy. It was not until the late 1990s that the principles and procedures on which MWs were determined and enforced were undertaken more seriously and systematically. The new approach was driven by combination of forces including the development of independent trade unions, increased industrialization, political pressure for greater equity in income distribution and international competitive pressures from 'cheap' labour. The trade unions, particularly the three main confederations, have thrown their weight behind improvements in the MW determination, making up for the lack of bargaining power of unions at the enterprise level. Between 2002 and 2006, the average real MW rose by nearly 20 per cent.

Although the formal sector generally pays the prescribed MW, a sizeable proportion of small businesses pay well below the MWs, taking advantage of the provision for exemption to the payment of the MW to be made for enterprises which can show incapacity to pay the prescribed amount. Encouraged by the employer association (APINDO), employers have taken advantage of this provision (Hadiz 1997: 177). Such exemptions seem to be granted freely. In Indonesia, for example, 30 per cent of full-time workers and 50 per cent of full-time casual workers earn less than the minimum wage (Saget 2006: 19). Unions' attempts at securing the MW through collective bargaining have in many cases been rebuffed by threats of dismissal of workers or plant closure. MWs are effectively excluded from application in the informal sector covering some 60 per cent of the workforce (Bird and Suryahadi 2002: 11; Alatas and Cameron 2003: 12).

Moreover, the MW has not operated as a wage floor. Increases in MWs have a significant effect on wages generally as reflected in average wages rather than mainly on those at the lower end of the wage scale (SMERU: 56). This, again, is an indication of the weakness of unions in collective bargaining and their reliance on legislation to raise wages generally *via* minimum wages policy.

Unions rely on membership dues to fund their activities. Dues are relatively high – 1 per cent of gross basic pay – a fact that may discourage paid-up membership, bearing in mind that the union development has been driven largely from above. Most dues are collected directly by the shop stewards at the workplace level, but in some 10 per cent of cases collections are on a check-off basis. In general, those unions affiliated to a federation send about 30 per cent of dues to the federation, retaining the rest at the branch. Where a confederation branch level exists, 20 per cent is sent to it, leaving the branch with half of the collections.

Finally, mention should be made of strikes. Measurement of the incidence and magnitude of strikes are subject to substantial anomalies (Perry 2005).[3] The broad picture reflected by time lost per member of the labour force shows that 0.6 working days per 1,000 workers per annum was lost in the 1980s on average, rising to 1.4 days (0.14 per cent) for the years 1990–2003. The highest figure, 4.5 working days, was in 1996. Since then, despite the relaxation of the repressive laws, the figure has trended sharply downwards in an environment of high unemployment. However, taking the total workforce as the basis of these figures understates the effect of strikes on the formal sector of the economy where industrial action occurs. Nonetheless, the magnitude of working days lost is still very small and cannot be regarded as a significant drain on the economy. Since 1994–96, close to the end of the Soeharto era when a large number of strikes occurred, the number of strikes has fallen to about 200 per annum. Moreover, the duration of worker involvement in strikes has generally been very short. Excluding 1998 when the duration averaged nearly 12 days, since the 1980s, strikes last on average 1.4 days.

These figures demonstrate the low level of strike activity. The confluence of high unemployment, weak union consciousness and the constraint of loss of income on workers explain this picture. New dispute machinery came into operation in 2006, and although mostly used by regional branches, the procedures appear to be slow and costly (Interview with Rekson Silaban, Chairman of KSBSI, December 2006).

Explaining the development, structure and strategies of trade unions

The Introduction to this chapter concluded with a number of questions, the answers to which are implicitly contained in the text that followed. We now turn to draw them together against the background of the contents of Table 14.5.

The advent of democratic government clearly affected the growth, structure and functions of trade unions. In the very early days of their scanty and insecure existence, trade unions were dedicated mainly to achieving independence from colonial rule. In these circumstances, drawing on Gospel, they would be classified as essentially political/revolutionary. Then, despite facilitative legislation, trade

Table 14.5 Explaining Indonesian trade union development, structure and strategy

Political context	
Degrees of liberalization and autonomy	
(repression, tolerance, support, indifference)	Support
Relations with the state (dependent, independent)	Independent

Markets	
Openness (imports + exports as % of GDP)	8
Degree of competition (high, medium or low)	Medium
Financial markets	
Openness to market financing structure (group, institutional, foreign, dispersed)	Medium Dispersed/group
Labour markets	
Demand elasticity (relates to ability of employers to pass on wage increases in prices – high, medium or low)	Low-Medium

Employers	
Concentration (2003) (top 100 companies as % value of total)	CR2 (0.51); CR4 (0.67)*
Employer organization membership (high, medium or low)	Low
Multinational (high, medium or low)	Medium
Unitarist or pluralist perspective	Pluralist

Sources: Asian Development Bank Key Indicators. Statistics Indonesia (2004), Jakarta, 'Indicators of large and medium-sized manufacturing'.

Note
* CR2 and CR4 show, respectively, the share of 2 firms and of 4 firms in the value of output of the total number of firms in manufacturing.

unions became embroiled in ideological and political conflicts rather than in attending to the needs of the workers more directly. This phase again shows unionism taking on a substantially political character, although overlaid by the religious and social base of *Pancasila*. Later, following a military coup in 1965, they were effectively repressed and incorporated into an authoritarian government intent on promoting its own agenda. It would be fair to categorize this form of unionism as statist/incorporatist.

We noted above that on the test of economic growth alone, the three decades of the Soeharto era could fairly be regarded as a golden age. There was economic prosperity from which large numbers profited, even if unequally. It has also been argued that through an 'administrative patrimonial' state, 'where power is located in the hands of a class of office-holders who are the main beneficiaries of rent extraction from a disorganized business class' (Huthcroft 1998: 52, quoted by Robison and Hadiz 2004), a class of powerful office holders came into being (Robison and Hadiz 2004: 12).

However, the Soeharto years showed that a prosperous economy in itself is not a sufficient condition for the development of independent trade unions as a force in promoting workers' rights. An authoritarian government on the pretext of *Pancasila* can effectively subvert the union movement into a state instrument.

The advent of political democracy in 1998 brought a comprehensive range of progressive labour laws consistent with ILO conventions, providing the potential for union growth and meaningful collective bargaining. This marked a new phase of essentially market unionism with the force of class-consciousness blunted by substantial unemployment and the large agricultural and informal sectors, and moderated by patriarchical and Islamic values (Hadiz 1997: 123–4) inherent in the *Pancasila* philosophy in favour of social harmony and against conflict.

This development came with considerable pressure on the Indonesian government from international institutions that included not only the ILO and ICFTU, as might be expected, but also from the World Bank and the IMF. However, despite these facilitative provisions for improving the economic plight of workers through trade union initiatives, other factors – economic, organizational, leadership, political – limited this potential. Relative to the size of the workforce, the growth in membership has been small. Moreover, trade unions have not been in a position to apply effectively restrictive practices of the kind noted by Gospel in European countries despite the employment rigidities in the legislation mentioned above.

The aftermath of the Asian Crisis left the economy depressed and foreign investors nervous, thus slowing down economic growth and the potential for securing more union membership and improvements for workers. In addition, there were difficulties associated with a lack of grassroots union commitment and a multiplicity of unions at the workplace. Its leadership at that level lacked experience in collective bargaining and have had to face the frustration and transaction costs of enterprise bargaining, mainly with small and medium sized employers unsympathetic to unionism. The low incidence of industrial action testifies partly to the weakness of unions.

In order to secure a wider spread of wage employment benefits, these circumstances have led unions to rely less on collective bargaining and more on politically determined minimum wage and other conditions of employment by 'legal enactment', to use the Webbs' term noted by Gospel. Here the unions face a dilemma common to most developing economies with a large informal sector, namely, raising the real minimum wage too quickly to a higher level slows down the inflow of labour to the formal sector, thus limiting potential union membership (Bird and Manning 2002).

Finally, although the unions have avoided being drawn into ideological and political conflicts, a feature of early years, the lack of unity among the peak union bodies has sapped the potential of constructive influence of union leadership. One such issue that continues to fester is the question of undue rigidity in working conditions relevant to investment and productivity growth. The ambivalence and vacillations of the government on this issue have not assisted in its resolution. Thus, all in all, there is a big gap between the potential benefits available to workers under the labour laws and 'the reality of industrial relations policies and practices' (Lindsey and Masduki 2002: 28).

Conclusion

The experience of trade unionism in Indonesia shows the confluence of a number of factors in its development – its colonial past; the form of government; its political ideology and its expressed religious doctrines; the influence of international institutions; the legal provisions relating to the role of trade unions; the state of the economy; its susceptibility to international economic forces and its reliance on foreign investment; the large informal sector; and the structure and leadership of the unions and the effects of a mainly top-down driven unionism on grassroots commitment. Each of these has been important in explaining the development of unionism in Indonesia. Their relative influences, some positive and others negative, have varied from time to time in determining the course of events for the trade unions.

The Indonesian trade union movement is still in its infancy and it would be unwise to predict its future with undue confidence. In some ways, given the turbulence of the environment in which it developed and the learning process which is still going on, it has done remarkably well. Some union leaders express optimism about the future and confidence in the spirit of partnership with the government (interview with Rekson Silaban, leader of one of the three largest confederations). Others see the development of a labour party as an important ingredient of trade union growth (interview with two KSBSI leaders, Silaban and Pakpahan). Nevertheless, there are indications based on the factors discussed, that trade unionism in Indonesia may not grow much beyond its present infant stage for some time to come. Furthermore, forces of global competition and the persistent decline in recent years in trade union density and trade union power in most developed countries, noted by Gospel, add to the case for a cautious outlook for trade unions in Indonesia in the near future.

Acknowledgement

We gratefully acknowledge advice and assistance from Alan Boulton, Carmelo Noriel, Asaneca Colowai, Lusiani Julia and Budi Setiawati of ILO Jakarta; Sutanto Suwarno and Guntoro of the Ministry of Manpower; Muchtar Pakpahan, Rekson Silaban and Chris Manning. However, we are solely responsible for what appears in this chapter.

Notes

1 The laws included *Labour Act 1948, Collective Agreement Act 1954* and *Labour Disputes Act 1957* as well many regulations and decrees (Boulton 2001: 7).
2 We are especially indebted to Asaneca Colowai of ILO Jakarta for valuable advice on this section.
3 This section draws heavily on Perry (2005). Since ILO and other international agency data are drawn from figures supplied by individual countries, it may be expedient for our purposes to rely on Indonesian official statistics as presented by Perry. The updated figure for the number of strikes in 2006 is 282.

Bibliography

Alatas, V. and Cameron, L. (2003) 'The impact of minimum wages on employment in a low income country: an evaluation using the difference-in-difference approach'. World Bank Policy Research Working Paper No 2985, February: 1–31.

Bird, K. and Manning, C. (2002) 'Impact of minimum wage policy on employment and earnings in the informal sector: the case of Indonesia', paper presented to the East Asian Economists Conference, Kuala Lumpur, November.

Bird, K. and Suryahadi, A. (2002) 'Impact of minimum wage policy on wages and employment in Indonesia', paper presented to the PEG-BAPPENAS, USAID Technical Seminar, Jakarta, 27–28 March 2002.

Boulton, A. J. (2001) *The Future Structure of Industrial Relations in Indonesia: Some Issues and Challenges*, Jakarta: International Labour Organization.

Caraway, T. L. (2004) 'Protective repression, international pressure, and institutional design: Explaining labor reform in Indonesia', *Studies in Comparative International Development*, 39(3): 28–49.

Ford, M. (2000) 'Research note: Indonesian trade union developments since the fall of Suharto', *Labour and Management in Development Journal*, 1(3): 2–10.

Ford, M. (2001) 'Challenging the criteria of significance: lessons from contemporary Indonesian labour history', *Australian Journal of Politics and History*, 47(1): 101–14.

Ford, M. (2005) 'Economic unionism and labour's poor performance in Indonesia's 1999 and 2004 elections', paper presented to the Association of Industrial Relations Academics of Australia and New Zealand Conference, Sydney, 9–12 February.

Ghellab, Y. (1998) *Minimum Wages and Youth Employment*, Geneva: International Labour Organization.

Hadiz, V. R. (1997) *Workers and the State in New Order Indonesia,* London: Routledge.

Hadiz, V. R. (1998) '*Reformasi Total?* Labor after Suharto', *Indonesia 66*, October: 109–24.

Hadiz, V. R. (2000) 'Globalization, labour and the state: the case of Indonesia', in C. Rowley and J. Benson (eds) *Globalization and Labour in the Asia Pacific*, London: Frank Cass.

International Labour Conference (2002) *Decent work and the Informal Economy*, Report VI. Geneva, International Labour Organization.

International Labour Office (1993) *Social Security for All: Restructuring the Social Security Scheme for Indonesia – Issues and Options*, Jakarta: International Labour Organization.

International Labour Office (1999) *Demystifying the Core Conventions of the ILO through Social Dialogue: The Indonesian Experience*, Jakarta: International Labour Organization.

International Labour Office (2000) *Labour Market Dynamics in Indonesia (KILM) 1986–1999*, Jakarta: International Labour Organization.

Islam, I. and Nazar, S. (2000) *Minimum Wage and the Welfare of Indonesian Workers*, Jakarta: International Labour Organization.

Kelly, P. (2002) *Promoting Democracy and Peace Through Social Dialogue: A Study of the Social Dialogue Institutions and Processes in Indonesia*, Geneva: International Labour Organization.

Lindsey, T. and Masduki, T. (2002) 'Labour law in Indonesia after Soeharto', in S. Cooney, T. Lindsey, R. Mitchell and Y. Zhu (eds) *Law in Labour Market Regulations in East Asia*, London: Routledge.

Manning, C. (1997) 'A new era of labour market regulation in developing countries: the case of Indonesia', *Asian Economic Journal*, 1(1): 111–29.

Manning, C. and Roesad, K. (2006) 'Survey of recent developments', *Bulletin of Indonesian Economic Studies*, 42(2): 143–70.

Mizuno, K. (2005) 'The rise of labor movements and the evolution of the Indonesian system of industrial relations: a case study', *The Developing Economies*, XLIII-I, March: 190–211.

Perry, L. J. (2005) 'Industrial disputes in Indonesia: a reassessment', *Labour and Management in Development Journal*, 6(1): 3–17.

Quinn, P. (2003) *Freedom of Association and Collective Bargaining: A Study of Indonesian Experience 1998–2000*, Geneva: International Labour Organization.

Robison, R. and Hadiz, V. (2004) *Reorganising Power in Indonesia: The Politics of Oligarchy in an Age of Markets*, London: Routledge.

Saget, C. (2006) 'Fixing minimum wages in developing countries: common failures and remedies', International Labour Organisation, October 2006.

SMERU (2001) *Wage and Employment Effects of Minimum Wage Policy in Indonesian Urban Labor Market*, Jakarta, SMERU.

Suwarno, S. and Elliott, J. (2000) 'Changing approaches to employment relations in Indonesia', in G. Bamber, F. Park, C. Lee, P. K. Ross and K. Broadbent (eds) *Employment Relations in the Asia Pacific: Changing Approaches*, St Leonards, NSW, Allen and Unwin.

15 Trade unions in Asia

A comparative analysis

Ying Zhu and John Benson

The trade union movement in Asia has undergone rapid transformation over the past two decades as many Asian economies have embraced the processes of democratization and globalization. Two important factors have led to these changes; the external influences of foreign capital and international trade with the acceleration of global competition, and the internal factors of democratization, economic and institutional reforms, and an increased awareness of individual rights among citizens in both developed and developing Asian economies.

However, the events surrounding the 1997–8 Asian Crisis highlighted the vulnerability of national systems to protect workers, and trade unions have been one of the important forces fighting for institutional reform in order to build up the protection networks for both employed and unemployed labour in many Asian economies. The chapters in this volume have illustrated the problems facing trade unions in Asia and their contribution in providing a measure of equity and social justice at the societal level, as well as protecting workers through workplace representation and bargaining at the industrial and enterprise levels. In this concluding chapter our task now is to compare and contrast the development of trade unions in these key Asian economies, as well as between these Asian economies and other more advanced industrialized economies. In order to achieve this goal we will address the key research questions presented in Chapter 1 as well as respond to the theoretical issues raised by Gospel in Chapter 2 concerning the nature, structure and strategies of trade unions. In carrying out this comparative analysis the framework provided by Gospel in Chapter 2 will be utilized.

As discussed in Chapter 1, 12 Asian economies were chosen for investigation and analysis. Clearly unions in these Asian economies are not homogeneous due to the differences in their social and political systems and stages of economic development. Hence, it is necessary to separate these Asian economies into two groups, namely the first group of developed capitalist societies including Japan, South Korea, Taiwan, Hong Kong, Singapore and Malaysia, and the second group of developing societies including China, India, Sri Lanka, Vietnam, Thailand and Indonesia. Within this latter group, China and Vietnam, as pointed out in Chapter 1, represents special cases of developing economies as they move from centrally planned to market-based economies. Given the importance of this transition, these two economies will be considered separately from the other developing economies.

Trade unions in developed Asian economies

Trade unions in the developed Asian economies conform to many of the characteristics common among trade unions in Western countries. Trade unions in these economies do have a history of a 'continuous association of wage earners for the purpose of maintaining or improving the conditions of their employment' (Webb and Webb 1894); and have been interested in securing and maintaining jobs for their members (Perlman 1928); and have attempted to counter delocalization and produce a sense of solidarity and belonging among workers (Veblen 1904; Tannenbaum 1951) when faced with the increasing pressure of regional and global competition. For example, in Japan, trade unions were prepared to accept lower working hours and to forego wage increases in an attempt to secure jobs for their members whilst in Korea and Taiwan a sense of local-oriented solidarity developed among newly established unions to promote job security and to fight against businesses moving offshore or introducing foreign workers into the domestic economy.

Yet, there are clearly some unique characteristics that exist widely among the trade unions in the developed Asian economies that separate them from their Western union counterparts. The most important difference is the degree of union independence. It is likely, at least by Western conceptions of independence, that Asian trade unions are dependent organizations, although the nature of this dependency varies considerably and can be related to the history, nature and structure of unions as well as to union strategies. For instance, the history and nature of enterprise unions in Japan would logically lead to unions developing a relatively strong dependent relationship with employers. In contrast, in economies such as Korea and Taiwan where unions developed along industrial lines within more centralized systems, there developed a relatively strong dependent relationship with the state during the pre-democracy period and then with the political parties, in particular the ruling parties, after democracy was introduced. Nevertheless, we have, in recent years, detected in all these economies a desire by unions and their members for a more independent trade union movement which appears to be paralleling the changing political landscapes in these countries.

Is such independence related to the various developmental stages that unions progress through? As discussed by Gospel in Chapter 2, Michels (1911) argued that unions had an inevitable tendency towards oligarchy as leaders came to entrench their position and subvert any original more radical purpose of unions. However, another way of viewing this came from Lester (1958) who suggested that as US union leaders matured from the earlier pursuit of radical reform they came to stress recognition by employers and other significant groups and consequently stability and partnership. In other words, it may be more strategic to pursue union objectives through other than direct confrontation.

258 Ying Zhu and John Benson

Our examples of trade unions in the developed Asian economies show that early stages of union movements accompanied by democratic movements, such as occurred Japan in the 1950s and 1960s and Korea and Taiwan in the late 1980s and 1990s, were marked by a confrontational approach in terms of industrial relations issues, as well as the fight for social justice and democracy. Following the development of national economies and more democratic institutions, the strategies of trade unions became more stable and cooperative and legal means and a social partnership approach became the norm. This development is more consistent with the later observations of Lester (1958). However, one exceptional case is Hong Kong where the union movement has not been strong or influential at either societal or enterprise level, despite the appearance of 'democratic' institutions.

One useful way to assess the underlying strategies of Asian trade unions is to utilize the framework developed by Hyman (2001) and outlined by Gospel in Chapter 2. In his research on European trade unionism, Hyman (2001) identifies three types of trade unions: market-oriented, class-oriented, and society-oriented unions. Hyman claims that unions exist and function within a social framework that they may aspire to change but which acts as a constraint on current choices (Hyman 2001: 4). In other words, unions are part of society. Therefore, all three models typically have some purchase; but in most cases, unions have tended towards a mixture of two of the three ideal types. How do the trade unions in the developed Asian economies fit into those models?

Based on the analysis presented in each chapter of this volume, we can see an ongoing transformation of Asian trade unions over time. For instance, unions with a strong focus on class struggle are not dominant among the mainstream unions in the developed Asian economies. This is not, however, to suggest that such unions do not exist, as the case of Japan would testify. In the early years of economic development in the developed Asian economies, the political orientation of unions was used by the ruling parties as a means to restructure trade unionism. This was certainly the case in Japan, Korea, Taiwan and Malaysia. Hong Kong and Singapore are somewhat different due to their city-state status, but political influence, for example, CCP and KMT influence in Hong Kong and the government and People's Party in Singapore, were also very strong.

Today the focus and approach of trade unions is more related to individual trade unions' particular political and economic goals for the benefit of their own group rather than any attempt at mobilization of the working class against the political and business elite. With the onset of globalization, market forces have become more powerful, leading to the mainstream unions in these economies adopting a more economic-oriented strategy with the emphasis on 'social partnership' and 'dual-responsibility'. But the trade union model in developed Asian economies, we would argue, is still different from the union movement in either Europe, where trade unions are regarded as agents of social integration with an emphasis on 'social partnership', or the United States, where unions operate as business entities with a focus on the market (see Hyman 2001: 3). To us, the actions and outcomes of trade unionism in the advanced Asian economies suggest a combination of both market-oriented and society-oriented unionism.

How then can we characterize the strategies and outcomes of trade unions in developed Asian economies? First, the most utilized mechanism of union action in these economies, namely collective bargaining, has shifted from a centralized industrial-based bargaining approach towards a more enterprise-based system in parallel with the decline in union membership and the economic downturn in the 1990s. Second, there has been an increase in enterprise-based joint consultative arrangements, with unions adopting more cooperative approaches, accompanied by the revision of related labour legislation and the introduction of more individualistic approaches to human resource management. In particular, the outcomes of joint consultative arrangements have been seen as an effective mechanism for the protection of short-term employees who work under extremely flexible employment arrangements.

Third, due to increasing competition in the Asian region, there has been increasing demand for a highly skilled workforce in the developed Asian economies and many less-skilled workers have become under-employed or unemployed. Trade unions in response to these developments have played a significant role as promoters and providers of training for those unskilled workers. In this and other industrial relations matters unions have taken a dual strategy. On the one hand, unions have attempted, through a variety of strategies, to influence industrial relations policy (and indeed a variety of social policy) at the national level and employment conditions at the enterprise level through industrial campaigns and public hearings. On the other hand, unions have nominated their own representatives to stand for national legislatures in order to initiate and draft legislation to protect the interests of workers.

The activity of the trade union movement in the developed Asian economies over the past two decades is characterized by several important outcomes. First, trade unions were part of a democratic movement to change the political landscape in Korea and Taiwan, as well as pro-democratic political movements in Japan and Hong Kong. The outcome has been reflected in greater political participation as members of legislatures, associations with certain political parties, as well as gaining seats within government advisory bodies.

Second, unions have influenced government policy to be more pro-worker (for example in Korea and Taiwan), agitating for the revision and reform of relevant laws such as legislation on labour standards, minimum wages, overtime pay and other social benefits, including unemployment benefits and minimum social support among these developed Asian economies. Third, by adopting a more cooperative approach towards industrial relations, trade unions have been involved in less industrial action and the number of strikes and hours lost due to industrial action has declined significantly in the past two decades in the developed Asian economies.

Overall, it appears that trade unions in developed Asian economies have adopted a hybrid approach, combining both market-oriented and society-oriented models. Although the general trend of union density has declined in these economies over the past two decades, the impact of the union movement has generally been positive in assisting society to become more democratic in terms of political participation and legislation that has a stronger emphasis on social justice and social partnership. In turn, trade unions, by focusing on partnership, not only helped these economies recover from the economic impact of the financial Crisis but have contributed to economic success through a focus on worker training and employability.

Trade unions in developing Asian economies

India, Sri Lanka, Thailand and Indonesia

By comparing the union movement in these developing economies from a historical evolution perspective we can identify a relatively common pattern of four phases of development. The first phase of union development commenced with the revolutionary characteristics of anti-colonialism and struggle for independence. (Although this was not strictly the case for Thailand, it was also the case for the more developed Malaysia.) At this time the union movement was closely associated with other 'independence movements' and political parties and their major activities included participation in the wider movements that were fighting for social justice and national independence.[1]

Soon after independence was achieved in each of these economies, the union movement shifted into the second phase with a political struggle for union independence and the right of workers to have true representation. In this phase, the state supported unions that were incorporated into their supporting structures, but suppressed other independent unions, as was clearly the case in Indonesia. During this period the union movement tended to be monopolistic, bureaucratic, dependent and divided with substantial challenges coming from 'unauthorized' or 'illegal' unions.

The third phase of union development has run parallel with the rapid economic growth of the past two decades and was marked by increasing industrial unionism and union concentration in key industries, locations and occupations. Union action in this phase was focused predominately on economic benefits such as wages, conditions and other aspects of working conditions. In addition, new legislation was passed to accommodate the demands of economic growth and inevitable rebalancing of the political power between capital and workers.

The fourth phase of union development in these four developing economies was associated with the increased intensity of globalization, the move towards neo-liberalism, increased international competition and the Asian Crisis. At this stage state policy shifted towards encouraging labour market flexibility. External influences such as the International Monetary Fund and, more generally, foreign capital, placed significant pressure on the need to reform economic and industrial policies and, in particular, the need to reform the industrial relations system. At the enterprise level, the increasing trend of adopting more individualistic HRM paradigms provided more managerial control over workers. Again, as with the more developed economies, these policies led to union decline in terms of density and membership. In this period, union action shifted focus from improving wages and conditions of employment to fighting for job security, workers' employability and social insurance.

Compared with unions in the developed economies, unions in these economies, with the exception of India, were relatively weak in terms of political influence. Three characteristics appear to represent the development and activities of unions in these economies. First, the unions developed strong links with political parties through their involvement in the revolutionary struggle for independence. Notwithstanding, as time passed there was an increasing awareness among unions that such political association could well jeopardize their independence. Hence, in more recent years most of the unions in these economies have attempted to distance themselves from the major political parties.

Second, trade union influence has been relatively weak, as can be seen by the low density and membership, as well as the low coverage of collective bargaining. Whilst globalization, international competition, economic restructuring and the increased emphasis on labour market flexibility have played a key role in union decline, it is also the case that the large pool of unorganized workers in the informal sector was, and remains, a key factor in the low level of union influence. In recent years, unions in these economies have started to address these problems by increasing their efforts to recruit workers in both the formal and informal sectors.

Third, the influence of neo-liberalism and global competition has taken the economies toward de-centralization and de-institutionalization. Collective bargaining was not strong at central or industrial levels in these economies, but mainly occurred at the enterprise level, which made high coverage more difficult. New and amended legislation in these economies was generally aimed at providing more autonomy to capital; and in this environment it became more difficult for unions to take industrial action.

In terms of Hyman's (2001) orientation approach, trade unions in these economies have shifted from a political-oriented union approach to a market-oriented form, with little society focus. This explains why, under the influence of globalization and neo-liberalist policies, the union movement has been in decline and why the social and institutional environments have weakened in recent years. It appears on the surface that these economies are now similar to the more advanced economies of Asia. Yet, it should be pointed out that the developed economies enjoy a certain level of industrial and institutional maturity with relatively sound social, economic and industrial infrastructures in place. They exhibit strong social networks to support the basic needs of working men and women. In contrast, the developing economies have not built the necessary basic social and legal protections for vulnerable workers. The adoption of a neo-liberal policy framework so quickly, along with the abandonment of the move towards institutionalization and social protection has meant that sustainable well-being for both society and individual citizens is less likely in the developing economies.

The trade union movement in the socialist transitional economies

The socialist transitional economies of China and Vietnam present another picture of trade unions in developing Asian economies. Like trade unions in other developing Asian economies, the birth of trade unions in both China and Vietnam was closely associated with the anti-colonialist struggle (Zhu and Fahey 2000: 285). Unlike the developing economies discussed above, trade unions in China and Vietnam, under the influence of Leninist principles, had the dual role of supporting management as well as representing workers' interests. In short, trade unions were used as a 'transmission belt' between the party and the 'masses' (Zhu and Fahey 2000: 285). They fulfilled four main official functions: to protect the interests of the party/state, management and workers; to help their members participate in the management of their own work units; to mobilize the labour force to raise productivity and the economy's performance; and to train and educate the workers to be better employees in the workplace and citizens in the society.

In both countries, a single official trade union organization, the ACFTU in China and the VFTU in Vietnam, dominates the union movement. These unions are under the control and support of the party/state and involved in the process of policy formation, law amendment and enactment. Under the peak body, there are industrial-sector based unions and location-based unions with both horizontal and vertical linkages with the grassroot enterprise unions. At the enterprise level, the union leadership is selected according to the Leninist principles of 'democratic centralism', with bottom-up selection from the primary union level through nomination and election. A sense of 'mass participation' underpins this process, although both the party and the management are intimately involved in the process of selection (Warner 1993).

In China, among a large number of SOEs and COEs, both trade unions and the union-guided Workers' Congresses have been and remain the major bodies representing the workers at the enterprise level (Zhu and Campbell 1996: 42). The Workers' Congresses are closely integrated into the trade union structure, with the trade union committee at the enterprise level becoming a standing body to deal with routine duties, such as consultation with management on key decisions, dealing with occupational, health and safety matters, training workers, participating in collective negotiation and mediating disputes between workers and enterprises (Zhu and Campbell 1996: 42). However, in DPEs and FIEs, trade unions do not appear to have such a major role. In these enterprises the low level of union density and membership are due to the general lack of enforcement of labour law and regulations.

In Vietnam, trade union representatives were originally closely associated with the party and with management, as either the deputy party representative or deputy director. The priorities of the union were to participate in administration, to educate workers and to defend workers' rights. In recent years, a new set of priorities has reversed this order, with the primary role being to protect the material interests of the union members. Similar to the situation in China, union density is high in SOEs and COEs, and low in DPEs and FIEs. In these enterprises both the employer and the employees have seen little effective outcome from union involvement in labour relations (Zhu and Fahey 2000: 290).

The major challenge that faces the trade union movement in China and Vietnam concerns the globalization process and market-driven economic reform. Trade unions are in the process of renewing their organizational structure and activities to undertake a more representative role in an attempt to protect their members' rights and interests. This is a substantial difference to the earlier role of trade unions in these economies where they existed only as part of the state sector with the major aim of promoting political unity. As Zhu and Fahey (2000) have argued, unions in Vietnam and China seem to be moving away from the 'classical dualism' of protecting the interests of both workers and management toward a range of alternative objectives, including 'corporatist dualism' for effective policy formation, 'participatory dualism' for continued reform, and even 'adversarial non-dualism' to protect workers in foreign-owned enterprises. These challenges require greater union democracy and political reform. In terms of Hyman's (2001) model, a hybrid model of union movement in China and Vietnam has developed which is a combination of market-oriented and society-oriented trade unionism. However, this classification is not static and the weight between these two elements has shifted from time to time due to the changing political, economic and social contexts.

Comparison of the Asian economies with advanced Western economies

The underpinning theoretical models of trade unions utilized above (Hyman 2001; Gospel 2005 and Chapter 2 of this volume) have provided a useful point of departure for our analysis. In this section we wish to make some comparison between the economies discussed in this volume and the more advanced Western developed economies. The 'logics of action' approach proposed by Frenkel and Kuruvilla (2002) provides a useful way to consider the question of whether there is a trend towards convergence or divergence of union structure. This approach provides a useful way to consider union strategy and to conceptualize the impact of globalization on employment relations by considering the logic of competition, the logic of industrial peace and the logic of employment-income protection.

Frenkel and Kuruvilla (2002) have argued that the strengths of the logics themselves are influenced by five related factors: the economic development strategy; globalization intensity; union strength; labour market features; and government responsiveness to workers. The underpinning literatures on these five factors have some common grounds with specific orientation and they guide us in extending our analysis to predict the trajectory of trade unions in Asia.

First, the trade union movement in Asian economies and other advanced industrial economies is facing increasing competition due to the influence of globalization and neo-liberalism. In most economies trade unions have adopted a degree of market orientation in Hyman's (2001) model or the logic of competition in Frenkel and Kuruvilla's (2002) approach. The overwhelming trajectory is a trend towards convergence. However, the detailed actions carried out by individual trade unions or the trade union movements in particular economies in response to such pressures are very different. While generalizations are difficult to formulate, it is the case that in the less-developed economies or in industries involving simple processing or lower value-added elements, there appears to be a propensity to adopt numerical and wage flexibility with the tendency towards the low-skill/ low-wage model. In contrast, in the more-developed economies or industries involving complex production processes or higher value-added elements, there is a propensity to adopt functional flexibility with a tendency towards the high-skill/high-wage orientation. This generalization is consistent with Frenkel and Kuruvilla's (2002) approach.

Second, the divergent path is also reflected through state regulation and policy priority. For certain Asian governments unions were sometimes seen (perhaps reluctantly) as a positive force for political democracy and the encouragement of political participation (for example Korea and Taiwan in the late 1980s and early 1990s). However, following the Asian Crisis the policy priority has shifted towards economic growth and attracting investment. Consequently unions are seen as obstacles and a policy of constraining unions has become more important. For other economies, such as China and Vietnam, the policy of economic reform has been driven by market forces and the logic of competition has dominated the policies on economic reform in general and employment relations in particular. As their economies have grown and become more competitive, the state has become concerned with maintaining political and social stability. Hence, re-introducing social protection policies and passing legislation to reduce inequalities has begun to dominate government policy, which is consistent with the logics of employment-income protection and industrial peace. Some economies, such as Thailand and Sri Lanka, have remained unmoved by economic or social pressures and the predominating logic of competition. Minimum social protection dominates these economies.

Third, by utilizing Gospel's (2005) historical-institutionalist framework we can identify different trajectories of institutionalization and de-institutionalization among these economies. As in most developed economies, in particular the Western advanced economies, the peak of institutionalization was reached decades ago and we have observed a trend of de-centralization and de-institutionalization in more recent years. However, in these countries the fundamental social protection network and legal framework had been built up over many decades. The rules of law and civil society were thus the cornerstone of social stability. In contrast, the lack of fundamental social protection networks and an independent legal framework is common among Asian economies. The trend of decentralization and de-institutionalization among the majority of developing Asian economies before they had achieved both industrial and institutional maturity and the early adoption of a neo-liberal policy framework has meant that the long-term sustainable development of the society could be under threat.

The two socialist transitional economies, China and Vietnam, have gradually institutionalized and place greater reliance on the rule of law after a period of marketization. Many new laws have been established and the enforcement of law has become a major priority of the state in order to achieve social stability and progress. This reversal was necessary for both these economies given the pressure they face to carry out further political reform in order to facilitate further economic reform.

Fourth, the characteristics of the union movement, such as union density and impact, union fragmentation and consolidation, union monopoly and democracy, and union bureaucracy and autonomy, determine the role of unions within their industrial context, the strategies that unions adopted in policy formation and law enactment at the national level, and the representation and bargaining at industry and enterprise levels. From the case studies presented in this volume some general propositions can be advanced:

- Union density is not always related to the impact of unions within the industrial relations system. For example, some economies had very high union density (China, Taiwan and Vietnam), but their unions' impact was not stronger than some other economies with relatively lower union density (Korea and India). To explain why this might be so we need to turn to other factors such as the historical evolution of unions, the political and legal environments that unions operate within, and the actions and decisions made by unions at both the society and enterprise levels.
- The trajectory of union fragmentation and consolidation has varied among the Asian economies. For example, unions in some economies had a long history of freedom of association and experience of union diversity (India), with the negative impact of union fragmentation in the past providing an impetus to the union movement to adopt strategies for union consolidation. In contrast, unions in the economies with a long history of a single official union body (Korea and Taiwan) fragmented when the societies embraced democracy and freedom of union association. Such fragmentation led to inter/intra-union competition and a dilution of union voice, and strengthened the power of employers.
- Union consolidation does not mean union monopoly. For many years, most Asian economies had a union movement under the control of peak bodies with strong political association with certain political parties (either ruling parties or opposition parties). Unions became a machine of bureaucracy without very much concern for democracy or self-determination. In recent years, however, there has been increasing awareness and pressure from union members to develop a more democratic institution and to provide more autonomy and self-determination for members and less intervention from either political parties or the union bureaucracy.

These union characteristics and related actions and strategies have influenced the outcome of industrial relations policies and systems in each of the economies discussed in this volume. In turn, these outcomes have influenced and been influenced by a range of factors related to the stage of political, economic and social development, the intensity of globalization and regionalism, shifts in ideology, and the level of awareness of labour and union's rights among citizens in general, and workers in particular in each Asian economy. Such a combination creates the complexity and divergence among the Asian economies on the one hand, as well as between the Asian economies and other advanced market economies on the other.

Note

1 For more information of the background of these four economies, see Budhwar (2003) for India, Lakshman and Tisdaell (2000) for Sri Lanka, Lawler and Suttawet (2000) for Thailand, and Hadiz (2000) for Indonesia.

Bibliography

Budhwar, P. S. (2003) 'Culture and Management in India', in M. Warner (ed.) *Culture and Management in Asia*, London and New York: RoutledgeCurzon.

Frenkel, S. and Kuruvilla, S. (2002) 'Logics of action, globalization, and changing employment relations in China, India, Malaysia, and the Philippines', *Industrial and Labor Relations Review*, 55: 387–412.

Gospel, H. (2005) 'Markets, firms, and unions: a historical-institutionalist perspective on trade unions', in S. Fernie and D. Metcalf (eds) *The Future of Trade Unions*, London: Routledge.

Hadiz, V. R. (2000) 'Globalization, labour and the state: the case of Indonesia', in C. Rowley and J. Benson (eds) *Globalization and Labour in the Asia Pacific Region*, London: Frank Cass.

Hyman, R. (2001) *Understanding European Trade Unionism: Between Market, Class, and Society*, London: Sage.

Lakshman, W. D. and Tisdaell, C. A. (2000) *Sri Lanka's Development Since Independence: Socio-economic Perspectives and Analysis*, New York: Nova Science Publishers.

Lawler, J. J. and Suttawet, C. (2000) 'Labour unions, globalization and deregulation in Thailand', in C. Rowley and J. Benson (eds) *Globalization and Labour in the Asia Pacific Region*, London: Frank Cass.

Lester, R. A. (1958) *As Unions Mature*, Princeton, NJ: Princeton University Press.

Michels, R. (1911; 1955 edn) *The Iron Law of Oligarchy*, New York: Dover Books.

Perlman, S. (1928) *A Theory of the Labour Movement*, New York: August M. Kelly.

Tannenbaum, F. (1951) *A Philosophy of Labor*, New York: Knopft.

Veblen, T. (1904; 1994 edn) *The Theory of the Business Enterprise*, New York: Dover Books.

Warner, M. (1993) 'Chinese trade unions: Structure and function in a decade of economic reform, 1979–89', in S. Frenkel (ed.) *Organized Labour in the Asia-Pacific Region*, Ithaca, NY: ILR Press.

Webb, S. and Webb, B. (1894) *History of Trade Unionism*, Deventer: Kluwer.

Zhu, Y. and Campbell, I. (1996) 'Economic reform and the challenge of transforming labour regulation in China', *Labour and Industry*, 7: 29–49.

Zhu, Y. and Fahey, S. (2000) 'The challenges and opportunities for the trade union movement in the transition era: two socialist market economies, China and Vietnam', *Asia Pacific Business Review*, special issue 6: 282–99.

Index

For Product Safety Concerns and Information please contact our EU
representative GPSR@taylorandfrancis.com
Taylor & Francis Verlag GmbH, Kaufingerstraße 24, 80331 München, Germany